PRODUCTIVE ARCHIVING

Contributors

Ernst van Alphen, Aleida Assmann, Jeannette Christensen, Annet Dekker, Sebastián Díaz Morales, Lars Ebert, Monika Huber, William Kentridge, Pablo Lerma, Inge Meijer, Santu Mofokeng, Merapi Obermayer, Mathieu Pernot, Walid Raad, Ana Paula Saab, Drew Sawyer, Carla Subrizi, Marjan Teeuwen, Daria Tuminas, Jeffrey Wallen, Michelle Williams Gamaker

PRODUCTIVE ARCHIVING

Artistic Stategies, Future Memories, and Fluid Identities

Ernst van Alphen (ed.)

Valiz, Amsterdam

CONTENTS

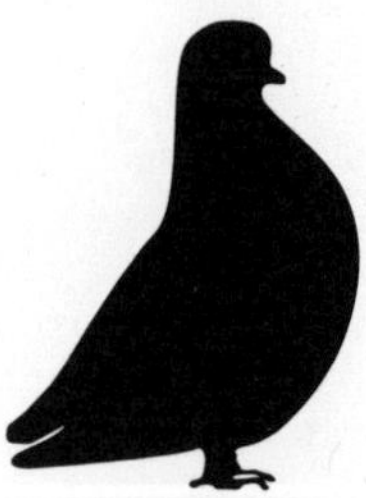

Archiving Identities

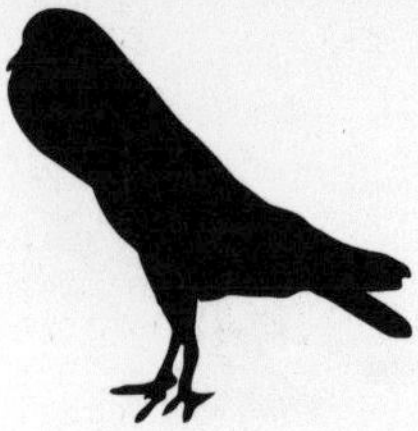

Archiving Memories and Histories

Archiving Objects

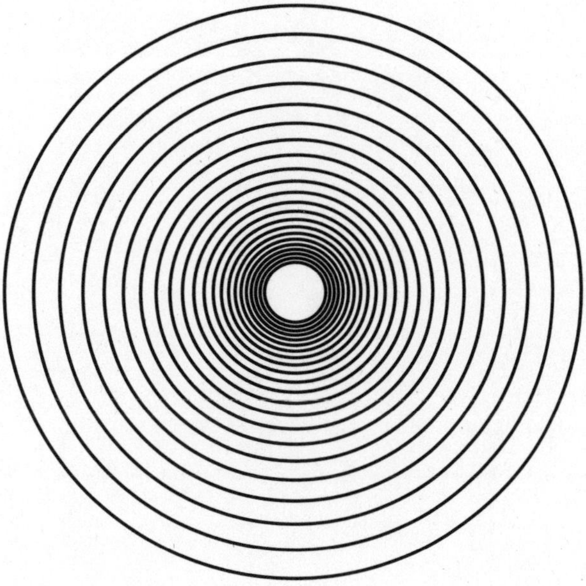

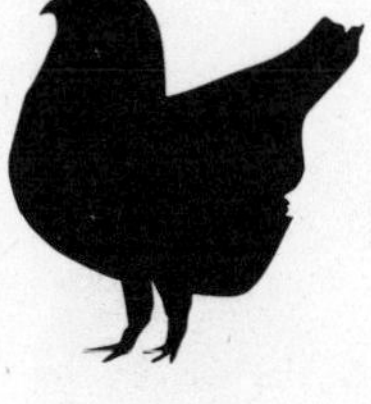

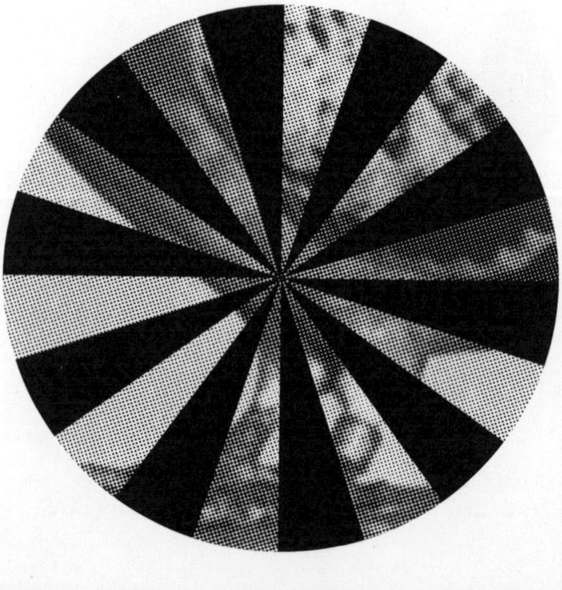

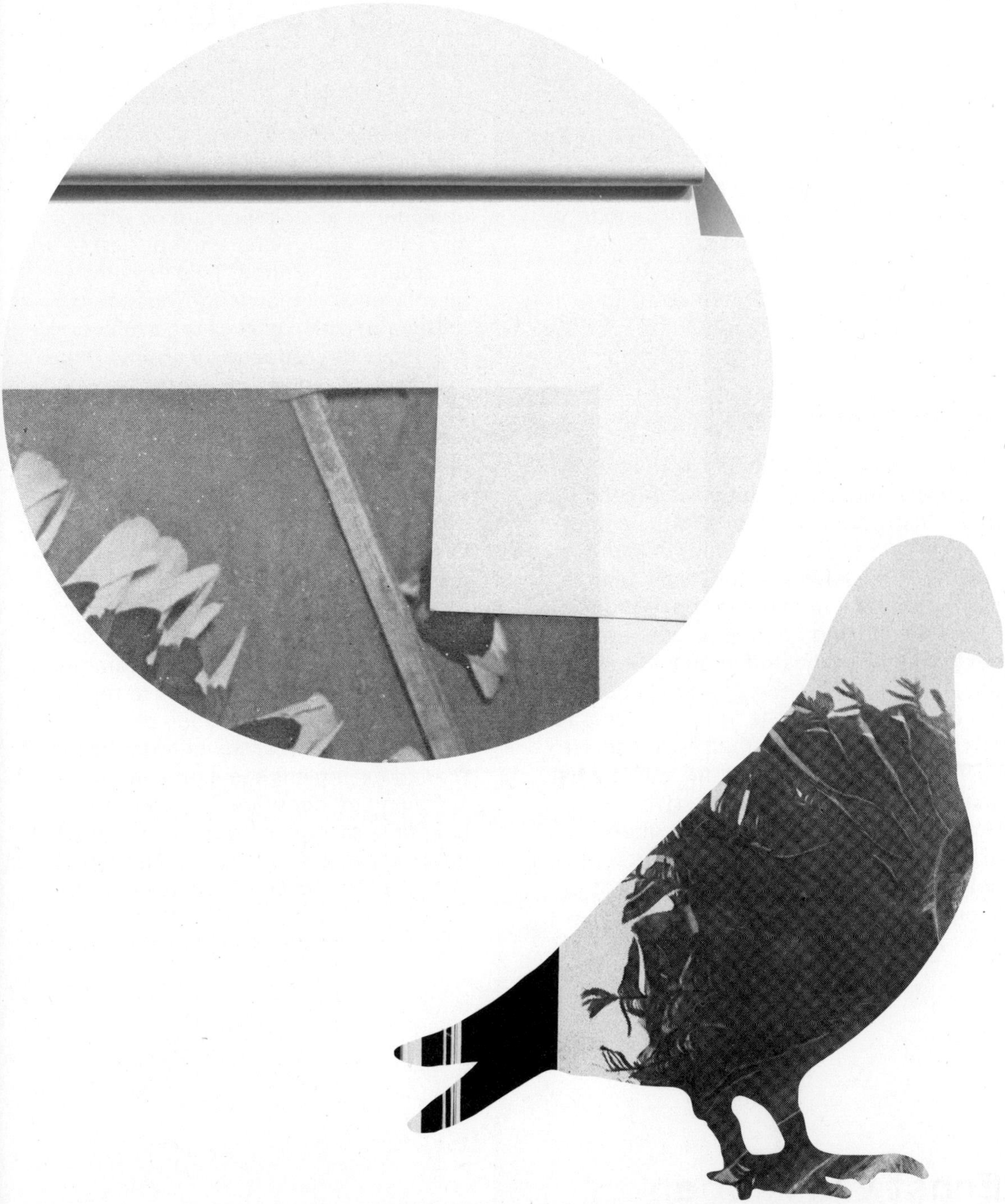

INTRODUCTION

When is Archiving Productive, and When is it Not?

Productive Archiving takes as its starting point three problems that archival organizations confront us with and that are usually overlooked: first, the inclusions in or exclusions from the archive; second, the loss of individuality and specificity in the archive; and third, when archiving becomes a form of pigeonholing.

Inclusions and Exclusions

The notion of the archive is used literally as well as figuratively. Literally, it refers to the institution or material site, in short, a building filled with documents and objects. Figuratively, it concerns a much more general and ungraspable notion of knowledge and memory practices not bound by or located in an institutional organization. Especially Michel Foucault's notion of the archive seems to be responsible for this figurative use. He used the term archive for the law of what can be said, or a set of discursive rules. Such a set of discursive rules consists of specific conceptual distinctions that determine what can be said and what cannot be said. In that sense, discursive rules also always imply exclusions. Those exclusions concern memories, documents, practices of knowledge production that are overlooked, not taken seriously, considered as unimportant or without any value. Exclusions are inherent to any archival organization. This explains why memories and knowledge 'outside the archive' are also part of the archive, in the sense of produced by archival rules of exclusion. 'Archive,' then, covers two kinds of knowledge: knowledge that can be articulated and objectified by convergent discursive rules, and knowledge that remains overlooked because of the same discursive rules, now working as rules of exclusion. As a consequence, an archival organization has by definition both an inside and an outside.

In recent years many social and artistic practices have had the ambition to include items or identities in the archive that were until then overlooked or excluded from archival organization. A good example is the listing, hence, archiving of identities that were for a long time grouped together as 'perverse,' now indicated as LGBTQ+. Although I will criticize the fact that identities are being boxed in by listing them in this way later in this introduction, one positive effect is

Ernst van Alphen

that identities that were for a long time unimaginable or invisible suddenly can be named. Until recently, they were excluded from the archival categories prevalent in Western societies. Their inclusion means that they are now acknowledged in their existence, because, as argued earlier, outside the archive there is no proof of that existence.

Many contemporary art practices foreground these exclusions from the archive by presenting them as yet another archive. Artists highlight this residue of the archive by collecting images that were until then not considered to be 'archivable.' These excluded images are still there but cannot be looked at because according to the accepted discursive rules they do not show or articulate anything worth knowing. An example of such an artistic practice transforming exclusions from the archive into an archive in its own right is *The Black Photo Album* by South African photographer Santu Mofokeng. I will discuss this photo album later in this introduction. Another example of an artistic practice based on an inclusion in the archive what has so far been excluded is the work of Lebanese artist Walid Raad. He has had great impact on the re-thinking of the archive and its effect. Raad and his fictional collaborators of 'The Atlas Group' donated work to the Archive of The Atlas Group. To give an example, *Missing Lebanese Wars*, consisting of plates and a notebook, was deposited in The Atlas Group Archive by a well-known (but fictional) Lebanese historian, named Dr. Fadl Fakhouri. Other fictive legatees of the archive are Asma Taffan (*Let's be honest, the weather helped*, 1992), and Habib Fathallah *(I might die before I get a rifle*, 1993). Walid Raad himself also donated work to the archive (*We decided to let them say, "We are convinced" twice*). The project of The Atlas Group unfolded between 1989 and 2004. In the 2004 Raad decided to end this so-called collaborative project. In 2006 a retrospective exhibition was organized that showed the complete Atlas Group Archive in one single place, the Hamburger Bahnhof in Berlin.[1]

By means of the works in The Atlas Group Archive Raad questions the mediation and archiving of information. This artistic, fictional archive enables the exploration of new epistemic and cognitive models. This new knowledge challenges the kind of knowledge that

1_The complete contents of the archive are published in the following book: *The Atlas Group (1989–2004): A Project by Walid Raad* (Cologne: Walter König, 2006).

is disseminated by the dominant mass media and by Western discourses about terrorism, colonialism and orientalism. The presentation of artistic works as belonging to an archive directs the attention to the cognitive conflicts and problems thematized by these works. Walid Raad explains why the archive as a *place* is the necessary framework for his cognitive project:

> I like to think that I always work from facts. But I always proceed from the understanding that there are different kinds of facts; some facts are historical, some are sociological, some are emotional, some are economic, and some are aesthetic. And some of these facts can sometimes only be experienced in a place we call fiction. I tend to think in terms of different kinds of facts and the places that permit their emergence.[2]

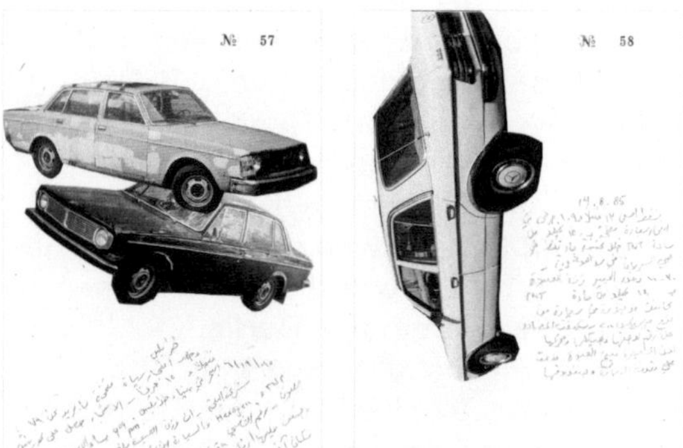

Walid Raad, *Already Been in a Lake of Fire*, 1985 (see pp. 48–57)

Besides fiction, the other place in the work of Walid Raad that permits these facts to emerge and become visible and knowable is the archive. Most people outside Lebanon know only vaguely that during the twentieth century wars have been fought, with the Lebanese (by Israel) an among the Lebanese themselves. One remembers especially its glorious past, namely the capital Beirut as the equivalent to Paris in the Middle East. The very destructive wars that have ruined the country have sunken into oblivion. As a result, they have no real existence any more, they are no longer present in our memories. By means of his artistic project, integrating fact and fiction, Raad includes and transforms forgotten histories into archival knowledge.

The documents and images presented by The Atlas Group are not inherently fake or fictional. The texts and photographs are not manipulated. But it is their montage and assembling into a narrative or specific historical situation that propels them into fiction. The montage of image and text, or of different images is a specific mode of producing knowledge. The texts and images are never presented at face value, but they always 'trouble each other.'[3] A good example of this use of montage is the *Notebook volume 38: Already been in a lake of fire*, donated to The Atlas Group Archive by the already mentioned Dr. Fadl Fakhouri. This file contains 145 photographic images of cars. These cars are of the same brand, model and color as those used in car-bomb attacks during the Lebanese wars of 1975 to 1991. Notes and annotations made by Fakhouri are attached to the images. They specify information such as the number

2_Gunilla Knape, 'Afterword,' in Walid Raad, *Walid Raad: I Might Die Before I Get a Rifle* (Göttingen: Steidl Verlag, 2011), p. 99.

3_Hélène Chouteau-Matikan, 'War, There, Over There,' in *Walid Raad: I Might Die Before I Get a Rifle* (Göttingen: Steidl Verlag, 2011), p. 104.

4_Chouteau-Matikan, 'War, There, Over There,' p. 105.

of casualties, the location and time of the explosion and the type of explosives used. The documentary information is all real and true. What is fictional however, is the bringing together of these different elements in the notebook of the imaginary character of Dr. F. Fakhouri. And of course, the notebook is an archival genre. By using the notebook as the framework presenting factual images and notes, they are assigned a cognitive status. It is thanks to this archival genre that the images and notes are no longer disparate elements without any cognitive value. They become knowable and visible objects through their newly acquired status as archivable objects. The fictional archive of The Atlas Group presents, in the words of Chouteau, 'latency, lapse, and speculation as vectors for historical truth equal to those of verification, authenticity and proof.'[4]

The Price to Pay when Included in the Archive

But once one is inside an archival organization, other problems arise: one does not exist in one's unique, individual specificity but as an example of how one is categorized in the archive. This is especially the case in the type of modern archiving that was developed at the end of the nineteenth century. As already concluded when discussing Foucault's notion of the archive: whereas in the old archive individuals were used to build or substantiate categories, in the new archive categories are being used to build or substantiate the individual. This leads to a situation wherein individual identity is the result of the interaction between human bodies, events and archives. This identity is then not seen as a subjective interiority, but as an objective exteriority.

One of the radical implications of this new, modern archive is that what, or who, is not in the records does not really exist. This drastic consequence is understandable when we realize that archival administrators do not observe, describe, and classify reality, but the other way around: they shape people and events into entities that fit the categorizations and are recordable. This kind of reification entails that there are virtually no other facts than those that are contained in records and archives.[5] The result of this archival practice is pigeonholing.

Archiving as Pigeonholing

Since the 1990s, a tension has emerged between the archive and narrative as symbolic modes used by human beings to provide meaning to their lives and identities. For centuries, the medium of the archive was considered only as a tool used by historians. Storytelling, however, was much more than just a tool: it was a medium of crucial importance for making sense of the past, the present and the future. But with the rise of the internet and other digital media the subordinated position of the archive has become a dominant one. The story we tell about ourselves has become of less importance than how we are registered by the State, the insurance company, in our medical files, et cetera. When one tells a story about oneself it implies that there has been a change, a development, a growth in who one is. In the 18th century the notion of Bildung was introduced in order

5_In archives interfaces function as the critical nodes through which archivists enable and constrain the interpretation of the past. The interface is a site where power in the Foucauldian sense is negotiated and exercised. It is power exercised over documents and their representation, over the access to them and over the uses of archives. On archival interfaces, see Margaret Hedstrom, 'Archives, Memory, and Interfaces with the Past,' *Archival Science* 2, nos. 1–2 (2002), pp. 21–43.

to stress the importance of growth and development. But *Bildung* has become an almost obsolete notion. We do not develop, transform, or build our identity but are pinned down on an identity that is fixed. This inclination to fixating identity is, for example, demonstrated by the recent classifications of gender and sexuality as LHBTQ and so on. I add 'and so on,' because again and again identities so far forgotten or marginalized are added to this listing; a recent addition was the 'I' of intersexuality. Identity is no longer seen as a transgression, as a classification you should challenge in order to be free, but as a box in which you feel understood and safe. The irony is that also the Q of queer has been added to this listing of identities. This is ironic, because queer, in fact, indicates the resistance against the pigeonholing of identities; but now, even queer people are boxed in by making them part of this list.

This boxing in of different genders and sexuality also contradicts the rather recent philosophical understanding of gender and sexuality as being the result of performative agency. In the 1990s, American philosopher Judith Butler argued that we are not born with a gender or sexual identity; we constitute these identities by performative behavior. This does not imply that we can 'adopt' a different identity every day when we wake up, as if wearing a different clothing style. Performative acting and behavior usually confirm the gender identities that are socially available to us; the margins to challenge these identities are rather small.[6] But although small, this theory of performativity implies that gender identity and sexual identity are not fixed and are not something we carry with us like DNA and only have to unearth or discover. This notion of identity suggests that we are not born *with* an identity but born *into* an identity.

The post-structuralist theory of performativity has become canonical in most of the humanities, especially in gender and queer studies and in cultural analysis, although it is rather abstract and difficult to understand. It is difficult because it does not immediately comply with how we 'live' our gender and sexual identity. The idea that we have an identity and that we only must discover our 'true' identity seems to reflect better how we experience who we are. The suggestion that we can 'build' our identity performatively, even if only marginally, does not seem to 'fit' with how we live and experience our gender and sexual identity.

So, it is understandable that the theory that gender and sexuality are performative suddenly being replaced by the opposite paradigm according to which identities are fixed categories that box in who we are, may be a bit puzzling. At first sight categorizing and classifying identities is not a problem, because it acknowledges difference. But as Iris van der Tuin has argued, categorizing is in practice *classifixation*; you can no longer escape the category that boxes you in.[7] There is no escape any more from this pigeonholing. This is quite a radical change in how subjects are supposed to reflect on their individuality, their individual subjectivity. For centuries it was common to work with a very limited number of identity distinctions, and to subvert or transgress them when these distinctions did not fit. For gender and sexuality, it was the distinction between man and woman, for sexuality between

6_See especially: Judith Butler, *Bodies That Matter: On the Discursive Limits of "Sex"* (New York and London: Routledge, 1993), and *Gender Trouble: Feminism and the Subversion of Identity* (New York and London: Routledge 1990), and *Undoing Gender* (New York and London: Routledge 2004).

7_Iris van der Tuin, *Generational Feminism: New Materialist Introduction to a Generative Approach* (Lanham: Lexington Books, 2015).

heterosexual and homosexual that you had to work with in order to build your own identity. Of course, in the case of many subjects these distinctions or, rather, oppositions, were too restrictive; they do not fit their self-experience. As a result, these distinctions had to be transgressed. It is precisely this narrative of transgression, this *Bildung*, that constituted one's own individual identity.

For a long time, namely since the beginning of modernity, there was another identity that was even more important than the identities of gender and sexuality. This was class identity. One was a farmer, belonged to the workers, lower-middle class, the middle class, the upper-middle class, or the upper-class, including the old nobility. Modernity also gave rise to capitalism and its promise that upward mobility between classes was possible—and downward mobility as well, if one did not put enough effort in going upward. This promise, in the US translated into the so-called American dream, and its Janus face of threat implied that class identity was not fixed but could be transgressed.

But in our times of neoliberalism, class as a notion that co-constitutes our identity, our class identity, has imploded. This does not mean that with neoliberalism the Marxist ideal of a classless society has been reached, but that people no longer consider class as an issue that constitutes their identity—even though the gap between those who are rich and those who are poor is only widening. But as a result, our notion of identity as such has changed: identity is no longer something we build by transgressing specific norms and distinctions. Identity is now our true self, which we have to discover within ourselves. As a result, identity also has another temporality: whereas identity-as-*Bildung* is future-oriented, identity-as-our-true-self is past oriented, because we carry that identity already within us and only have to release it. Class identity is no longer the model to understand who we are, but our gender identity and sexual identity have become the model. As if we were nothing more than our gender and our sexual object choice.

So far, I have not mentioned one other crucial component of identity: ethnicity. The rise of modernity in the nineteenth century did not only make class identity dominant; it also brought more wide-spread colonialism and the notion of ethnic (racial) identity. Ethnic identity is the Janus face of class identity, because it is also seen as fixed, something we are born with instead of born into; it is not considered to be the result of performative behavior. It also brings about a boxing in of different identities, e.g., Jewish, African, Asian, Caucasian. Although the racial theories on which these ethnic identities are based are nowadays very contested, one still must check one of these boxes when one tries to get a visa to enter the United States. Although the notion of ethnic identity has in the last century been very contested because it resulted in anti-Semitism and racism, it remains a given, even now in the twenty-first century. One should fight racism and anti-Semitism and yet accept the idea that ethnicity determines our identity. As a result, we are getting more and more used to the idea that identity is something we are born with. And gender and sexual identities can be understood as comparable to ethnic identities: we are born with them and they can be archived by neat classifications in different boxes.

Archiving from a Performative Point of View

The rise of the archive and the decline of narrative and storytelling as symbolic systems with which we try to give meaning to our life, the past, the present, and the future, developed simultaneously with this changing notion of identity. I will not relate these two fundamental changes as chicken and egg, as the one causing the other. For the rise of the archive can also be considered the result of the rise of digital media, which are also fundamentally archival. Whatever the cause of the increasing role of archival organization is, it necessitates serious reflection on the possibilities and problems of the archive as institution, and the effects of archival thinking, either harmful or productive.

Because of the conventional, privileged status of narrative in our culture but also in scholarship, we know much more about the importance, possibilities, and effects of storytelling than about archiving. For a long time, the archive was considered to be a practical tool to be employed by scientists, scholars, and administrative institutions. The fact that archival organization is also employed by how we think and organize the world was acknowledged only more recently. We make sense of the world and direct our lives, by making lists, by categorizing, and by making groups of people belonging together, based on these categorizations. Like narrative, the archive is also a special mode of thinking. The project 'Productive Archiving' intends to explore the possibilities and problems of the archive, the harmful and productive effects of archival thinking.

The medium of the archive is usually understood in terms of its referential efficiency: an archival list, for example, does not refer generally or metaphorically, but refers to all items, all individuals, and, in the case of a holocaust memorial, to all victims, by explicitly naming them all. This quality of archival organization makes the archive as medium into an ideal or perfect instrument for referential objectivity.

The referentiality of archives is, however, less perfect than it seems when we consider it from a performative and political point of view. This became clear, for instance, during the Second World War because of the role archival organizations had in tracing Jewish inhabitants in countries such as the Netherlands, Belgium, and France. Whereas in the Netherlands 75 per cent of the Jewish population were deported, in Belgium and in France the percentage only added up to, respectively, 40 and 25 per cent. There are several reasons for these major differences. One of them is the fact that Dutch municipal archives were perfectly organized, which made it rather easy for the Nazis to find out who was Jewish and who was not. Municipal archives in Belgium and France, by contrast, were rather messy and had all kinds of systemic and organizational imperfections. In those countries the Nazis had much more difficulty in tracing Jewish inhabitants. In this respect, the imperfection of messy archives saved the lives of many people. In the case of World War II, the more perfect, that is well-organized, the archive, the more deadly it was.

This example suggests that there is no reason to idealize the archival medium. Important as archival organizations may be for cultural memory and scholarly projects, this kind of organization can also be used for counter-productive, even deadly purposes. Genocides such as the Holocaust, for example the one performed by the Khmer Rouge in Cambodia, were organized as enormous, deadly archival projects. Not only people were categorized based on their ethnic, religious, sexual, or class identity, in the case of the Holocaust also the belongings of these people were categorized and archived for future use. Death camps and concentration camps were archival machines. I will come back to this in the chapter about the Ringelblum Archive in the present book.

Conceptualizing the Archive

Before introducing the contents of the book, I will first explore some theoretical and historical understandings of the archive, i.e., those of the French philosophers Jacques Derrida and Michel Foucault. In his book *Archive Fever* Derrida argues that the archive marks an institutional passage from private to public. Even private archives, such as family archives, demonstrate this, not in being publicly accessible, but in what they store, as private archives usually also store that which is storable and worth storing in the eyes of the public or culture at large.[8] It is in the archive that the singularity of stored objects and documents is or, rather, becomes, representative of the category under which the objects have been classified. The status of the archive as a place of transition of private to public, has fundamental consequences for the nature of that place. It implies that not everything can be included in an archive. Archiving is a selective procedure.

Because it intersects with the public realm and with the law, the archive is ruled by the functions of unification, consignation, and classification. The acts of unification and consignation imply that the archive is not passive; it is not a place that stores indiscriminately. Rather, it introduces distinction between archivable and non-archivable content, and based on that distinction, one might say, the archive actively produces its own content. According to Derrida, consignation is power: the power to decide what is archivable and what is not. Each object is not just stored because of its singularity, but because of what it means and does in relation to the other stored objects.

Foucault differentiates between the role of archives in the classical and in the modern period, because what changed radically in the modern period is the so-called 'threshold of description,' the minimum of importance a piece of information must have to be worthy of archiving. This threshold was lowered dramatically in order to include common people. In the words of Foucault:

> For a long time ordinary individuality—the everyday individuality of everybody—remained below the threshold of description. To be looked at, observed, described in detail, followed from day to day by an interrupted writing, was a privilege [...]. The disciplinary methods reserved this relation, lowered the threshold of describable individuality and made of this description a means of control and a method of

8_Jacques Derrida, *Archive Fever: A Freudian Impression*, trans. Eric Prenowitz (Chicago: University of Chicago Press, 1996). For a discussion of how and why archival records are socially constructed and maintained entities, see: Ciaran Trace, 'What is Recorded is Never Simply "What Happened": Record Keeping in Modern Organizational Culture,' *Archival Science* 2, nos. 1–2 (2002), pp. 137–59.

domination. [What is archived] is no longer a monument for future memory, but a document for possible use. And this new describability is all the more marked in that the disciplinary framework is a strict one: the child, the patient, the madman, the prisoner, were to become [...] the object of individual descriptions and biographical accounts.[9]

Foucault argues that a variety of new ways of examining and describing individuals was developed. The question thus emerges in what sense this accumulation and processing of new data differed from the knowledge production in earlier centuries, since scientists from long ago also had an obsession with classifying objects and archiving the results of these classifications.[10]

Foucault's answer is that while it is true that plants, animals, and even human beings had been the subjects of study before the examination regime was in place, they entered a field of knowledge as general categories, as a species for example, and not as singular individuals.

> What was innovative about the new archives was precisely that they objectified individuals not as members of a pre-existing category, but in all their uniqueness and singularity. Far from being archivable in terms of their shared properties, human beings became linked to all the unique series of events (medical, military, educational, penal events) which made them who they are as historical individuals—a history which could now take the form of a file while the individual became a case.[11]

In other words, whereas in the old archives individuals were used to build or substantiate categories, in the modern archive categories are being used to build or substantiate the individual. This leads to a situation in which human bodies, events and archives interact, and it is this interaction which brings about individual identity: this identity is then not seen as a subjective interiority, but as an objective exteriority.

Artistic Archiving is Productive Archiving

In the project 'Productive Archiving' we focus mainly on artistic practices that reflect on and challenge the three mentioned problems inherent to archival organizations and archival thinking, namely exclusions from the archive, the loss of individuality and specificity, and pigeonholing. It is not by accident that most of the contributions to this project are artistic, or that they discuss artistic practices that rethink, and then refigure the archive. It is especially artists who challenge the problems inherent to archival organization and archival thinking. Although the earliest examples of such archival artworks go back to the 1930s, it is since the 1960s that archival principles have increasingly been used by visual artists to inform, structure, and shape their works. Their aesthetic practices consist of archival enquiry or construction, and the works are built out of archival materials. This use of the archive for art does not, however, imply

9_Michel Foucault, *Discipline and Punish: The Birth of the Prison*, trans. Alan Sheridan. (New York: Pantheon, 1977), pp. 191–92.

10_For clear descriptions of the history of archival science, see Fernanda Ribeiro, 'Archival Science and Changes in the Paradigm,' *Archival Science* 1, no. 3 (2001), pp. 295–310, and Hermann Rumschöttel, 'The Development of Archival Science as a Scholarly Discipline,' *Archival Science* 1, no. 2 (2001), pp. 143–55.

an unreflected instrumentalization of the archive as artistic medium. On the contrary, these artworks interrogate the principles, claims, potentials and effects of the archive. They usually interrogate the self-evidentiary claims of the archive by reading it against the grain. The interrogation by these artists may take aim at the structural and functional principles underlying the use of the archival record; or it may result in the creation of another archival structure as a means of establishing an archaeological relationship to history, evidence, information, and data; a structure that gives rise to its own interpretative categories.

Quite some contemporary art practices that model themselves on the archive make use of the book, resulting in a so-called artist's book. Although the archive as institution is usually not associated with the medium of the book, books quite often contain archival organizations. Administrative records, for instance, cannot only be found in filing cabinets but also in book form. Books and tablets are perhaps the earliest media for the organization of recollection. In that sense certain art practices that make use of the book can also be seen as archival.[12]

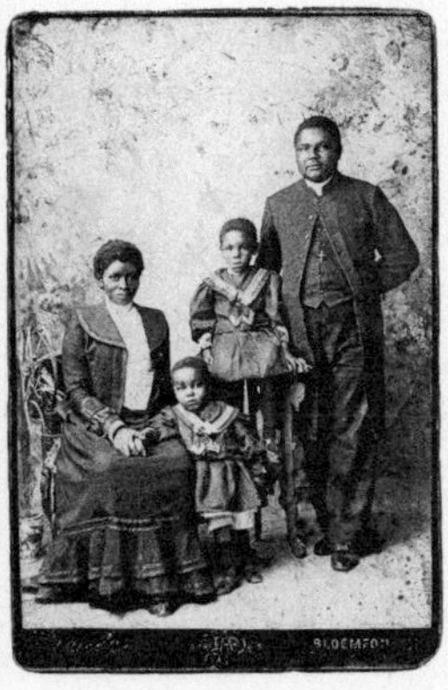

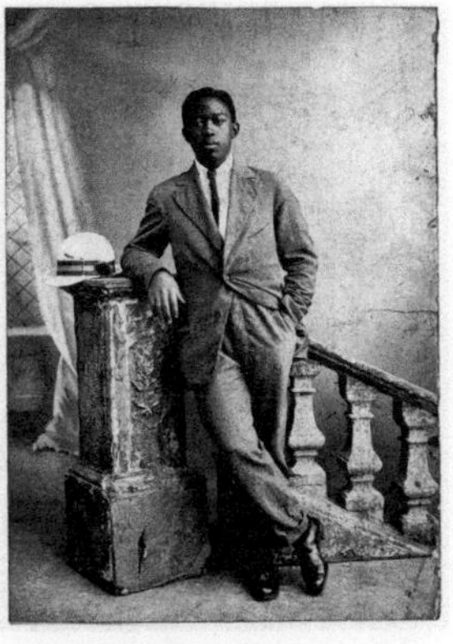

Santu Mofokeng, Images from *The Black Photo Album / Look at me: 1890–1950* (see pp. 118–123)

An example of such an archival book practice transforming exclusions from the archive into an archive in its own right, is *The Black Photo Album* by South African photographer Santu Mofokeng, mentioned above. *The Black Photo Album* is the result of an investigation of images that were commissioned by black working- and middle-class families in South Africa between 1890–1950. It was in this period that South-Africa developed and implemented a racist political system. In this era, it was still common practice to depict African people in the same visual language as animals, as part of the fauna in their own natural habitat. In the ideologies of authoritative knowledge, they were considered as 'natives' and the official, 'archivable' images had to confirm such a notion of African people. The photographs commissioned by black people and representing them as bourgeois families did not fit this ideology and were excluded from the archives of official knowledge.

These images remain scattered in the private domain and are largely invisible. In the words of Santu Mofokeng:

> They have been left behind by dead relatives, where they sometimes hang on obscure parlour walls in the townships. In some families they are coveted as treasures, displacing totems in discursive narratives about identity, lineage and personality. And because, to some people, photographs contain the 'shadow' of the subject, they are carefully guarded from the ill-will of witches

11_Manuel DeLanda, 'The Archive before and after Foucault,' in *Information is Alive: Art and Theory on Archiving and Retrieving Data*, ed. Joke Brouwer and Arjen Mulder (Rotterdam: V2_Publishing and NAi Publishers, 2003), p. 11.

12_See for a history of different media used for recollection Sonja Neef, *Imprint and Trace: Handwriting in the Age of Technology* (Chicago: Reaktion Books, 2011).

and enemies. In other families they are being destroyed as rubbish during spring-cleans because of interruptions in continuity or disaffection with the encapsulated meanings and history of the images. Most often they lie hidden to rot through neglect in kists, cupboards, cardboard boxes and plastic bags.[13]

Mofokeng's *Black Photo Album* reverses the exclusion of these images from the authoritative public domain. He collects these images and the stories about the subjects of the photographs. It is important that images that have so far been excluded from public archives are now presented within the archival genre of the artist's book. But photographs from *The Black Photo Album* are shown within the context of the gallery and the museum too. Mofokeng presents them in a new format in combination with the stories. By doing this the neglected memories and images are inserted into the public domain, and form the archive from which they had been excluded until now. This reanimation of the invisible exclusions from the archive implies much more than bringing to life almost forgotten memories. By making these images into archival objects, the ideology that subjected African people to the lower orders in the 'family of men' is rewritten.

Dutch artist Inge Meijer also presented her archival project *The Plant Collection* (2019) in the form of an artist's book. She researched the archives of the Stedelijk Museum Amsterdam and discovered something remarkable. Many of the images that documented the exhibitions after the Second World War showed plants as part of the exhibition. Meijer investigated the vanished and subsequently forgotten vegetation in the museum during the period between 1945–1983. It turned out that director Sandberg had started a new kind of museum display, which was continued by the directors who succeeded him. In those days there was even one special guard who was responsible for taking care of the Stedelijk Museum's plant collection. In the late 1980s, this practice gradually came to an end. In her book *The Plant Collection* Meijer has collected images that include plants from the official exhibitions' installations documentation. What we see in these images is not just insignificant details; they point to a buried and largely forgotten history. Meijer is currently

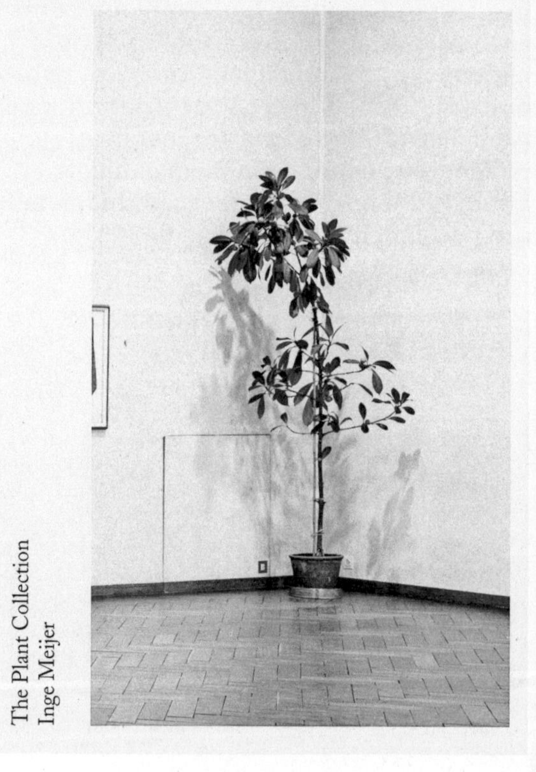

13_Santu Mofokeng, *The Black Photo Album / Look at me: 1890–1950* (Göttingen: Steidl Verlag), p. 230.

making a similar kind of book, this time based on the collection of photographs of plants in the MoMA in New York.

In her contribution to this book, Annet Dekker discusses another significant archival artist's book: Anne Geene's *No. 235/Encyclopedia of an Allotment* (2010). This book looks like a taxonomic work, but it doesn't focus on the conventional categories of plant and animal life; categories such as insects, mammals, or garden plants are not used. The book has three parts; the third part, for example, contains all kinds of measurements, such as the group behavior of snails, the speed of ducks, the camouflage of frogs, and the effects of sunlight on leaves. Her approach seems to be modelled on that of a scientist or biologist. But being an artist as well, her taxonomic look is based purely on what can be seen, on visual similarities, contrasts, and patterns. Important is that not only the book itself is an archive, but she also deals with the photographs in her taxonomic collection

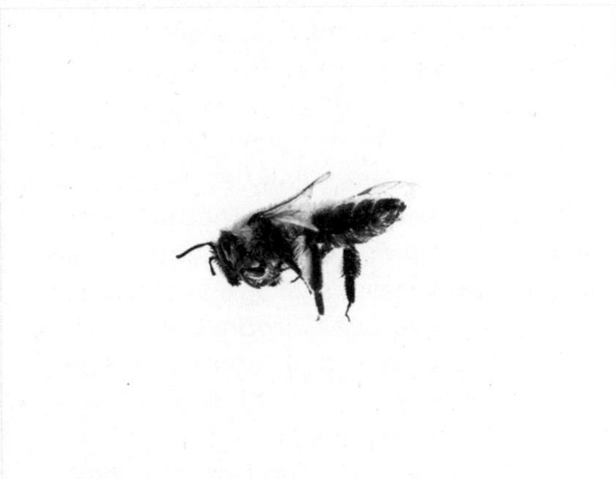

Anne Geene, *Insecten van de vensterbank* [Insects from the windowsill], from: *Perceel Nr. 235. Encyclopedie van een volkstuin*. Rotterdam, 2010 (see pp. 212–221)

as archives. As Dekker quotes her: 'I see photography as an information carrier with which different stories can be told.' The same can be said about archives.[14] Dekker concludes that the difference between this artistic taxonomy and scientific taxonomies is that the former leads to completely new, surprising insights, e.g., that she had to reconsider

> snails not as loathsome enemies who are after my precious lettuce, but as interesting nodes in a community that perhaps move according to certain unknown (at least to me) rules.[15]

Overview over Parts and Chapters

Aleida Assmann makes a useful distinction between functional archives and storage archives. Functional archives store what is needed in the present. Medical files, police and tax office files, and those of insurance companies are good examples of functional archives. Also, the way users of new media such as Facebook are being archived happens within a functional archive: the resulting data are being sold to companies, so that the users can be targeted for advertising. In Assmann's words: 'Functional archives are the infrastructure and control instruments that guide and support the present.'[16] This present is not the present in which acts of memory are being performed, but in which the state controls its subjects and capitalist companies reach out to their potential clients. Within Foucault's distinction between the classical and the modern archive, one could say that the modern archive is exclusively

14_See for the photographic image as archive, Ernst van Alphen, 'Introduction,' *Staging the Archive: Art and Photography in the Age of New Media*. (London: Reaktion Books, 2014), pp. 7–20.

15_Annet Dekker, 'Archival Absurdity, or a Walk in the Park,' this book, p. 00–00.

16_Aleida Assmann, 'The Archive as Laboratory of the New,' this book, p. 00–00.

functional. The storage archive is then the equivalent of what Foucault calls the classical archive. Assmann defines storage archives as based on a different logic: they come into being when what is no longer of interest or relevant for the present is sorted out but not immediately thrown away: it is stored in an archive, a museum, a library. The primary function of storage archives is history, or the enabling and activation of memory.

Archiving Identities

The first section of the book presents contributions that discuss or challenge the archiving of identities. My own chapter on the Ringelblum archive in Warsaw is a good example of the usefulness of Assmann's distinction. This archive came about in the ghetto of Warsaw during World War II. To concentrate all Jewish inhabitants based on their Jewish ethnicity is an archival procedure. The category of Jewishness is a specific box on the basis of which ghettos, concentration camps and deathcamps were organized. This was a functional way of

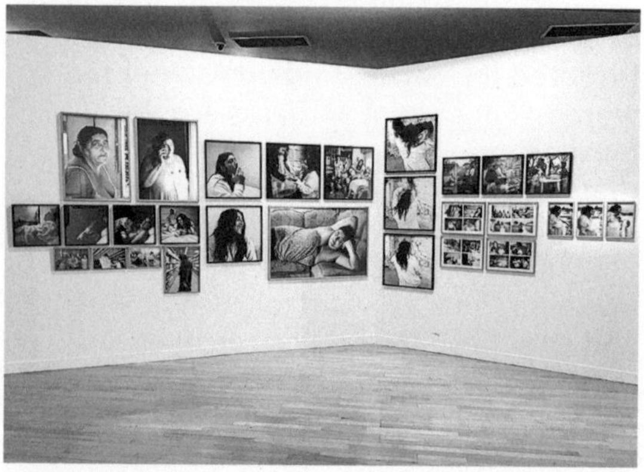

Mathieu Pernot, *Les Gorgan*, installation (see pp. 70–87)

archiving because it had to isolate, and them kill, European Jews. This intention was not focused on the past, but on the present and future. The chapter deals with the question of how the archive of the ghetto in Warsaw can function as a counter-archive, countering the deadly archival practices of the Nazis.

My text on the French artist photographer Mathieu Pernot relies on Assmann's distinction between functional and storage archives too. Pernot's work does not consist of individual images, but of assemblages of photos in book or exhibition form. In the case of his projects with Roma people and families he does not make a representation of a family through photography, but a photographic history: it is a history of images, of practices of photography that were used to represent Roma people. His books as well as exhibitions are then an assemblage of images and photographic genres, instead of a storage or collection of individual images.

By doing this Pernot has rewritten the archival registers that were traditionally used to portray Roma people. Whereas the kind of archival collections used to portray Roma were so far functional archives, especially ethnographic or anthropometric archives, Mathieu Pernot has revisited these archives and transformed them into a storage archive. His storage archive *Les Gorgan 1995–2015* enables the viewer to imagine and see real, individual people with their own histories and memories.

The short film *The Bang Straws* (2021) by Michelle Williams Gamaker is not modelled on the archive as such but critiques the archiving of identities in twentieth-century Hollywood studio films. It returns to Sidney Franklin's 1937 film *The Good Earth*, which was one of cinema's most notorious cases of casting discrimination, with German-Austrian-American actress Luise Rainer winning the high-profile lead of O-Lan, the farmer's wife. Despite Chinese-American actress Anna May Wong's talent and evident desire to play O-Lan, MGM refused her the lead due to the anti-miscegenation Hays Code, offering her the minor role of sex worker Lotus instead, which she refused. To play O-Lan, Rainer wore racist 'yellowface' make-up, as so many Hollywood actors did, winning an Oscar for her performance.

The Bang Straws questions the structural violence on film sets and the lack of agency for actors of color. 'Bang straws' is an obsolete term for farm hands who threshed the grain. The film begins with an image of Rainer trapped under straw; in this image, Rainer becomes a nebulous straw figure, devoid of race or gender. In *The Bang Straws*, Chinese performer Dahong Wang (who plays herself) auditions for a screen test for the character of O-Lan in *The Good Earth*. The violence of the casting process is a recurring motif in Williams Gamaker's work; this process is violent, because based on the pigeonholing of identities. The protagonist of *The Bang Straws* expresses it as follows: 'They are interested in my body, not in me.' The film also subtly weaves in a Covid-19 narrative to address the racism that ensued for people of Chinese heritage at the start of the pandemic.

Like Williams Gamaker, Merapi Obermayer challenges the boxing in of identities in her personal short text 'Does the fact that I fall for men make me a woman?' In her case she even refuses all identity distinction, for identity feels to her like a stigma. She can only live in what she calls 'an androgynous society.' Having grown up with her parents in the last leper colony in the Netherlands, she has suffered from ghettoizing identities in the most extreme way. Her identity of being the child of a father who suffered from leprosy did not only put her into a specific conceptual box, but also isolated her into a real place, a colony. As a result, she has a fundamental distrust of any identity, for identity has been pigeonholing to her in an almost literal sense. Even the basic distinction between man and woman has performative effects that she, with this extraordinary background, experiences as harmful. Although her personal background is different than that of many of us, it does not mean that her experience

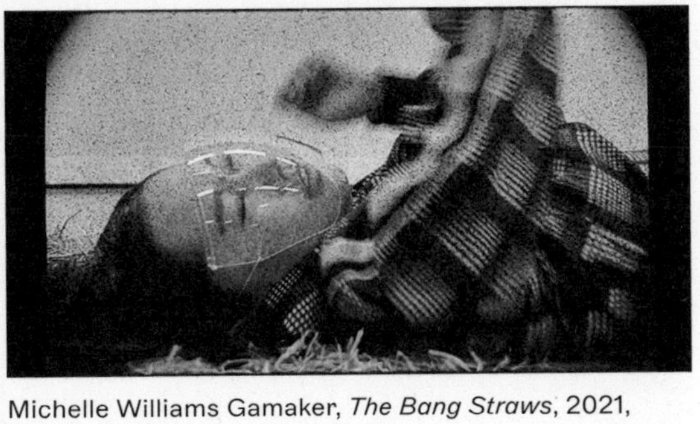

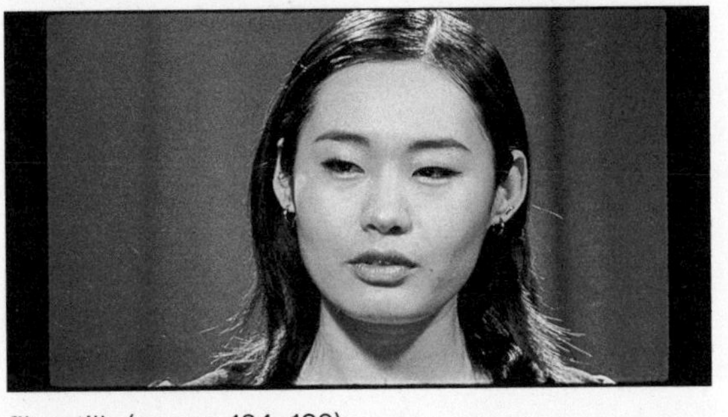

Michelle Williams Gamaker, *The Bang Straws*, 2021, film stills (see pp. 124–129)

of the pigeonholing of identities is unique. I would like to suggest that it is emblematic; it is thanks to her exceptional experience that she understands the harmful effects of pigeonholing as such.

In his essay on artist Pablo Lerma, Drew Sawyer argues that Lerma's archival works challenge the homogenizing effects of the archive. Archives are not objective but subjective, because the inclusion or exclusion of materials is often based on biases or existing categories. For his installation *It Doesn't Stop at Images*, for instance, Lerma collected thousands of images from the IHLIA's archives in Amsterdam of the Dutch gay magazine *Homologie*. After researching these images Lerma concluded that even this archive followed the stereotypes of gay culture. It is dominated by the dominant forms of masculinity and male beauty. Being himself married to a man and having three children, Lerma was especially interested in images of care and of queer families, but there were almost none in this archive.

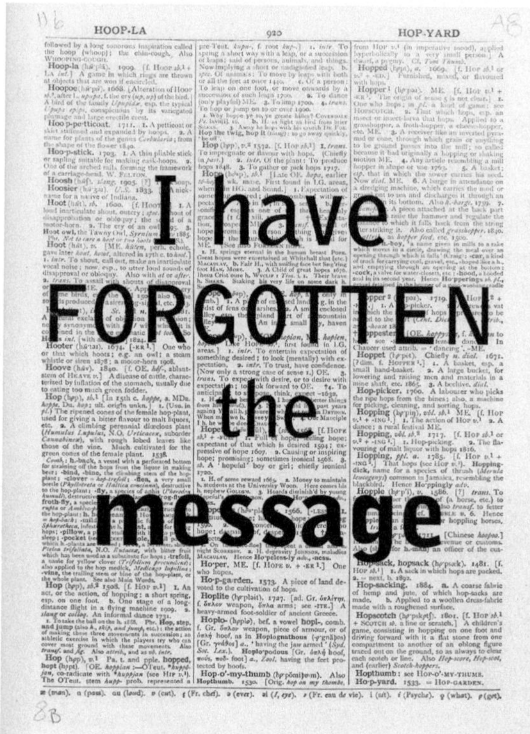

William Kentridge, *Waiting for the Sibyl*, 2020, page from the book (see pp 190–199)

For some time now, South African artist William Kentridge uses old dictionaries and encyclopedias for his works. For his works on paper, he superimposes texts and images on pages from these old archival books. His animated film *Sibyl* (2020) was also made on such pages as background on which new images were created and superimposed. This film was first conceived for, and developed from, his chamber opera *Waiting for the Sibyl*, which was commissioned by the Teatro dell'Opera di Roma in 2019. The fact that he uses pages from old dictionaries for his recent work can be understood as Kentridge's renegotiation with the colonial past of Africa. Western notions and paradigms of knowledge were also imposed on colonialized cultures. As a result, Western notions of time and space were introduced into cultures that so far experienced time and space differently. Although this important element of colonialization was considered to be the equivalent of modernization, the price to pay for this modernization was high. Kentridge's superimposition of images and texts of old archival books, introduced into Africa as part of colonialization, is a way of challenging the colonial identity of African countries.

Archiving Memories and Histories

When identities are being archived it concerns mainly, but not exclusively, functional archives. The IHLIA, the LHBTQI archive in Amsterdam, for instance, is a storage archive, not a functional one. However, the archiving of memories and histories takes place especially in storage archives. But even when memories and histories are being archived in a storage archive, it is almost impossible to escape the homogenizing effect of the archive and its stereotypical classifications.

It is especially this problem of homogenization and classification that is challenged by artistic archival practices. They use or make archives in order to explore alternative historical narratives and knowledge. As Daria Tuminas makes clear in her discussion of the exhibition about photographic archival materials she curated, 'Pass it On,' 'the artists' main goal is not to purely represent the archive, but rather to create an artwork based on it. [...] An attempt to construct an archive is counterbalanced by a simultaneous attempt to deconstruct it.'[17] The four artists who participated in Tuminas' exhibition 'Pass it On' (Lebohang Kganye, Marianne Ingleby, Pablo Lerma, Inge Meijer) are interested in what Allan Sekula has called the semantic 'availability of pictures,'[18] implying 'the potential of the archival meaning to change over time and for history to be rewritten.'[19]

The work of German artist Monika Huber is related to, but differs slightly in one respect from the photographic archival practices discussed by Tuminas. Huber works on images by overpainting them. She has created an archive of images she takes from television coverage of worldwide public protests, the responses to them and their consequences. But she does more than collect those images into her archive. She paints over parts of the images in order to draw attention to the key scenes. Because the photographic image as well as the archive is supposed to register 'everything,' especially photos are often hard to read because of this non-selectivity. Huber's overpainting helps us to focus and concentrate on what we see. But there is more to it; television coverage, but also snapshots of the world consist of fleeting images; they snap and cover fleeting, instantaneous events and they are gone, have disappeared before we have realized what we have seen. By imposing painterly gestures on these fleeting images, Huber arrests them because painterly time and photographic time are fundamentally different. Her painting is not a snapshot of the world, but a gesture performed by an artist in the present of looking at the images of worldwide protests. Huber's painterly impositions on the images in her archive suggests that looking at these images should not be fleeting, like the images themselves, but slow and engaging. We should be *aware* of what we see, and if possible, act upon it. Looking at an image is not the same as seeing the image; with her overpainted photos Huber makes us see.

H401 (Herengracht 401) in Amsterdam is an archival space full of collections, archives and interiors embodied with a great diversity of potential memories. During World War II the house functioned as a hiding place. Hence, nowadays the archival nature of this house can be used to tell its heroic

17_Daria Tuminas, 'Pass It On: Private Stories, Public Histories,' this book, p. 00–00.

18_Allan Sekula, 'Reading an Archive: Photography between Labor and Capitalism,' in *The Photography Reader*, ed. Liz Wells (New York: Routledge, 2003), pp. 443–52.

19_Daria Tuminas, 'Pass It On: Private Stories, Public Histories,' p. 00–00.

history. But the interiors, collections and archives in this house have been carefully curated by the people who lived there and who made them. These archival collections are foremost self-representations of the people responsible for them. They need critical readings and alternative perspectives in order to unveil different memories and narratives not necessarily included in the self-presentation of the archivists living in this house. This includes the stories about sexual abuse that recently came to light, having taking place in the same house. These stories are not heroic but traumatic. The people presently responsible for the house have experienced that especially artistic research could make the archival space, full of potential memories, productive again. Instead of retelling the same heroic story, the archives should be challenged to tell other and different stories. And this can best be done by artists. Artistic research is employed as a method to discover something that is not intended and that is not already known, although hidden in this archival space.

Argentinian artist Sebastián Díaz Morales takes yet a different archival route. The word 'archive' does not only refer to ordered collections of books, documents, and objects, but also to the building in which those collections are housed. An archive has also an architectural dimension. This suggests that architecture does not only provide space to people, but also to memories. I already implied this when I wrote about H401 as an archival space. In Díaz Morales' video works *Pasajes*, he takes a walk through architecture as a means of archiving and collecting memories. In his *Pasajes I & II*, memories of the last Argentinian military dictatorship (1976–1983) are being archived by means of a walk through 'guilty spaces.' spaces were 'things' have happened and where the regime performed their dictatorship in the cruelest ways.

This notion of memory in relation to architecture resonates with the famous view of memory presented by Frances A. Yates, who traced the theories of memory from antiquity on, before the invention of print came along to assist us in memorizing. She focused especially on the art of memorizing by means of a walk through a house. Each room becomes the storage space for specific memories, and space becomes the host of time. This architectural practice in the service of memorization was especially used in rhetoric. In order to memorize the order of one's argumentation one could best walk through the subsequent spaces of an architectural building, imaginary or not. Many artists have taken up Yates' vision, among whom the Italian writer Italo Calvino.[20]

Sebastián Díaz Morales too steps into Yates' footsteps, consciously or not. The passages in his *Pasajes* are not just passages through architectural space but at the same time through time lost.

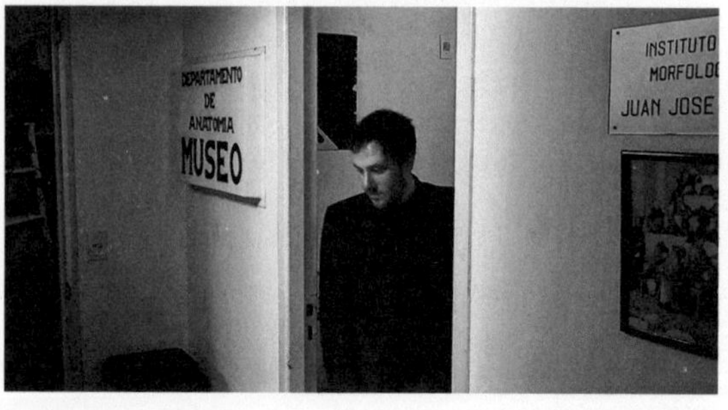

Sebastián Díaz Morales, *Pasajes* [Passages], 2012, film still (see pp. 172–189)

20_Francis A. Yates, *The Art of Memory* (Chicago: The University of Chicago Press, 1966).

The architecture activates memories of events that took place in these spaces. Of course only the people who are knowledgeable about these buildings in Buenos Aires and the specific events that took place there will recognize buildings and particular memories connected to them, but that is not necessarily the point of these passages through architecture. The point is that the viewer is affected by the burden of memory that architecture may carry, and how architecture is archival in several respects.

When addressing the relationship between memory and architecture, the work of Dutch artist Marjan Teeuwen imposes itself. Some of her works are literally titled *Archive*, others *Destroyed House*. But her destroyed houses are archival as well. By constructing architectural spaces, all her work demonstrates an important characteristic of archival organization. Architectural organization is the equivalent of archival organization here, because both are the result of ordering, making order out of disorder, bringing order out of chaos. Whereas architecture organizes and orders space, archives order memories and our potential connections to the past. For her destroyed houses Teeuwen re-uses debris and materials from the house. With these materials she makes architectural constructions in the house. These constructions are not creations *ex nihilo* but re-orderings of what was already there. This re-ordering evokes archival organizations, of which memory is one of the prime examples.

Her interventions in ruined houses create order and structure in chaos. Her creation of harmonious order out of chaos and destruction is, however, not an end in itself. It embodies the ordering activity of memory. This ordering activity is even intensified in her photographic practice. The photographs she makes of these destroyed houses are much more than documentation of temporary installations. Making use of how linear perspective in the photographic image imposes a very specific order on space, she intensifies that ordering quality of the photographic image. Her temporary installations, and the photographic images she makes of these installations, help us to understand how the temporality of trauma distinguishes itself from the temporality of memory, and most importantly, how it contributes to the transformation of trauma into memory.

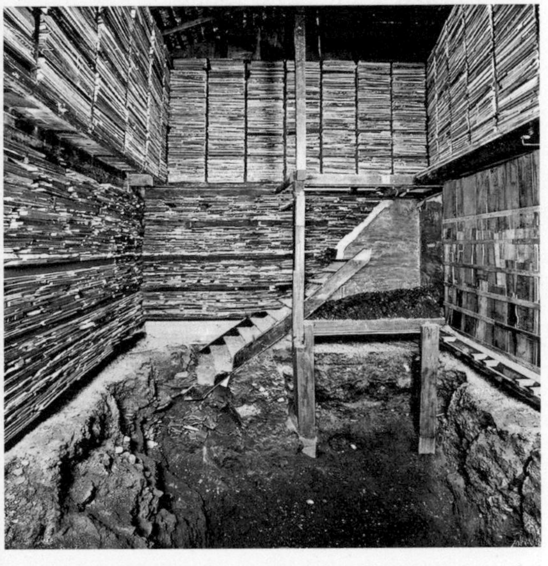

Marjan Teeuwen, *Destroyed House Kyoto*, 2020
(see pp. 38–45)

Archiving Objects

The last part of this book concerns the archiving of objects. I already discussed the archival books of Anne Geene and of Inge Meijer. Geene archives the plants and animals in her allotment garden 235 in the allotment garden association 'Eigen Hof' (Own Garden) in Rotterdam. Meijer has collected those images of exhibition documentation from the archives of the Stedelijk Museum Amsterdam that include plants. But Meijer has done more than that. In her work *A Garden Revisioned* (2019–ongoing) she literally and materially takes care of the collection of negatives and contact sheets of an abandoned photo studio she found in a building that was a 'wedding palace' in the South-Korean city of Gwangju. The wedding images were meant for the family album, or the wedding album as a sub-genre of the family album. Within that context we look at dear family members on the so-called most beautiful day of their lives. We look on the basis of the conventions of the wedding image and the wedding album. Meijer's work on and with this found archival collection alters our mode of looking. She makes this archive productive again by taking care of these images not only in the literal, material sense of the expression, as preserving, but also as transforming our mode of looking at images.

According to the most common notion of the archive, it is a storage of documents and objects from the past. In the archival artistic practice of Italian artist Gianfranco Baruchello, however, the archive is all about times to come. Since the 1960s he has made a great diversity of works all based on the appropriation, disassembling, assembling, accumulation of images and texts, listing them, or making montages of them. His encyclopedias, his paintings as well his drawings are the result of this procedure. All his works should be considered as, to use his own term, 'small systems.' For him archives are not objective systems that make inventories and order the past or the world; no, they create new, possible worlds. As Carla Subrizi explains, Baruchello's small systems or archival constructions combine differences and similarities as starting points for worlds to come. With his small systems he does not record existing organizations of the world, but he tries to provoke new ones.

When the archive is used in this way, or when an archival practice succeeds in realizing this potential of the archive, it is utterly productive. This book discusses a variety of problems archival organizations confront us with. Avoiding the archive because of these problems, is not an issue, because archival organization is a basic symbolic mode on the basis of which we organize our life, the past, the present, and the future. And we should not confuse the classical archive with the modern archive, or the functional archive with the storage archive (Assmann); each kind of archive brings with it different kinds of problems. What this book suggests is that it is best to explore constructive and creative solutions for these problems. Especially artistic archives seem to be able to develop these possible solutions, because they are more conscious of the conventional problems to archival organization.

Let me conclude by saying a few words about the series of images titled *Point of Departure* by Jeannette

Christensen. They all show navels. Although they are our point of departure into life, we do not give them much attention. That is why they all belong to one category, that is how we pigeonhole them. But this series shows that they are all different, they all have their own tiny characteristics and features. These images suggest that our individuality cannot be found in an archive but in our navel.

THE ARCHIVE AS A LABORATORY OF THE NEW

Where Remembering and Forgetting Meet

Aleida Assmann

The term 'archive' has made an astonishing career in recent years. For a long time, archives led a shadowy existence; they were regarded as shy of publicity, and dusty; an archivist was imagined to be a pale specialist with sleeve protectors. This changed abruptly when famous philosophers and historians such as Derrida and Foucault, but also artists of different media and orientations took up the term. Since then, the word has circulated with many new meanings. It is therefore advisable to first define more accurately in what sense we are to speak of archives in the following.

Two Forms of Archives

I understand archives as places where remembering and forgetting meet. To describe this more precisely, I distinguish between functional archives and storage archives. Functional archives store what is needed to act in the present. Expiry dates are inscribed in every functional archive. In a doctor's office, for example, files of deceased patients are disposed of; the same applies to folders in an office that has been vacated for a successor. Functional archives are the infrastructure and control instruments that guide and support action in the present. Neither administration nor political power can do without them. When the presence of an organization, bureaucracy or political power ends, the value of this information instantly decays.

Memory archives follow a completely different logic. They only come into being when what is no longer of interest or relevance for the present or the future is sorted out but not immediately thrown away. Such an attitude first prevailed in human history after the French Revolution, when institutions such as the monarchy, clergy, and nobility were forcibly abolished. However, their traces were not erased in the process, but were specifically secured in new institutions.

At that time, a new consciousness arose for that which is past and from which no normative force emanates any more, but is still of interest: history.

The founding saint of the storage archive in this new sense was Abbé Grégoire, who coined the term 'vandalism' in the last years of the eighteenth century. Only 'barbarians and slaves,' he wrote, 'hate the sciences and destroy the monuments of culture. Free men love and preserve them.' At the same time, this gave rise to a new concept of culture that separated itself from the political, and with it new civic values that were given their sacrosanct shelters in new kinds of museums, archives, and libraries. The French Revolution unleashed an enormous acceleration of modernization. What was thereby eliminated from the present at an ever-faster pace did not simply disappear, however, but now became 'historical' and thus gained a whole new meaning as 'culture.' This new way of dealing with the past did not prevail everywhere in the world. On the contrary, it is specific to Western modernity and created the basis for important cultural resources in the nineteenth century, of which I would like to mention only three here.

First: The Recognition of the Alterity of the Past

The first point concerns a new form of selflessness in dealing with the past. It is the attitude that protects the past from the grasp and desires of the present, which otherwise has always been and continues to be claimed for the legitimization of power. According to a phrase by German historian Arno Borst, these new historians are characterized by the fact that they 'acknowledge the diversity of times.' But only where sources are listed, secured and interpreted in this new framework does it become possible to acknowledge the alterity of times. In order to recognize an anachronism, one must know the difference between the present and a past era. This cannot be done without archives, which are the prerequisite for this invaluable cognitive achievement and the basis of historical education. Only this education makes it possible to expand one's knowledge of one's own past, to think critically beyond the narrowing of traditions handed down and a one-sided image of oneself, and thus also to recognize the foreign in one's own.

Today, for example, if we take a look at the archives of the programs of the Vienna Festival, we are inevitably struck by this alterity of history. We learn, for example, that this important departure into a new future and the revival of Vienna as European Capital of Culture in the early 1950s was even about more than a successful program of events, namely the restoration of a long and proud history of origins that masked the traumatic ruptures of the immediate past. Already ten years after the end of WW II, people were betting on the unshakeable continuity of this 'genius loci that has been at work on the shape and soul of Vienna for a millennium.' The city is praised as a meeting place, 'whose spirit and culture, landscape and buildings of the past speak the language of all peoples and are of such harmonious diversity that all good spirits of every kind can feel at home here in earnest and cheerfulness'. To today's ears, this special emphasis on Vienna's hospitality tacitly overlooks the fact that until recently 'all good spirits in earnest and cheerfulness' could by no means feel at home here, but that many Viennese artists, actors, and musicians were persecuted for racial reasons and had to flee into exile. Examples of this are the author Stefan Zweig or the Viennese pop star and violin virtuoso of the 1930s Albert Rosé and his daughter Alma, to whom the plateau on the first floor of the Neue Burg is now dedicated as a place of remembrance.

Secondly: The Reappraisal of a Denied History

When the winds of history turn and a change of political system is imminent, unjust regimes immediately set about destroying their archives. This is how the apartheid regime in South Africa destroyed tons of incriminating material before it left, and the civil rights activists in the GDR had to go on a hunger strike to secure the Stasi files. In such cases, the information value of the files is reversed. In the historical archive, the documents that previously served political persecution become the basis for coming to terms with history, condemning the perpetrators, recognizing and rehabilitating the victims and enlightening society.

In this context, securing sources means even more than expanding our historical knowledge and self-image; it means bringing not only a forgotten, but a concealed and denied history into the present and making it the basis of a new present and future. Acknowledging and accepting this denied history is the prerequisite for effectively bringing it to a close, and only this prevents this injustice from being repeated. Looking at the history of black people in the US that has been repressed from the white archive, civil and human rights activist James Baldwin put this key insight in a succinct formula: 'Not everything can be changed, but nothing can be changed until it is dealt with.'

Thirdly: The Archives of Art

As these references already show, the material conditions for remembering and forgetting are within the framework of society, politics, science and the arts. If we take musicians as an example, their archives consisted exclusively of sheet music, initially handwritten and later reproduced in engravings, until the technical possibility of sound recordings. What did early collections of sheet music look like? Who had access to them? What was their range? Before bourgeois singing and music societies began to play a role in the history of music archiving by following the changes in music history with interest and archiving sheet music, it was noble patrons who took on this task. Before the age of printed music, these archives only ever benefited small circles.

One example is Baron Gottfried van Swieten (1734–1803), who was a passionate collector of sheet music. He did a lot of research in London in the circle of Georg Friedrich Händel as well as in Berlin in the circle of Bach's sons and brought his treasures to Vienna, where he became director of the royal court library.

With this private collection of sheet music, he made Haydn, Mozart and Beethoven happy and thereby triggered significant artistic innovations. The musicians became acquainted with Bach's polyphony, which helped them overcome the gallant style popular in Vienna.
This music archive also made Mozart's arrangement of Händel's great oratorios possible. Without this important service of noble music archives, there would have been no recourse to the compositions of older masters, and without this recourse certain innovations in the work of the younger masters would not have been possible. Against this background, one can imagine what the great treasure of collected sheet music in the Weimar library of the Duchess Anna Amalia meant for contemporary musicians, who could draw their inspiration from it. Since most of this treasure was burnt in 2004, this chapter of music history has been closed forever.

Verdi knew how important such archives are for artistic creation and innovation and said:

> To return to the old is to progress. The archive is a passive resource, but one that must be actively secured, maintained, sorted and, above all, interrogated. But like the oracle at Delphi, it is always the question that triggers the answer. It is the current questions and search movements of the artists that set this creative exchange in motion. Their questions are like a wake-up call that once again calls up latent information from oblivion, uses it and lets it shine.

As can be seen here, the concept of memory has always encompassed both: remembering and forgetting.
The distinction of cultural memory into the poles of memory and functional memory shows the complementary structure of memory, in which remembering and forgetting are always close to each other and intertwine in many ways.

For much that has been forgotten is not lost forever, but only temporarily withdrawn from us and thus became inaccessible. What has sunk to the unsorted bottom of the forgotten in personal memory can, however, rise to the surface again under certain circumstances, like the deeply forgotten sensation that Proust's madeleine suddenly releases in him again after many years. What we call forgetting is usually a latent memory to which we have lost the password; when it is accidentally hit, a piece of sensually lived past returns, completely unexpectedly. Latency comes from the Latin *latere*, which means to hide and conceal. What Proust's 'mémoire involontaire' is for the individual, we may conclude, is the archive for cultural memory: a space of latency and thus a fund and background for memories that have their hour behind them, but perhaps also still ahead of them.

Already Been in a Lake of Fire

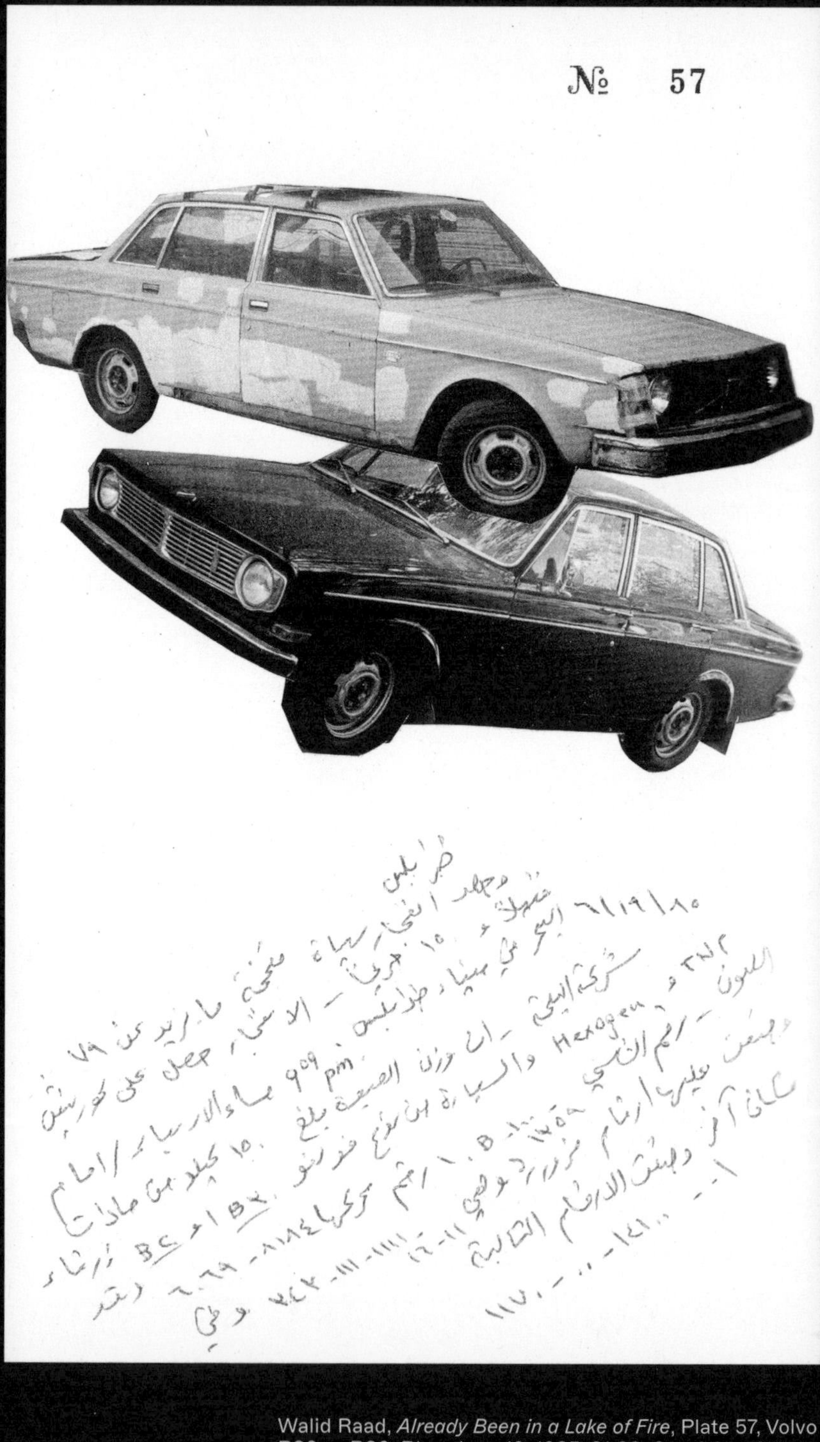

Walid Raad

Walid Raad, *Already Been in a Lake of Fire*, Plate 57, Volvo B20 or B30, Blue, June 19, 1985, 21:09, Corniche of the sea, Tripoli, 79 killed, 150 injured, 150 kg. of TNT Hexogen

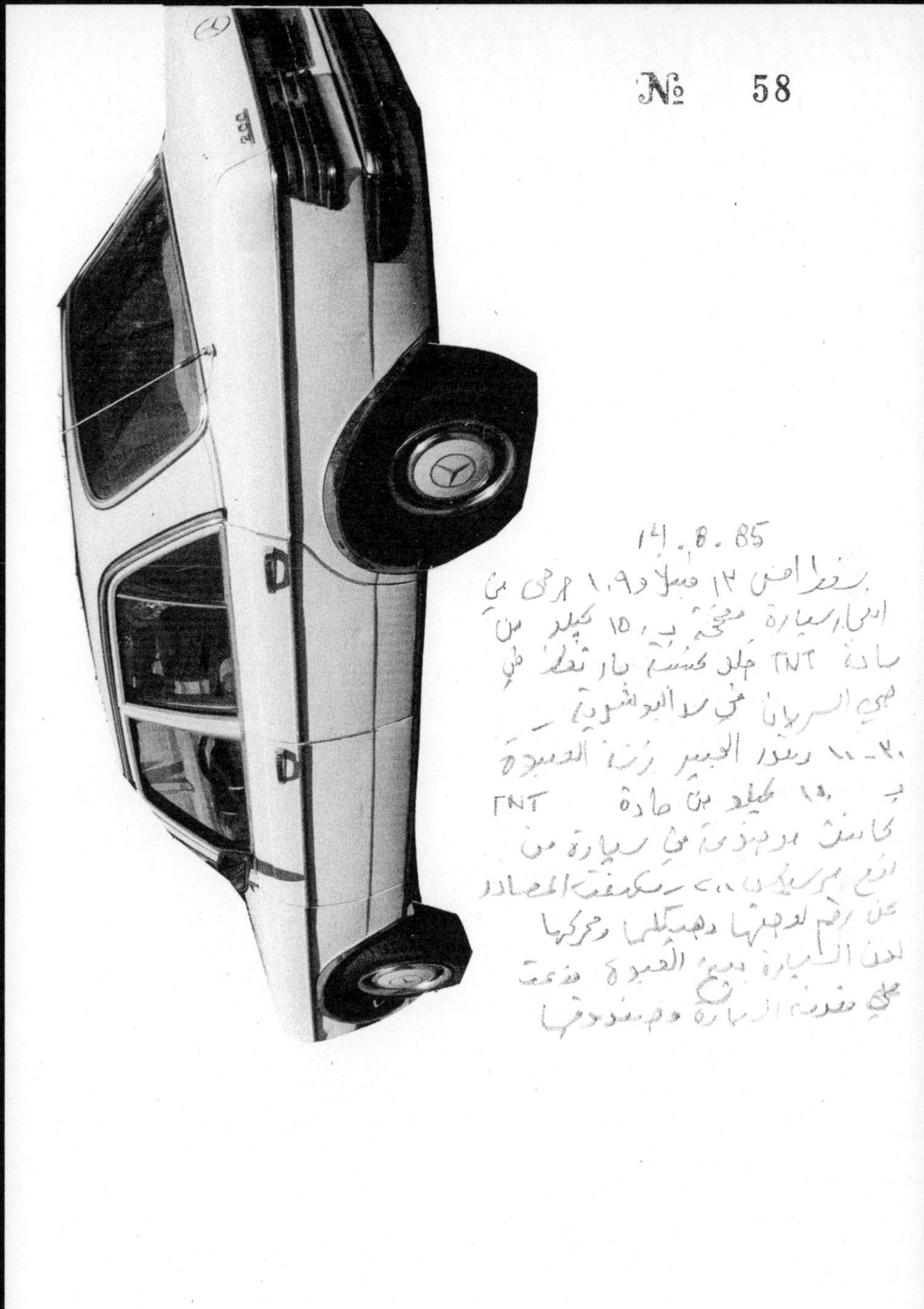

Walid Raad, *Already Been in a Lake of Fire*, Plate 58, Mercedes 200, Beige, August 14, 1985, 10:30, Beirut, Mar Takla, 13 killed, 109 injured, 150 kg. of TNT

Destroyed House

Marjan Teeuwen

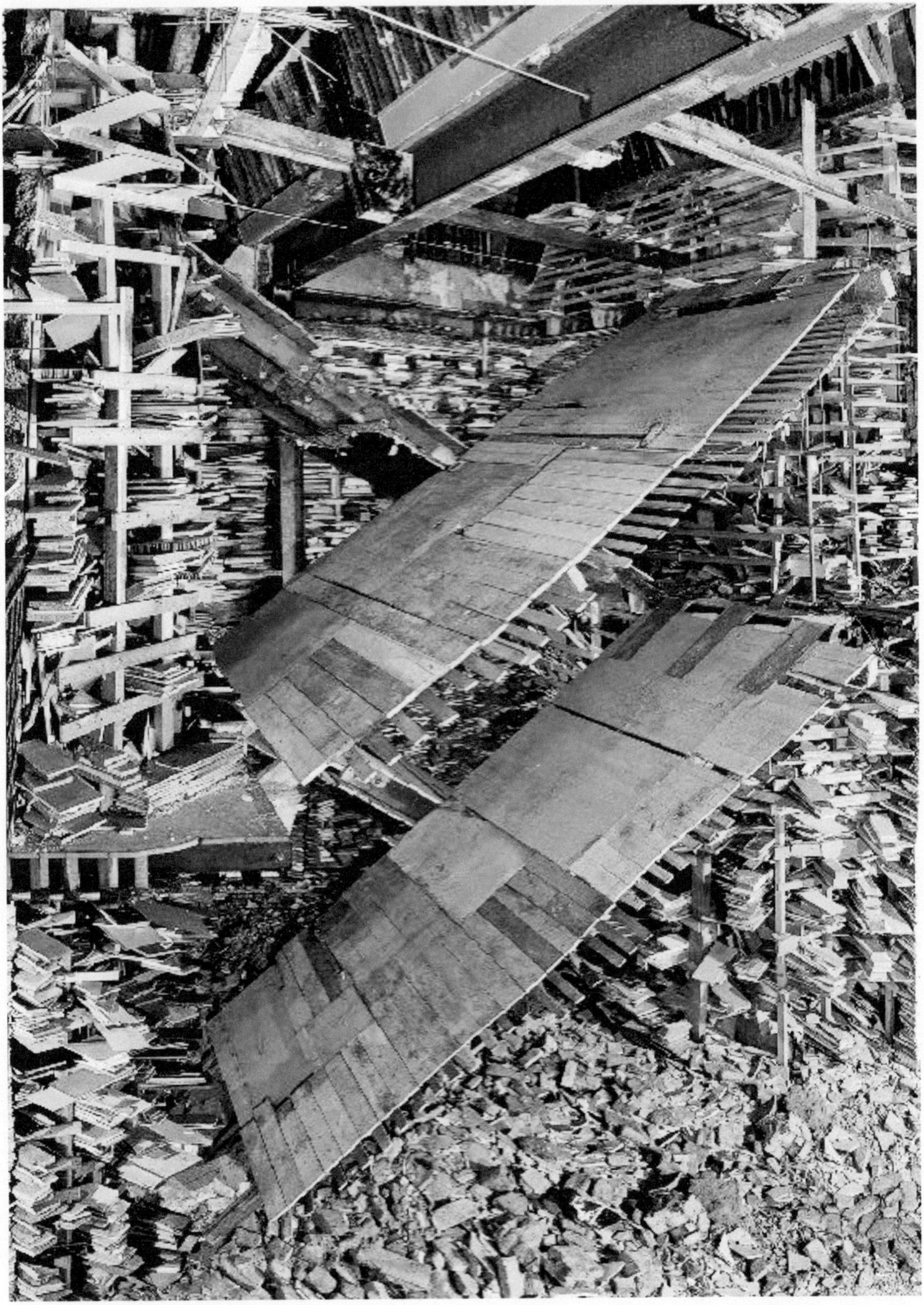

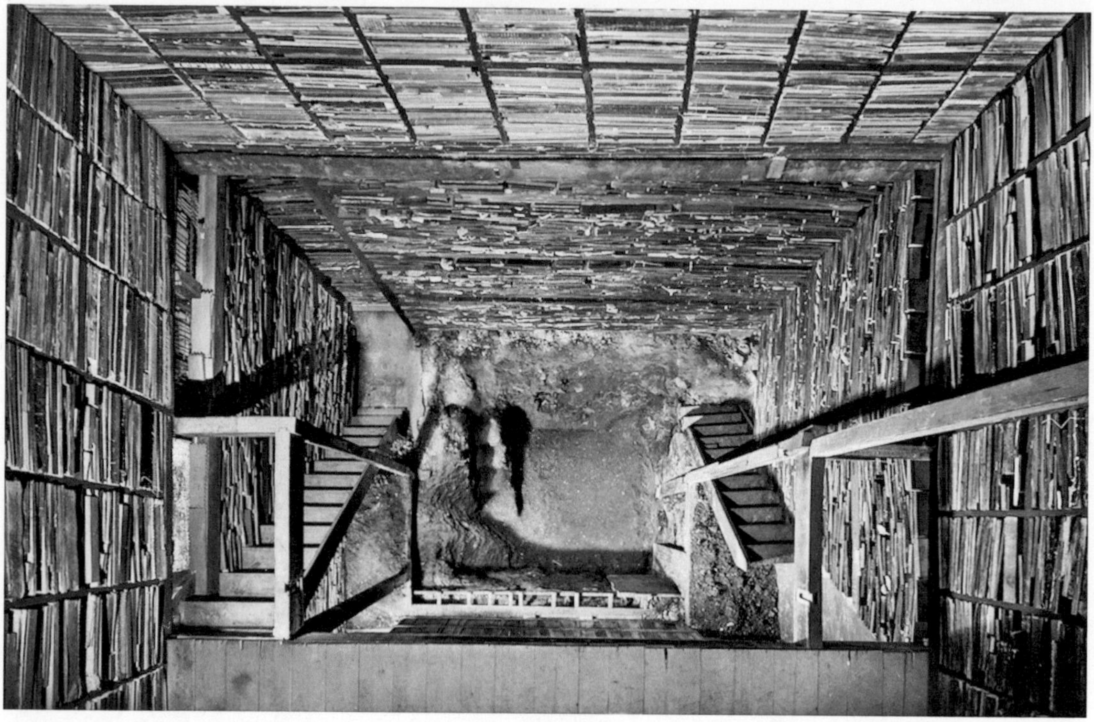

Marjan Teeuwen

Marjan Teeuwen,
Destroyed House Kyoto,
2020

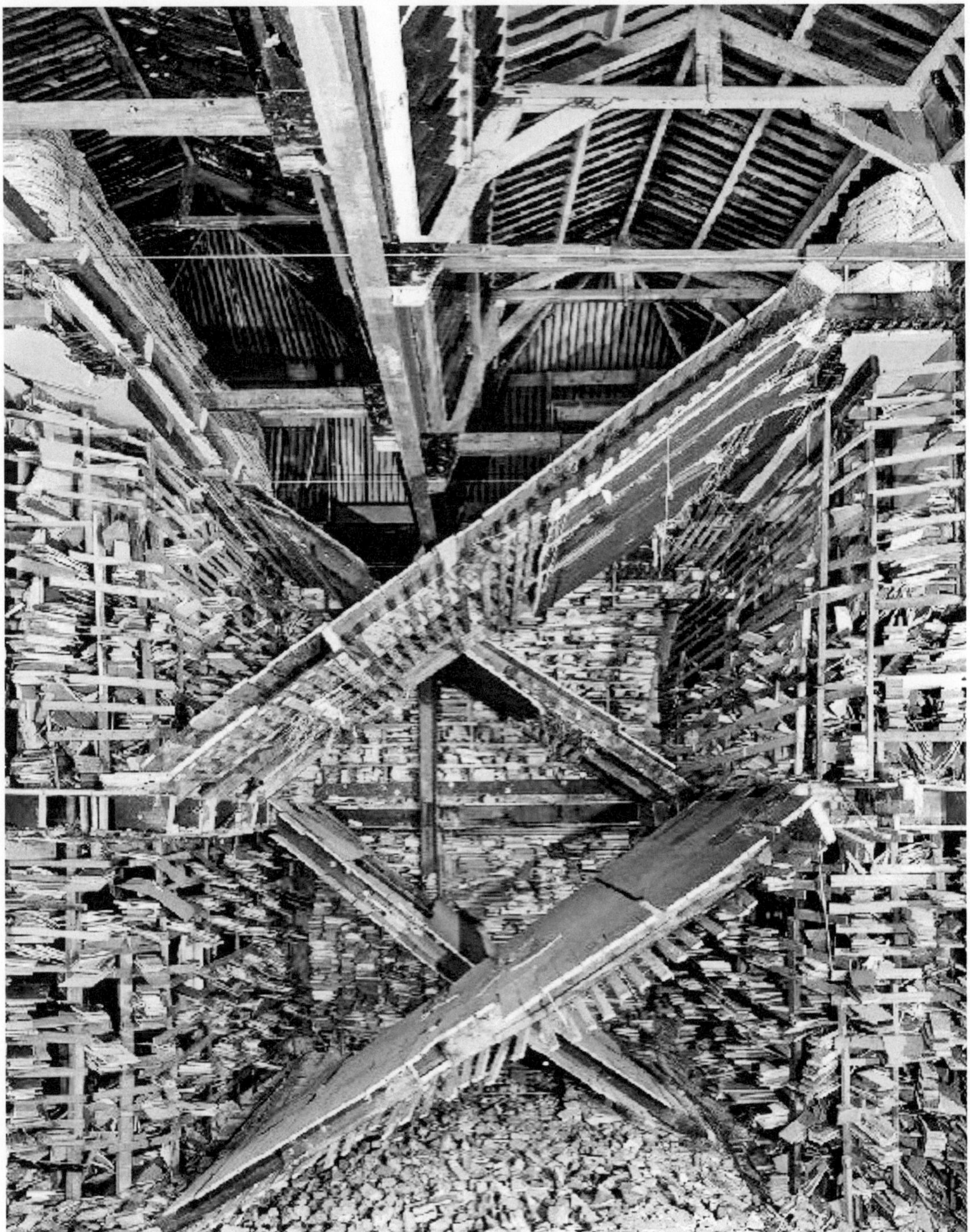

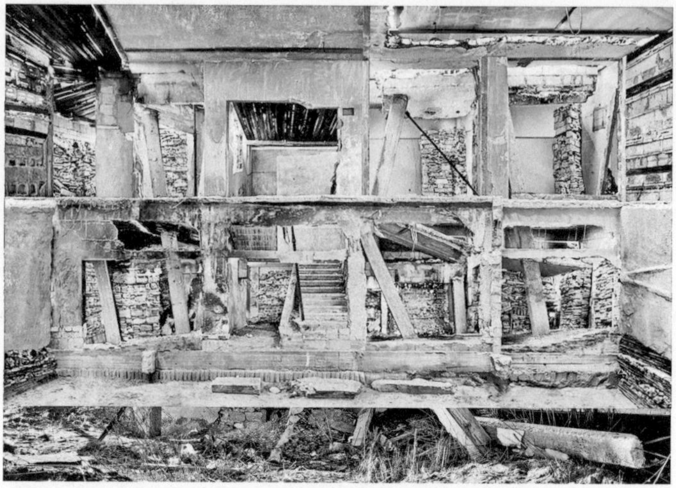

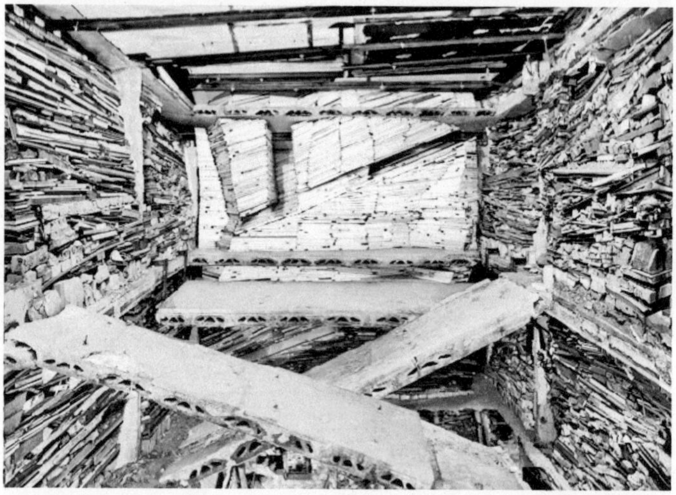

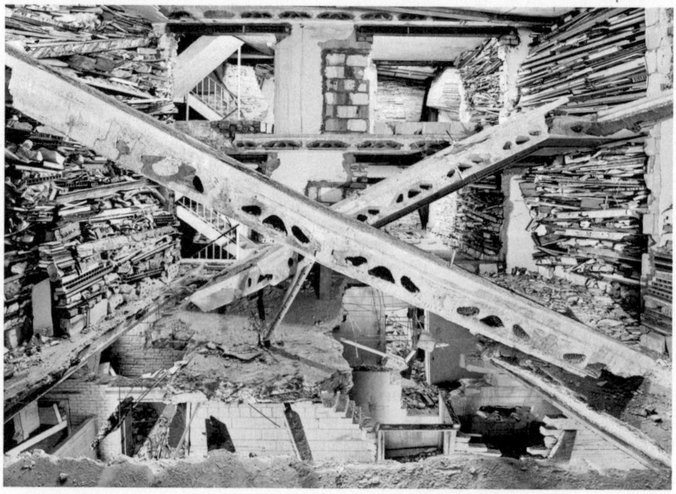

Marjan Teeuwen

Marjan Teeuwen,
Destroyed House Kyoto,
2020

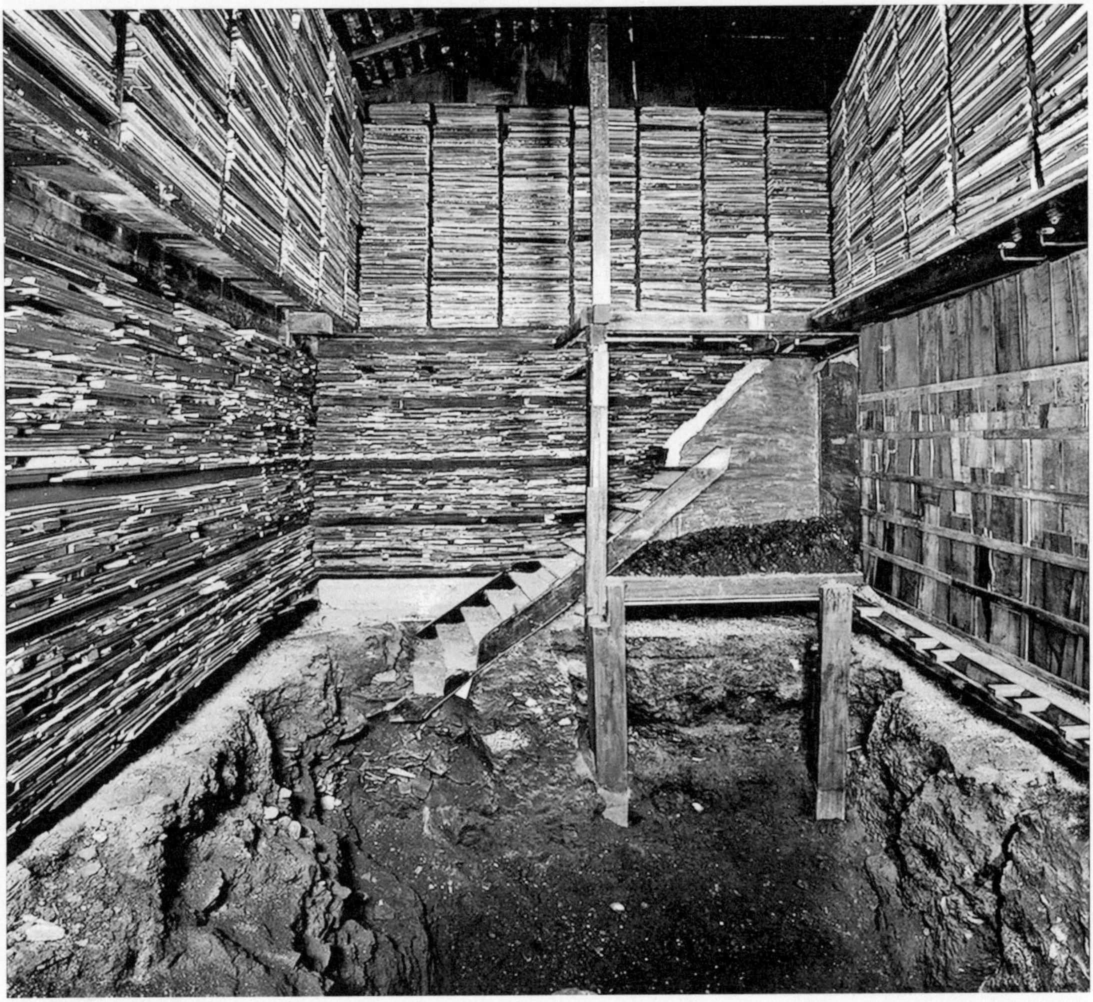

Marjan Teeuwen

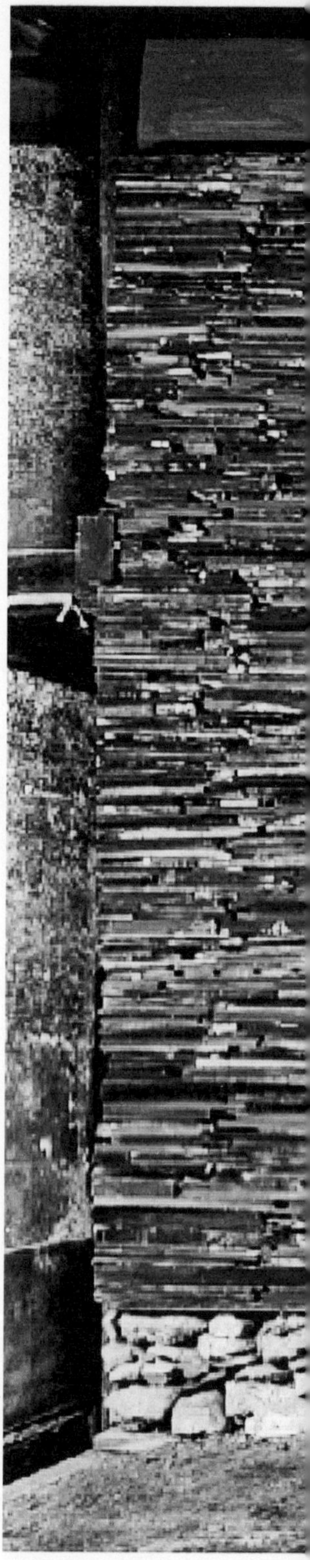

Marjan Teeuwen,
Destroyed House Kyoto,
2020

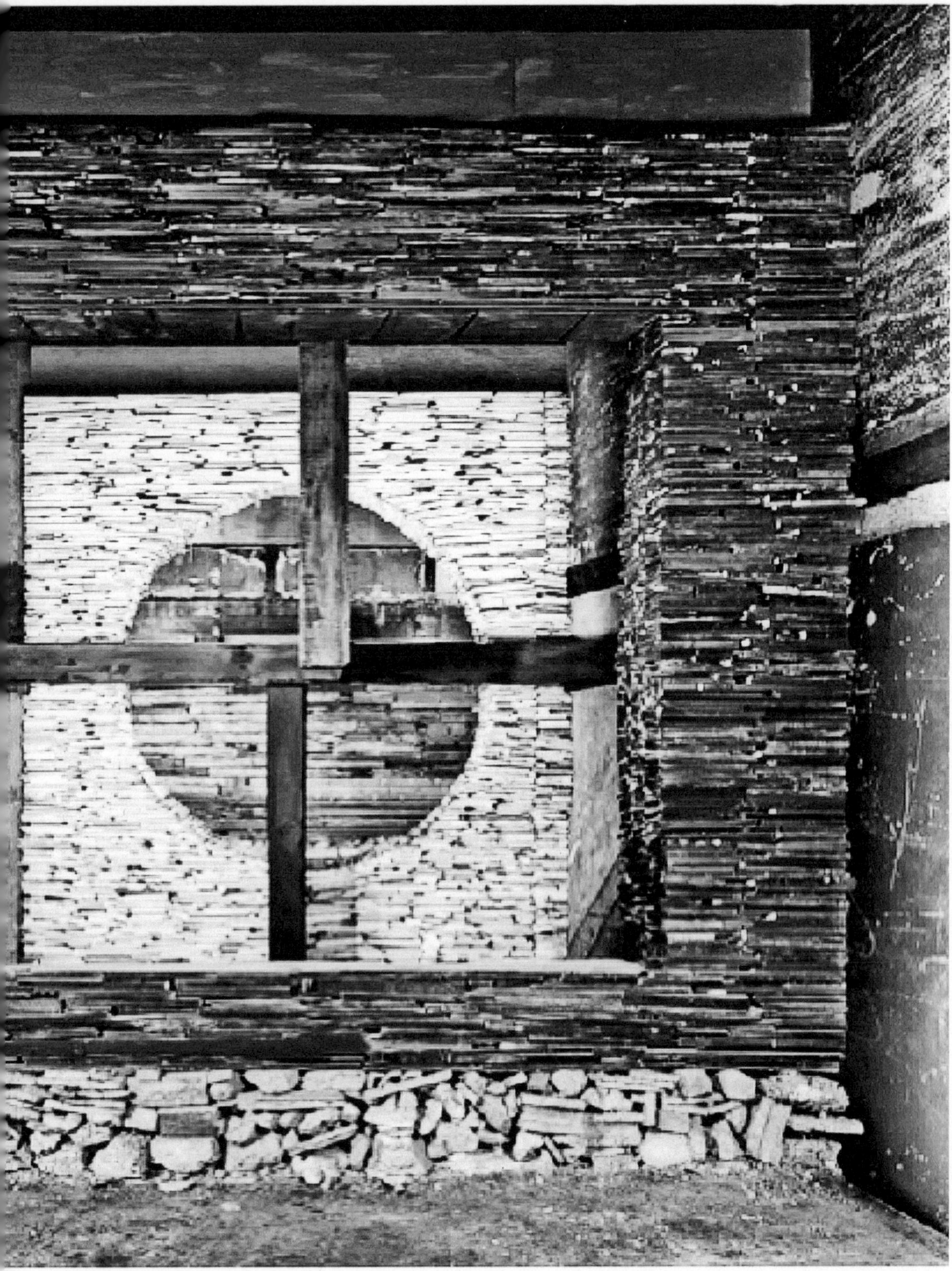

Archiving Identities

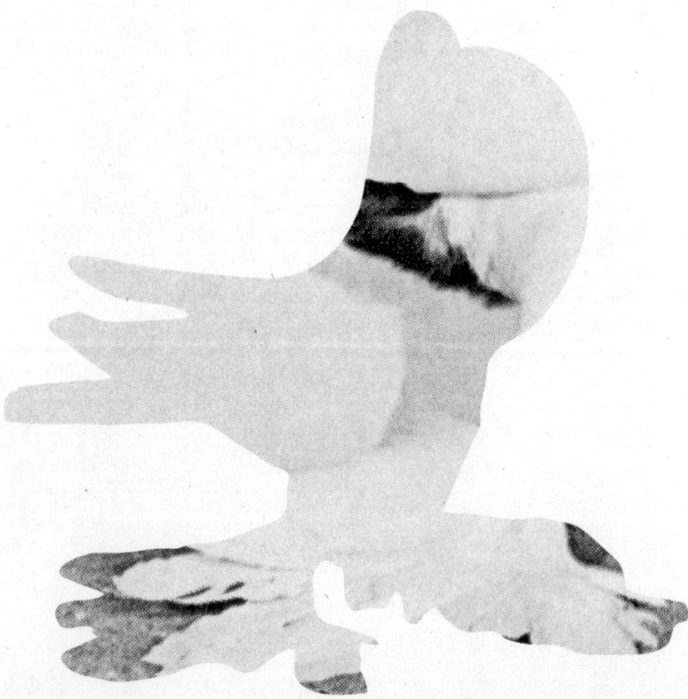

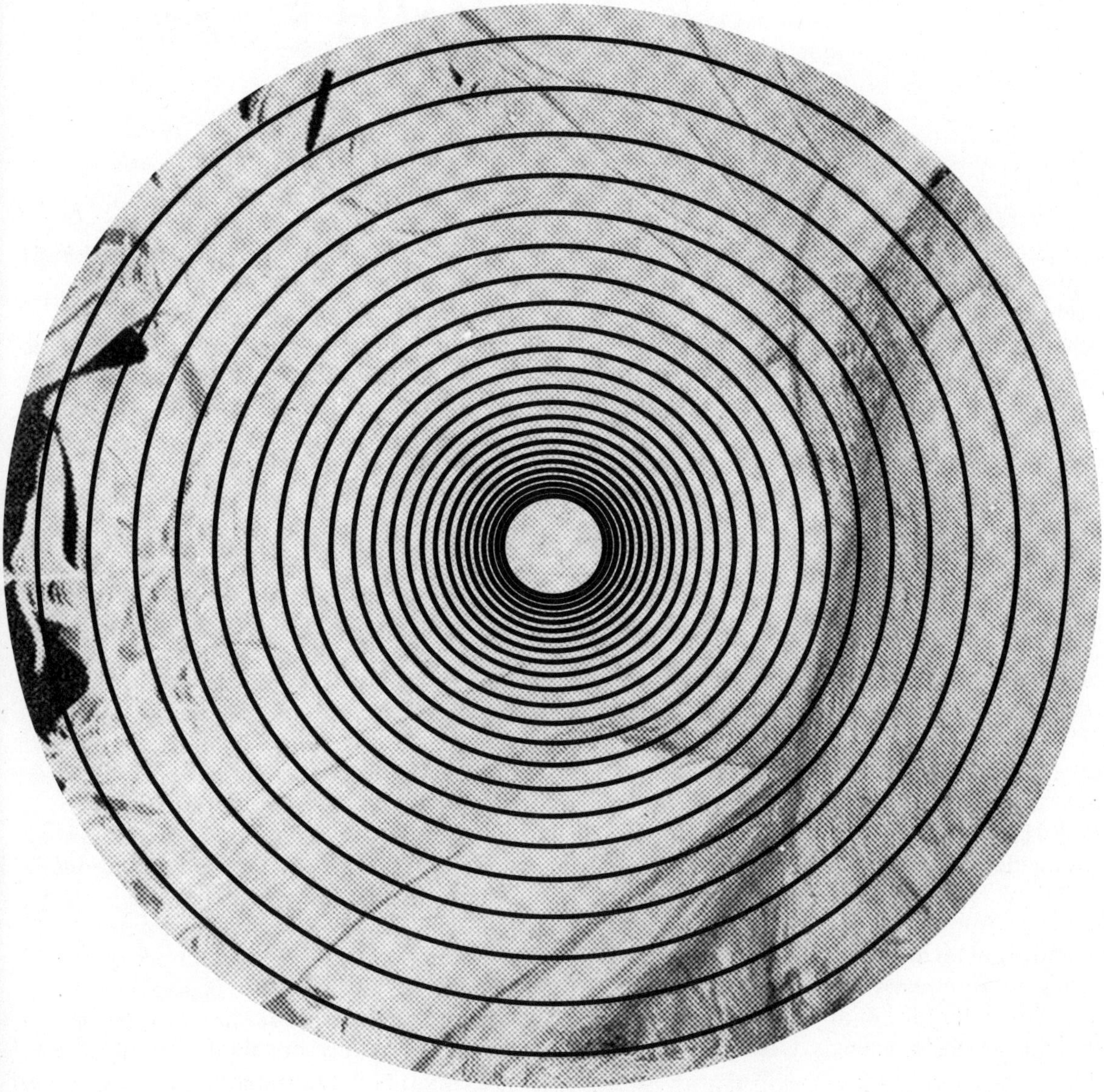

THE LURE OF THE ARCHIVE

The Atlas Project of Walid Raad

The last thirty years have been described as 'the era of the witness,' a time when the systematic collection of testimonies has proliferated.[1] This period could with equal validity be called 'the era of the archive.' Not only has the collection of documents and the establishment of archives increased dramatically, but the archive is now one of the central topics of thought throughout the humanities. For literary studies in particular, both engagement with archival documents and attention to the 'archive' have shifted from the margins to the center of the field. The American professor Jane Gallop even notes—disparagingly—the remark of a recent job candidate that in a literature department it is now 'impossible to get published without archival work.'[2]

The *lure* of the archive has also changed. The archive appeals to the desire to come into contact with the material of history, and to touch and read that which is not accessible to everyone, and may have been overlooked or ignored. But a shift has taken place at the conceptual level, and the scholarly desire today is often less to unearth this or that particular content in an archive than to engage with the archive itself, both as an institution and as a constitutive and transformative force. In literary studies the concern is no longer primarily with the work itself but with the discursive systems that regulate what is enunciated and written, with what is seemingly supplemental and other within the literary work, and with transformations in the forms of recording, assembling, and disseminating information and memory. All of these tendencies might be described as a shift towards the archival. Our reading practices have changed, and they have done so in part through an engagement with the archive.

What I am describing therefore is not just a change in conceptual frameworks or a turn to theory, but also transformations in the nature of experience and memory in the era of the archive. The archive is a transformative force, and not simply a repository for information collected or produced elsewhere. Here is a stark example (which I have written about elsewhere).[3] In the former East Germany, with the Stasi collecting information on a large number of its citizens, the person who has fallen under suspicion—whether a committed political dissident or merely someone who did not sufficiently support the regime—often comes to resemble and accept the portrait of him- or herself assembled out of archival fragments by the Stasi. This happens in two ways: one openly confesses one's 'crimes' in order to put an end to the humiliating, frightening, and exhausting process of interrogation;

1_Annette Wieviorka, *The Era of the Witness* (Ithaca: Cornell University Press, 2006), trans. from the French by Jared Stark (*L'Ère du témoin*, Paris: Plon, 1998), p. 96.

2_Jane Gallop, 'The Historicization of Literary Studies and the Fate of Close Reading,' *Profession* 2007, pp. 181–86, this quotation p. 181.

3_See Jeffrey Wallen, 'Narrative Tensions: The Archive and the Eyewitness,' *Partial Answers: Journal of Literature and The History of* Ideas 7, no. 2 (2009), pp. 261–78.

Jeffrey Wallen

and one begins (or continues more sharply) to think critically and antagonistically—that is, to think almost in the manner described in the accusations that have been made. The archival portrait becomes the person's own reality, and the eyewitness to the repressive power of the Stasi, in response to this power, becomes a product, even a function of the archive.

There are many avenues for trying to grasp the shaping forces of the archive. The work of artists—and a very large number of artists have engaged with archives in recent years—can be particularly illuminating, since artworks not only reflect on these forces but necessarily put them into play, and play with them. In this short space I cannot provide a full overview or introduction to modern artists' fascination with the archive, or in Hal Foster's words, to 'an archival impulse at work internationally in contemporary art.'[4] Here, I will focus only on two artists—Arnold Dreyblatt and especially Walid Raad, whose works are especially perceptive in interrogating, reimagining, performing, and displaying archives, and in giving us ways of reading archivally. Raad's work also engages with the archive as an institution and a mechanism of collection, registration, and storage, and challenges us to think differently about what structures the archive.

In his 2004 essay on the 'archival impulse,' Foster discusses three artists (Thomas Hirschhorn, Tacita Dean, and Sam Durant), and argues that while this impulse is 'hardly new' and extends throughout the twentieth century, the current turn to the archive has a new and distinctive character. These artists, he argues, 'seek to make historical information, often lost or displaced, physically present'; the task of the artist is to revive and investigate that which has escaped sufficient notice, and above all to emphasize and to rethink the materiality of these archival objects. Additionally, the 'archival impulse' now involves critical reflections on the space and the function of the archive:

> [...] the work in question is archival since it not only draws on informal archives but produces them as well, and does so in a way that underscores the nature of all archival materials as found yet constructed, factual yet fictive, public yet private.[5]

The repeated 'yet' underscores the awareness of the artists' archives as navigating or negotiating between the poles of the objective and institutional ('found,' 'factual,' and 'public') and the constructed or personal. And yet, the strong historical and critical awareness that underlies

4_Hal Foster, 'An Archival Impulse,' *October* 110 (Fall 2004), pp. 3–22, this quotation p. 3.

5_Foster, 'An Archival Impulse,' pp. 4–5.

these projects is for the most part not directed toward a rethinking of the archive itself—that is, of archives as functioning institutions for the collection, registration, storage, and retrieval of information. The emphasis is still largely on the *collection* that the artist has put together, and on the archival *material* that is (re)displayed for us.

Foster emphasizes the differences from earlier archival art projects, such as Richter's *Atlas* (begun in 1961), but the key terms he cites from each artist—'collection' (Dean), 'combination' (Durant), and 'ramification' (Hirschhorn; or 'mutations of connection and disconnection,' as Foster elaborates)—also bring out the continuity with Richter's project. As Benjamin Buchloh explains in his astute analysis of Richter's *Atlas*, the project involves the accumulation or collection of a vast amount of material, but 'cannot be identified either with the private album of the amateur or with the cumulative projects of documentary photography'; it is not governed by the earlier rules of collecting.[6] Concurrently, *Atlas* takes 'as the principles of a given work's formal organization photography's innate structural order (its condition as archive),' but nevertheless what 'does come to mind' is only 'the archival organization of materials according to the principles of an as yet unidentifiable discipline.' This 'archival impasse' (as Okwui Enwezor terms this lack of coherence or the inapplicability of the former logics governing both the organization and accumulation of photographic images) only tangentially engages or disturbs the mechanisms of any archive on which the artist may draw.[7] The archive remains primarily the artist's own collection and redisplay of historical material that might potentially have been archived elsewhere.

Christian Boltanski, the artist of the last few decades perhaps most associated with the 'archive,' sidesteps this impasse. His work, especially since the mid-1980s, often creates an archive of the faces of the dead or the traces of the absent, and the destruction of the Holocaust hovers as an historical specter. Boltanski repurposes the materials that survive, and the earlier archival activity that produced these materials, such as the processes of photographing, cataloguing, and preserving the faces he redisplays, is largely overwhelmed by the power of the artist's new archive, which haunts us as a memorial, stressing the absence of the lives the objects metonymically invoke.

Only rarely is there a dynamic engagement on more or less equal terms between past and present, bureaucratic and artistic archival activities. For the past thirty years one can see in Berlin Boltanski's piece *The Missing House*, which inscribes on the outside walls of the two remaining buildings information about the people who lived in the (now missing) house on Große Hamburgerstrasse when it was destroyed by aerial bombing in 1945. In the original exhibition in 1990, however, there were vitrines set up in front, 'arranging the copious archives concerning the missing occupants in glass boxes outside,' with 'more than one hundred and fifty facsimile documents.'[8] These archival documents also registered the Jewish occupants of the building before they were deported or forced to leave a few years earlier (a fact which Boltanski was unaware of when he began the project), and whose

6_Benjamin Buchloh, 'Gerhard Richter's *Atlas*: The Anomic Archive,' *October* 88 (Spring 1999), pp. 117–45, this quotation p. 118.

7_Okwui Enwezor, 'Archive Fever: Photography between History and Monument,' in *Archive Fever: Uses of the Document in Contemporary Art* (New York: International Center of Photography, 2008), pp. 11–47, this quotation p. 14.

8_Catherine Grenier, *Christian Boltanski* (Paris: Flammarion, 2010), p. 194.

living spaces were then given to 'proper' Germans.[9] The layers of archival activity, the bland registrations of the ordinary details of who lived in which apartment, radically disturb the more immediately visible play of presence and absence. In the 1990 version of this piece, but not in what we see today, the archive as a space staged by the artist remains in tension with the archives that produced and continue to produce the documents of who lives where.

The social functions and guiding logics of an archive most pertinent for discussions of photography and art are acutely explored by Allan Sekula in his seminal essay 'The Body and the Archive' (1986). Sekula asserts that at the end of the nineteenth century 'the institution of the photographic archive received its most thorough early articulation in precise conjunction with an increasingly professionalized and technological mode of police work and an emerging social science of criminology,' and he goes on to explore why 'the model of the archive' was 'of such import for these linked disciplines.'[10] Seeking to counter this history of the photographic archive as inherently an apparatus of control if not repression that he has laid out for us, Sekula praises those artists who take 'an aggressive stance' against the 'authoritative and official' uses of the 'instrumental realist archive.'[11] The authoritative and the artistic archive square off here in clear opposition, with it being evident to viewers where we should position ourselves with regard to the fault lines that are exposed. The stance of the artist I shall consider here is less easy to characterize, but I will argue it is all the more powerful for the ways in which it burrows into the archive and thereby reshapes our reading practices.

Walid Raad's Atlas Group Archives provide materials about the Lebanese Civil Wars (1975–1991). These works radically shake up the 'archival impulses.' The violence and disruption of war necessarily arouse desires for archival evidence. One vector of these desires is to see that which has been hidden from view, and to confront that which we have not been able to grasp: marks of trauma; unofficial, non-public histories; accounts and documents that have been submerged or are not accessible to a Western audience. Whatever we may have previously seen could not have given us adequate knowledge. The American media, for instance, focused on that which affected Americans (the car bombing of the marine base and the embassy; the taking of Westerners as hostages; bombed-out hotels); and we all know that the media filter and control what we see. The archive lures us with the promise of more authentic documents and the hope of a greater truth than what we have encountered in media images.

On the other hand, we also want to critique the desire to see the authentic or the true. Part of the lure of looking at archival material about the Lebanese wars is to have our critical sophistication aroused and confirmed: to engage with a trace, a supplement, a substitute, a reproduction, an aftereffect of that which we cannot access immediately and directly. The frame of the archive appeals to our knowledge that photographs cannot provide us with historical truth or the exact measure of what took place, or transport us to an originary moment;

9_Abigail Solomon-Godeau, 'Mourning or Melancholia: Christian Boltanski's *Missing House*,' *Oxford Art Journal* 21, no. 2 (1998), pp. 3–20.

10_Allan Sekula, 'The Body and the Archive,' *October* 39 (Winter 1986), pp. 3–64, this quotation p. 17.

11_Sekula, 'The Body and the Archive,' p. 62.

it appeals to our knowledge that trauma is precisely that which cannot be directly documented or made visible; and to our suspicion of the libidinal desire for images of violence. Embracing an archival perspective also helps us to grasp the processes of de-subjectification, of transformation into something other than a human subject, that are at the center of collective violence. Walid Raad's work plays on all of these lures of the archive.

Let us now turn to some images of his work. The series *Let's be honest, the weather helped* purports to show where bullets hits buildings in the neighborhood of Beirut in which he lived in the early 1980s. What we see are buildings—or in one case a tree—with lots of colored circles, like Band-Aids covering the wounds made by the bullets. The bright green, orange, and purple circles enliven the black-and-white photographs and sometimes almost completely blot out the underlying building.[12] The accompanying text tells us:

> I collected bullets and shrapnel. I would run out to the streets after a night or day of shelling to remove bullets from walls, cars, and trees. I kept detailed notes of where I found every bullet by photographing the sites of my findings, and by placing colored dots over the bullet holes

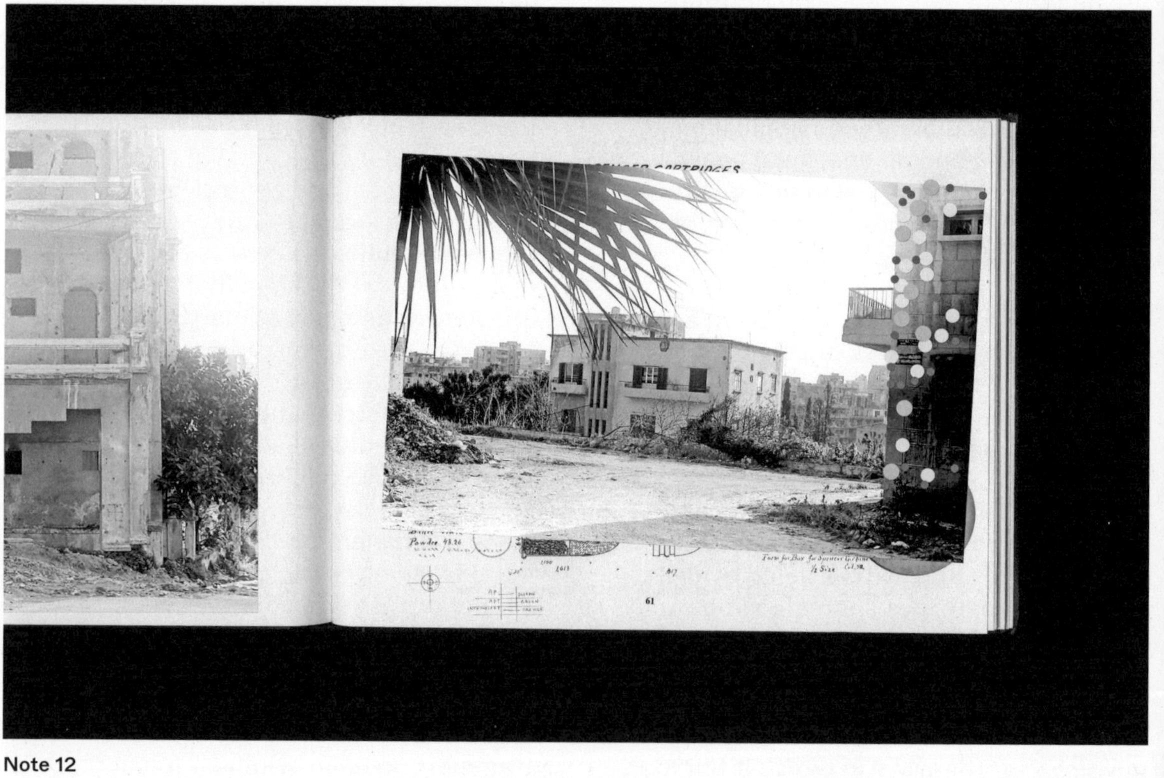

Note 12

12_This picture from the series 'Let's be honest the weather helped' can be found on the Atlas Group website, and the link for this image contains the words Saudi Arabia (each picture contains the name of a different country, or a group such as NATO, though the pictures are not titled with these names), purporting to be the country of origin for the bullets whose damage is being marked: www.theatlasgroup.org/data/images/raad-note/001_SaudiArabia_Full_Page4.jpg.

in my black and white photographs. The color of the dots corresponded to the mesmerizing hues I found on the bullets' tips. The colors were also faithful to the distinct code devised by manufacturers in different countries to mark their cartridges and shells.[13]

The colored dots mark (and cover over) the sites of damage, and mark the location where each item in a collection was found. The bullet is here also a toy, and an aesthetic object, as we see in the beautiful pictures of each type of bullet. It is presented as intact, with its colorful tip, before it was fired, as if one could return to a moment before the shooting. The colors also purport to mark the country of origin of the bullet, like a play on the *provenance* of the collection (a key aspect of art since the work of Marcel Broodthaers, Hans Haacke, and others), and we are told how each bullet came into his collection ('gift from best friend,' 'found in tree,' 'purchased from vendor').[14] The collection performs a tracing of the arms trade (on the website, each picture is labeled with a country). Profit, responsibility, and historical context are reinscribed onto the picture.

Each dot is a deflection: it points to, but prevents us from seeing, the damage of war. The works continually play with the structures of psychoanalysis, but any secure hierarchical logic that would determine, for instance, which images represent the traumatic event and which are only screen memories is put into doubt. Rather than providing a stable ground for interpretation or critique, the archival material reveals that each act of charting, collecting, and tracking is also a substitution and displacement: that of the bureaucrat or witness who marks the damage of war each day no less than the 'boy' who pastes dots on pictures of buildings and who lovingly notes the characteristics of each country's bullets. The photographs themselves are pasted over diagrams that look like weapons' schemata. The act of making the notebook is highlighted as inherently palimpsestic, with it no longer being possible to privilege any particular layer as the proper basis for interpretation.

The seriousness of the subject matter has led most commentators to underestimate the playfulness of Raad's work. In fact, Raad makes explicit, extends, and plays with our implicit understanding of what we think we might learn from going into the archive. We want to know, for one thing, more about the traumatic effects of car bombs on the people of Beirut. Mike Davis, in writing about car bombs, stated that 'Beirut became to the technology of urban violence what a tropical rainforest is to the evolution of plants.'[15] We know that trauma cannot be viewed directly, and that what we have seen on television or read in newspapers is inadequate, but we also know that the archive cannot give us direct access to historical truth or to the essence of an ineffable experience, and cannot provide an exact measure of what happened. The Atlas Project takes this knowledge as its program: deflection from an origin, the serial reproduction of events, a substitute image for the open wound, a displacement of the incidental for the essential, a parody of the drive to gain knowledge through measurement, and a mixing of registers (the handwritten annotation and the newspaper

13_Walid Raad, *The Atlas Group (1989–2004): A Project by Walid Raad*, ed. Kassandra Nakas and Britta Schmitz (Cologne: Walther König, 2006), p. 126.

14_Walid Raad, *Scratching on Things I Could Disavow* (Cologne: Walther König, 2007), pp. 135–43.

15_Mike Davis, 'The Poor Man's Air Force: A History of the Car Bomb (Part 1),' www.tomdispatch.com/post/76140/.

photograph; the picture from a magazine and the personal photograph; the archival commentary and the diary entry).

In the series *My neck is thinner than a hair*, one sees pictures of the effects of car bombs. Raad writes,

> The only part that remains intact after a car bomb explodes is the engine. Landing on balconies, roofs or adjacent streets, the engine is projected tens and sometimes hundreds of meters away from the original site of the bomb. During the wars, photojournalists competed to be the first to find and photograph engines.[16]

The photographs purport to be taken by photojournalists in the 1980s and Raad claims to have found them 'in the archives of An-Nahar Research Center (Beirut, Lebanon) and The Arab Documentation Center (Beirut, Lebanon).'[17] The wrecked engine—not the 'target' of the bomb (wounded people and damaged buildings)—is at the center of a group photograph.[18]

The description presents it almost as a game—who can be the first one to arrive at the destination, to find the sought-after object—but the photographs belie this description. The photographs present literally a displacement—the distance of the engine from the original

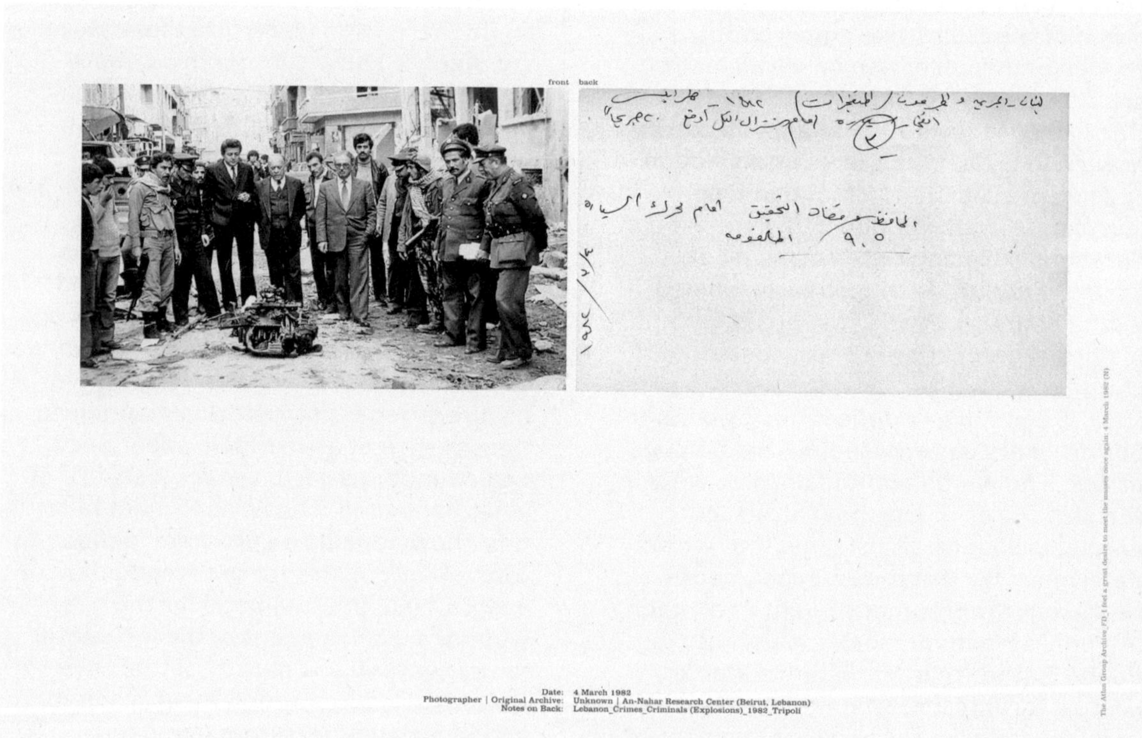

Note 18

16_Raad, *The Atlas Group (1989–2004)*, p. 96.

17_Raad, *The Atlas Group (1989–2004)*, p. 96. But in *Scratching on Things I Could Disavow*, Raad writes that these same photographs were 'found in the archives of the Lebanese daily newspapers *Annahar* and *As-Safir*' (p. 100).

18_www.theatlasgroup.org/data/images/volume-57/Neck_Engines_ALL8.jpg.

site of the bomb—while refocusing the gaze on this destructive displacement itself, with a crowd of Lebanese surveying what remains of the engine and the car. This refocusing implicates and unsettles our own gaze as well.

In another series of pictures that documents the car bombings in Lebanon, *Already been in a lake of fire*, one sees a very different interplay of destructive force and documentary reframing. These images, purportedly from a notebook put together by Dr. Fadl Fakhouri—who, according to the Atlas Group, was 'the foremost historian of the Lebanese civil wars until his death in 1993'—present attractive cutout photographs of the make, model, and color of each car used in a bombing.[19]

Handwritten (in Arabic) and typed (below in English) statistics regarding the quantity of explosive material, the number killed, the date and place accompany each picture. The depiction of an intact vehicle engages the fantasy for a time before the bomb exploded (and before the war). Presenting the vehicles almost in flight, mounted at a slight angle, heightens their attractiveness as pure and even whimsical object of desires, removed from the usual advertising context. But the cutout is also a radical reframing, forcing the viewer to imagine the car's destructive potential when turned into a bomb, on the particular date and place that accompanies the picture.[20]

The Atlas Project presents counter-archives, alternatives to and contestations of official archives, and performs a repurposing: each series moves away from a typical goal and toward a new one. These series are also interpolations, inserting new material into other texts. The camera's gaze as displacement and interpolation is most directly presented in the video *I only wish that I could weep*, which is described as video shot by 'Operator #17,' who was supposed to be manning a surveillance camera along the 'Corniche, a seaside boardwalk in Beirut,' and who each evening just before sunset would divert his video camera from its surveillance function to record the sunset, and then refocus it on its proper targets. The diversion of the camera from a policing to an aesthetic function expresses a yearning for other aims (and here we are told that the operator was from east Beirut, unable habitually to see the seaside of west Beirut), but the poignancy here is less a matter of two competing purposes, or the transformation of surveillance into something else, than of one activity taking place alongside the other. The footage is more like an interpolation, unseen by others and by history, into the usual fabric of purposeful daily activity, though here of course that norm is marked as a destructive, perverted one, directed more toward death than life.

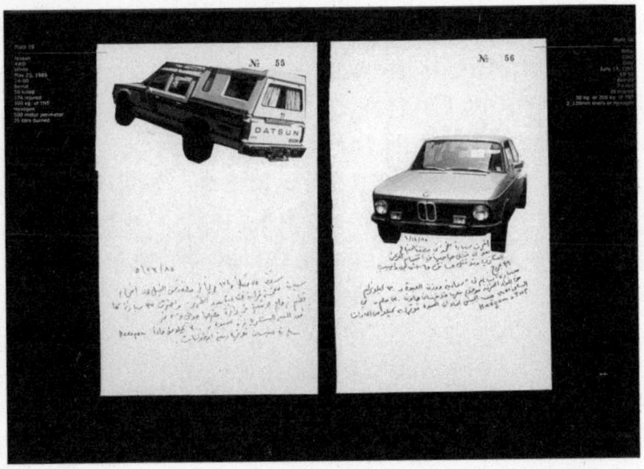

Note 20

19_Raad, *Scratching on Things I Could Disavow*, p. 86.

20_www.theatlasgroup.org/data/images/volume-38/L55_56.jpg.

Missing Lebanese wars, purportedly also from the notebooks of Dr. Fadl Fakhouri, is to my mind Raad's most extreme (and acute) example of playing against our archival expectations. It is a series of photographs of the finish of horse races taped onto pages from a notebook, with handwritten comments about the bets and the winner, and the archivist's transcription of these notations typed onto the margins.[21]

There are several layers of perversity here, in this allegory of the historian's work. These groups of historians at the track bet not on which horse will win the race, but on the margin of error in recording the photo-finish. And rather than simply betting on the distance of the discrepancy, which could be easily measured, they bet on the time interval—how many ten thousandths of a second early or late the photograph was apparently taken, which can only be approximately calculated (we are given the elements of the calculation, but not the process of calculation itself: the photographs document the distance between the finish line and the horse's position when the photograph was taken, and then, apparently using the average speed of the horse, this distance as measured on the photograph is converted to a time interval). The bets are almost random guesses at an imperfectly measurable error, as in a sense they 'correct' the official record.[22] Moreover, the winner—the historian, not the horse—is acerbically profiled by Dr. Fakhouri. All the usual tools of the historian, and all the typical forms of registration, measurement, and documentation, are turned slightly away from their normal functions.

Perhaps even more perverse than the activity of placing these bets is that of collecting and archiving the results. As opposed to the records of the racetrack habitué, which will help him to progress from luck to skill (the knowledge gained of the *history* of each horse informs the future), this notebook serves no apparent useful function. No knowledge is gained through repetition; it does not provide anything useable to improve the future, or to inform us about, by bearing witness to, the past. Critics discussing Raad's work, and particularly this series, usually emphasize that the 'documents provoke a questioning of historical facts' and highlight that 'any representation misses its target,'[23] or stress his

> ... concern with the limits of historical forms of representation and the failure of these forms to

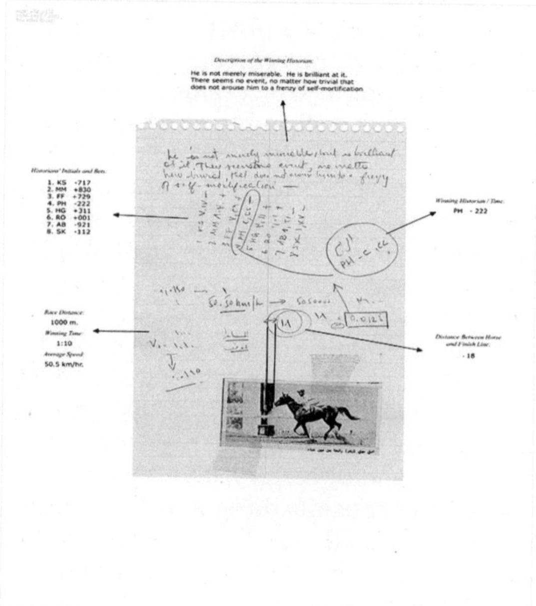

Note 21

21_www.theatlasgroup.org/data/images/volume-72/plate132.jpg.

22_But even the documents are themselves subject to revision, and hardly present an official or even fixed record. The version of *Missing Lebanese Wars* in *The Atlas Group (1989—2004)* is identical to what is on The Atlas Group website, but the plates presented in *Scratching on Things I Could Disavow* sometimes contain small differences in the numbers from the seemingly identical document in the other edition (compare for examples p. 71 of *The Atlas Group (1989–2004)*

> register specific aspects of experience (psychological, perceptual) that are strongly affected by the violence of war, yet nevertheless remain unintelligible or simply unmarked by traditional forms of documentation (like photography or film).[24]

But what the plates of this series register and represent is perhaps more striking. The archival *activity*, as a response to the random, disruptive effects of violence—and it is not surprising that this series is bluntly named *Missing Lebanese Wars* rather than Raad's usually more poetic titles—is here laid bare in its basic structures. The powerful gesture of The Atlas Group Archive, a gesture which is not diminished by reading the small print that puts into question both the artifactual status of the documents and the institutional status of the archive, is to subsume these materials into an organized archive. The imprimatur of The Atlas Group Archive—and in Lebanon as opposed to London, institutions for archiving are much less widespread or established—provides a new frame, another viewing and a further possibility of significance for these records of a purposeful documentary activity without a conventional goal or guiding purpose. Walid Raad's work pushes us to see and engage the 'exterior scaffolding' of modern memory.[25]

with p. 29 of *Scratching on Things I Could Disavow*).

23_Britta Schmitz, 'Not a Search for Truth,' in *The Atlas Group (1989–2004)*, pp. 41–46, this quotation p. 43.

24_Vered Maimon, 'The Third Citizen: On Models of Criticality in Contemporary Artistic Practices,' *October* 129 (Summer 2009), pp. 85–112, this quotation p. 99.

25_Pierre Nora writes, 'Modern memory is, above all, archival [...]. The less memory is experienced from the inside the more it exists only through its exterior scaffolding and outward signs.' See Pierre Nora, 'Between Memory and History: *Les Lieux de Mémoire*,' trans. Marc Roudebush, *Representations* 26, no. 1 (Spring 1986), pp. 7–24, this quotation p. 13.

'DOES THE FACT THAT I FALL FOR MEN ALSO MAKE ME A WOMAN?'

1

Let me say it straight away: I'm in for an androgynous society. It must have been somewhere around 1985 that I asked this question at a meeting of men and women: 'Does the fact that I fall for men also make me a woman?' Nobody knew the answer right away. They just laughed.

Vulnerability is too often associated with weakness. In your vulnerability, in accepting it, you can find peace. Men are often not given that. How can we explore and accept another notion of vulnerability?

I grew up alternately in two different environments and in a situation where gender roles played no role. I had to survive physically and mentally. I did notice that they were there and sometimes I made an effort to understand them and to subjugate myself to them. From the age of six until I was twenty, I stayed with nuns in a boarding school for girls, where there were also some boys. But they left as soon as they became a danger to the girls. I spent my school holidays in the only and last leper colony in the Netherlands. My parents had to live there because of my father, who contracted the disease in Indonesia.

I owe my mental and physical survival to three people: a nun, a teacher, and Uncle Bloem, the one who became my mentor. He was a friend of my mother, and he also had the disease.

All three helped me keep my wits about me and gave me the tools to not completely lose my humanity, or to rediscover it later. They taught me to think analytically, to let go of categorizing people, to see vulnerability as a place where one can find everything that makes us human, where humus thrives best, from which one learns and tastes life. Only there would I find comfort for a life that would never be without pain.

Vulnerability continually brings forth new life.

Merapi Obermayer

Without those three helpers I was completely on my own. Eating, drinking and sleeping... in the boarding school that wasn't even guaranteed. The punishments also included abstinence.

2

Vulnerability is a reality based on facts. Invulnerability is a non-existent reality that stems from our desire to escape vulnerability. The fact that we desire it makes us believe that it really exists. An accumulation of certainties and inner, social, and institutional machinations, which one must create over and over again, must help maintain that belief and turn it into a daily reality. This is called 'resilience.' In my youth, I tried for years to make that 'non-existent reality' possible. I did it in my own way, though.

Our lives take place between these two realities in which we repeatedly place ourselves in a new role. What makes people unable or afraid to embrace vulnerability? That it always ends up in the wrong hands? Vulnerability is not only about yourself, but also about the other. Invulnerability means shutting the other person out.

3

We cannot help but classify people according to their characteristics, ethnic origin and gender. Until now it has been clear: boys, girls, men, and women.

The rest was slurred over. Vulnerability falls under femininity and invulnerability… (that non-existent reality): that is something men are allowed to fasten their teeth in.

While women can and must breathe freely, men are forced to hold their breath and must always prove themselves. The result is that both groups feel unfree toward each other and themselves. Today, they no longer know how to relate to each other. Progressive insight is so rapid that even the use of language lags behind today's reality. New words have to be created, new titles of address.

4

For me vulnerability was all about transience in the most literal sense, mainly due to my birth and stay among leprosy patients and of course, the past war. On top of that, my life was all about shame and fear. My parents belonged to the lowest European class. They were the children of comfort girls to white European soldiers who served in the colonial army. In a report that I once read, my parents and I were described as 'colonial leftovers.'

My stay in a boarding school was also shameful; all children suffered from this. Children of color and of Jewish background were doubly affected. We were put apart, got black numbers in our clothes and had to work the hardest because we were paid very little. At school, the decent children were not allowed by their parents to play with us. We were trash. The color didn't matter, our stay was enough to be ashamed of. We were only allowed to visit a classmate under strict conditions. My life was a mess. I had to draw the fragile lines myself.

5

Partly because of these experiences, I am averse to groups and especially today's identity politics that is closely linked to victimhood. The question 'who and what am I?' or 'who and what are we?' cannot be answered without 'the other.' By placing the other in a permanently powerless position—'shame on you!'—no dialogue or advancing insight is possible. This is what the imposition of shame does: it deprives the others of their autonomy and creates new forms of power and violence through emotional blackmail transcending the generations.

6

Individualism is an attitude to life, a vision, not a capitalist product of, say, Western society.

It is a perspective, a 'point of view' from which we look at each other and from which we develop a parallel attitude to life, based on the dignity of the human being. By living side by side, we do not take each other's breath away, so that the possibility of the exchange of thoughts and feelings remains without the danger of an all-too-direct exchange.

The meaning we give to independence, individualism, and relationship is derived too much from the functional point of view. This has nothing to do with the recognition of the human being as an individual in relation to the other. That is why I don't want to talk about matriarchy and patriarchy, male and female singularity, but about human beings. Fortunately, I am not the first one. I will join the queue.

My starting point is the human creature as a creative being in all its facets. This is how I see it.

7

As human beings we have always tried to bend reality to our will. Yet we failed in all our attempts. Therein lies our hope. What hope? It has to be based on something. There are two keys that give access to that hope. One is for daily use; it is stored in the memory of each individual person and does not go beyond a generation. The other is stored in the memory of humanity that transcends generations and will continue to do so, especially with today's technology.

8

I'm still not able to accustom myself to my own face.
Surprised and lost
my hands go through my hair
I'm still not able to accustom myself to my own face,
a face that would always betray me.

9

My parents wanted Uncle Bloem to tutor me. At school I was bored to death; and moreover, I was often too tired to take in the lessons. Instead of giving me regular tutoring he came up with another plan to help me get over my and his boredom at the same time. Life in the leper colony was just boring. It was a kind of lockdown.

He taught me tricks to absorb the ordinary learning material quickly and efficiently in-between jobs. That worked out successfully. Soon after, he started giving me a practical education in 'thinking freely,' year after year during all my school holidays.

He saw it as his task to free my questions from the prison of fear. You only could create peace in your mind by daring to ask, to let yourself be questioned, he once said.

Vulnerability itself doesn't make one anxious. It is just what it is.

What is frightening is the image you have of it, what is being presented to you: 'you mustn't want to be like that!' Hiding your failures from the outside world behind a so-called laughing face results in more and more complicated constructions.

The first thing uncle Bloem did was to teach me to walk upright. Like all the children in the boarding school, I walked with my head bowed, my arms hanging heavily along my body. Fear, shame, and enforced humility held us under its spell. I had to get rid of this. Walking with a bowed head had to be a choice, my choice.

According to him, I could only think freely with my eyes fixed on the horizon.

10

The 'visible world' as an expression of an 'invisible reality'... . What we artists shape is the concentrated energy that scientists can perceive through a microscope.

Without mentioning the word, Uncle Bloem taught me all about vulnerability. In this way he proved that vulnerability is a fact-based reality that we all have to deal with.

11

If I had been healthy, he said, I should have been a man and therefore strong and tough. In the war I did not have to fight, so I did not have to kill anyone. Only in war do men find out how vulnerable they are.

Since women are not readily available in wartime, men must appeal to their own feminine qualities in order to survive mentally. After which, life goes on again.

According to him, it was no coincidence that the most beautiful poems by men were only written after a war, after they could finally come home, tired of fighting.

Now he could live as a woman, or at least... It was her role he did not like: to breathe freely, but only within the limits set by men who had to hold their breath while they were alive. In his position he could just be human, no social demands were asked of him.

By giving himself an attitude, but also by analyzing how things really were, disconnected from conceptions and norms, he got over the shame of his illness and the death of his body. He never wanted to be photographed, though.

Once I saw him become shy. He asked me to help him pee. We were in the woods behind the cottages. The toilet was too far away and there was no nurse at hand. He couldn't get his zip open with those finger-stubs. I was about ten years old. This was the first time I would see a penis up close. There we stood, fumbling. The zip almost got stuck. Judging by the jet, it was really urgent. Then I pulled the lace out of my shoe, fastened it to the zip in such a way that he could put it around his wrist and pull the zip up and down. Now he could walk down the forest path on his own and feel less confined.

12

My father suffered from having to live like a 'woman.' As a result, he always knew better and we always agreed with him so that he could retain some of his masculinity, i.e., his sense of power. He was an adult child who wanted to be recognized as a man, but could not be, not any more. The illness had taken its toll. My mother turned out to be the only adult in the family.

So, I learned something about the difference between men and women. That you had real differences, based on the physical reality and also roles related to that physicality, but mainly based on our needs and desires, transformed into opinions. The rest I had to find out for myself.

Uncle Bloem only wanted to give me tools to be able to continue in the boarding school so that I would not break. He gave me a sexless education where I could choose for myself which role I wanted to have, that of man, woman, or human being.

13

How do morality, attitudes, and our role play relate to vulnerability? These three things take place in the area between the existing reality and the non-existing reality that is driven by human desire. Nature in itself knows no paths. It is we ourselves who make the paths, paths that place us outside nature, to which we will return one day.

14

What exactly is shame? The shame resulting from an act is the only real shame. Seeing the pain, bowing to that pain, is an acknowledgement of the other. This kind of shame is important for a society. Those directly involved who feel this shame, who do not shun this feeling and who are prepared to face it... .

We cannot do without these feelings of shame. But that also requires a willingness to forget or even forgive.

A society with citizens who are unwilling to do so, who base their identity on victimhood, might just as well abolish itself.

But what is the other shame? That shame that was imposed on me? That shame we impose on others? That shame we cannot express in clear language? The fact that my parents were called colonial bastards gave the nuns the right to claim my body. My body was not sacred, not a temple, it was full of shame and yet they could not keep their hands off it! My body did not arouse lust, but sin. As if there was a need to be defiled through me and then to pray for forgiveness. As a child, it greatly confused me.

There were a few other children. We didn't talk to each other about this. You noticed it in the bathroom. When you saw a flannel with remnants of an abrasive and a girl had rubbed her lips and fingers red. I always managed to get hold of Vaseline.

15

At the exhibition 'Shame! and Masculinity,' I saw a painting by Marlene Dumas showing two naked girls [Marlene Dumas, *Beauty as Burden*, 1998, ink wash and watercolor]. Their posture: was it shyness, was it shame? I could hardly look at them. Yet I forced myself to. It brought me back to that bathroom. Adolescent girls, Jewish, Indo-Europeans and even one with a very dark skin; under the watchful eyes of three nuns we were forced to undress. When naked we held our knees together, almost like X-legs. One nun put the chair against the bathroom door. The other two squeezed our breasts. You had to bend over so they could look inside your anus. One girl had her period, blood ran down her thighs. Remarks were made... .

I stood there with clenched fists. Refused to bend down. Then one of the nuns took the scrubber and hit me on my back with the handle. It was that particular moment that I decided to go into hiding, to go into hiding in my own body. Why be ashamed of a body if it wasn't mine? My mind, my brain were not to be touched! I became detached from my body, talked about 'that body of mine.' At the same time, I understood that I had to continue to care for it because I had no other place to live.

My brain, my mind, were my everything. With this I could communicate with uncle Bloem. Uncle Bloem who saw his body disappearing before his eyes!

When the parade was over, we were squeezed into a shower-cubicle, stuck together. In another one you had a garden hose that was always ready to be used for cleaning the floor. First, we were sprayed with boiling hot water, then cold, then boiling hot again. Our screams even reached the corridor. That was when the little nun intervened. I saw the desperation on her face. For one Jewish girl it was too much. She knew all the stories about the war. We never spoke a word about it. In spring, we would secretly pick flowers from the garden and put them on the spot where she was found with her wrists cut, a week after the so-called 'shower incident.' We knew better.

16

Shame, shame and more shame. I had dealt with that radically. Maybe that's one of the reasons why, once in Amsterdam, I had no trouble earning my living by being a nude model at art academies. I was in great demand because I could distance myself from my body. When I saw the painting by Marlene Dumas, going back in time, I felt the shame, the humiliation and it felt like NOW. A few days later I went looking for a photo book by David Hamilton. The man who, like no other, knew how to portray naked young adolescent girls, dreamy, blurred... cliché, but still. The way I would have liked to remember myself at that age: inquisitive, curious and yes, above all, vulnerable. When I was six, I already knew everything about the human body and didn't like it. At twelve, I saw my body as a useful instrument, a house, a hiding place. Now I felt purified.

Finding that vulnerability again, in which wonder and pain can live side by side rather than in opposition to each other, is not possible without confrontation. In the present, you find the strength to face them.

Like I found it when I saw the painting by Marlene Dumas. I no longer felt like that child abandoned by adults.

17

There was once a tree on the leper colony's site. According to the manager, it was dead. He wanted to cut it down because it posed a danger to the patients. Especially in the autumn, when there was a storm. Uncle Bloem was vehemently against this. He claimed it wasn't dead at all. That was, well, a doubtful assertion. The behavior of the birds spoke volumes. For their nests they used twigs from dead trees. There had not been a bird near this tree, yet they had been busy building, in other trees. He had seen them flying off and on with dead twigs that did not come from this tree. The tree was not dead enough for a nest. It was brain dead.

Uncle Bloem's argument had woken up the occupants. The manager then gave in. After which a battle for prestige began. The tree became a beacon of hope. Maybe there was a resurrection. One patted it, smelled it, made incisions in the bark to see if any wound fluid came out, one was busy with it. Uncle Bloem did none of that. He only watched the behavior of the birds. And did so for two years!

I was there when the happy event took place.

Uncle Bloem, while waving his arms excitedly, lost his balance. Lying down in the grass he said: 'Leaves! buds!' That was enough to summon everyone to the tree. And indeed, a young twig was budding! Somewhere in the middle of the trunk, exactly where the tree could still feel pain!'

The patients repeated the sentence again and again. The manager stood there asking himself: 'What's wrong with this people? There were still plenty of trees!'

One, seeing his confusion, shouted in his ear: 'He's still able to feel pain! He belongs to us!'

The battle was won, but not for long. The twig grew and grew, it produced some tiny leaves and that was it.

The decision came with arrival of the autumn.

There have been times when I wanted to be like that tree: brain dead. Sometimes it happened. Yet there were always new leaves budding, enough for the birds to nestle in me again. After which life went on.

I have resigned myself to the fact that such moments are part of me. Pain and wonder, no longer opposite each other, but next to each other.

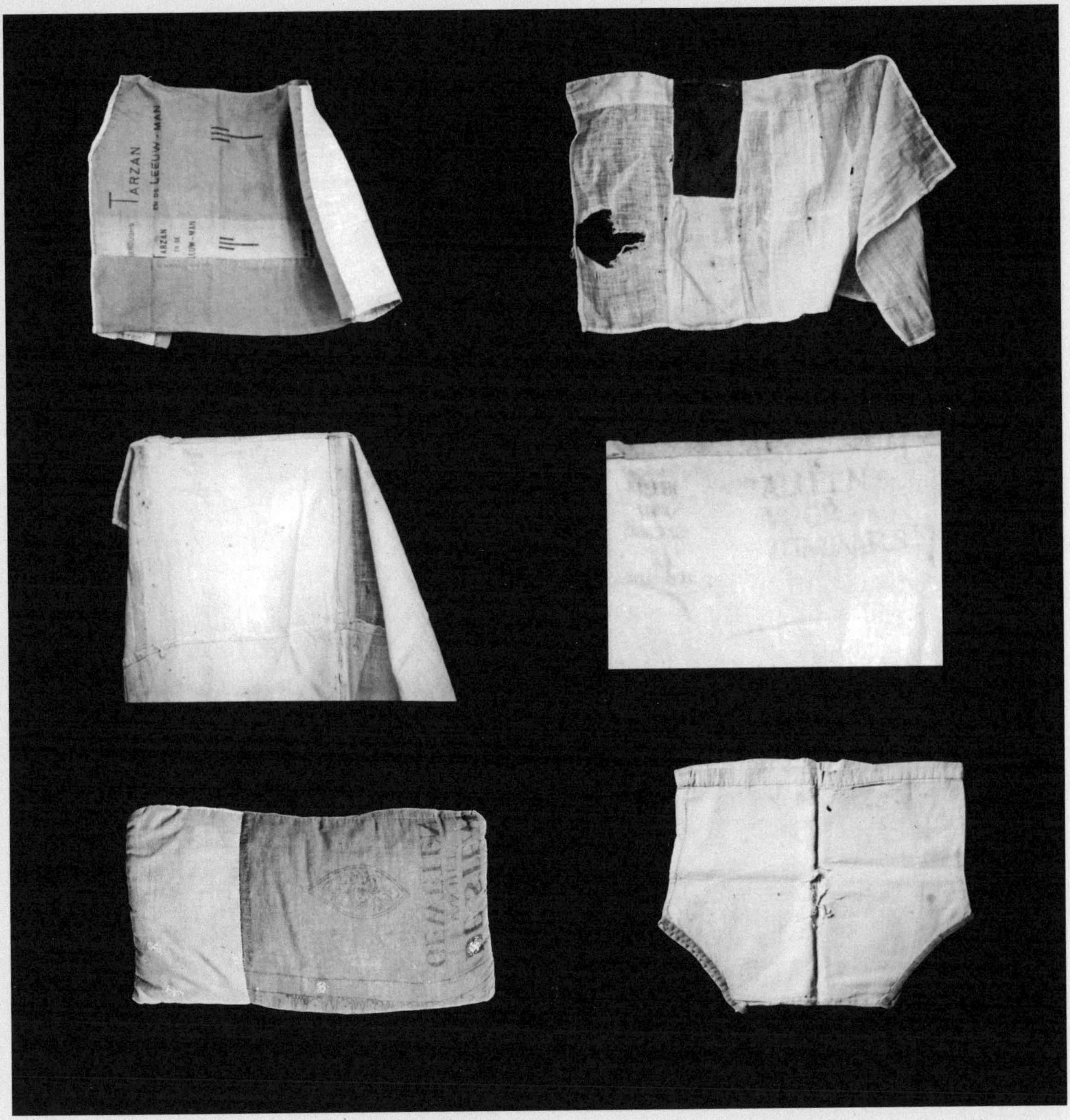

Merapi Obermayer

My life began on September 6, 1947 in a leprosy colony in Pelantungan on the island Java in Indonesia. The struggle for independence was in full swing. My parents had lost everything. Besides their own clothes they had nothing to dress me at my birth.

Luckily there was the library. They soaked the linen from the books and sewed baby clothes of it. The titles they have deliberately picked out.

We fled to the Netherlands at 1953. After we went ashore in Rotterdam my parents saved the clothes at the very last minute from the hands of the Dutch social workers who wanted to send them with the garbage men for being unhygienically and not being relevant for our stay in our new homeland.

I got them back as a gift of war when my parents found out that books and the writing of poems and shorts stories had become an integral part of my artistry.

<u>The titles were</u>:
blouse: *Tarzan en de Leeuw-Man* [Tarzan and the Lion Man], author: Edgard Burroughs
nappy no. 1: No title: but the colours of the Indonesian flag
nappy no. 2: *Alleen voor zondaars* [For sinners only], author's name became unreadable
pillow: *The dictates of one's conscience*, author: Hall Caine

These clothes represent everything life stands for: strength, conscience, freedom, and yes... humour, not unimportant in a war in which monuments of oblivion are scarce.

TRANS-FORMING FUNCTIONAL ARCHIVES INTO STORAGE ARCHIVES

The Photographic Monuments of Mathieu Pernot

Transforming Documents into Monuments

Mathieu Pernot's work can be appreciated for his individual images, as they are very remarkable. But it makes more sense to see his images as part of series or montages as presented in his books or on the walls of a gallery or museum. It is in those contexts that his individual images acquire extra dimensions that they do not have when one focuses on them without the other images and the texts that frame them. The full impact of his images, books, and exhibitions can be best understood not in relation to what they do show but to what they relate.

The most important medium to which his photographic images relate is the archive. The archive as a medium is comprehensive, and the genres of photography within that archive are divers. They range from family albums and travel albums to the archives of photo studios (mainly portraits), the identity images of the police and other state institutions, and scholarly archives of ethnographic images. Pernot's work relates to all these archival genres, not in each work but to one or two of these genres in each project. More importantly, his response to the archival collections and genres to which he relates is itself also presented in an archival format: the (artist's) book and the exhibition.

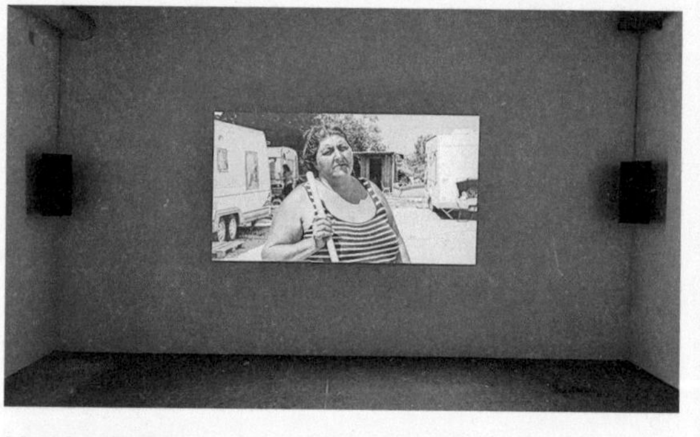

Mathieu Pernot, installations of different 'chapters' of *Les Gorgan*

Ernst van Alphen

Of course, the book and the exhibition are not by definition archival; they are both often used for narrative purposes: to tell stories. But I contend that Pernot's books and exhibitions are always archival and that they rewrite the archive(s) to which they relate.

Pernot's work is strongly informed by history and sociology; he researches the institutional organization of identity, memory, and society at large, by focusing on one specific institutional organization: the archive. A good example is his most recent book and exhibition *La ruine de sa demeure*, which took place at de Henri Cartier Bresson Foundation (2022). The book as well the exhibition begins with the family album of his grandfather René Pernot, who lived in Lebanon's capital Beirut. The grandfather made the archival album in 1926 and devoted it to the travels he made from Beirut through the Middle East, a kind of alternative *grand tour*, not to ancient places in Italy and Greece but to eastern areas, which also constitute the cradle of Western civilization. Places that figure in the album and were visited by the grandfather are Beirut, Tripoli, Baalbek, Damas, Homs, the castle Kalaat el Hosn in Syria, and Palmyra. An important detail is that the original album of the grandfather is not 'represented' in the book. Instead, it begins with a kind of facsimile of the album which is slightly smaller than the rest of the book. The facsimile has a different status in the book, the rest of which shows the work of grandson Mathieu Pernot who stepped into the footsteps of his grandfather. He visited the same places as his grandfather, but almost a hundred years later. His trip also went to the city of Mosul in Iraq, although his grandfather had not been there on his *grand tour*.

The difference between the photographs made by the grandfather and the grandson is shocking. René Pernot's images are typical tourist images showing archeological sites, seascapes and landscapes, local inhabitants, and friends and/or family members in picturesque locations. Mathieu Pernot's series of images begins with the house in the old town of Beirut where his grandparents lived and where his father was born and grew up. The house has survived the enormous explosion that ruined the old center of Beirut in august 2020. Only the balustrade of one of the balconies on the fourth floor fell off the building and is now, as one of the other images shows, used as fencing to prevent people from entering the building. Pernot was able to make

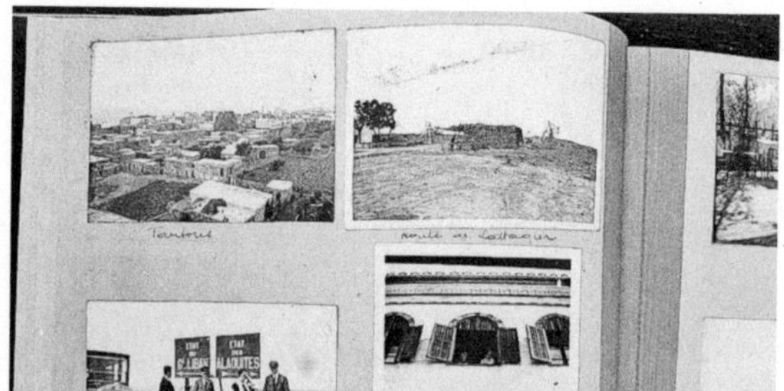

Two pages form the Family album of the grandfather of Mathieu Pernot

images of the spaces of the apartment of his grandparents. In the book these images are combined with images of the family album showing the same spots but then with his grandparents, his father and his aunt. The new pictures are combined with the old family photos in such a way that they resonate with each other, because they show the same elements, like the same tile floor, a door, or a buffet. The issue of resonating images is not to show the similarity between old and new images (because that is rather evident), but the transformation that takes place from the images of the family album to the images of Pernot himself. Whereas the former document the private realm, the latter transfer that private realm to a public one that can be seen by all viewers. I will return to the transformation that takes place here later.

The rest of the book as well as of the exhibition revisits the places that were part of Pernot's grandfather's *grand tour*. But the glorious past of the visited places has been hit by a succession of recent wars; the places that once looked picturesque are now ruins. The remains of houses, apartment buildings, landscapes, severely damaged by explosions and gunfire are overwhelmingly present in most of Pernot's images. And the local inhabitants that could be seen in the grandfather's album have transformed into survivors who try to rebuild their ruined existence. The series of images as shown in the exhibition and in the book becomes a monument of the Middle East, commemorating the glorious past of the region ruined by war after war.

This qualifies Pernot the artist as a modern historian. Michel Foucault describes the modern historian in his

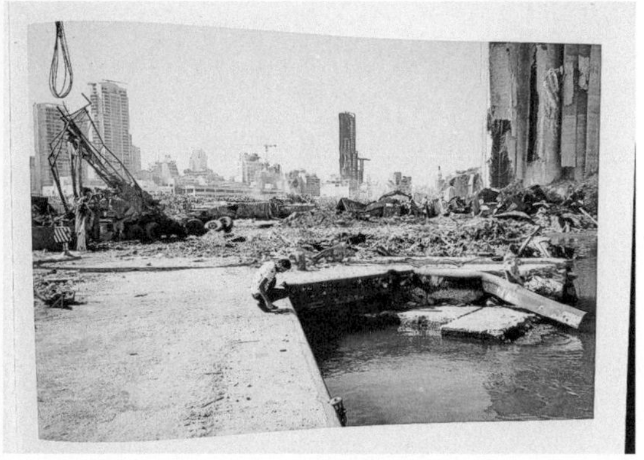

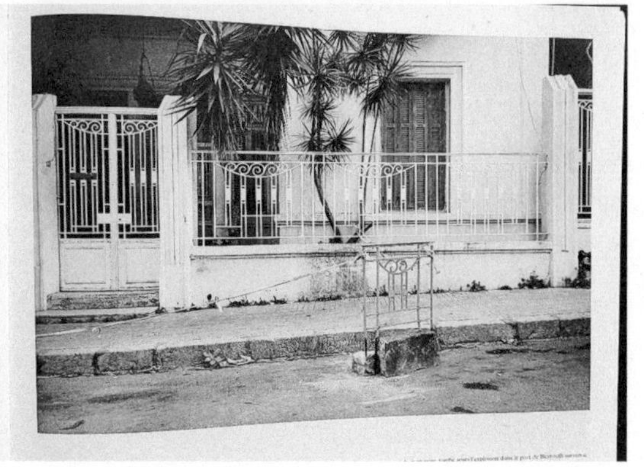

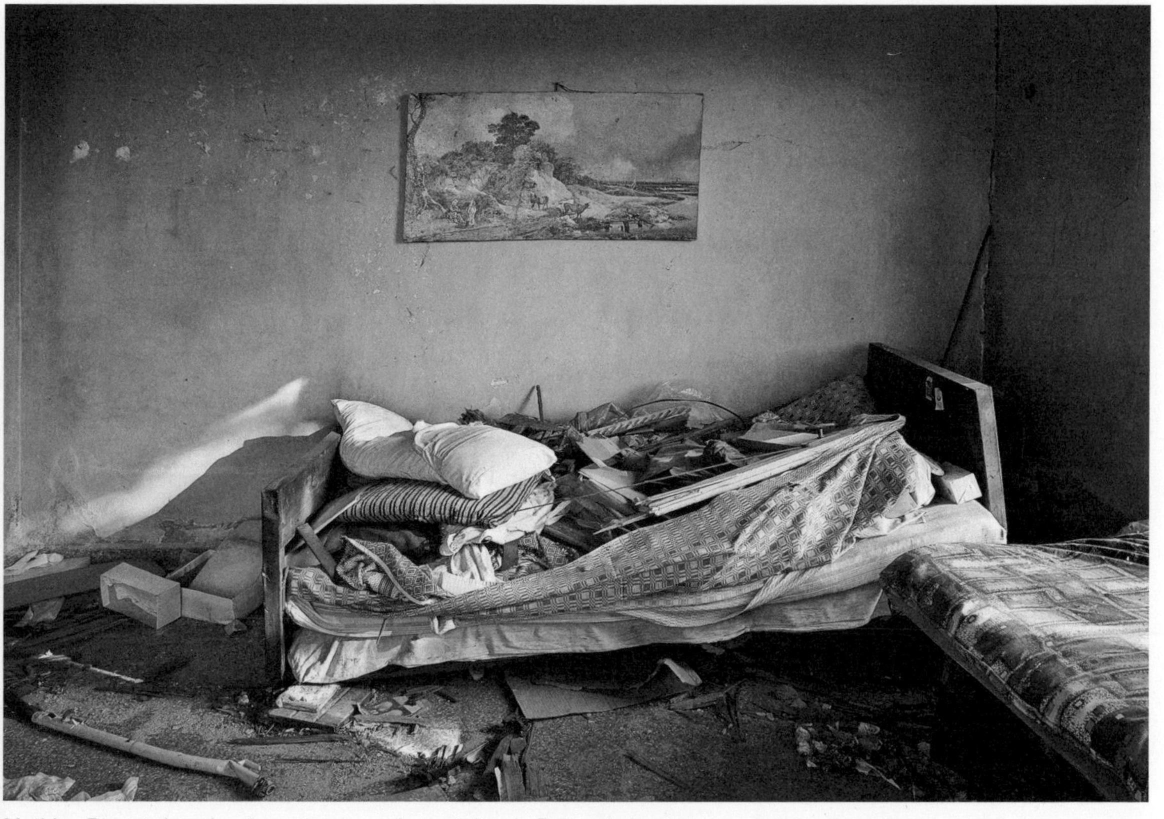

Mathieu Pernot, *La ruine de sa demeure*, photos taken in Beirut, Lebanon

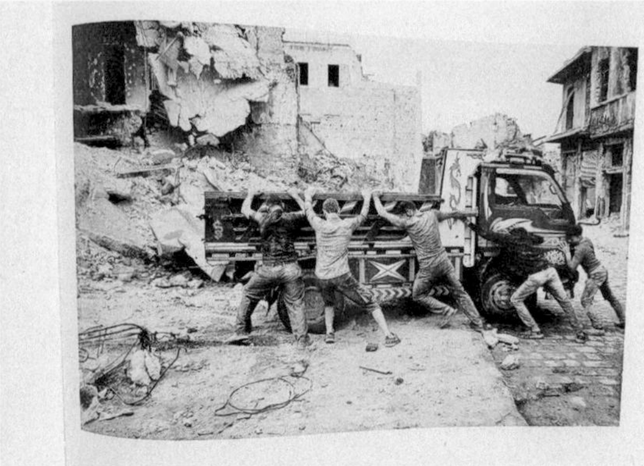

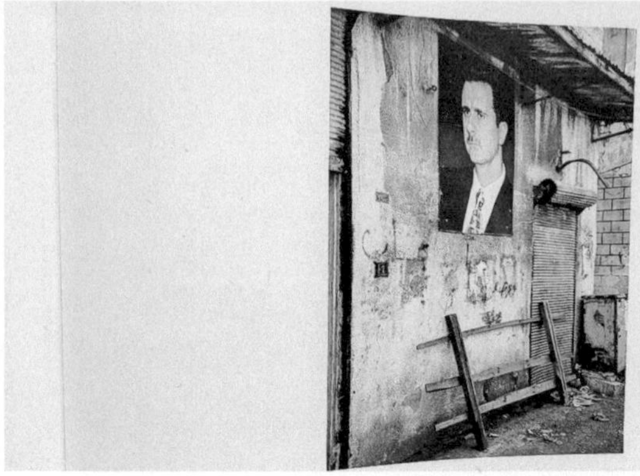

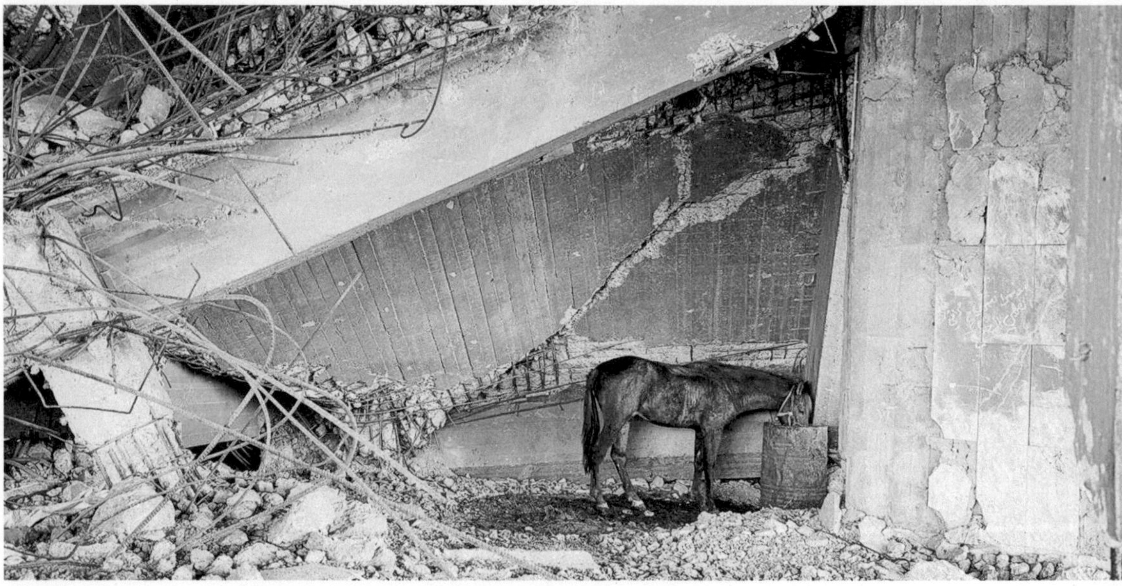

Mathieu Pernot, *La ruine de sa demeure*, photos taken in Syria

Introduction to the *Archaeology of Knowledge* as follows:

> To be brief, then, let us say that history, in its traditional form, undertook to 'memorize' the *monuments* of the past, transform them into *documents*, and lend speech to those traces which, in themselves, are often not verbal, or which say in silence something other than what they actually say; in our time, history is that which transforms *documents* into *monuments*. In that area where, in the past, history deciphered the traces left by men, it now deploys a mass of elements that have to be grouped, made relevant, placed in relation to one another to form totalities.[1]

Pernot's photographic practice is well described by the way Foucault characterizes the practice of modern history: '[...] it now deploys a mass of elements that have to be grouped, made relevant, placed in relation to one another to form totalities.' It also makes clear that his photographic practice is an archival practice: he makes his photographs relevant by placing them in relation to each other, by means of which he forms a new totality. This new totality is the monument that commemorates the 'mass of elements' grouped together and made relevant in relation to one another.

According to the common notion of photography, a photographic image is a representation of the world it shows. This would imply that Pernot's photographs in *La ruine de sa demeure* show representations of places and people that are all unique and specific, because each image is different. But seeing the whole series of images, one is struck by what these images have in common, not in how they differ. This implies that Pernot's photographic use of the archival principle suggests that this notion of photography is irrelevant. His images, as being part of his books and exhibitions, together form a *discourse on*, not a representation of the world they show. A discourse is much more specific, more articulated than a representation, especially when that representation is an image. In an interview with Etienne Hatt, Pernot has said the following about why his images should be seen as discourse instead of representation:

> Every photograph is a discourse on the world, an idea we have about it. A postcard of housing developments and a photograph of a block imploding are two different discourses about the same place.[2]

Every photograph is a discourse on the world because it never exists as a unique isolated image. It always belongs to a specific genre or category, for instance, that of postcards showing housing developments, an image as part of a family album or of a travel album. In the archive, the archived objects or documents exist as examples of the category under which they are catalogued; they never exist as unique, as specific, or as individual. The distinctions made within the archive between different categories are what articulates discourses on the world.
At the end of the book as well as of the exhibition *La ruine de sa demeure* the viewer stumbles upon photographs Pernot found in ruined houses in Mosul in Iraq. These images have the same status

1_Michel Foucault, 'Introduction,' *The Archaeology of Knowledge & The Discourse of Language*, trans. A.M. Sheridan Smith (New York: Harper Torch Books, 1972), p. 7.

2_Etienne Hatt, 'Making Images Dialectical, Interview with Etienne Hatt,' *Art Press* 408 (2014).

as those of Pernot's grandfather's family album; they are found documents and they also belonged in a family album, but after the houses and the families were destroyed, these images have become homeless. The people in the images are not known to us, hence, the images do not refer to anybody anymore; they are just images. The ruination that caused their homelessness can also be seen in the images: traces of water and light and of the destruction that took place in the houses where they were found are visible in the images. Those photos of family members-we-do-not-know are grouped together with Pernot's images and the images of his grandfather's family album and that of his *grand tour*, combining big histories with small histories. The result is an archival collection of images that forms a totality that functions as monument, not only for the wars that destroyed the glorious past of the Middle East, but also of Pernot's family history and of those families whose lives were disrupted by those wars.

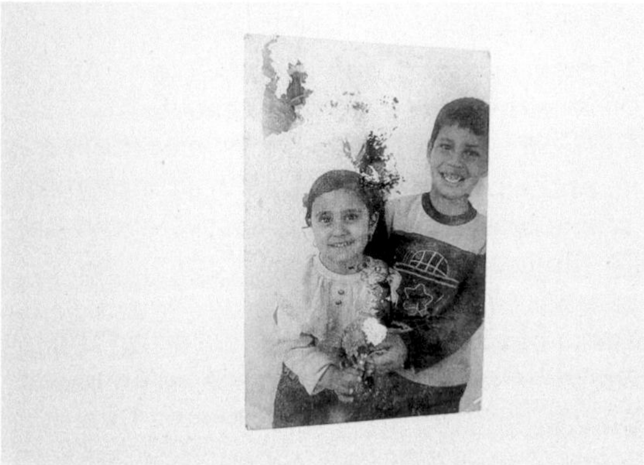

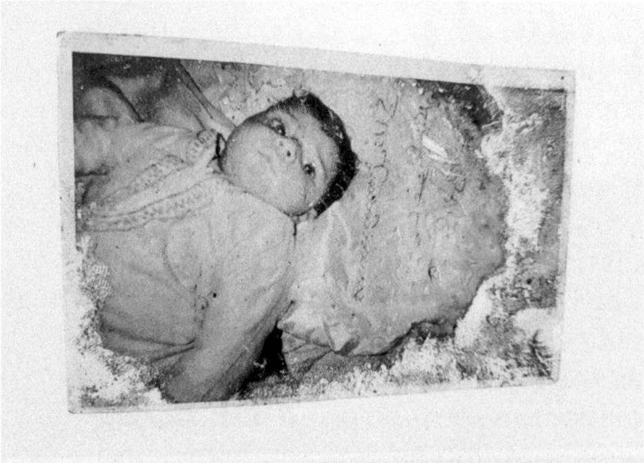

Photos from family albums found by Pernot in destroyed houses in Mosul

It is important, however, not to idealize and romanticize the archival genre of the family album. Although devoted to individual human beings and their singular lives, the images that are included in this archival genre are very conventional. This is beautifully demonstrated by Christian Boltanski's book *Sans-Souci* (1991). Here, found snapshots of several Nazi families have been reproduced. Although the represented people probably did not know each other, the book presents itself as a photo album of one family. As in 'real' photo albums a sheet of cobweb paper is inserted between the pages.

The intriguing and disturbing effect of *Sans-Souci* is caused by the fact that traditional meanings of the family photo album overrule the subjectivities that are supposed to be represented *in* the snapshots. The Nazi soldiers in these photographs do not show any signs or symptoms of the ideology and destruction of which they partake. We only see affectionate friends, lovers, husbands and fathers. So, Pernot's transformation of his grandfather's images and family album into a monument is not an idealization of those images and the archival genre they are part of. His work commemorates these images because it is only in the monument that the temporality of these images is extended; otherwise, they would be lost and disappear into oblivion, like the images Pernot found in the destroyed houses of Mosul.

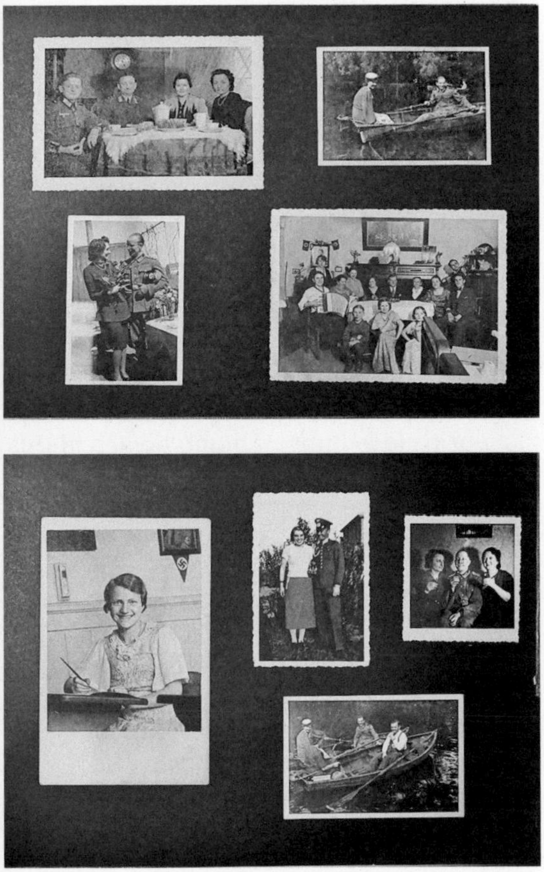

Christian Boltanski (1944-2021), two pages from *Sans-Souci* (1991)

Transforming Functional Archives into Storage Archives

So far, I have argued that Mathieu Pernot's photography should be understood as an archival practice. With his images he revisits specific archival forms of organization and by doing so he revises the signification of such an archival organization or better, the kind of discourse on the world such organizations produce. However, it is important to differentiate between different kinds of archives, and as a result, between different functions of the archive, in order to better understand Mathieu Pernot's interventions in archival organization.

As already explained in the Introduction to this volume, Michel Foucault differentiates between the role of archives in the classical and in the modern period. What changed radically in the modern period is the so-called 'threshold of description.' In the modern period this threshold was lowered dramatically in order to include common people.[3] Until then the archive was the exclusive domain of privileged classes. Foucault argues that a variety of new ways of examining and describing individuals was developed.[4] Although it is true that plants, animals, and even human beings had been the subjects of study before the examination regime was in place, they entered a field of knowledge as general categories, as a species, for example, and not as singular individuals. The modern examination regime is focused on the individual, but its uniqueness is explained in terms of external facts, instead of an inner subjectivity:

3_Michel Foucault, *Discipline and Punish: The Birth of Prison*, trans. Alan Sheridan (New York: Pantheon, 1977), pp. 191–92.

4_For clear descriptions of the history of archival science, see Fernanda Ribeiro, 'Archival Science and Changes in the Paradigm,' *Archival Science* 1, no. 3 (2001), pp. 295–310 and Hermann Rumschöttel, 'The Development of Archival Science as a Scholarly Discipline,' *Archival Science* 1, no. 2 (2001), pp. 43–55.

> What was innovative about the new archives was precisely that they objectified individuals not as members of a pre-existing category, but in all their uniqueness and singularity. Far from being archivable in terms of their shared properties, human beings became linked to all the unique series of events (medical, military, educational, penal events) which made them who they are as historical individuals—a history which could now take the form of a file while the individual became a case.[5]

In other words, whereas in the old archives individuals were used to build or substantiate categories, in the modern archive, categories are being used to build or substantiate the individual. This leads to a situation in which human bodies, events, and archives interact, and it is this interaction that brings about individual identity. This identity is then not seen as a subjective interiority, but as an objective exteriority.

As I already mentioned in in the Introduction, in her contribution to this book Aleida Assmann makes a useful distinction between functional archives and storage archives that does not differentiate archival practices in different periods, but different functions of the archive. Functional archives store what is needed in the present. Medical dossiers, police and tax office files, and those of insurance companies are good examples of functional archives. Also, the way users of new media such as Facebook are being archived happens within a functional archive: the resulting data are being sold to companies, so that the users can be targeted for advertising. In Assmann's words: 'Functional archives are the infrastructure and control instruments that guide and support the present.'[6] This present is not the present in which acts of memory are being performed, but in which the state controls its subjects and capitalist companies reach out to their potential clients. Within Foucault's distinction between the classical archive and the modern archive, one could say that the modern archive is exclusively functional. The storage archive is then the equivalent of what Foucault calls the classical archive. Assmann defines the storage archive as based on a different logic: they come into being when what is no longer of interest or relevant for the present is sorted out but not immediately thrown away: it is stored in an archive, a museum, a library. The function of storage archives is first history, but also the enabling and activation of memory.

When we use Foucault's and Assmann's distinction for a better understanding of Mathieu Pernot's archival practice, it remains at first ambivalent which kind of archive best characterizes his work. He is himself much aware of this when he answers the following to Etienne Hatt's question about the authorship of the images he uses:

> It's not for me to establish ratings and hierarchies, but it may be useful to distinguish between different uses of preexisting images. There are artists who collect images without doing anything to them, and those who invent different classification systems in order to reinterpret them; others appropriate the initial documents as the raw material of a conceptual or plastic process, and finally, there are

5_Manuel DeLanda, 'The Archive before and after Foucault,' in *Information is Alive: Art and Theory on Archiving and Retrieving Data*, ed. Joke Brouwer and Arjen Mulder (Rotterdam: V2_Publishing and NAi Publishers, 2003), p. 11.

6_Aleida Assmann, 'The Archive as Laboratory of the New,' this book, pp. 00–00.

> those artists who produce imaginary archives. I find it difficult to define myself precisely with regard to these approaches and I guess some of my projects could fit into several categories. .... My work is a sort of montage between the images and those I find.[7]

The archives to which Mathieu Pernot relates and that he uses are not at all imaginary, but real. He uses two kinds of archives frequently: the family album and the ethnographic archive. The family album is an ambivalent kind of archive, however. At first it seems to be a storage archive: all the images made by one family of that family are collected in the album and the album enables activating memories of one's youth or other phases in life. But as I just argued on the basis of Boltanski's artist's book *Sans-Souci*, it is at the same time a functional archive because it usually only selects images in which the members of the family are smiling, happy, and confirming the impression that life is good. From this perspective the family album is a performative genre (and not just a storage) because it creates a very specific kind of image of a family.

In order to better understand Mathieu Pernot's archival practice, I will focus on one specific project: *Les Gorgan 1995–2015*. As usual in his practice, this project was realized in the form of a book as well as an exhibition. The exhibition was at the Rencontres de la photographie d'Arles in 2017 and at the Musée national de l'histoire de l'immigration in Paris in 2018. Both are emblematic for Pernot's archival practice. When we approach his work from this perspective it also means that *Les Gorgan* does not offer a representation of a family through photography, but a photographic history: it is a history of images, of practices of photography that were used to represent Roma people. The book as well as the

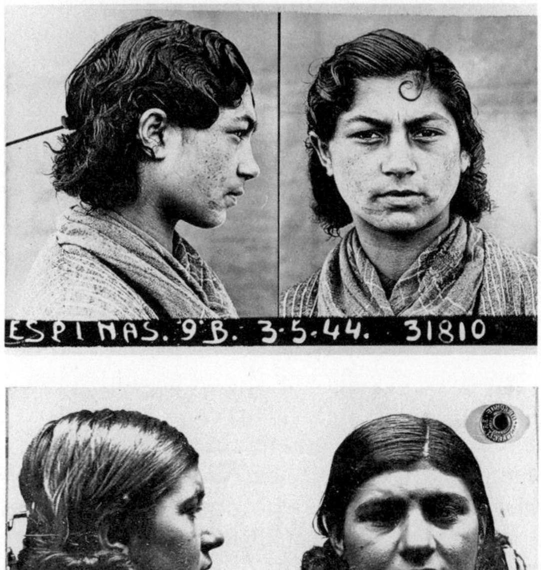

Anthropometric photos of Roma individuals in the provincial archives of Bouches du Rhône

7_Étienne Hatt, 'Giving Form to History: Interview with Mathieu Pernot,' *VU mag*, no. 5, 2010

exhibition are then an assemblage of images and photographic genres, instead of a storage or collection of individual images.

Pernot's engagement with Roma is longstanding. At a certain moment the grandfather Bitschieka Gorgan told him that he had been deported to Buchenwald. When Bietschika told him his story, Pernot started doing research about what had happened in France with the Roma community; he discovered the existence of the Saliers camp in Camargue, not so far from the place where he was living at the time. In 1998 Pernot discovered hundreds of anthropometric portraits of Roma people in the provincial archives of Bouches du Rhône. Anthropometric portraiture is a kind of photography introduced in the late-nineteenth century and used by ethnography and the police. The photographs measure the physical traits of 'others,' that is of non-Western people, but also of criminals and mad people. Among these archival images he discovered the anthropometric images of the Gorgan family, the Roma family he had been working with since a branch of this family had been deported to the camp Saliers fifteen kilometres from Arles, and their grandfather had subsequently been deported to Buchenwald. Anthropometric photos were made of everyone who entered the camp Saliers. The same was done by the Nazis in Auschwitz: those who were not immediately gassed, where first photographed before they were sent to the barracks and most of those images can still be found in archives of Auschwitz.[8] On the basis of these archival images Pernot did the project *Un camp pour les bohémiens. Mémoires du camp d'internement pour nomads de Saliers* (2001). In the book and the exhibition, he did not only show the original anthropometric images of Romas and of the camp, but also photos he had made himself in 1998 and 1999 of survivors of the camp Saliers and of the site in the present where the camp had been located.

After he had finished this project, Pernot kept in touch with the Gorgan family and continued to photograph them at various moments. He had been following the family for twenty-five years when he began working on *Les Gorgan 1995–2015*. When we browse through the book, many of the images seem to belong to what is called 'humanist' photography. This photographic movement, which was especially strong in France, is concerned with everyday human experience in the broadest sense, rather than with newsworthy events as in photojournalism. Nowadays it is considered to be dated and rather conservative, because it affirms the idea of a universal human nature, instead of diversity. But a closer look at the book and the exhibition makes clear that *Les Gorgan 1995–2015* is not at all humanist, but rather conceptual: it is not *about* the Gorgan family but about different archival, photographic genres in which Roma such as the Gorgan family

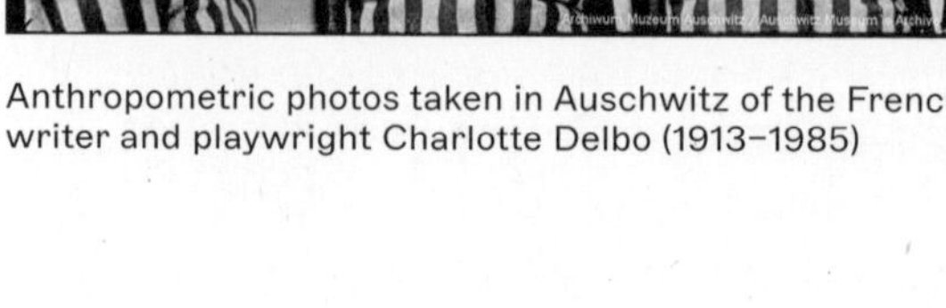

Anthropometric photos taken in Auschwitz of the French writer and playwright Charlotte Delbo (1913–1985)

8_Part of the archives of Auschwitz was taken by Russians and taken to Russia.

are being represented. The project does not just repeat or allegedly document these photographic histories; instead, it attempts to intervene in them while showing them.

In the history of photography Roma were often the subject of anthropomorphic photography. In thoses case they were not considered to be individual people but examples of a species. The project *Les Gorgan 1995–2015* is not structured and based on a taxonomy, but on the individual members of the Gorgan family. Each member is given his or her own chapter, and in each chapter a different kind of images is shown. Those family members are: Johny, Ninaï, Rocky, Giovanni, Mickaël, Jonathan, Priscilla, Vanessa, Ana and Doston. The chapters devoted to the individual members of the family contain images made by the family themselves, probably coming from their family album, and images made by Mathieu Pernot. Most of the chapters begin with a classical identity image made in a photography booth, requested by Pernot. Some of the images belong to the genre of the portrait, others to 'snapshots' showing the Gorgan family in their own living context as is customary in photos in a family album. And one more thing: the chapters are never devoted to one single, pregnant moment that catches the real nature of these individuals in a single image; instead, the images were taken over the course of more than twenty years and they demonstrate how each image represents them differently. There is no singular or universal human nature to be seen in any of these images. His project needs many images over time and belonging to different photographic genres; the images need to show the variety and complexity of Roma individuals.

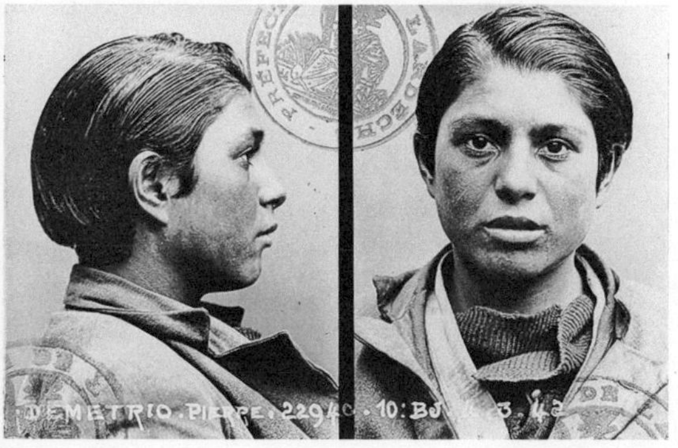

Anthropometric photos of Roma boy in the provincial archives of Bouches du Rhône

When Clément Chéroux compares Mathieu Pernot to earlier generations of photographers who have made representations of Roma (Robert Doisneau, Jean Dieuzaide, Hans Silvester, Michèle Brabo, Lucien Clergue), he argues the following:

> Mathieu Pernot proposes a quasi-meta-photographic approach, unrelated to folklore and myths, a *look* that is conscious of the *look*, which means it is completely open. Undoubtedly, he has kept the benevolence of the humanist but he has lost the candor of it. He is a photographer who has read the complete Foucault, he uses appropriation as a critique of representation. To conclude, his *humanism* is rather postmodern. [9]

Pernot's postmodern humanism implies that he does no longer believe in a universal human nature but rather in the diversity of human peoples and human beings. But even more importantly, in

9_Mathieu Pernot propose une rapproche quasi méta-photographique, loin du folklore et des mythes, un *regard* conscient du *regard*, c'est-à-dire parfaitement dessillé. Il a sans doute conservé la bienveillance de l'humaniste, mais il en a perdu la candeur. En photographe qui aurait lu tout Foucault, il utilise l'appropriation comme critique de la représentation. Son *humanisme* est en somme assez postmoderne. Clément Chéroux, 'Trouer l'éternité' [Piercing Eternity], in Mathieu Pernot, Clément Chéroux, and Johanne Lidskog, *Les Gorgan 1995–2015* (Paris: Atelier EXB/ Editions Xavier Barral, 2017), pp. 205-211

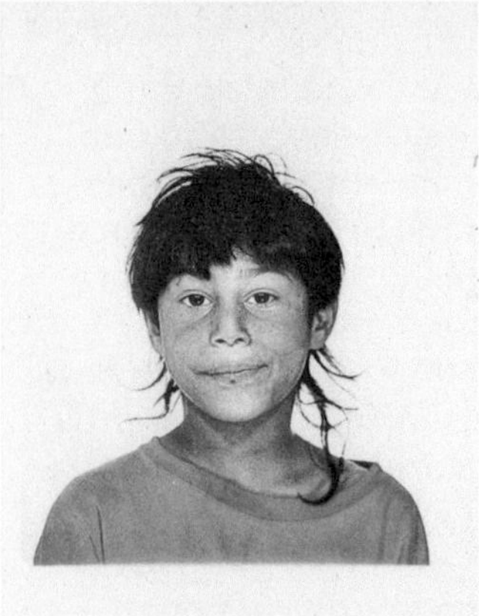

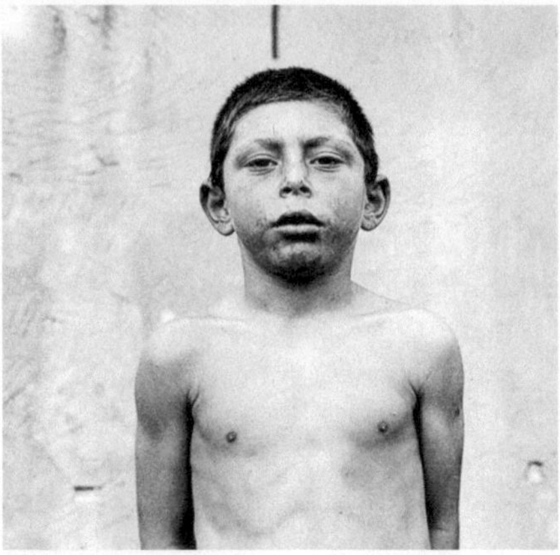

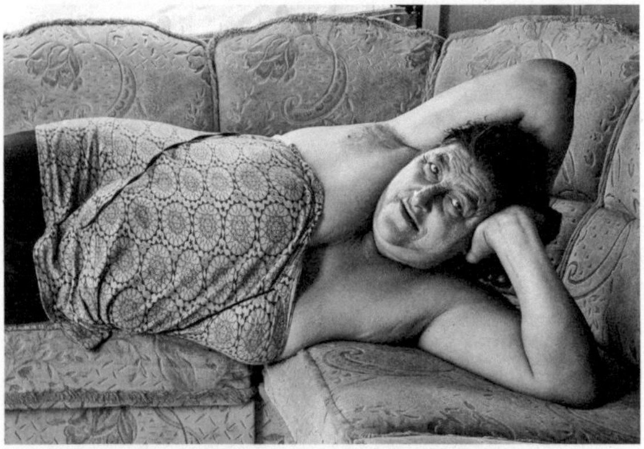

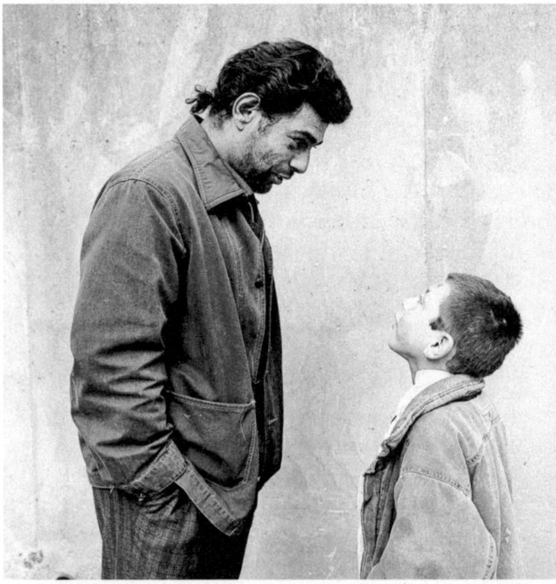

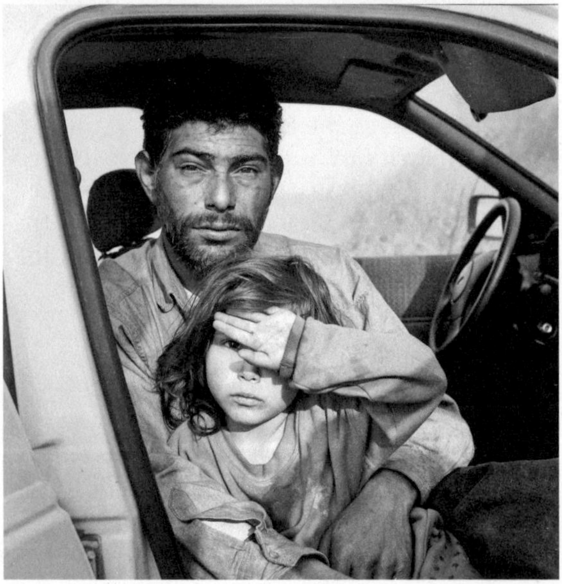

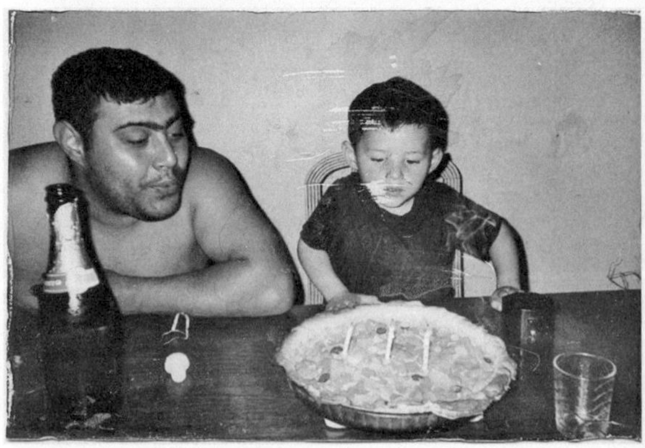

Different photos of the members of the Gorgan family, made by themselves or by Mathieu Pernot. The last image shows the tombstone of Jonathan for which the family used a photo taken by Mathieu Pernot.

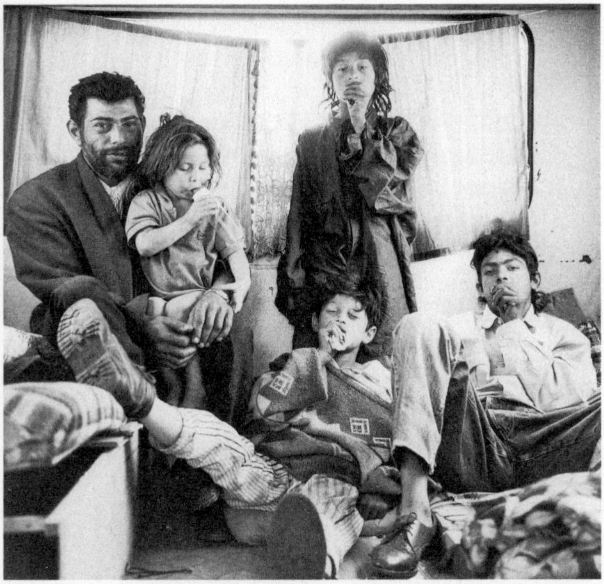

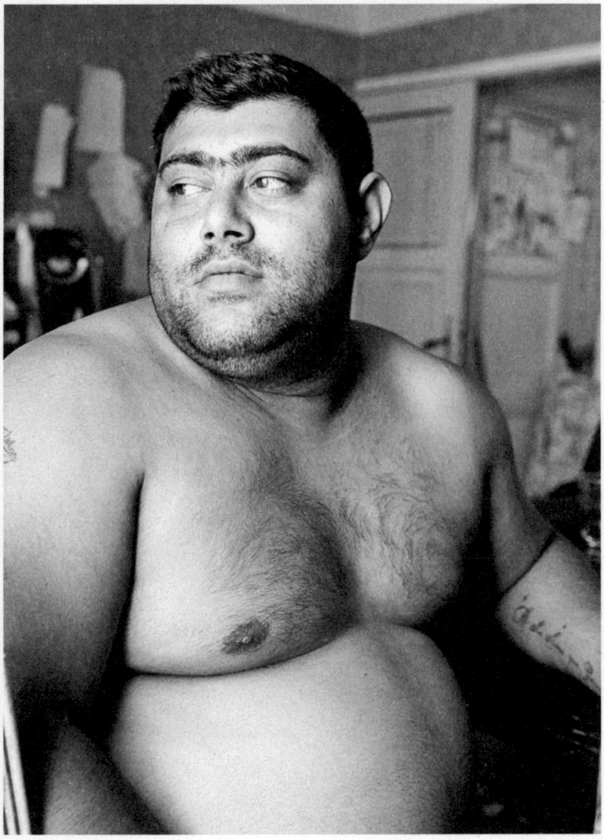

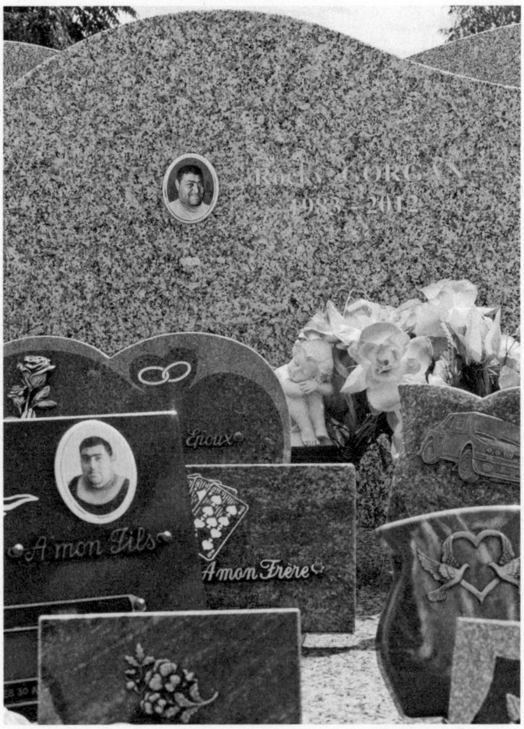
A mon Fils
A mon Frère

order to convey that notion of humanity he needs an archival photographic approach. Because only this approach denaturalizes the photographic image; it demonstrates that a photograph is not a slice taken out of the world before the camera. Photography should be understood in its difference from the reality it shows. That is why Mathieu Pernot's projects focus on the specific ways photographic genres and archives determine the world or the persons we see in the photographic image. It is only through the understanding of that mediation that we pay attention to the photographic image, instead of the illusion of the world it shows.

Let me conclude by comparing Mathieu Pernot's archival photographic projects to that of the German artist August Sander whose *major corpus* is also photographic as well as archival but done in the decades in which Nazism was rising, the 1920s and 1930s. Originally a portrait and documentary photographer Sander applied archival principles to the photographs he made. First having had a photo studio in Linz, Austria, later in Cologne, Germany, Sander joined the 'Cologne Progressives,' in 1920. Although his work includes many different genres, such as architecture, landscape, and street photography, he is best known for his portraits. As an artist, he had plans to document contemporary German society in a series of portraits. This resulted in his series titled *Menschen des 20. Jahrhunderts* (People of the Twentieth Century). In this series, he intended to show a cross-section of German society during the Weimar Republic. He inventoried his contemporaries by a standard procedure. As in a modern archive he used a classificatory system to order the series. He divided it into seven categories: the Farmer, the Skilled Tradesman,

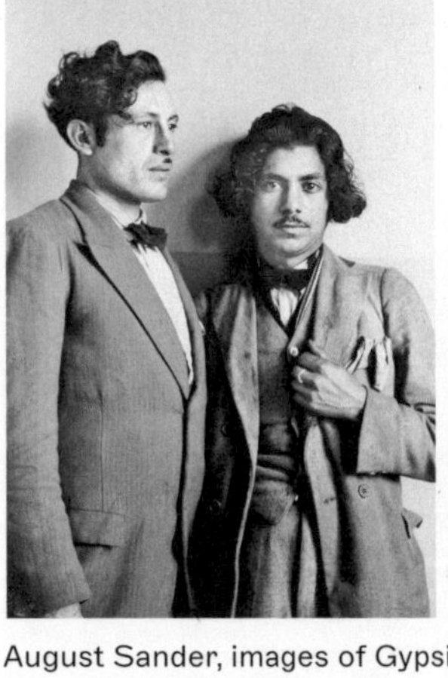

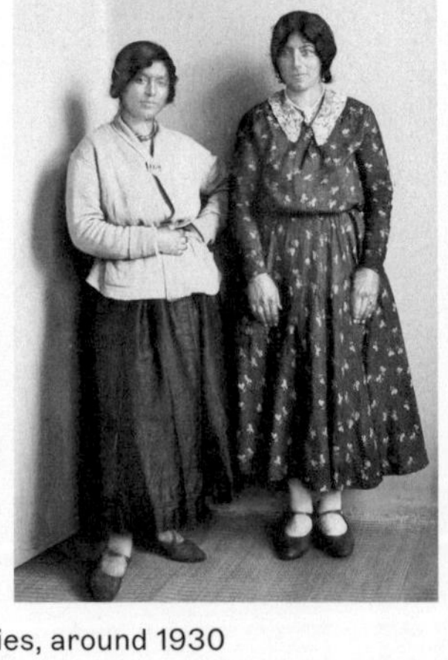

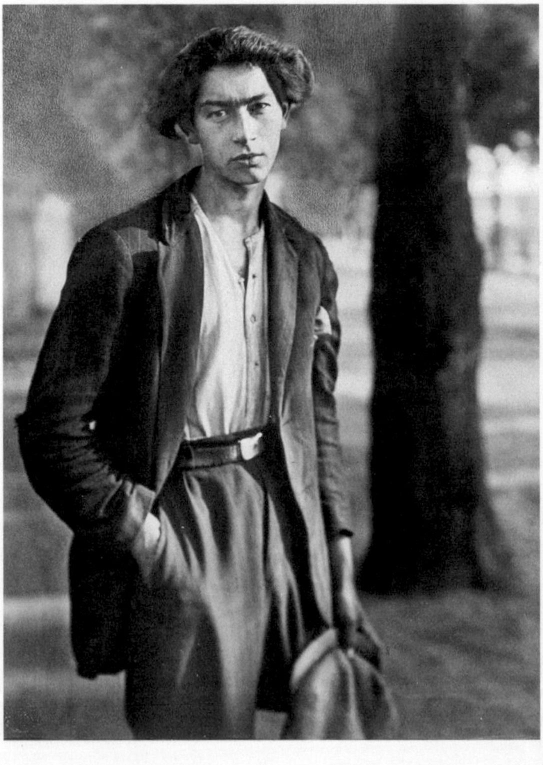

August Sander, images of Gypsies, around 1930

Woman, Classes and Professions, Artists, the City, and The Last People (meaning homeless people, veterans, and so on). In the end, Sander's archive contained over 40,000 images. Most of these show the subjects in full length. They are always facing and acknowledging the camera. The space in which their portrait is taken is usually their own 'natural context': the space in which they live or work. For instance, the pastry cook is portrayed in his kitchen, road workers in the street, a widower with his two children in the living room, circus artists in front of their circus wagon. This supplementary role of the spatial context is crucial, because otherwise the identity of the classified subjects would still be too ambiguous.

In 1929 Sander published sixty images from his *Menschen des 20. Jahrhunderts* in a book titled *Antlitz der Zeit* (Face of our Time). Under the Nazi regime his work was seen as *entartet*, degenerated, and in 1936 his book *Antlitz der Zeit* was seized and the photographic plates were destroyed. We can only speculate now which aspects of Sander's work were the reasons for the Nazis to condemn it as degenerated and have it destroyed. But from a certain perspective is it amazing that they did, because the archival art project of Sander and the political project of Nazism have key elements in common: they both use a typological mindset. Whereas Sander's archival project classified on the basis of occupational categories, the politics of Nazism used racial categories such as Germanic, Jewish, Slavic, gipsy. But what they have in common is an inventorial, encyclopaedic approach to humanity.

In both cases a specific identity, considered to be essential, is projected onto human beings on the basis of a classificatory system. With his classifications Sander, too, pursued the goal to pin down the identity of human beings, most often on the basis of their occupation or profession. The archival structure of his project took away, however, any identity he tried to institute on the basis of these categories, since the identity we are supposed to see in those images is not the result of who or what these subjects are, but foremost of the classificatory system imposed upon them. Not from an aesthetic point of view, but from the point of view of his epistemological pursuit of pinning down the identities of the photographed subjects, his project was doomed from the start.

Sander's photographic archive *Menschen des 20. Jahrhunderts* contains so many different categories that the ambition to overview modern society overshoots its goal. Whereas the categories employed by the Nazis to regulate German and later also European society were very restricted (jews, gipsies, homosexuals, Jehovah witnesses, political enemies), those of Sander are more or less endless. The ultimate effect of this endless proliferation of categories is that each category ends up showing individuals. When we look at some of the images Sander made of Roma people, it is clear that he portrayed them in more or less the same way as he did with the individuals demonstrating other categories of people. These images do not follow the model of ethnographic or anthropometric photography. But whereas Sander usually portraited his models in their own 'natural context': the space in which they live or work, in the case of his images of Roma people the spaces are rather undefined, an empty wall or room. This could mean that Sander tries to say that Romas have no conventional context because they are nomads. But as portraits these images do not differ from the way he portraited other people in his *Menschen des 20. Jahrhunderts*.

In one of Sander's portraits we see a young gypsy standing in an empty country lane with his hat in his hand. The background is not focused, probably because the exposure was taken with the lens set wide open. This creates the impression that the photo was taken in a photo studio with a painted stage set as background. These kinds of portraits are not ethnographic but utterly bourgeois.

In contrast with Sander or Santu Mofokeng, whose work I already discussed in the Introduction, Mathieu Pernot never employs the genre of the studio portrait to portray the members of the Gorgan family. His images are more casual and more difficult to fit into a conventional photographic genre. In contrast with Sander's images of gypsies, he portrays the Gorgan family members systematically in their own context. This context is always defined, specific and part of their private world. And very important, many images in the Gorgan project were made by the family themselves and given to Mathieu Pernot to include in his book or exhibition: the Gorgan family were not just the object of his project; they were collaborators in it. As a result, to use the words of Clément Chéroux once more, Mathieu Pernot shows real persons, instead of characters.[10] By doing this he has rewritten the archival registers which were conventionally used to portray Roma people. Whereas the kind of archival collections used to portray Roma were so far functional archives, especially ethnographic or anthropometric archives, Mathieu Pernot has revisited these archives and transformed them into a storage archive. His storage archive *Les Gorgan 1995–2015* enables the viewer to imagine and see real, individual people with their own histories and memories. This transformation is Pernot's intervention in archivism.

10_Chéroux, 'Trouer l'éternité.'

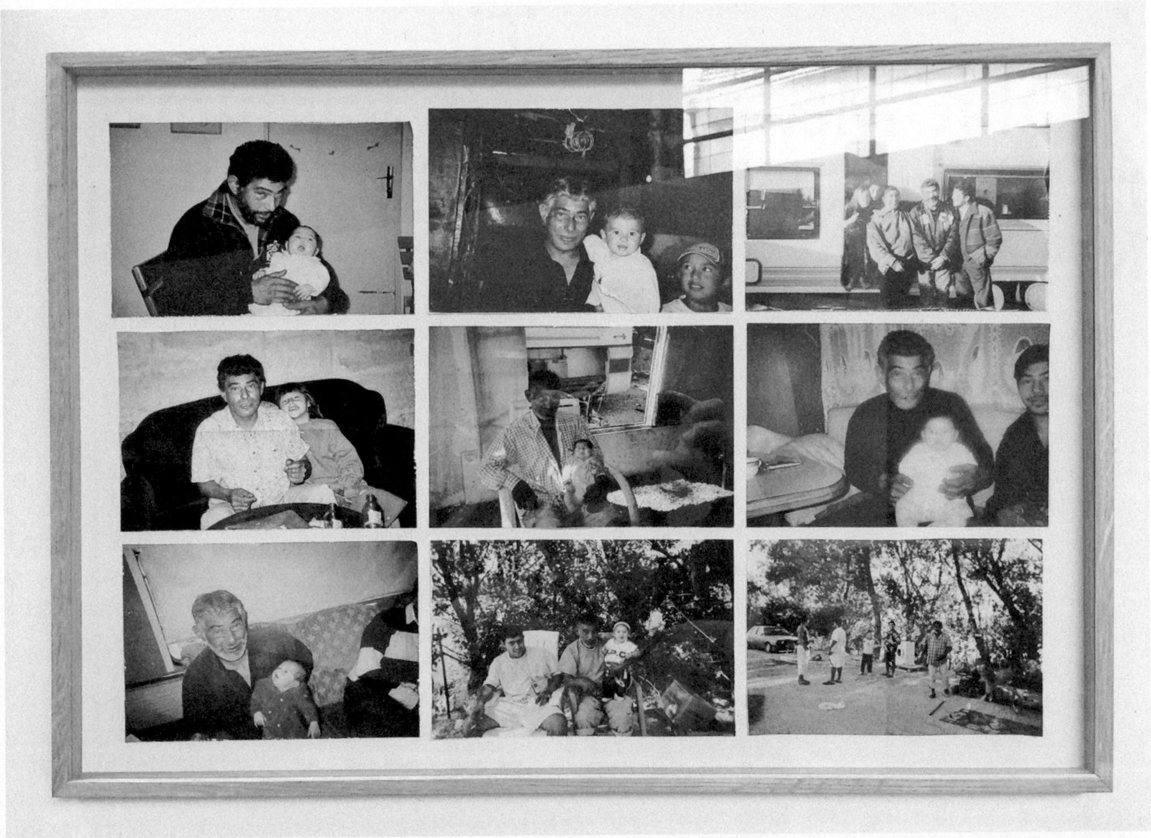

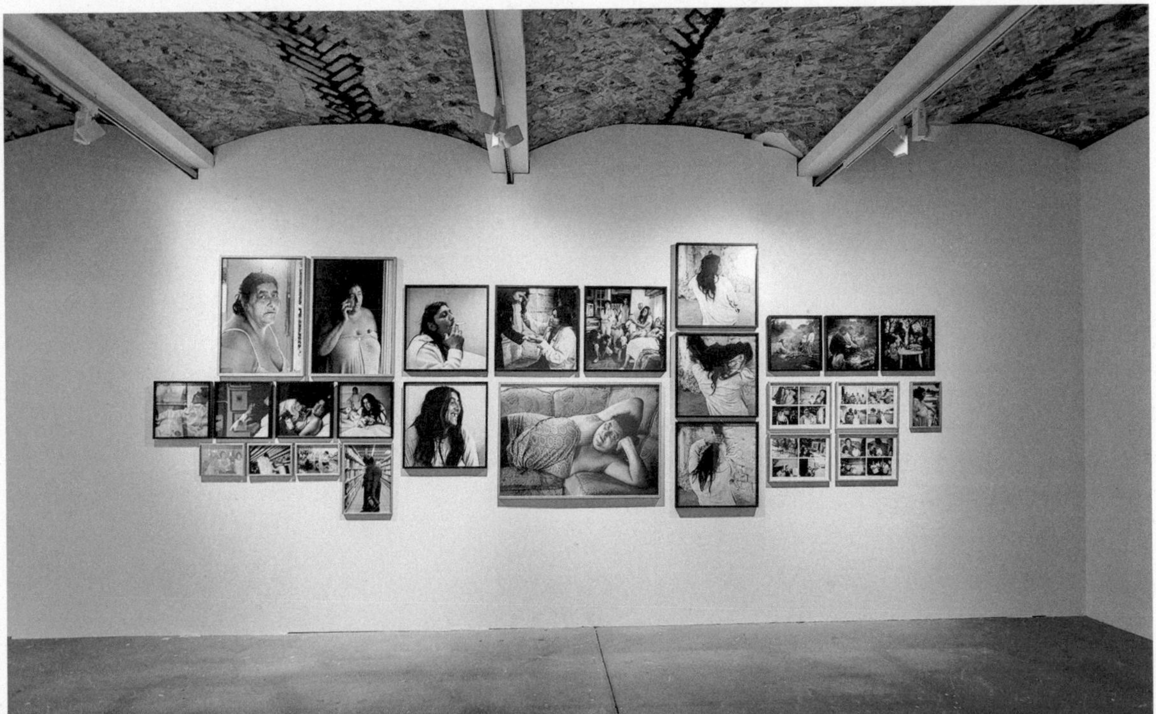

Mathieu Pernot, *Les Gorgan*, installation

A MONUMENT FOR FUTURE MEMORY

The Ringelblum Archive as a Classical Archive

'During this war every Jew is a separate, individual world.'
Emanuel Ringelblum

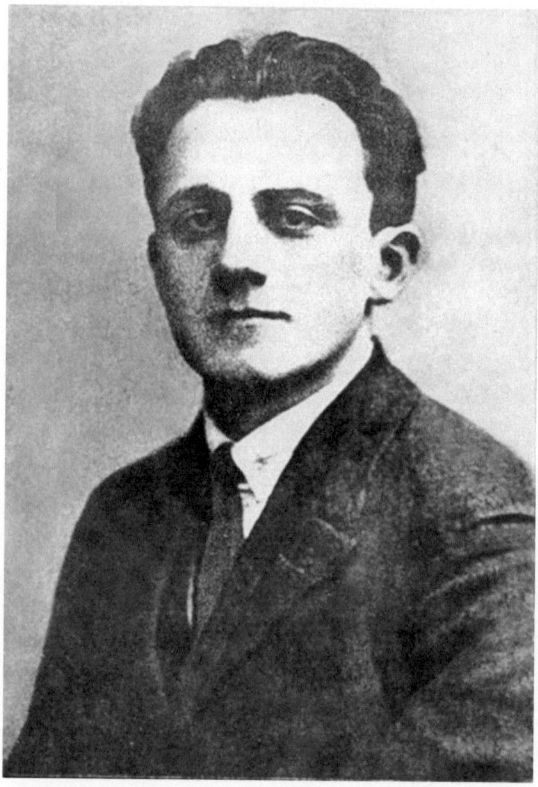

Ernst van Alphen

The story about the underground archive of the Warsaw ghetto is strangely enough not very well known to a wider audience. Whereas people all over the world know about the diaries of Anne Frank and of the house in Amsterdam where she and her family hid and were caught by the Nazis, not many people know about the archive that was put together in the Warsaw Ghetto and stored the narratives, everyday objects and facts of the lives of the Polish Jews in the ghetto. What makes this archive extraordinary is that its main purpose was not scientific or historical, but rather the very act of archiving was in itself an act of resistance.

The archive bears the name of its initiator, the historian Emanuel Ringelblum who was the head of a group that used the code name *Oneg Szabat* or *Oyneg Shabes* (Hebrew for joy of the Sabbath).

They began to work on the archive in November 1940. Ringelblum's collaborators included journalists, economists, teachers, writers and rabbis, and numbered between fifty and sixty people. The archived material was stored in milk cans and metal boxes and hidden in different parts of the ghetto. One part was retrieved from the ruins of the Warsaw ghetto in 1946, the second part in 1950.

The third part has not been found yet despite numerous efforts. The archive is now housed in the building where Ringelblum and his associates worked after Nazi Germany had occupied Poland and established the ghetto for Polish Jews in Warsaw. This building was then home to the Central Judaic Library and now houses the Jewish Historical Institute. It is one of very few buildings that survived the fire started by the Nazis, which almost completely destroyed this part of the city. Of Ringelblum's *Oneg Shabbat* team of associates only three people survived: economist Hersz Wasser, his wife Bluma, who was involved in Hebrew education, and writer Rachela Auerbach.

Imprisoned in the Warsaw ghetto, Ringelblum and his associates knew very well what their fate was going to be besides hunger, cold, lack of any resources and overcrowding.

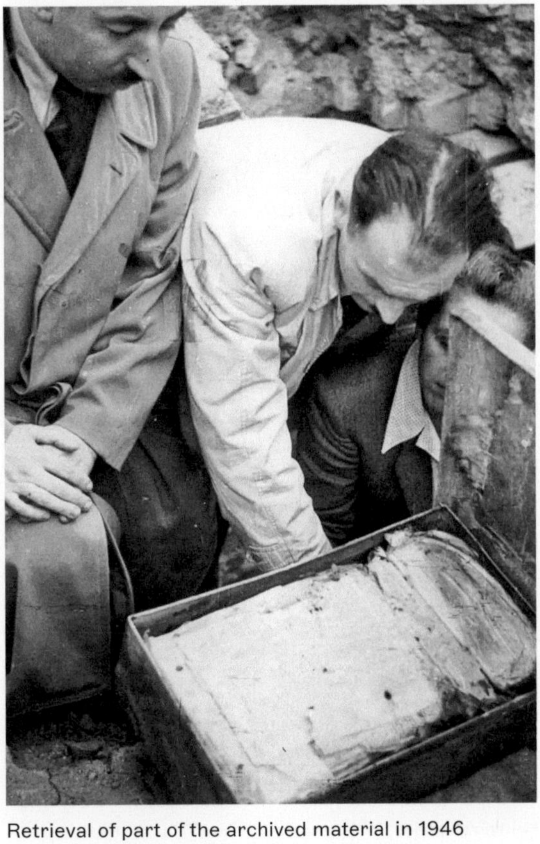

Retrieval of part of the archived material in 1946

The systematic mass murder of Jews performed by the Nazis in Poland was going to include those who were for the time being isolated in the ghetto. The stories of the genocide of Jewish people also reached the Jewish ghettos in Poland, and most people became aware that the ghetto was the purgatory or limbo of the extermination camps. How is it possible that under these circumstances Ringelblum conceived and decided to organize the archival project of collecting facts and stories of Polish Jews, in November 1940? When I imagine the situation in the ghetto, it seems more plausible that people despaired, became utterly depressed, and even committed suicide. And quite a number of people in the ghetto did just that. Although Ringelblum's situation was literally hopeless in all respects, he began his archival project as an act of resistance. What most probably inspired him were the lessons of his teacher Isaac Schipper, a famous Jewish historian. Schipper had argued that 'what one knows about murdered peoples is usually what their killers choose to say about them.'[1] So, if the Nazis were to win the war, then they would write about the murder of European Jewry as one of the most glorious chapters of world history. Ringelblum's response to this seems to have been to obstruct 'these German plans to distort or obliterate the memory of Polish Jewry,' by taking control over the material on the basis of which the history of Polish Jews could be written,[2] by collecting and preserving whatever he and his associates could find.

Schipper's general remark about murdered peoples and their killers and how killers want to have control over how the people they murdered are going to be remembered, is particularly true for the Nazis. After having liquidated the European Jews, Adolf Hitler intended to build a museum of the Jewish people, the so-called Central Museum of the Extinguished Jewish Race. In Czechoslovakia the Nazis brought Jewish

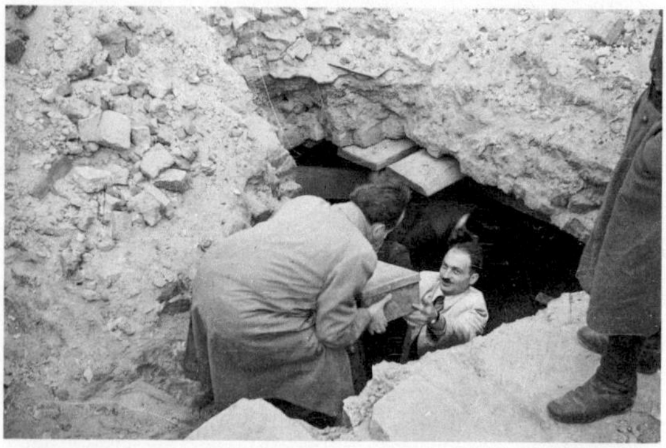

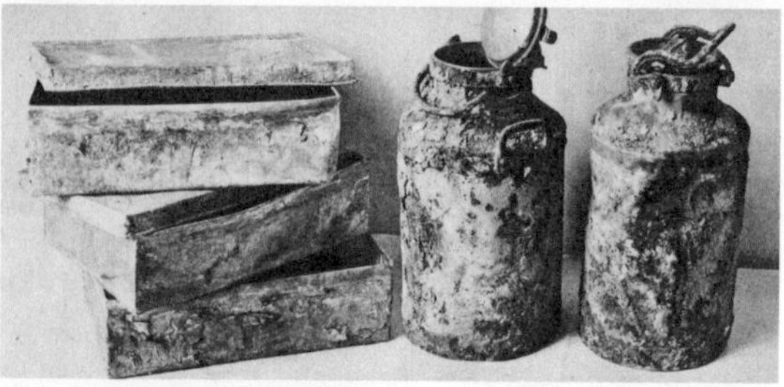

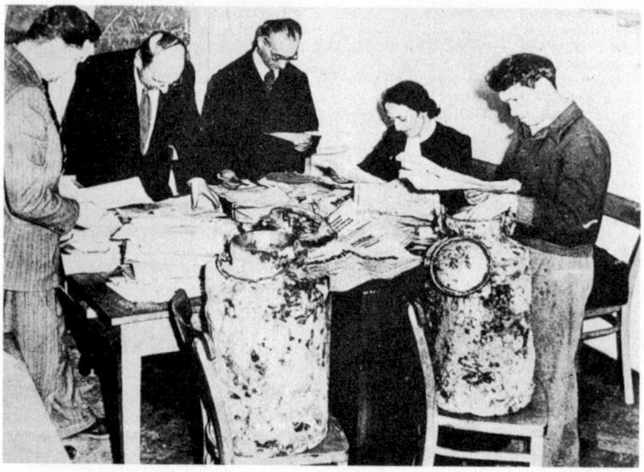

Retrieval of part of the archived material in 1946

1_Samuel D. Kassow, 'Foreword,' in *The Ringelblum Archive: Underground Archive of the Warsaw Ghetto*, vol. 1, ed. Katarzyna Person (Warszawa: Jewish Historical Institute, 2017), xv.

2_Kassow, 'Foreword.'

religious artefacts from 153 provincial communities to Prague for the collection of this institution. Included were 5400 religious objects, 24,500 prayer books and 6070 artefacts of historical value. After the end of the war, it became the core of the collection of the Jewish Museum of Prague.[3]

Adolf Hitler was a perverse genius in understanding that it mattered to remember European Jewry, and even more importantly, that it mattered how they were going to be remembered, who would shape this memory and for whom. Like Ringelblum, he wanted to be in control over the production of memory. He could be in control by establishing a museum: after having killed all European Jews, he would create his Central Museum of the Extinguished Jewish Race. One could wonder why? Why would he not have reached his goal once all the European Jews had been killed? Hitler's museum project suggests that liquidation was not enough, because even after their destruction the Jewish people could live on in memory of the living, in living memory. That which was to remain had to be dealt with effectively, so that possible continued existence of the Jews in memory was totally controlled. In terms of the linguistic distinctions of the verb tenses used to talk about the past (in some of the languages), we could say that it was only then that the present perfect of European Jewish culture was transformed into past simple or *preterite* (in French *passé défini*) of that culture.[4]

Hitler's planned museum of the extinguished race proves the point of Ringelblum's role-model Isaac Schipper that it matters which agent is in charge of the production not only of historical knowledge but also of memory. Museums and archives can also be used as media and counterforces that challenge other narratives about the past, especially the dominant ones. Ringelblum used the archive as a model for cultural resistance. But the fact that people such as Schipper and Ringelblum were convinced that archives could be used critically as counterforces, does not guarantee that Ringelblum's archival project was also successful in creating the conditions for productive memorialization of Polish Jewry. What is it in this archive that enables it to be an active means of resistance? The fact that Jewish instead of German sources were collected by Ringelblum does not seem to be any guarantee. It is not only what is stored in the archive that matters, but also the very organization of that archive that determines how it can and will be used. What is it that enables us in the present to have memories of the Holocaust past that differ, and are in that sense counter memories in relation to the prevalent narratives about that event?

Archival Organizations Employed by Nazism

This is a crucial question because many archival organizations have the opposite effect. I am now no longer talking about archives in the literal, institutional sense, but in a more conceptual one. I think we must examine this because collecting, storing, listing, categorizing, does not only take place in archives and museums, but is also a symbolic mode human beings use to impose order on the world and on their experiences in and of that

3_See *Encyclopedia of the Holocaust*, ed. Israel Gutman (New York: Macmillan, 1990), p. 118.

4_See Ernst van Alphen, *Staging the Archive: Art and Photography in Times of New Media* (London: Reaktion Books, 2016), pp. 209–11.

world. Also, our thinking is based on these archival principles: we collect, list and categorize all the time, arranging our ideas and experiences. And with our thinking as archiving machines, we also structure many dimensions of societal and political order on the basis of archival principles. From this perspective, ghettos and concentration camps are prime examples of archival organizations too: they are the result of the application of a very limited number of categories, such as Jews, Roma, homosexuals, political enemies. And having been categorized on the basis of these distinctions, people were collected and stored in ghettos and concentration camps. Their very diverse individual identities were reduced to one single category.

Alain Resnais' 1955 documentary on the Holocaust, entitled *Nuit et brouillard* (*Night and Fog*) demonstrated well in which sense concentration camps were archival machines. Whereas the first half of the film presents the camps factory-wise, the second half presents the camps as monstrous archives and storages. Of course, both are presented as intimately related: the camps are factory-like archives, and archive-like factories. What the factory and the archive according to Resnais have in common is that in both efficiency is the highest value. What kind of efficiency though?

Within the archival organization a complete depletion of individual identity has taken place. As the voice-over tells us, at arrival all the inmates had to leave their names. Instead, they became numbers, not only in the administrative records of the camps but by having the number tattooed on their forearms. Thus, the intimate, carnal relationship between archival organization and the depletion of identity was established. The film ends with color footage showing nature overgrowing the remains of the camps. There is no trace of human life. Life and identity have been depleted efficiently, or so it seems.

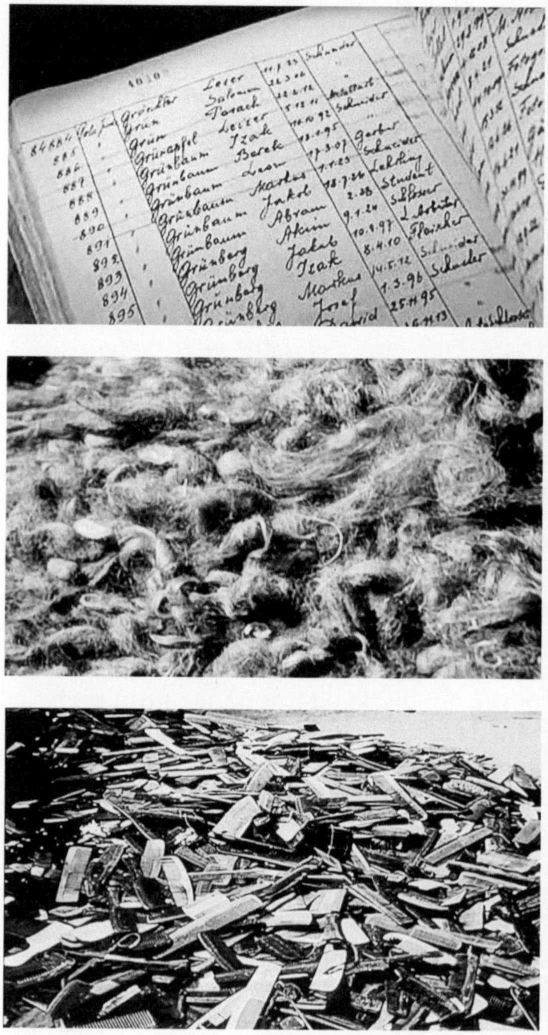

Alain Resnais, *Night and Fog*, 1955, film stills

The understanding of concentration camps as monstrous archival machines implies that one defines the Holocaust as a *method*. The Nazis employed the archival organization as their method for genocide. They were good at it; they were master-archivists. The most notorious concentration camp, Auschwitz, the name of which has become synonymous with the Holocaust as such, was modelled on archival principles.[5] Archival principles were crucial in the way the Nazis ruled Germany and the occupied territories, but also in the organization of the concentration camps and in their execution of the 'final solution.'

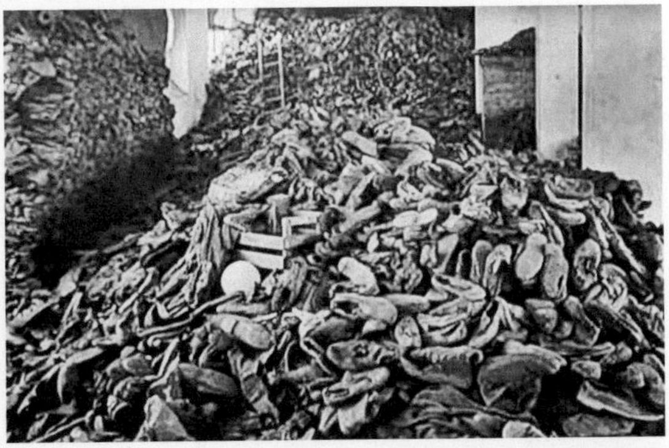

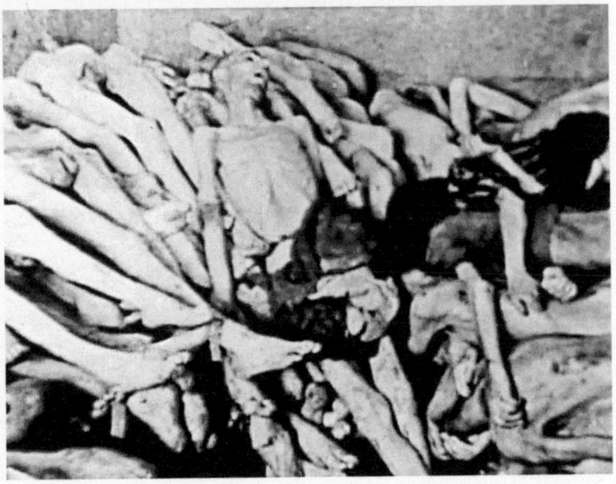

Alain Resnais, *Night and Fog*, 1955, film stills

The Nazis pursued what they called a 'restlose Erfassung,' which means total registering, without loose ends; an expression that also connotates 'all-embracing seizure.' This ambition leads to a fanatic policy of counting, listing, and conducting censuses.[6] Keeping the registry of the inhabitants of the German Reich up to date was the main task of the Bureau for Publications of the SS Security Office, the so-called *Sicherheitsdienst*. But the census did not stop with the registration of all inhabitants of the *Reich*; it was also performed in the camps where those who were no longer seen as fellow citizens ended up.

Let me explain in more detail which structural principles of the camps can be characterized as archival. In many concentration camps the Nazis were fanatic in making lists of all the people who entered the camps. It was thanks to the existence of these lists that after the liberation in many cases it was possible to determine if the detainees had survived the Holocaust, and if not, in which camp and on which date they had been killed.

Upon arrival, new detainees of the camps were transformed into archived objects with a number instead of a name: the inscription classified them as traceable elements within a collection. Upon entering the death camps, they were also sorted into groups: men with men, women with women; children, old people and pregnant women to the gas chambers. Artists, musicians, architects form Western European countries were usually sent to camps like Theresiënstadt. Selecting and sorting on the basis of a fixed set of categories are basic archival activities.

5_For a more elaborate discussion of the concentration camps as monstrous archival machines, see the chapter 'Depletion' in Ernst van Alphen, *Staging the Archive*.

6_For a discussion of the role archiving played in Nazi Germany, see Eric Ketelaar 'Archival Temples, Archival Prisons: Modes of Power and Protection,' *Archival Science* 2, nos. 3–4 (2002), pp. 221–38.

As we have seen in Resnais' *Night and Fog*, the same procedures were applied to the belongings of the Holocaust victims. In Auschwitz their possessions were sorted and stored in warehouses: heaps of suitcases, of pairs of glasses, of shaven hair, and other categories of objects. The primary aim of archiving of belongings was re-use by the German population. However, as has already been mentioned, Hitler also had the idea of the museum in mind. The archived belongings of the people who had entered the camps were going to became part of the museum's collection.

If the archive can be used as a genocidal tool, how then to imagine it can serve as cultural resistance? How does Ringelblum's archive differ from the way the Nazis employed archival principles and how is it possible that his archive is productive in creating the conditions for the production of memory—a counter-memory that resists the one constructed by the Nazis? When I say that archives create the condition to produce memories, I distance myself from the idea that archives *contain* memories, that archives are rich treasuries full of memories. For sure, archives (and museums) house historical objects, documents and narratives, but this is not the same as saying that they contain memories. Memories do not come to us from the past in any direct or unmediated way, rather they are performed in the present that establishes a relationship with the past.[7] So, archives should be evaluated in terms of how they enable the production of memory in the present, and what kind of memories are the result. It is in the use of the archive that acts of memory are performed.

The Classical versus the Modern Archive

In order to answer the questions raised above, it is important to come back to Michel Foucault's understanding of the archive already explained in the Introduction: Foucault differentiates between the role of archives in the classical and in the modern period. For, what changed radically in the modern period is the so-called 'threshold of description,' the minimum of importance a piece of information must have to be worthy of archiving. This threshold was lowered dramatically in order to include common people. In the words of Foucault:

> For a long time ordinary individuality – the everyday individuality of everybody – remained below the threshold of description. To be looked at, observed, described in detail, followed from day to day by an interrupted writing, was a privilege... . The disciplinary methods reserved this relation, lowered the threshold of describable individuality and made of this description a means of control and a method of domination. [What is archived] is no longer a monument for future memory, but a document for possible use. And this new describability is all the more marked in that the disciplinary framework is a strict one: the child, the patient, the madman, the prisoner, were to become [...] the

7_See Mieke Bal, 'Introduction,' in: *Acts of Memory: Cultural Recall in the Present*, ed. Mieke Bal, Jonathan Crewe, Leo Spitzer (Hanover, NH: University Press of New England, 1999), vii–xvii.

8_Michel Foucault, *Discipline and Punish: The Birth of Prison*, trans. Alan Sheridan (New York: Pantheon, 1977), pp. 191–92.

9_For clear descriptions of the history of archival science, see Fernanda Ribeiro, 'Archival Science and Changes in the Paradigm,' *Archival Science* 1, no. 3 (2001), pp. 295–310 and Hermann Rumschöttel, 'The Development of Archival Science as a Scholarly Discipline,' *Archival Science* 1, no. 2 (2001), pp. 143–55.

object of individual descriptions and biographical accounts.[8]

Foucault argues that a variety of new ways of examining and describing individuals was developed. The question thus emerges in what sense this accumulation and processing of new data differed from the knowledge production in earlier centuries since scientists from long ago had an obsession with classifying objects and archiving the results of these classifications too.[9]

Foucault's answer is that while it is true that plants, animals and even human beings had been the subjects of study before the examination regime was in place, they entered a field of knowledge as general categories, as a species for example, and not as singular individuals.

> What was innovative about the new archives was precisely that they objectified individuals not as members of a pre-existing category, but in all their uniqueness and singularity. Far from being archivable in terms of their shared properties, human beings became linked to all the unique series of events (medical, military, educational, penal events) which made them who they are as historical individuals – a history which could now take the form of a file while the individual became a case.[10]

In other words, whereas in the old archives individuals were used to build or substantiate categories, in the modern archive, categories are being used to build or substantiate the individual.

This leads to a situation in which human bodies, events and archives interact, and it is this interaction which brings about individual identity. This identity is then not seen as a subjective interiority, but as an objective exteriority. All the facts about people accumulated in the files and dossiers, extracted from us via a variety of examinations (medical reports, bank statements, educational degrees), provide people with an identity. This identity is not a matter of interiorized representation, like an ideology, but of an external body of archives within which we are caught and that compulsorily fabricate an objective identity of and for us. This 'archival identity' may perhaps have little to do with our own sense of our identity, but this may not be the case for an insurance company, for example, for whom archived medical facts are the key to our identity, whether we like it or not.[11]

One of the radical implications of the modern archive is that what, or who, is not in the records does not really exist. This drastic consequence is understandable when we realize that archival administrators do not observe, describe and classify reality, e.g., the unique identities of individuals, but the other way around: they shape people and events into entities that fit the categorizations and that are recordable. This kind of reification entails that there are virtually no other facts than the ones contained in records and archives.[12]

10_Manuel DeLanda, 'The Archive before and after Foucault,' in *Information is Alive*, eds. Joke Brouwer and Arjen Mulder (Rotterdam: V2_Publishing and NAi Publishers, 2003), p. 11.

11_DeLanda, 'The Archive before and after Foucault,' p. 12.

12_In archives interfaces function as the critical nodes through which archivists enable and constrain the interpretation of the past. The interface is a site where power in the Foucauldian sense is negotiated and exercised. It is power exercised over documents and their representation, over the access to them and over the uses of archives. On archival interfaces, see Margaret Hedstrom, 'Archives, Memory, and Interfaces with the Past,' *Archival Science* 2, nos. 1–2 (2002), pp. 21–43.

The Ringelblum Archive as Classical Archive

Foucault's differentiation of the role of old, classical archives and the role of modern archives enables me to assess the difference between the Ringelblum Archive and the archival organization of ghettos and concentration camps. It is against these Nazi archival gestures that Ringelblum tried to organize the archive in such a way that it would work as a counterforce. The archival practice of the Nazis is the extreme case of the modern archive: a very restricted number of categories were used to substantiate human beings. Their individual identities were reduced to one single, racial category.

In opposition to this very reductive use of the notion of identity, which made all Jewish people not similar but identical, Ringelblum used the archive to substantiate all the people who had ended up with the 'Jewish' identity, attributing to them a great variety of individual characteristics. He declared provocatively: 'During this war every Jew is a separate, individual world.'[13] His formulation of how he understood Jewish people in his archival project, is what positions his archive explicitly as a means of cultural resistance, as a counter-archive. It is this war that necessitated him to understand every Jew as a separate individual world, because the Nazis did exactly the opposite: they understand all Jews as belonging to one category and having one unified identity: Jewishness. In the words of Bożena Keff: 'The "Jew" is a construct superimposed on the faces of individuals to produce a uniform mask.'[14] By using the archive for his goal of dealing with Jews as separate individual worlds, Ringelblum assigns a role to the archive, which is within the Foucauldian framework not modern but classical. For in old, classical archives individuals were used to build or substantiate categories. Whereas in the old archives of elite persons like kings, nobleman, or important, powerful families, the category of sovereign or the family was substantiated by the specific person who was at that moment the sovereign or head of the family, the racial category of Jew was substantiated by Ringelblum as a form of resistance, by the individual worlds of each Jewish person. By doing this the restricted nature of that category was deconstructed and undermined. It demonstrated that this category was not unified at all, but contains an enormous number of varieties, differences, and specificities.

How exactly did Ringelblum succeed in his archival act of resistance? How did he organize his archive? First of all, by not being rigorous, that is, by not restricting himself to one exclusive form or subject:

> With regard to the form of the materials, the archive includes not only personal writings (accounts, journals, diaries, letters), but also newspapers, official documents (German and Jewish), public documents (posters, announcements, a school timetable), candy wrappers, poetry and prose, as well as many other types of documents. The topics touched on are similarly diverse, ranging from the misery of life under German occupation, i.e., indirect extermination through so-called liquidation operations, to relations between Jewish institutions, German regulations, etc.[15]

13_Emanuel Ringelblum, *Kronika getta warszawskiego wrzesień 1939 – styczeń 1943*, ed. Artur Eisenbach, trans. Adam Rutkowski (Warsaw: Czytelnik, 1983), p. 476.

14_Bożena Keff, 'Churban Forschung,' in *Letters to the Oneg Shabbat*, ed. Paweł Śpiewak (Warsaw: Jewish Historical Institute, 2017), p. 54.

15_Marta Janczewska, 'Numbers and Words: On Death Figures in the Ringelblum Archive,' in: *Letters*, p. 29.

From the perspective of the modern archive, Ringelblum's archive seems to be utterly messy, because it lacks a clear principle of selection and organization. And not only are the included materials extremely diverse; a systematic and orderly classification of the materials is also missing. Of course, it has been argued that Ringelblum and his associates had no time for classifying the materials they were collecting. All they could do was hide the materials in the milk cans and metal boxes and bury them in different places. Although the lack of order in the archive is probably not intentional, it now contributes to its status of classical archive. Bożena Keff has described the Ringelblum Archive as 'a multi-voice chronicle, each voice adding to the chorus':

> Through their stories, letters, and notes, the male and female narrators describe a portion of reality. What emerges is necessarily a collective work. The record covers the whole ghetto and, virtually, a much larger expanse, as it also includes voices from letters, postcards, and messages to and from family, friends and acquaintances.[16]

Although Keff talks only about the testimonial writings in the archive, the characterization as 'multi-voice chronicle' indicates that the archive does not impose a unified, coherent meaning on the lives and identities of the people isolated in the ghetto. A good example are the texts in the archive written by the historian Marian Małowist. Writing about young people and Polish-Jewish intellectuals in the ghetto he also writes about Catholic Jews in the ghetto who found themselves in a completely alien community. They identified themselves first of all as Catholic and as Polish, not as Jewish. The Jewish identity has been imposed on them by Nazism when they were imprisoned in the ghetto.[17]

The Ringelblum Archive as Memorial

In 2017 a permanent installation or exhibition, entitled 'What we could not shout out to the world' was opened in that Institute, presenting a small selection of the original materials in spaces that have first of all a symbolic function. These spaces refer back to typical archive and library furnishings, alluding to the original function of the building as Judaic library as well as to the archival workings of Oneg Shabbat.

Aneta Faner and Piotr Duma designed the installation, which they intended to function as a symbolic space—a memorial to the Ringelblum Archive. In fact, the memorial consists of three symbolic spaces. The first one is a space with

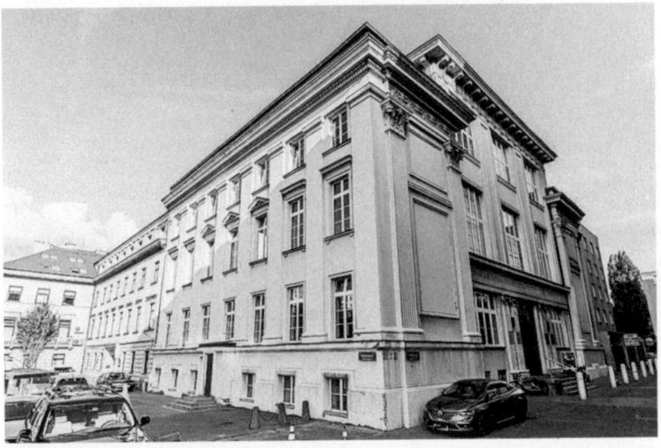

Jewish historical institute, Warsaw

16_Keff, 'Churban Forschung,' p. 53.

17_See Eleonora Bergman, Tadeusz Epsztein, and Katarzyna Person, 'Introduction,' *The Ringelblum Archive*, xxxi.

a large table with 25 seats, for each of the main 'archivists' responsible for the creation of the collection. The second symbolic space is the reconstructed brick cellar, in which parts of the archive were hidden. This cellar is 'cut' in half with a corridor running through it. Visitors can walk through the corridor. On the walls of the corridor are glass panes that show a glimpse of the geological cross-section of the cellar that held the Ringelblum Archive. The third symbolic space consists of the space surrounding the reconstructed cellar featuring a presentation of life in the ghetto, using original material from the Archive.

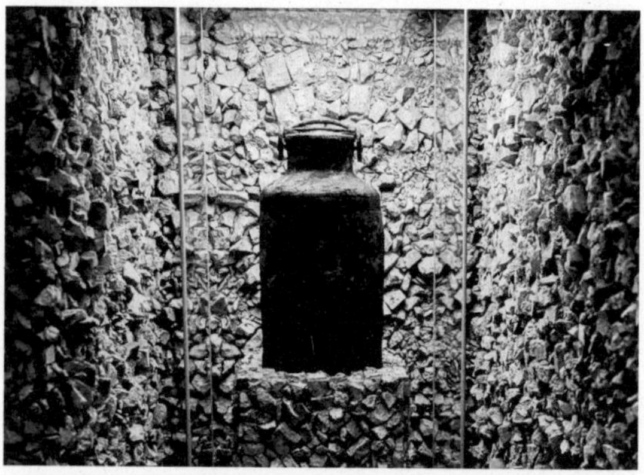

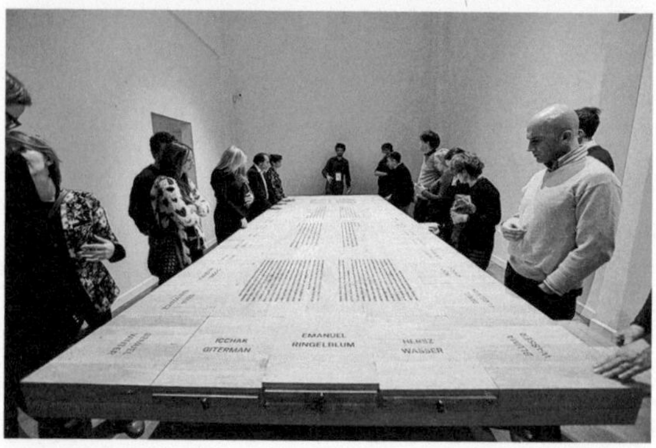

Jewish historical institute, Warsaw

Aneta Faner and Piotr Duma explicitly state that the main aim and mission of the installation is symbolic; it commemorates the Ringelblum Archive and is a kind of 'sanctuary.' But another function fulfilled by the installation is more conventionally archival, namely to provide information about the Holocaust. This function is usually phrased (also by Aneta Faner and Piotr Duma) as the moral obligation to let the world know about the Holocaust. Although many Holocaust museums already exist and many books have been published about the event, it is also true that many people still do not know about the Holocaust. So, this obligation to let the world know is still extremely important.

What does it mean to combine a symbolic function with the mission to provide information? In other words, in what way can an archive be symbolic? This must be understood, for the referential, historical function of providing information about the Holocaust requires a different focus, or attention, other than the attention needed for commemoration. The referential function of the archival materials also seems to be challenged by the fact that the historical meaning of it is in a certain sense limited. As Krzysztof Środa remarks in his 'reading' of the Ringelblum Archive, the archival materials are rather repetitive, and in many cases too detailed or already known. It is impossible to read the Ringelblum Archive as a historical novel about a past one is not yet familiar with.[18] But of course, as Środa explains, an archive is not a book one reads, but more like an encyclopedia that can be consulted.[19] This sheds a different light on the referential function but does not answer the question of how it can be

18_Krzysztof Środa, 'The Ringelblum Archive: A Reading,' in Śpiewak, *Letters to the Oneg Shabbat*, p. 139.

19_Środa, 'The Ringelblum Archive,' p. 142.

combined with the symbolic function of commemoration.

The preservation of the Ringelblum Archive by means of the exhibition opened in 2017 has an archival as well as commemorative function. However, one could argue, the archive created and organized by Ringelblum already had those two functions. His archival project was the result of a moral duty towards the Polish Jewish community. He wanted to give meaning to all their individual lives, by building a memorial out of words. These words do not only refer to what happened, but they are also future-oriented. In the words of Abraham Lewin: 'We want our sufferings, these "birth pangs of the Messiah," to be impressed upon the memories of future generations and on the memory of the whole world.' The words of Marta Janczewska articulate even more explicitly in which sense the referential, historical function of words is at the same oriented towards the future: 'Here is a group of people who stake all of their hopes on words, they cast into earth a "treasure of words" to be read in better times.'[20]

Janczewska's terse statement implies that words point toward a future, because they only have meaning when they are being read or heard. We are living in the 'better times' of the future, because the Holocaust now belongs to the past. But the archival memorial built out of words, depends on 'that bit of attention and focus that those of whose deaths we are reading deserve.'[21] That attention and focus in the present is precisely what the recent exhibition of the Ringelblum Archive is able to create as a condition for its symbolic function as memorial. The facts, the information, the narratives, included in an archival, referential organization have now, as Ringelblum already intended, also symbolic value. It is not because all the details of individual Jewish lives are so 'interesting' or 'historically meaningful,' but because Ringelblum's cultural resistance has transformed the unified category of Jewishness into a myriad of individual lives and identities against the logic of Nazi genocide.

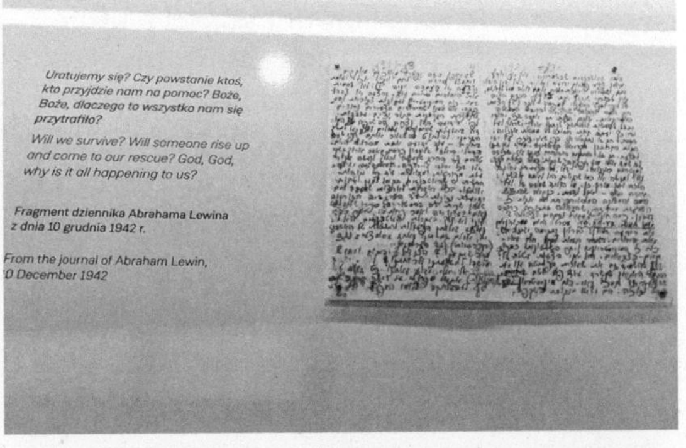

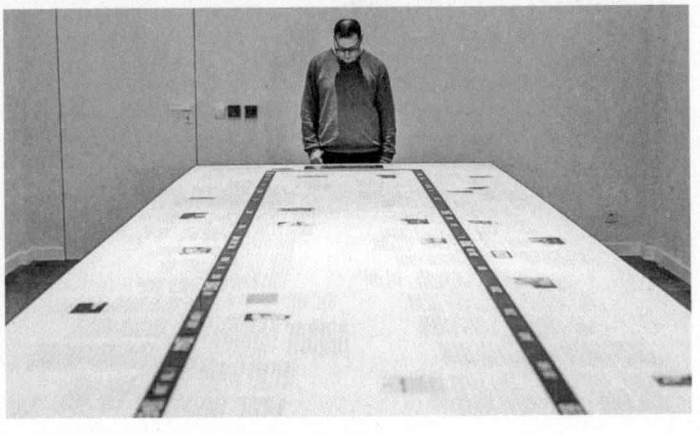

Jewish historical institute, Warsaw

20_Marta Janczewska, quoted in Tomasz Pietrasiewicz, 'The Ringelblum Archive Exhibition: Chronicle of a Journey,' in Śpiewak, *Letters to the Oneg Shabbat*, p. 106.

21_Środa, 'The Ringelblum Archive,' p. 140.

POSTCARDS FROM THE ARCHIVE

Pablo Lerma's Queer Poetics

In October 1989, at the height of the AIDS crisis and so-called 'culture wars' in New York City, the artist and activist David Wojnarowicz penned a polemic for the catalogue of *Witnesses: Against Our Vanishing*, an exhibition of work by artists responding to the epidemic, organized by the photographer Nan Goldin. Even before the show had opened, his six-page text, 'Postcards from America: X-Rays from Hell,' caused controversy between the non-profit gallery and the National Endowment for the Arts over the exhibition's funding. In it, he rebuked not only the government and others for failing to address the disease, but also individuals and institutions, including museums and galleries, on both sides of the political spectrum for censoring or excluding queer experiences. In the end, Wojnarowicz's essay was a call against the invisibility of a community whose lifestyle did not align with hegemonic ideas of 'normality,' or at least how those ideas were imagined and managed by the country's elites.

The artist Pablo Lerma's archival project *It Doesn't Stop at Images* (2020–ongoing) derives its title from Wojnarowicz's essay, which still feels as urgent more than thirty years later amid another pandemic. In the same paragraph in the essay where Lerma borrowed his title from, Wojnarowicz argues for the importance of images that show a diverse range of experiences, even if producing and revealing those images might be dangerous for their makers or subjects. He discloses:

> Sexuality defined in images gives me comfort in a hostile world. I have always loved my anonymity and therein lies a contradiction because I also find comfort in seeing representations of my private experiences in the public environment. [...] I find that when I witness diverse representations of 'Reality' on a gallery wall or in a book or a movie or in the spoken word or performance, that the larger the range of representations, the more I feel there is room in the environment for my existence, that not the entire environment is hostile.[1]

Today, some images of queer experience have indeed become normalized in many parts of the world, thanks in large part to activists such as Wojnarowicz. Therefore, it remains all the more necessary to reflect on these histories and interrogate the archives that hold them.

To explore a history of queer images, Lerma turned to IHLIA LGBTI Heritage, Amsterdam, the largest

1_David Wojnarowicz, 'Postcards from America: X-Rays from Hell,' in *Witnesses: Against Our Vanishing*, ed. Nan Goldin (New York: Artists Space, 1989), p. 2.

Drew Sawyer

archive dedicated to LGBTQI+ histories in Europe.[2] The center's origins date back to University of Amsterdam in 1978, where it was founded by a small group of students and teachers, who, like Wojnarowicz, demanded a space for queer representation. They not only formed study groups, but also started the magazine *Homologie*—from which Lerma draws his materials—and the Documentation Center of Gay Studies, which was soon named Homodok. *Homologie* and Homodok were created from the energies of liberation struggles across the globe during the 1960s and 1970s that sought to dismantle oppressive structures and official institutions, both from within and from outside. Numerous individuals and grassroots organizations started publications and archives dedicated to queer culture and history in the 1970s throughout North America and Europe.[3] Out of necessity and amidst separatist or essentialist mindsets, these alternative institutions were set up to save material and share stories of lesbian and gay lives neglected by the media and the official versions of history. These archives have often focused on other forms of historical remains, such as art, popular culture artefacts, anonymous pamphlets and zines, and various forms of 'ephemera.'

For the installation of *It Doesn't Stop at Images*, Lerma collected thousands of photographs from IHLIA's archives of *Homologie*, the Dutch magazine that ran from 1978 until 1997. He then divided the material into three separate themes. The first consists of photographs of public figures, dissecting the construction of shared queer histories and heroes. Featured among these images are portraits of historical figures as well as contemporary celebrities. The second group contains photographs that center on desire and representations of the body. Here, Lerma acknowledges the stereotypes of gay culture, pointing to its obsessions with dominant forms of masculinity and beauty. The third grouping contains photographs that show forms of relationships and community—there are images of gatherings and demonstrations, as well as couples embracing.

Lerma presents these groupings in three vitrines that recall institutional forms of display. Spreads of the original publication often appear on top of a matte black board at the base of each case. Facsimiles of photographs hover above the magazines on the first sheet of glazing, while the second layer of glass not only protects the photographs below but also reflects the viewer's visage when looking from above. Together, the

2_LGBTQI+ is an inclusive acronym for people who identify as lesbian, gay, bisexual, transgender, queer, intersex, and other nonbinary identities.

3_In 1974 in New York City, for example, a group of scholars associated with the Gay Academic Union, including writer Joan Nestle, founded the Lesbian Herstory Archives, which has similarly grown into one of the largest collections of its kind. The Union also created its own publication, *Gay Academic Union Journal: Gai Saber*, which ran briefly from 1977 to 1978.

presentation creates a three-dimensional collage that echoes strata in sedimentary rock formations. The cultural anthropologist Gayle Rubin has similarly discussed the queer archive through geologic metaphor in which 'queer knowledges' appear as 'sedimented layers':

> In the geologic record, certain strata are fossil rich, partly because of the conditions that produce luxuriant life forms and partly because of the conditions that favor their preservation in fossil form. Similarly, there seem to be periods in which social and political conditions have favored the abundant proliferation of queer knowledges, while other conditions dictate their preservation or destruction. And it is up to succeeding generations to ensure that such sedimentary formations are identified, excavated, catalogued, and utilized to produce new knowledge. Unfortunately, because of the lack of durable structural mechanisms to secure the reliable transfer of queer knowledges, they are often instead lost, buried, and forgotten.[4]

It Doesn't Stop at Images visualizes and expands this analogy. While publications during the 1970s and 1980s like *Homologie* embarked on their own form of archiving, creating a space for sharing images and stories of contemporary queer life as well as historical examples, Lerma's project shows how these archives themselves are becoming artefactual layers requiring not only preservation but also critical inquiry.

The installation draws the viewer's attention to everyday pictures in *Homologie*, validating their importance as images and records of queer experiences despite the ephemeral nature of magazines. It also reveals how *Homologie* participated in the construction of a particular white, gay identity and history through images, while the title of the work, *It Doesn't Stop at Images*, points to what is still absent—the broader social and political world beyond the confines of the publication and its pictures. Yet, by divorcing the photographs from their original contexts and accompanying captions and essays, Lerma also opens up the archive and images to new potential readings.

In his previous work, Lerma has been similarly attuned to the structures, silences, and poetics of the archive. His project *Greenfield* (2018), for example, is built from a discarded collection of photographic negatives and prints from a defunct studio in Greenfield, Massachusetts, kept in envelopes with notations. Lerma came across this material at a flea market in 2016. The resulting book is divided into two sections: the first onc contains a collection of commissioned texts that imagine different stories based upon the found images and the second part presents the collection of images in groupings alongside information written on the original envelopes. While archives control the meaning of objects through selection, classification, and interpretation, Lerma allows multiple stories to emerge through the commissioned essays that are juxtaposed with his attempts to catalogue the materials. More recently, Lerma created a counter-archive of vernacular photographs that draw attention to the lack of representations of gay men within histories of photography and archives. Similar to *It Doesn't Stop at Images*, the project *A Frame of Darkness*

4_Gayle Rubin, *Deviations: A Gayle Rubin Reader* (Durham, NC: Duke University Press, 2012), p. 354.

(2019) assumes multiple forms through appropriating, juxtaposing, and recontextualizing found photographs of men and landscapes.

Whereas Lerma's previous projects have involved the absence of queer archives or the creation of fictitious ones, *It Doesn't Stop at Images* works with an existing archive that is built around the politics of visibility during the gay liberation struggle and its aftermath. Yet, like all of Lerma's works, it still reminds us of the subjective and seemingly arbitrary nature of all archives—that meaning is always produced and controlled by something or someone. The French philosopher Jacques Derrida has discussed this aspect of archives in his influential text *Archive Fever*. 'There is no political power without control of the archive, if not of memory,' he writes. 'Effective democratization can always be measured by this essential criterion: the participation in and the access to the archive, its constitution, and its interpretation.'[5] Lerma's interventions in archives such as IHLIA LGBTI Heritage not only make visible materials that are not easily accessible to the public, but also allow for counter-memories to form through the process of selection, classification, and presentation.

In this regard, Lerma's practice builds on what art historian Hal Foster has called the 'archival impulse' in contemporary art.[6] Like Lerma, artists working in this vein often use archives to develop 'alternative knowledge or counter-memories' and 'make historical information, often lost or displaced, physically present,' writes Foster. 'To this end they elaborate on the found image, object and text, and favor the installation format [...].'[7] Using fragments or obscure traces to embark on new explorations, these artists, like Lerma, invite the spectator to participate in the production of meaning. Some of these artists have explored queer histories, such as Tom Burr, who often investigates the intersection of sexual—in particular homosexual—identity with public and private sites. He has, for the most part, avoided institutional settings like archives, concentrating instead on in-between sites that have fostered and contained gay sexual activity and identity. An early project, *Unearthing the public restrooms* (1994) traces the history of public toilets, from their inception at the turn of the twentieth century until their later transformation into 'tea rooms,' known as sites for gay cruising. Burr employs photographs that mimic the medium's uses as objective historical evidence. Yet, they provide no information about the queer uses of the restrooms. It is only through Burr's reframing that such meanings are accrued or recovered.

Lerma similarly uses the magazine as a public site for the production of a marginalized, yet collective gay identity, and both artists also use the language of institutional architecture and modes of display, like the vitrine and photographs. In addition to the vitrines, Lerma places a selection of images from the three thematic categories into a plexiglass markerboard that recalls free-standing chalkboards found in school classrooms. On a nearby wall, he also hangs three enlarged photographs drawn from each section, which all feature men with their eyes closed. Once again, the selection and grouping of photographs are associative, hinting toward the utopian aspirations of many queer projects imagining new pasts, presents, and futures.

5_Jacques Derrida and Eric Prenowitz, 'Archive Fever: A Freudian Impression,' *Diacritics* 25, no. 2 (1995), p. 11.

6_Hal Foster, 'An Archival Impulse,' *October* 110 (2004), pp. 3–22.

7_Foster, 'An Archival Impulse,' p. 4.

This presentation echoes, but differs from, the archival strategies used by artist Henrik Olesen in projects such as *Some Gay-Lesbian Artists and/ or Artists relevant to Homo-Social Culture Born between c. 1300–1870* (2007). That work, which consists of two freestanding double-sided panels and a wall-mounted display, visually resembles art historian Aby Warburg's *Mnemosyne Atlas* (1924–1929). Instead of Warburg's 'afterlife of antiquity,' Olesen's work centers on gay cultural history between the fourteenth and nineteenth centuries, using reproductions of paintings and sculptures, photographic portraits, medical illustrations, and images of cross-dressing and sodomy, among other subjects. The edited arrangements refer to a time when homosexuality was easily communicated through innuendo and subtext, before becoming pathologized in the late-nineteenth century. Headings such as 'American Male Bodies,' and 'Anal Sex in England' are quasi-scientific, but Oleson also revels in the pleasures of historical discovery and free association, just as Lerma does.

While Oleson and Burr work as historians to reconstruct fragmentary histories, Lerma's interventions provide personal narratives into the homogenizing effects of the archive. Underscoring the subjective nature of all archives—how the inclusion and exclusion of materials is often based on biases or existing categories—Lerma selected materials based explicitly on his own experiences. Being married to a man and having children, he was particularly interested in finding images of queer families and relationships. This first 'chapter' of the project focuses on *Homologies* in part because Lerma now lives in the Netherlands and was interested in exploring the social construction of homosexuality in his current country of residence. He is now working on additional chapters that explore materials related to other places where he has lived: one will delve into a publication from San Francisco, since he lived in the United States for almost seven years, and another will focus on Spain, where Lerma was born and raised.

It Doesn't Stop at Images, like all of Lerma's archival projects, foregrounds the personal and the intuitive over historical or scientific methods of classification and interpretation. Scholar Ann Cvetkovich has argued that queer history in particular 'demands a radical archive of emotion in order to document intimacy, sexuality, love, and activism—all areas of experience that are difficult to chronicle through the materials of a traditional archive.'[8] But how to document feelings? Cvetkovich discusses how emotions and sexuality can only be archived indirectly, and thus art and cultural artefacts can function as important archival practices.[9] Although Lerma culled the archive as a researcher would, collecting images in the manner of an archivist, he displayed the results of his work without the signs and citations of conventional exhibitions and publications of historical materials. Instead, he has created an 'archive of feelings,' a collection that articulates personal passions and experiences, both intimate and political. In the end, this too is what Wojnarowicz called on artists to do: to make public the private or the personal. He finished his essay 'Postcards from America' with a bit of hope, suggesting that 'with enough gestures we can deafen the satellites and lift the

8_Ann Cvetkovich, 'In the Archives of Lesbian Feelings: Documentary and Popular Culture,' *Camera Obscura* 17, no. 1 (2002), pp. 109–10.

9_Ann Cvetkovich, 'Photographing Objects as Queer Archival Practice,' in *Feeling Photography*, ed. Elspeth Brown and Thy Phu (Durham, NC: Duke University Press, 2014), pp. 273–96.

curtains surrounding the control room.'[10] *Homologie* was one of those gestures, constructing and making visible aspects of gay life, history, and culture for readers in the Netherlands and beyond. *It Doesn't Stop at Images* returns the archive and the magazine to its original liberatory potential, reminding us that our work indeed doesn't stop at just images.

10_Wojnarowicz, 'Postcards from America,' p. 11.

It Doesn't Stop at Images

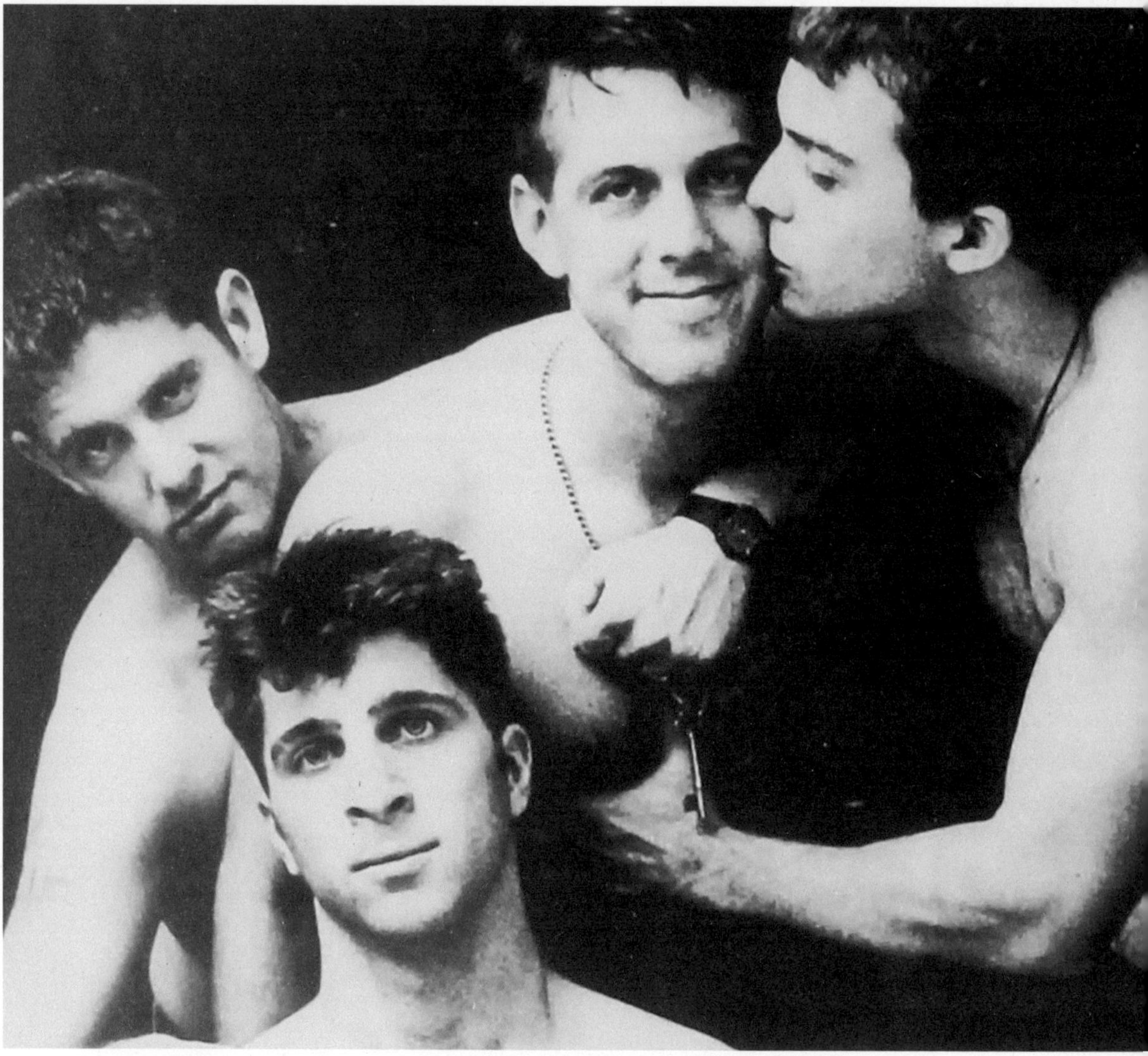

Pablo Lerma

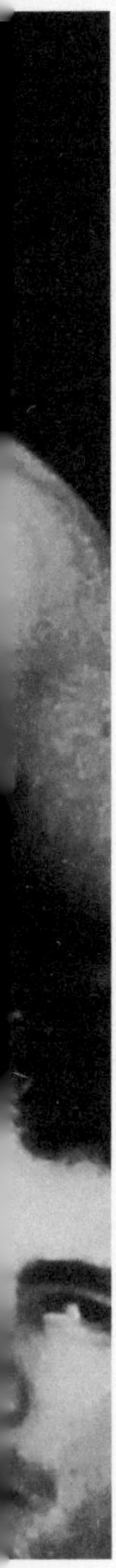

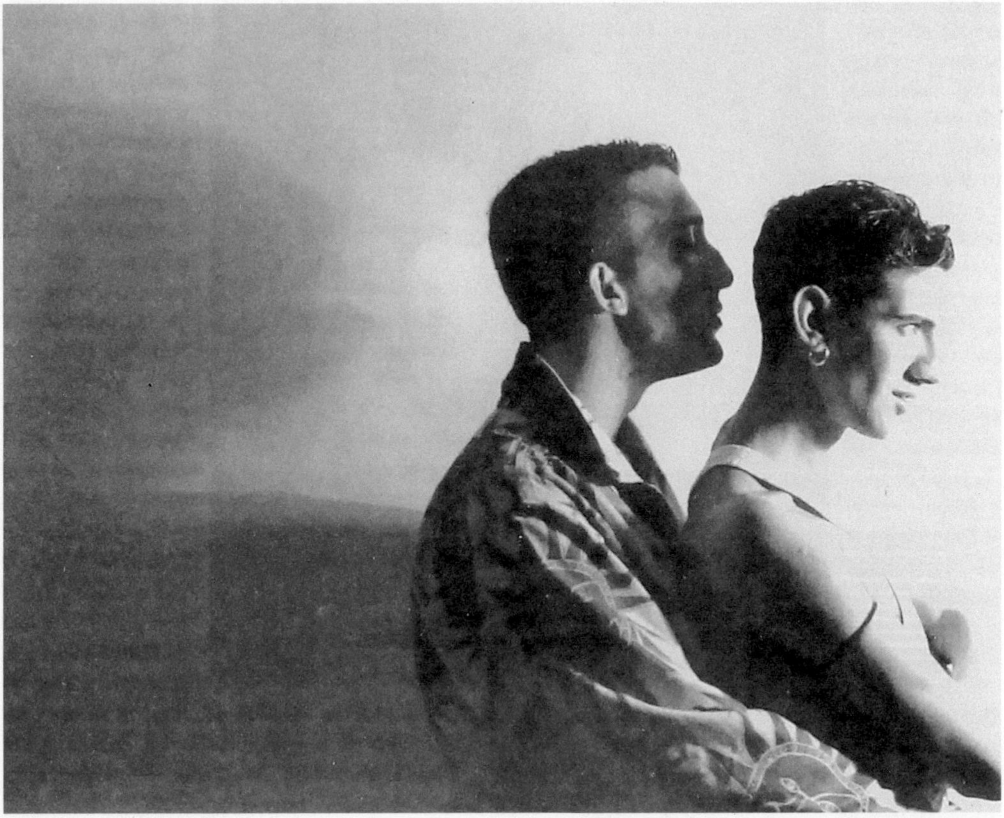

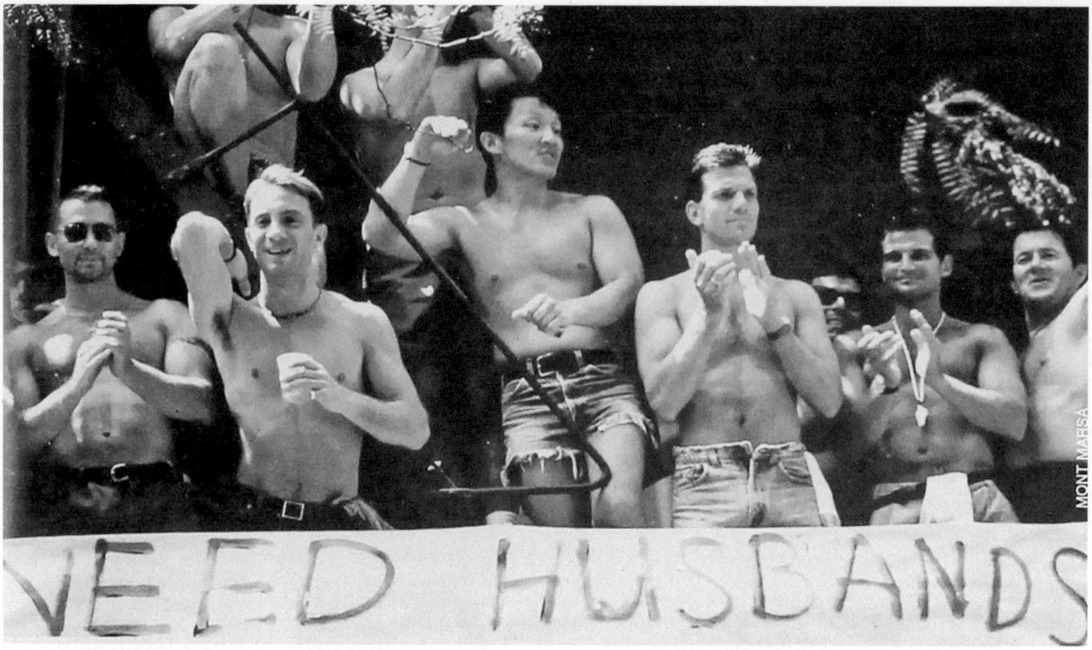

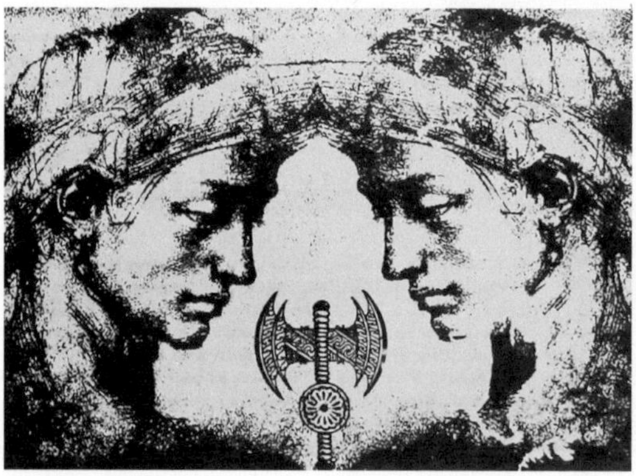

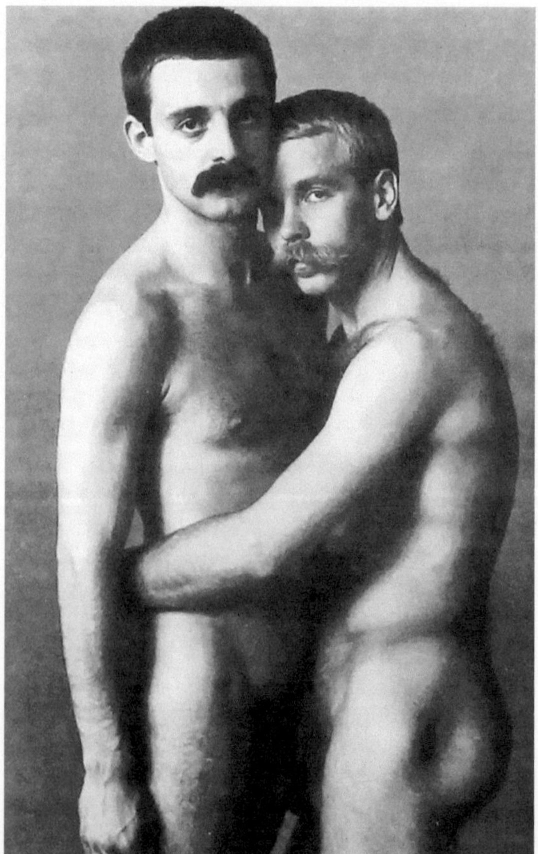

Pablo Lerma

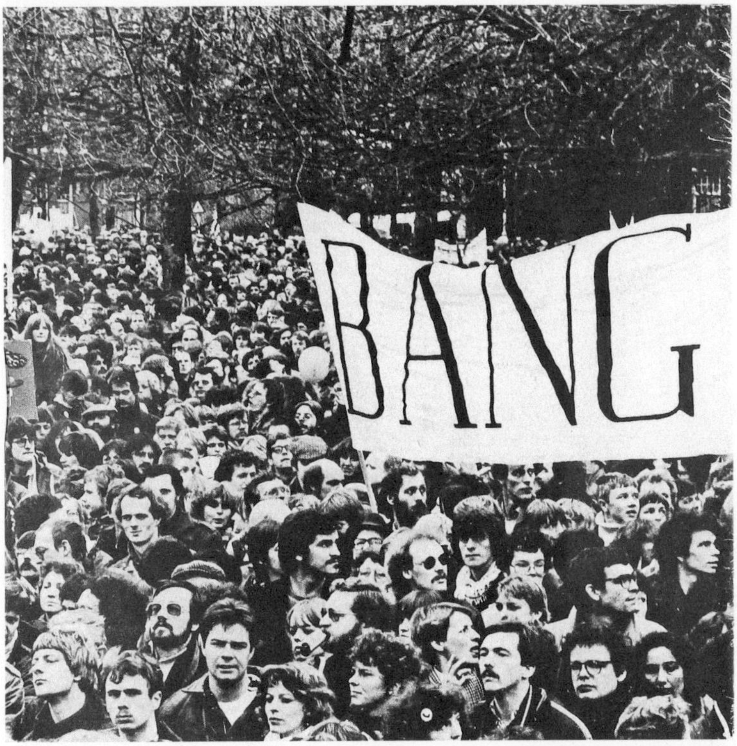
BANG

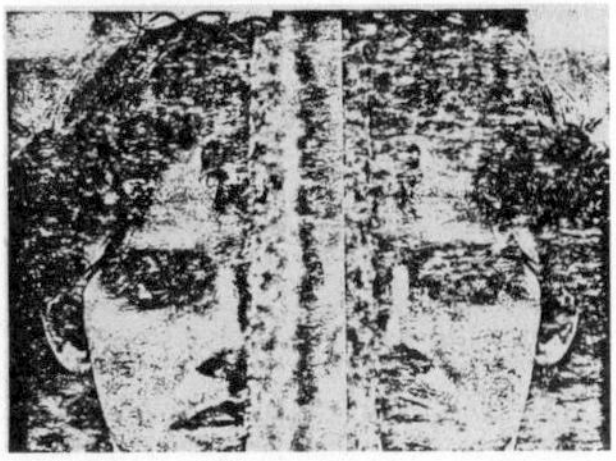

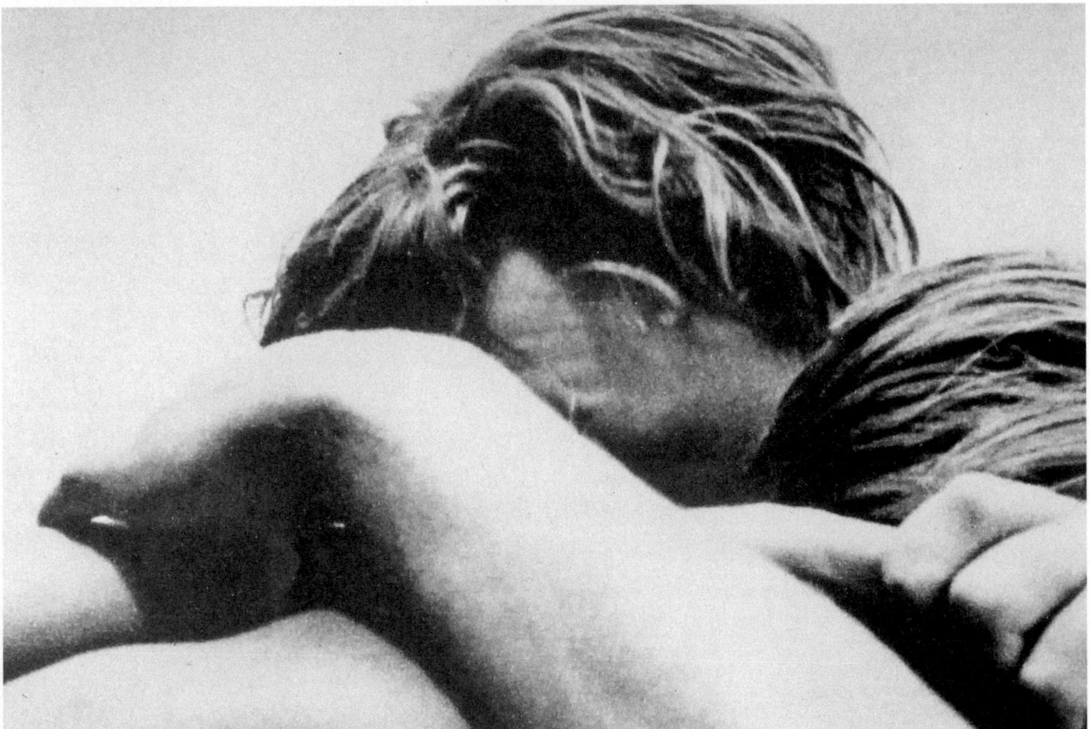

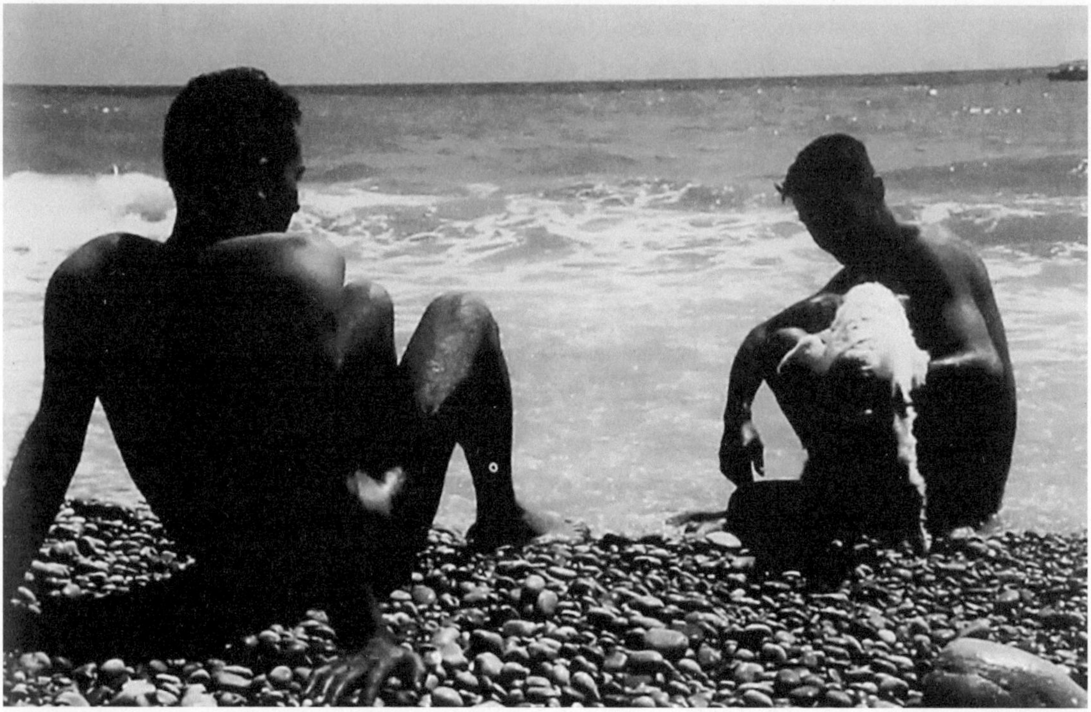

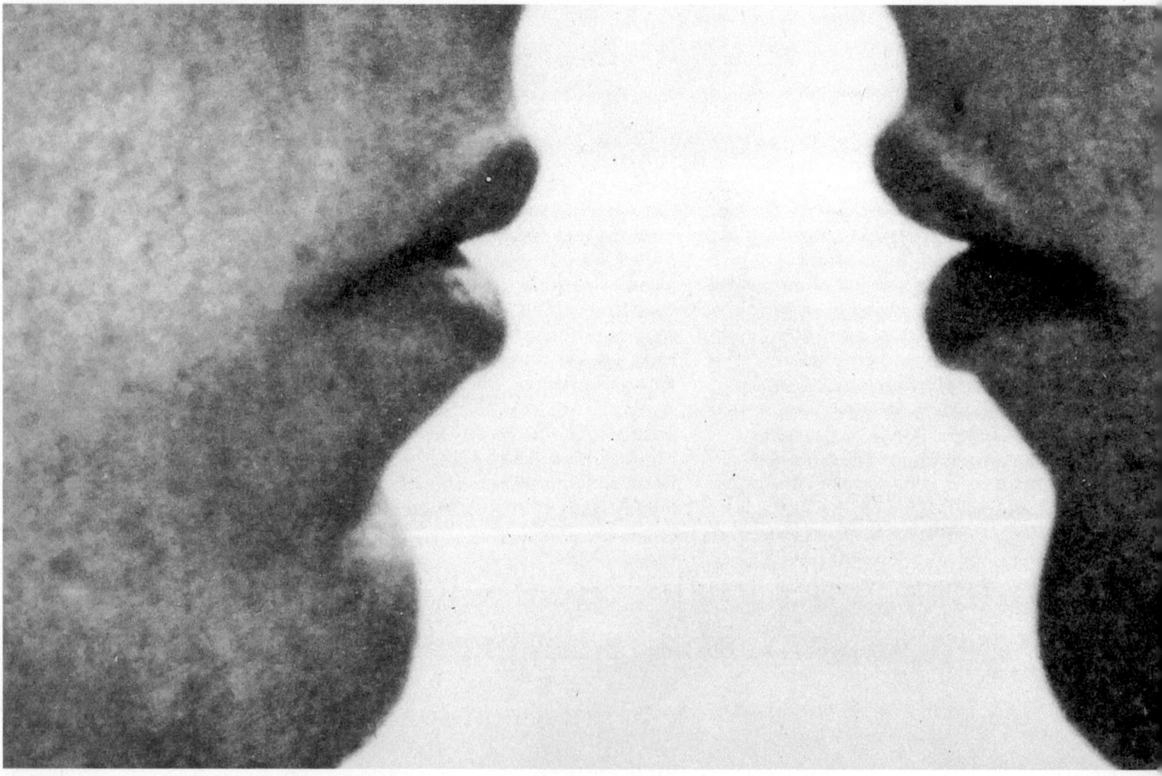

Pablo Lerma

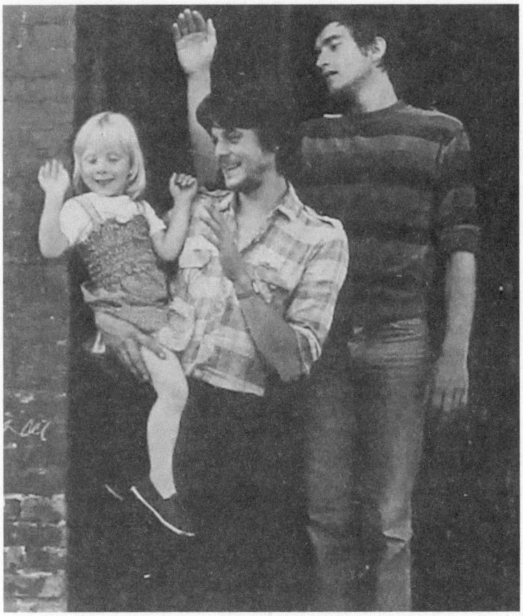

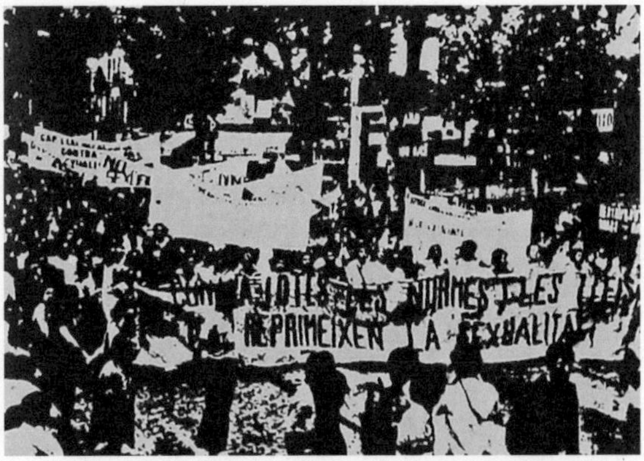
REPRIMEIXEN

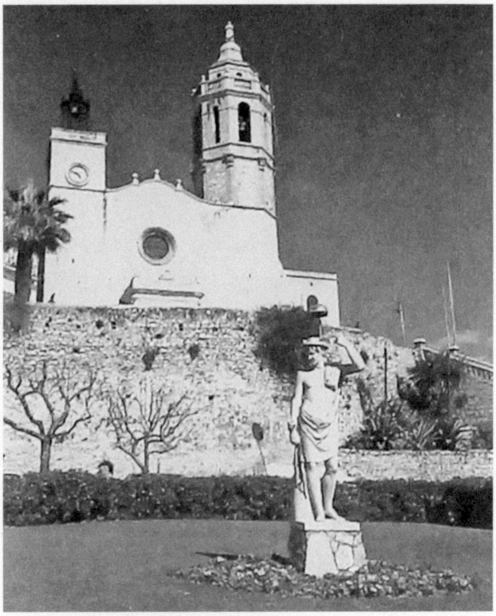

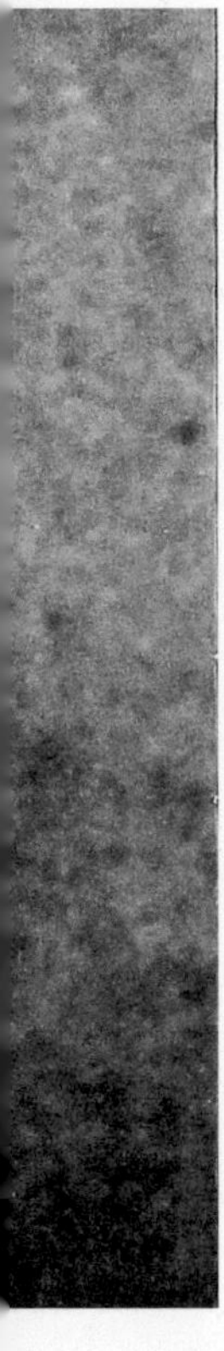

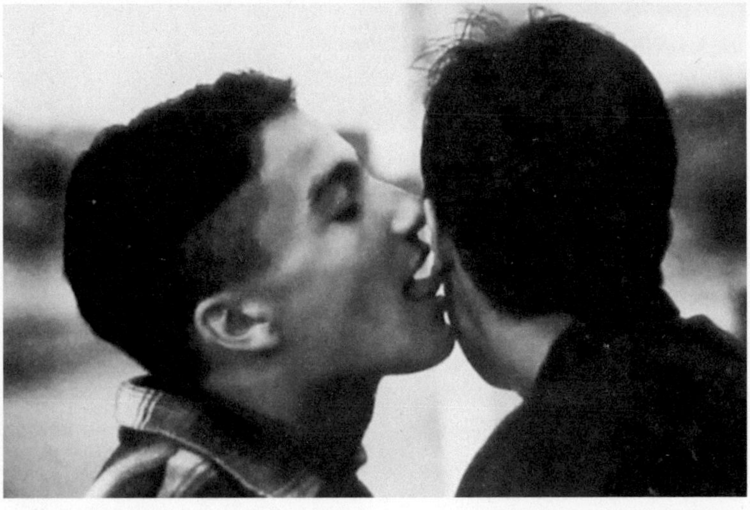

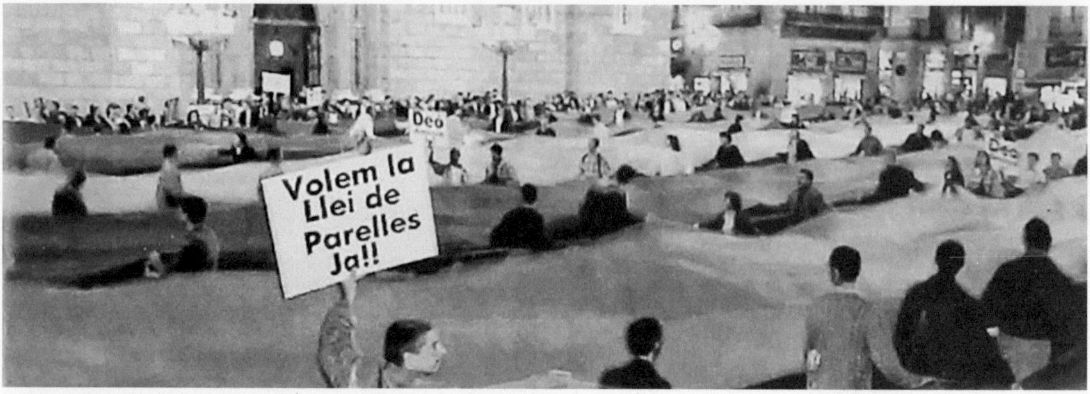

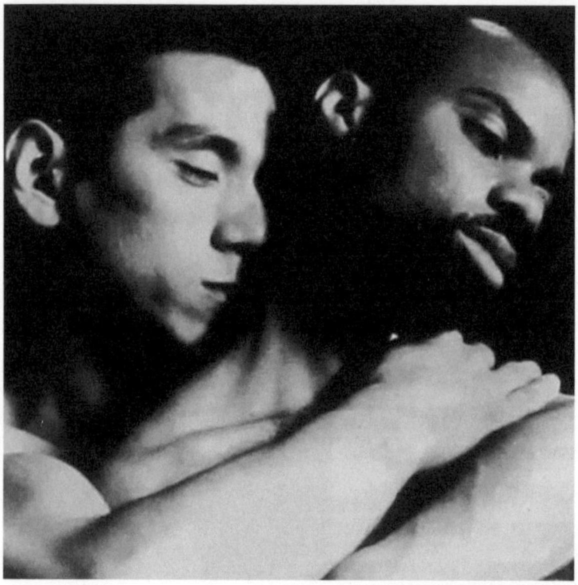

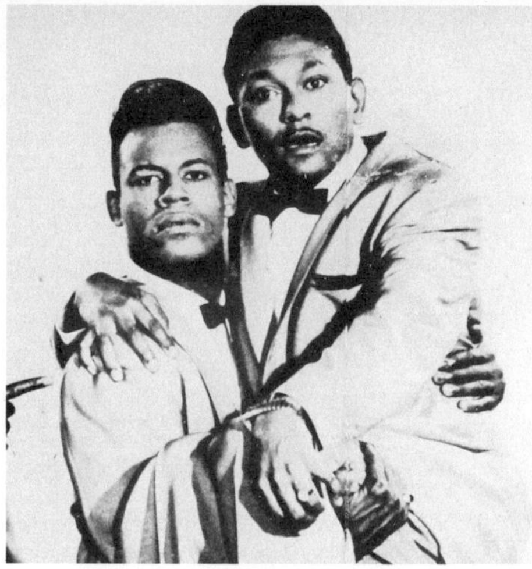

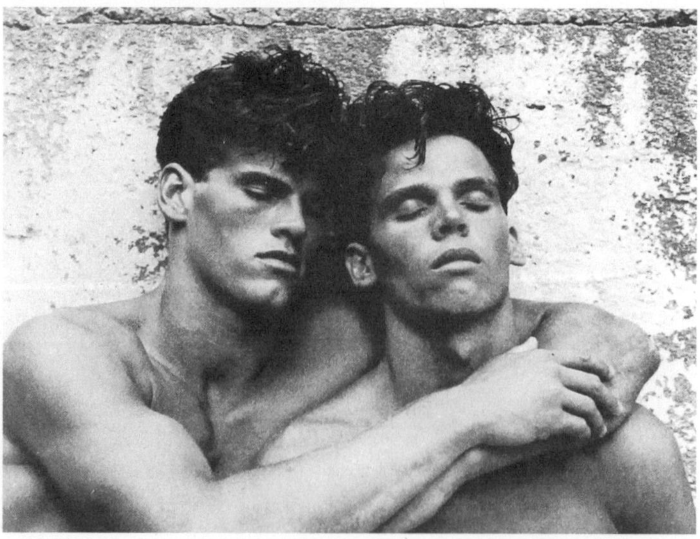

Pablo Lerma

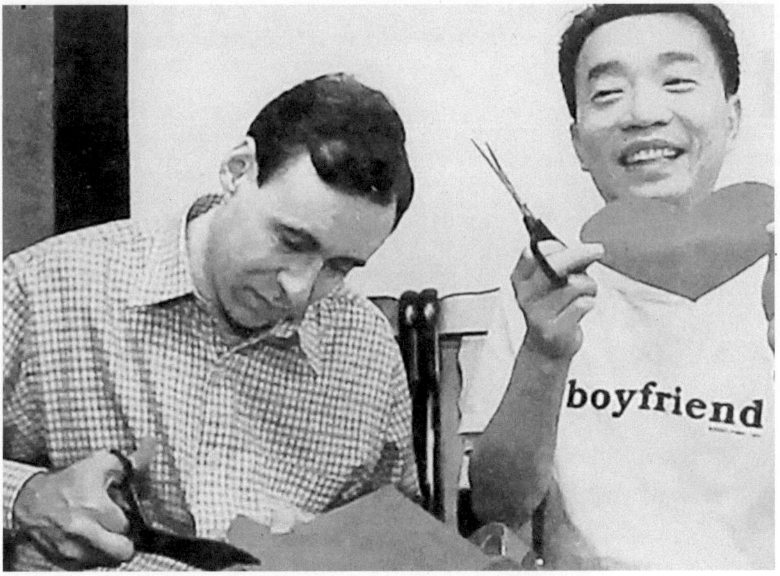
boyfriend

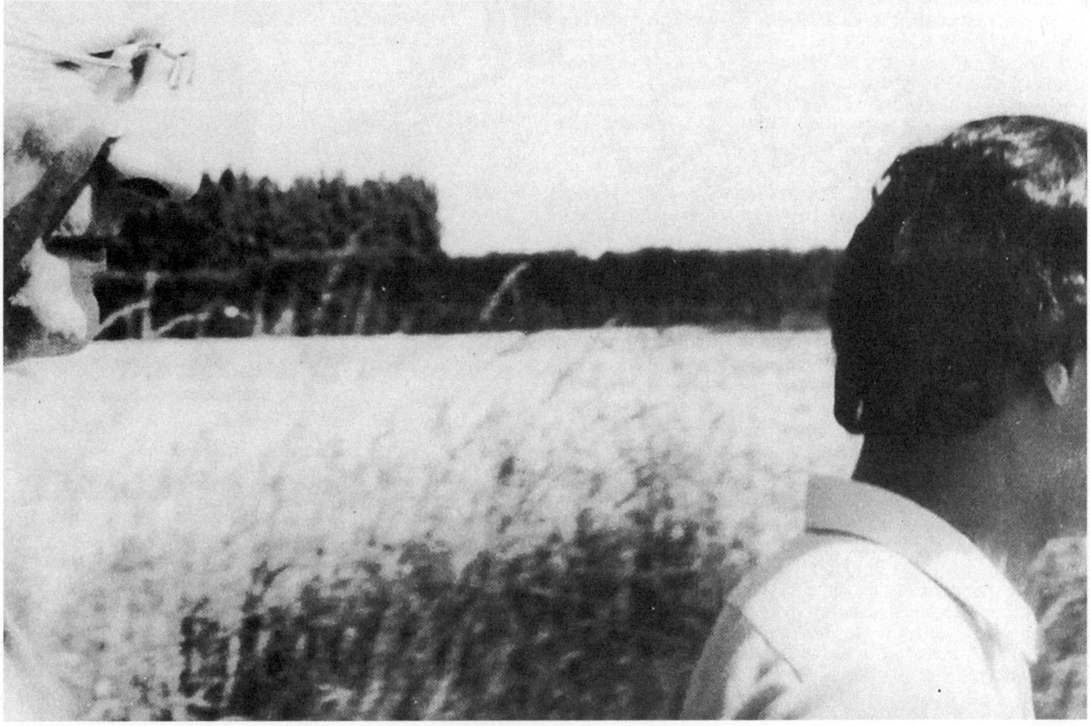

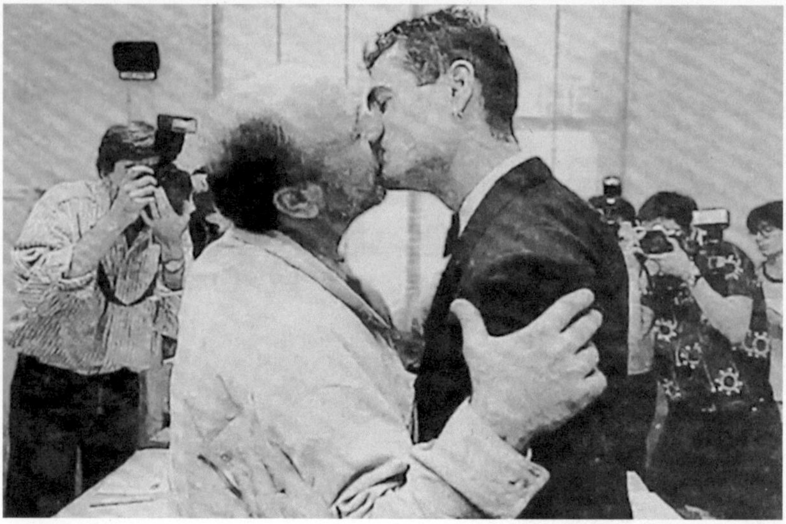

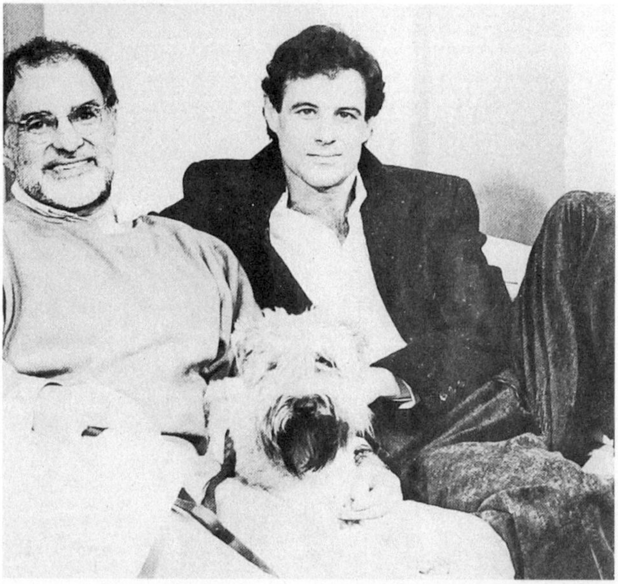

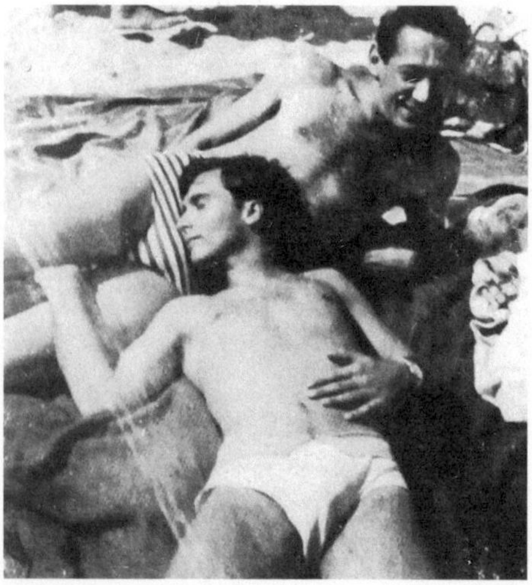

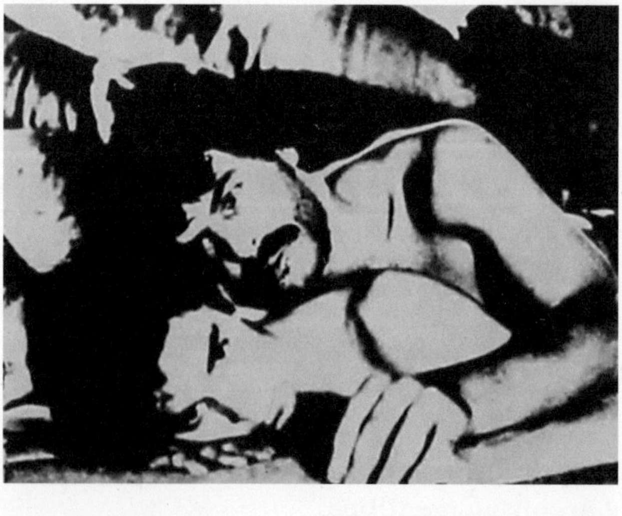

Pablo Lerma

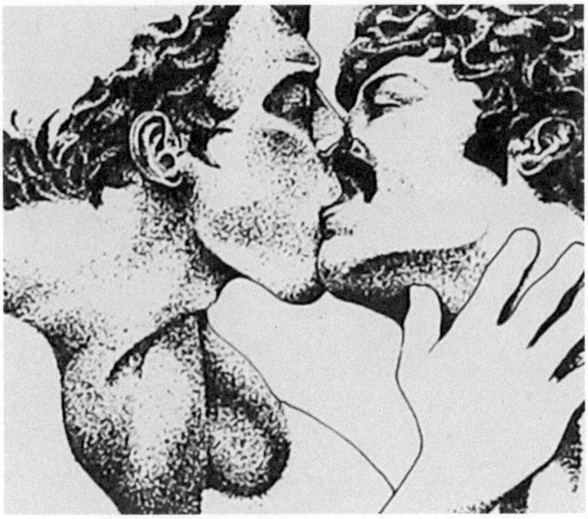

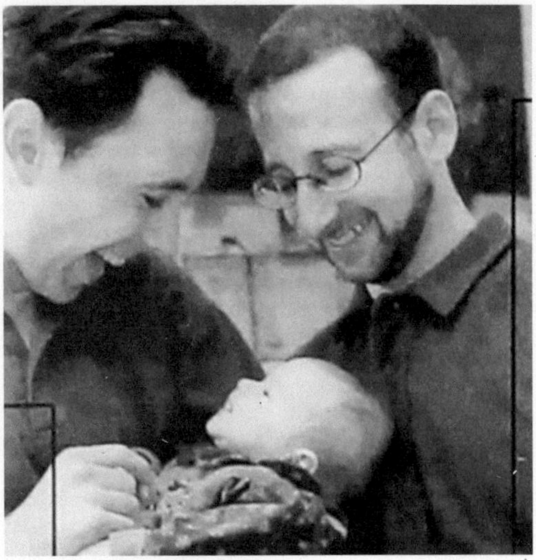

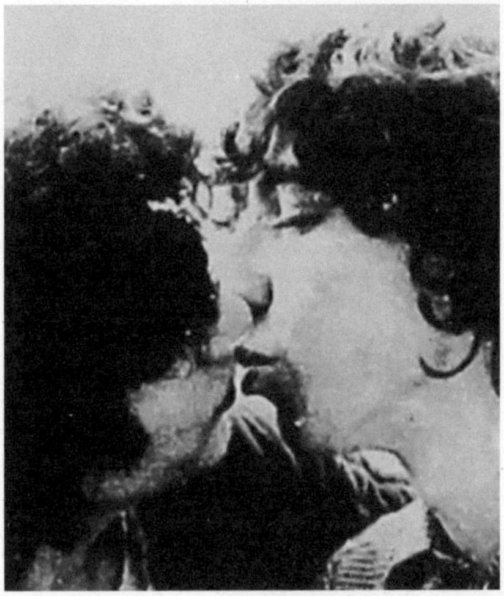

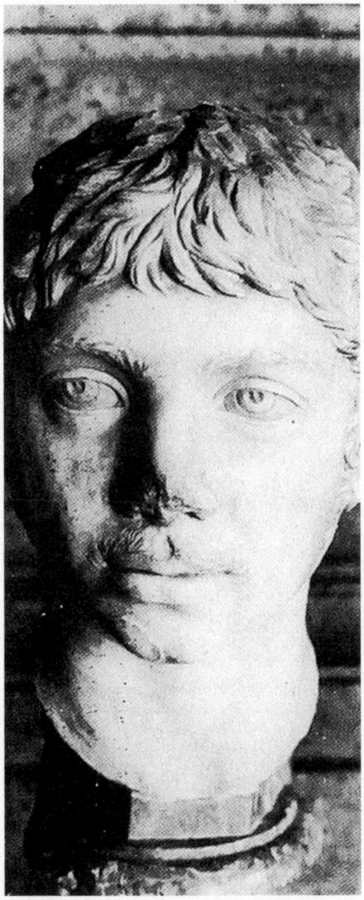

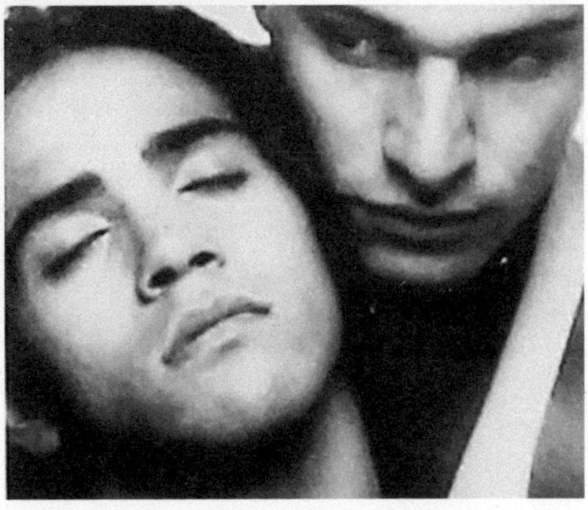

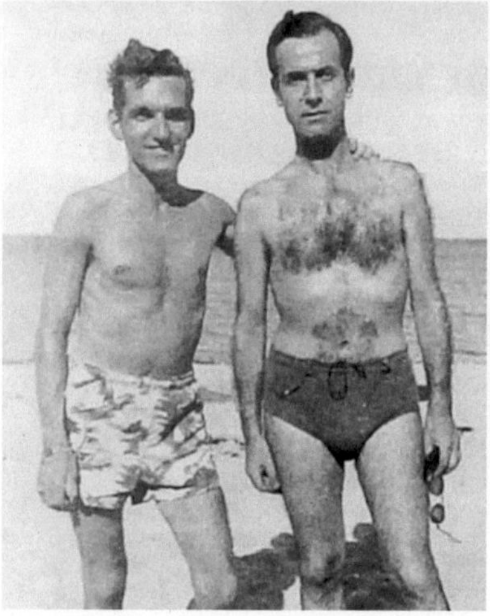

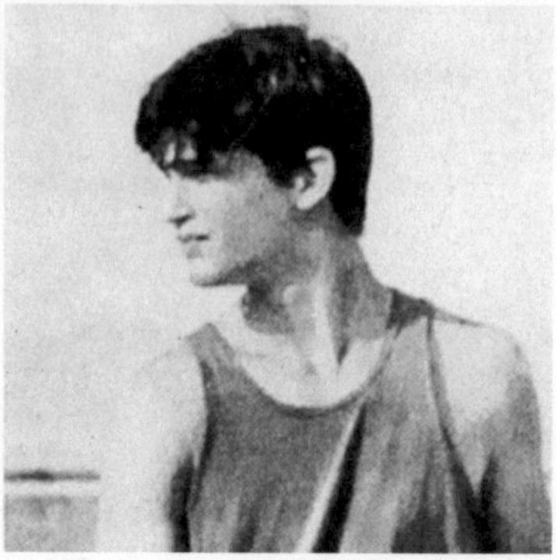

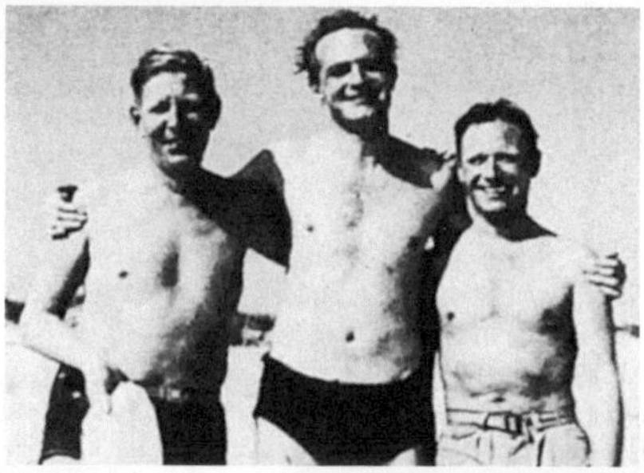

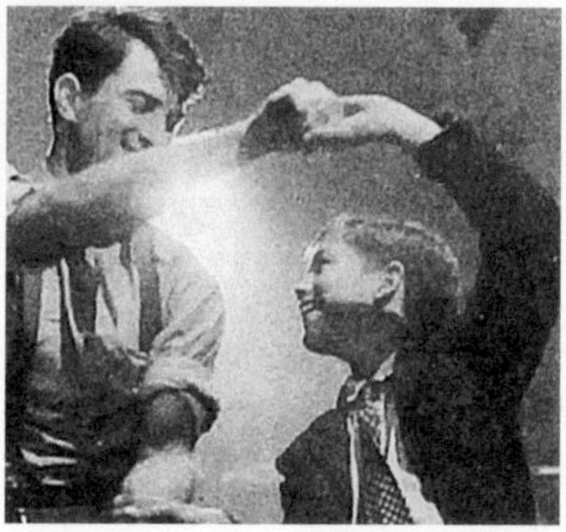

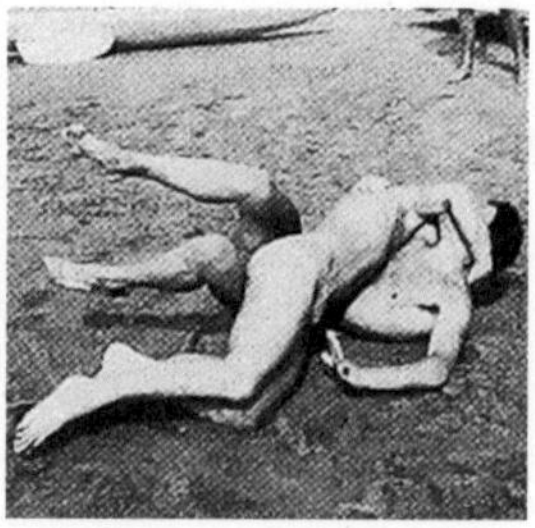

Pablo Lerma

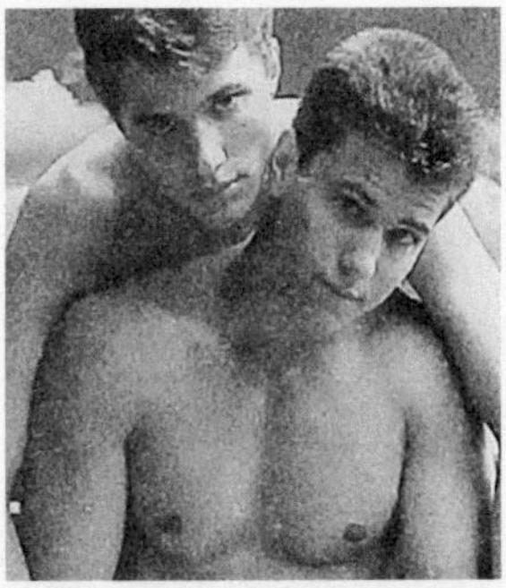

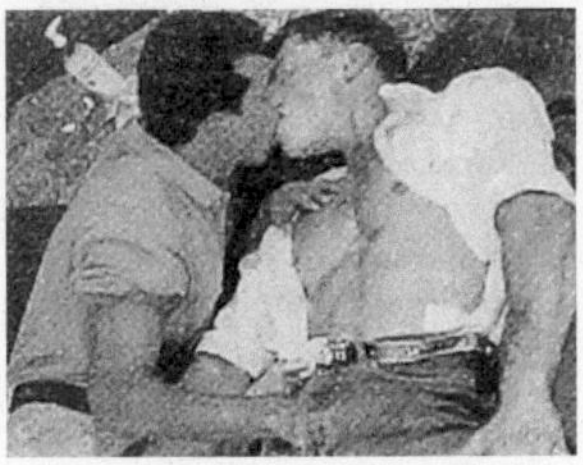

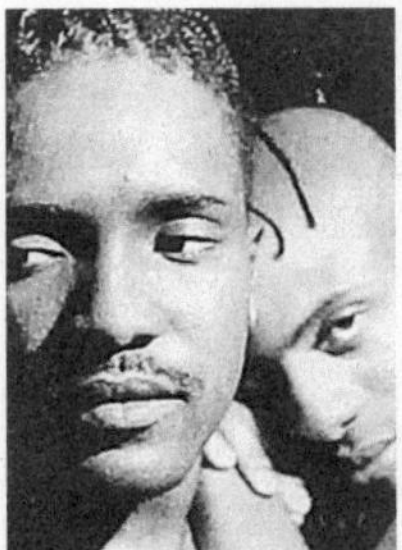

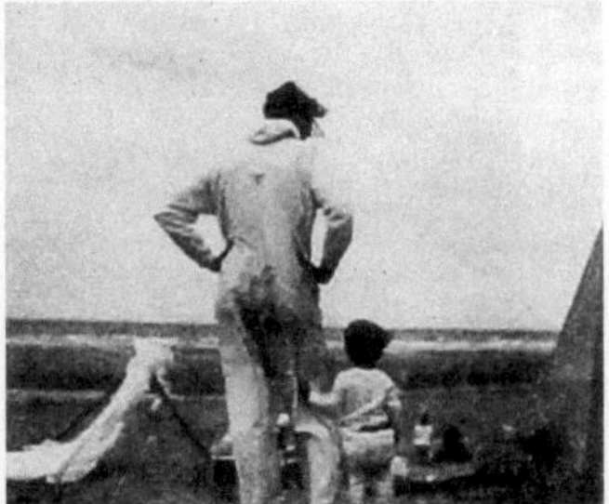

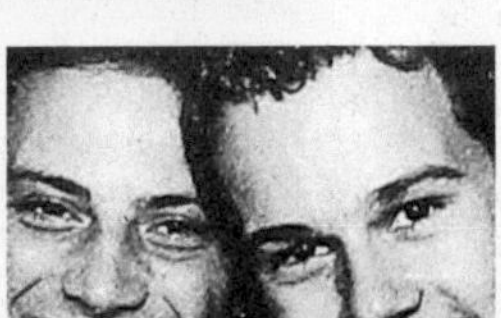

The Black Photo Album / Look at me: 1890–1950

Santu Mofokeng

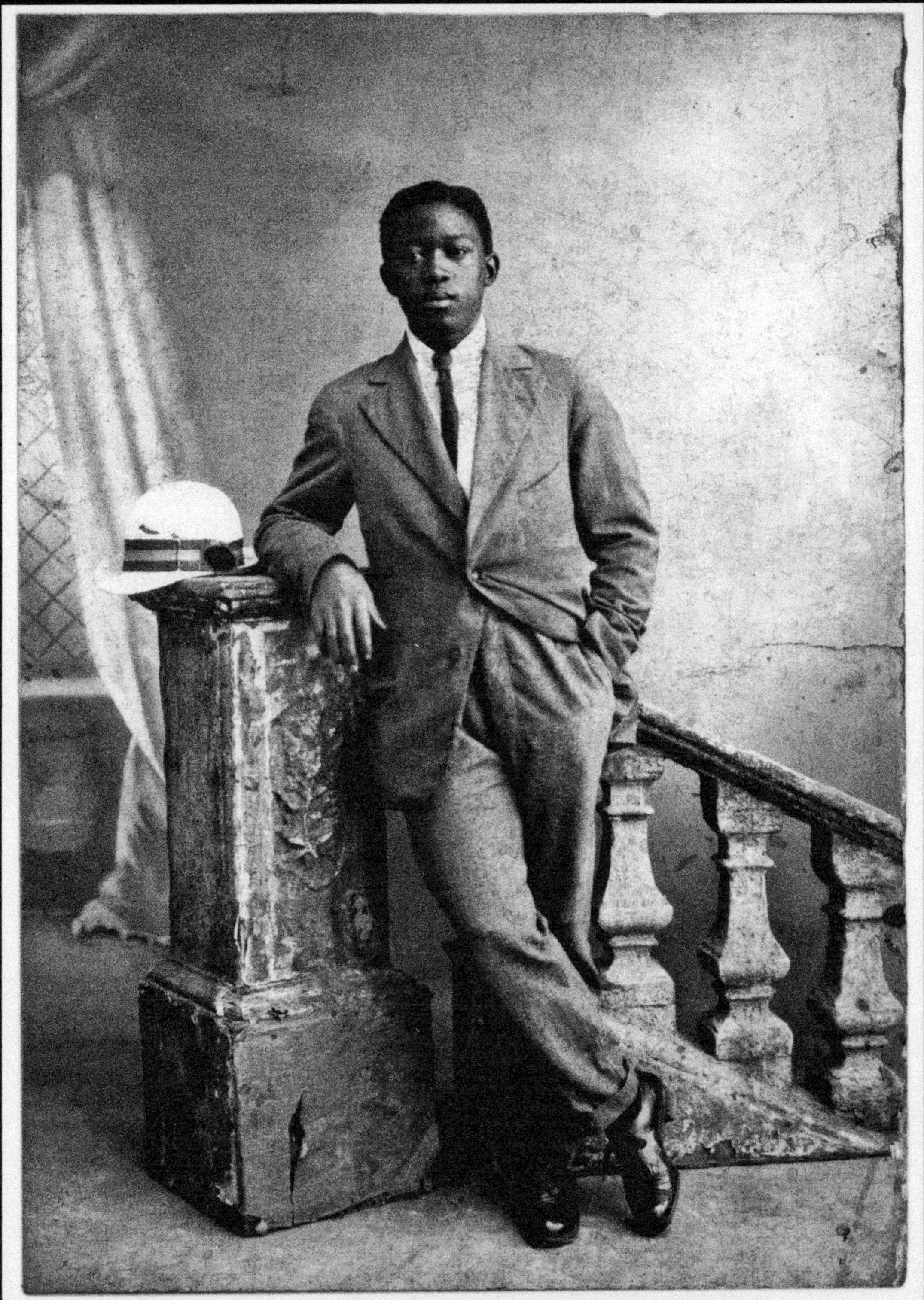

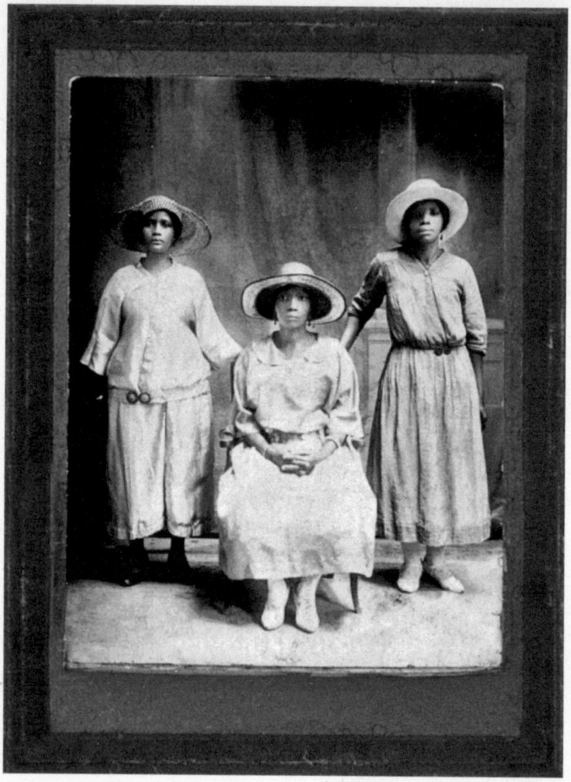

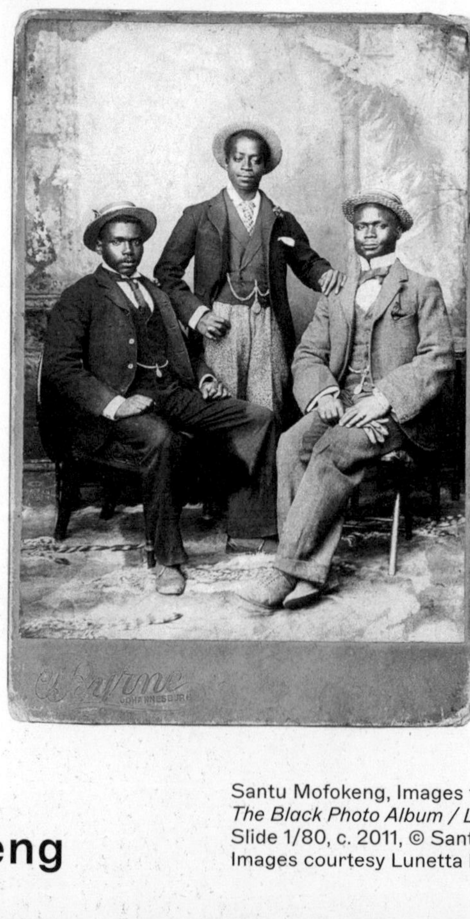

Santu Mofokeng

Santu Mofokeng, Images from:
The Black Photo Album / Look at me: 1890–1950,
Slide 1/80, c. 2011, © Santu Mofokeng
Images courtesy Lunetta Bartz, MAKER, Johannesburg

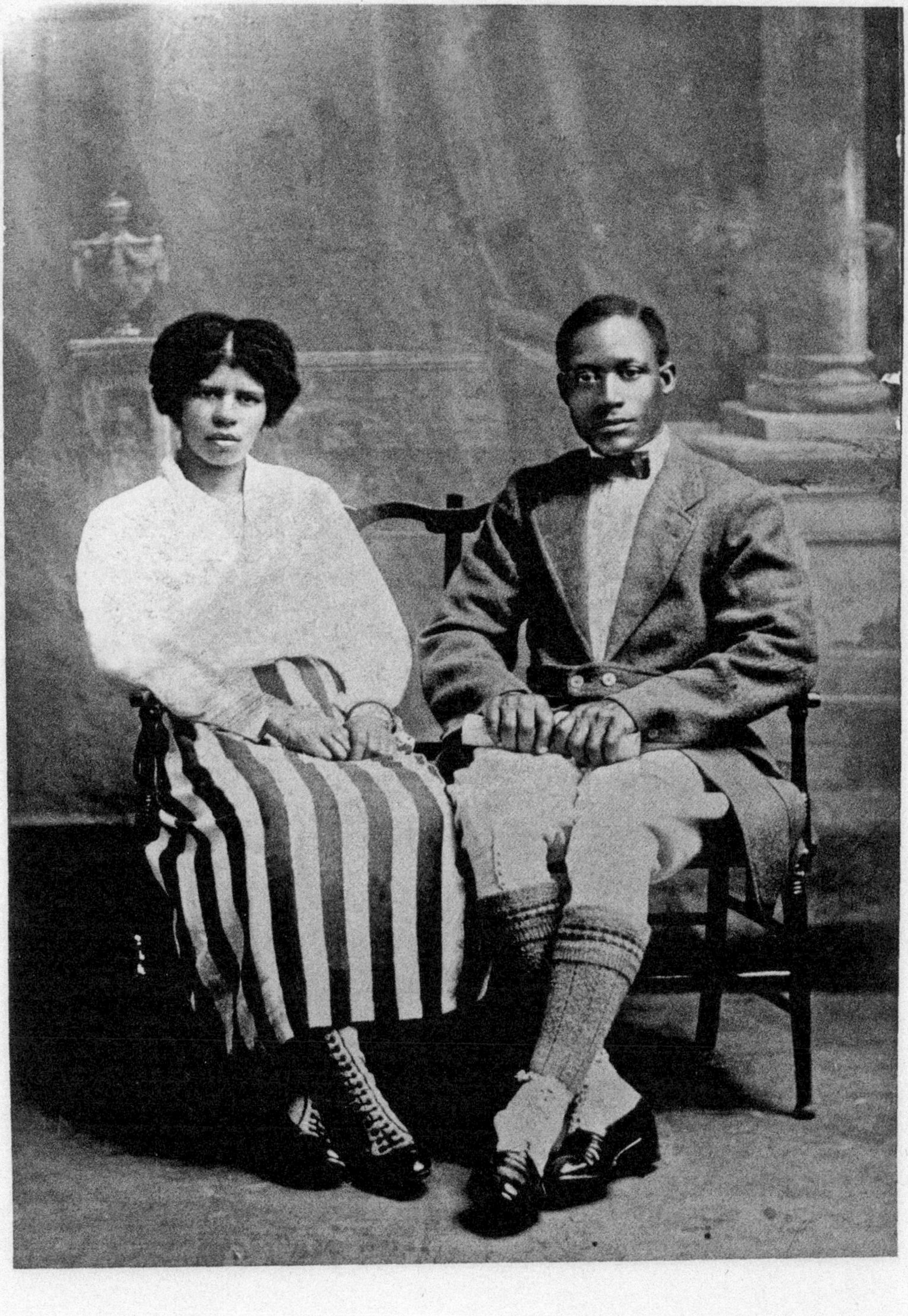

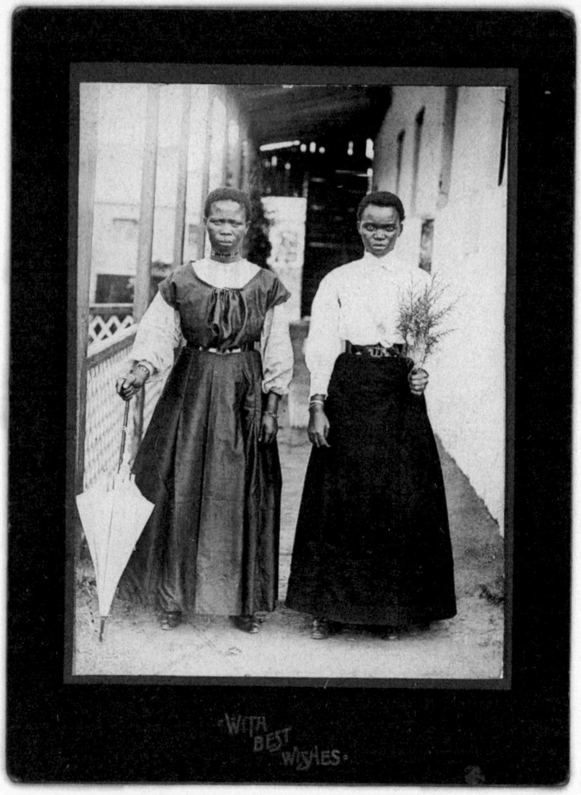

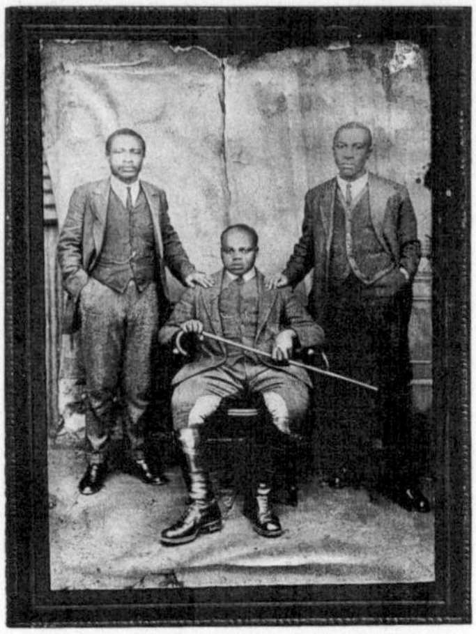

Santu Mofokeng

Santu Mofokeng, Images from:
The Black Photo Album / Look at me: 1890–1950,
Slide 1/80, c. 2011, © Santu Mofokeng
Images courtesy Lunetta Bartz, MAKER, Johannesburg

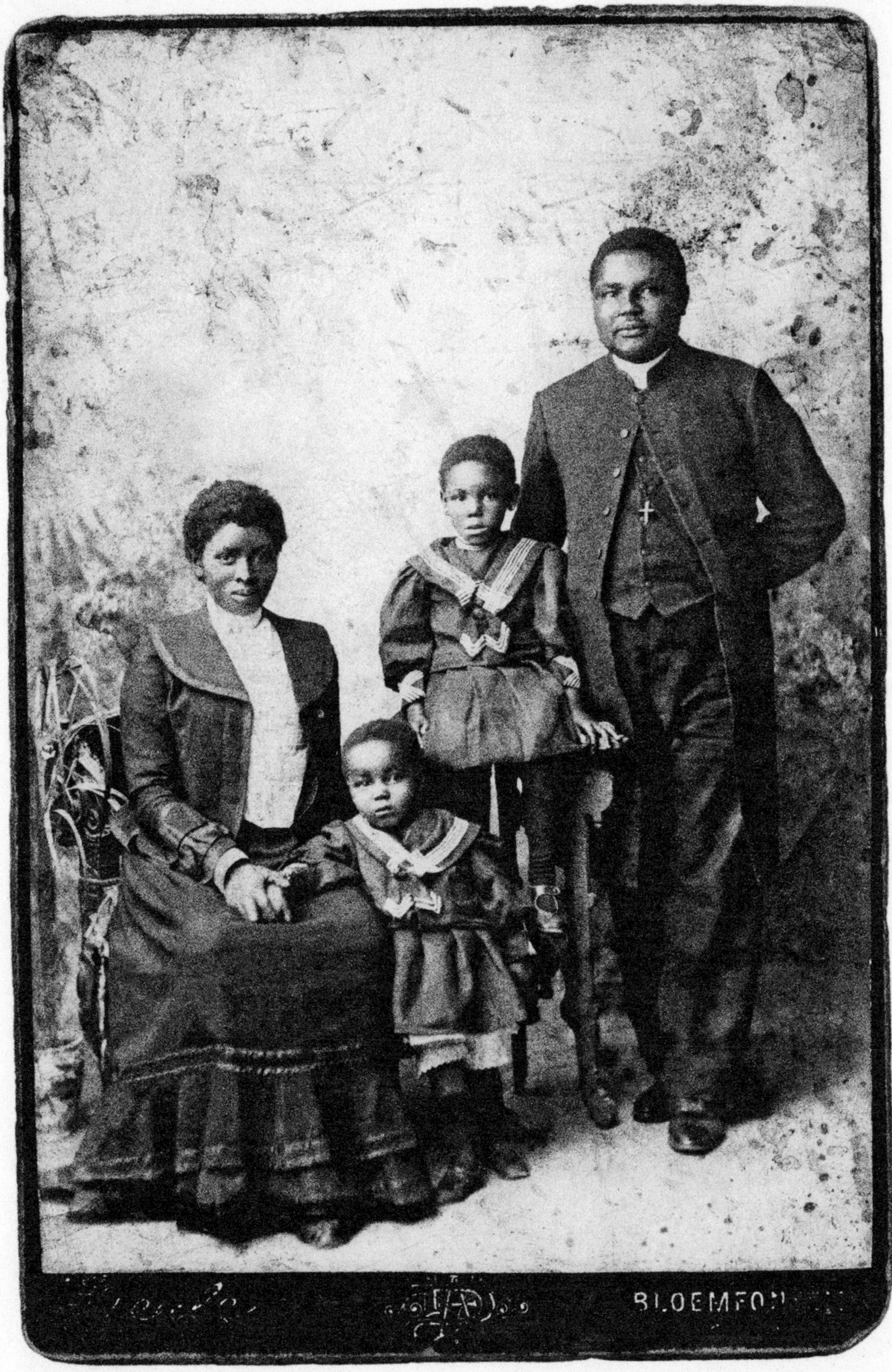

The Bang Straws

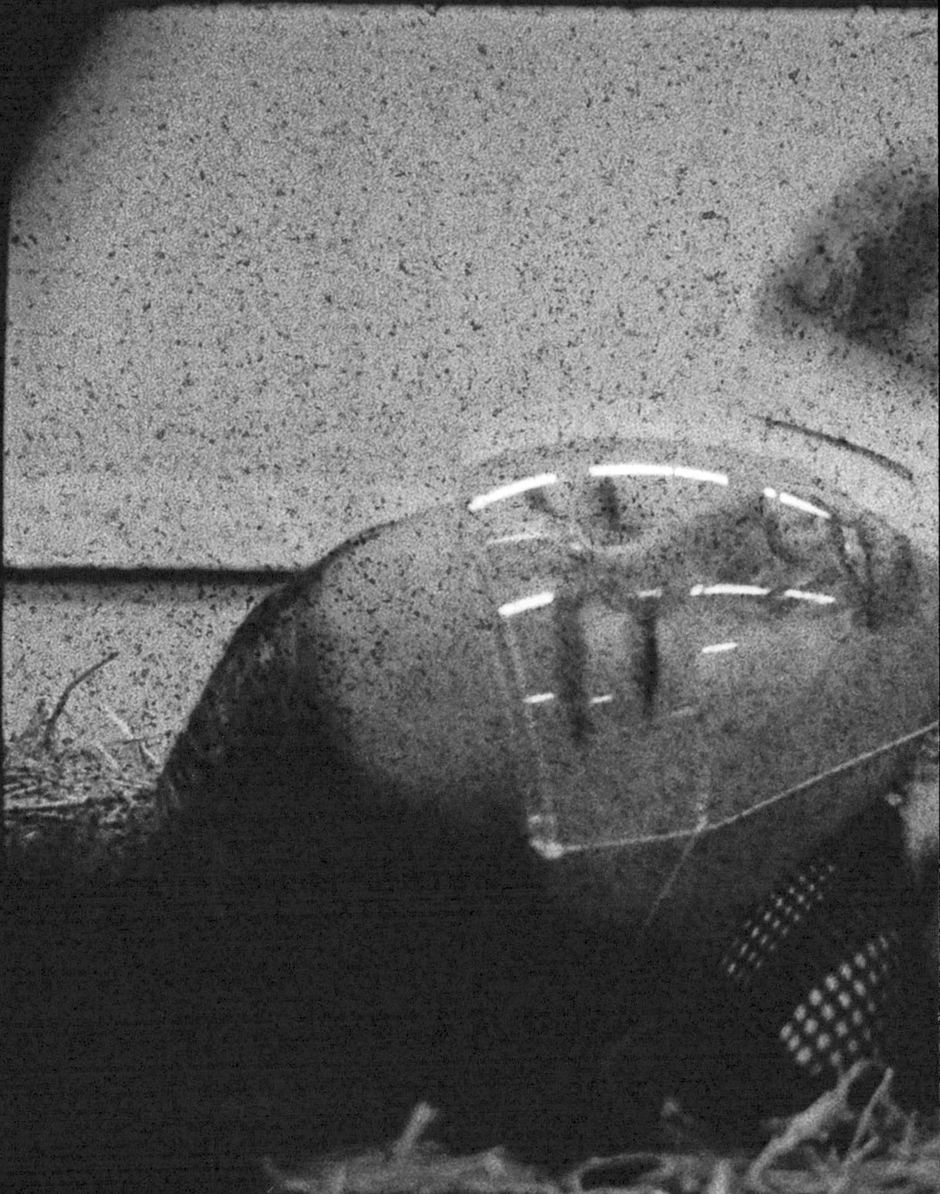

Michelle Williams Gamaker,
The Bang Straws, 2021
film stills

Michelle Williams Gamaker

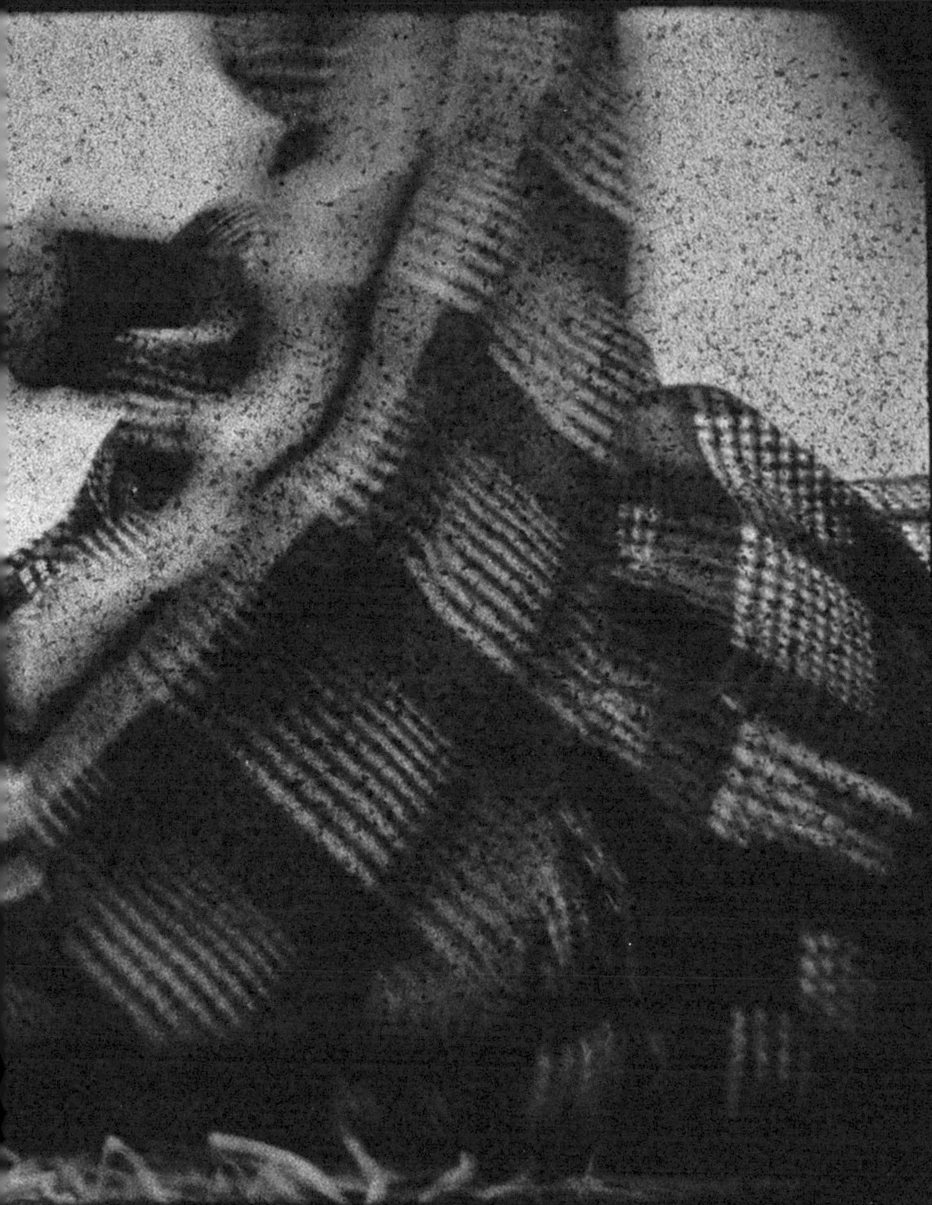

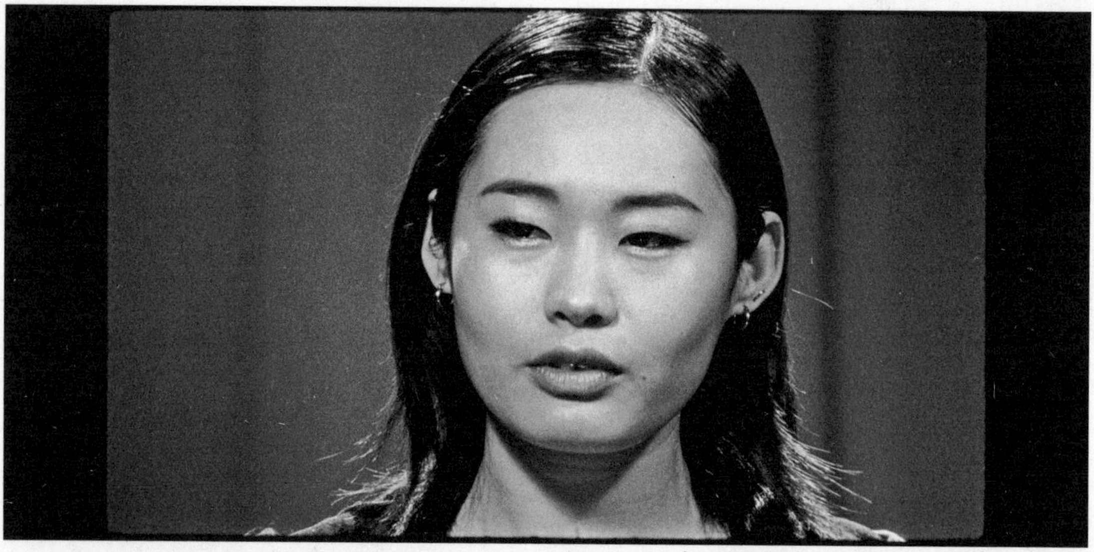

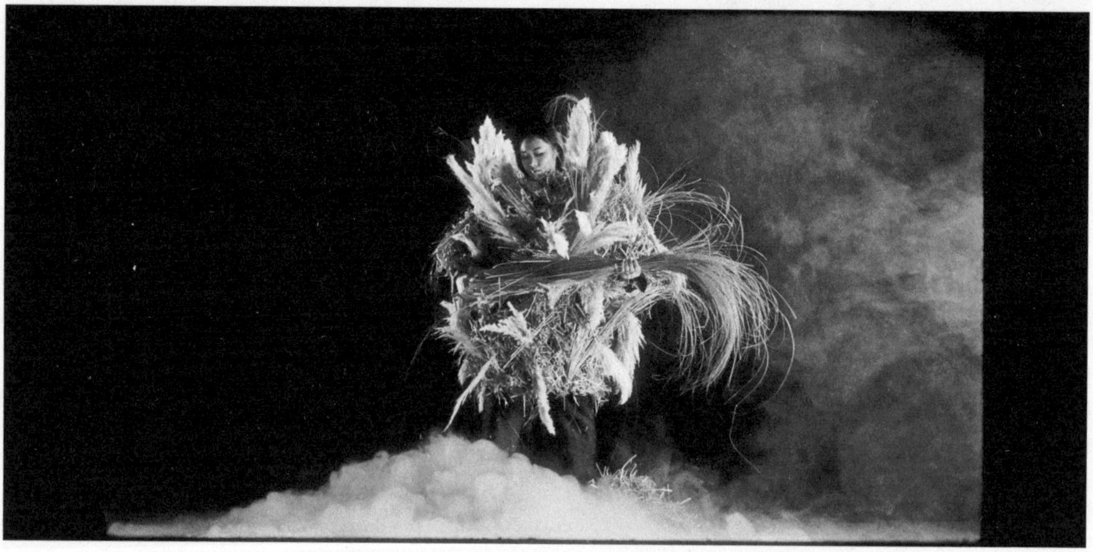

Michelle Williams Gamaker

Michelle Williams Gamaker,
The Bang Straws, 2021
film stills

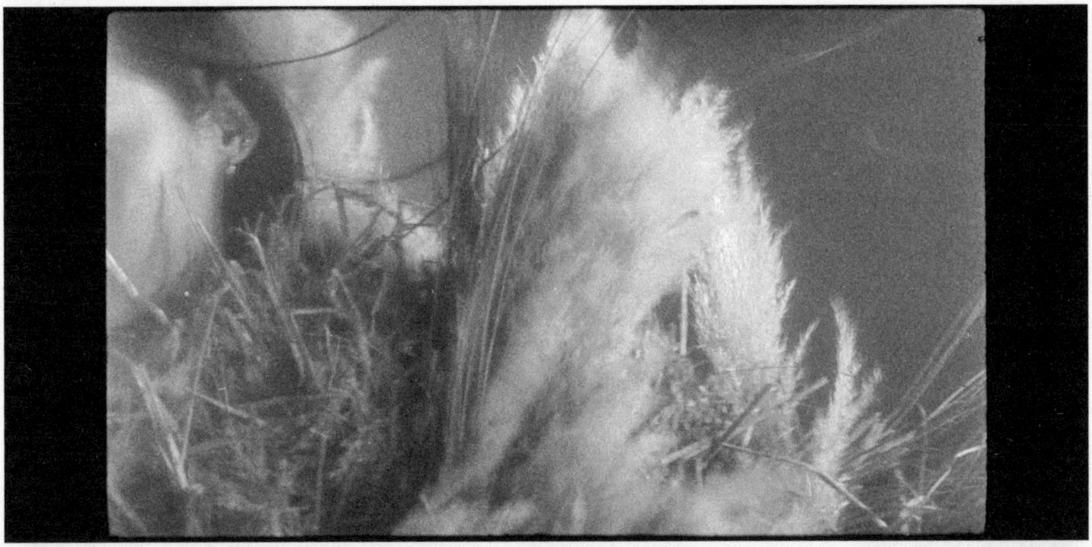

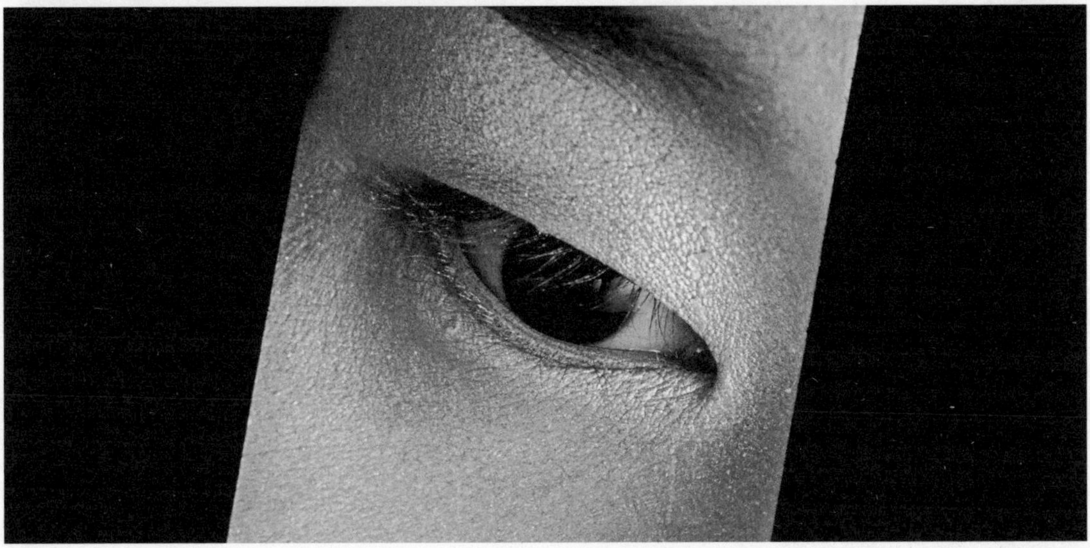

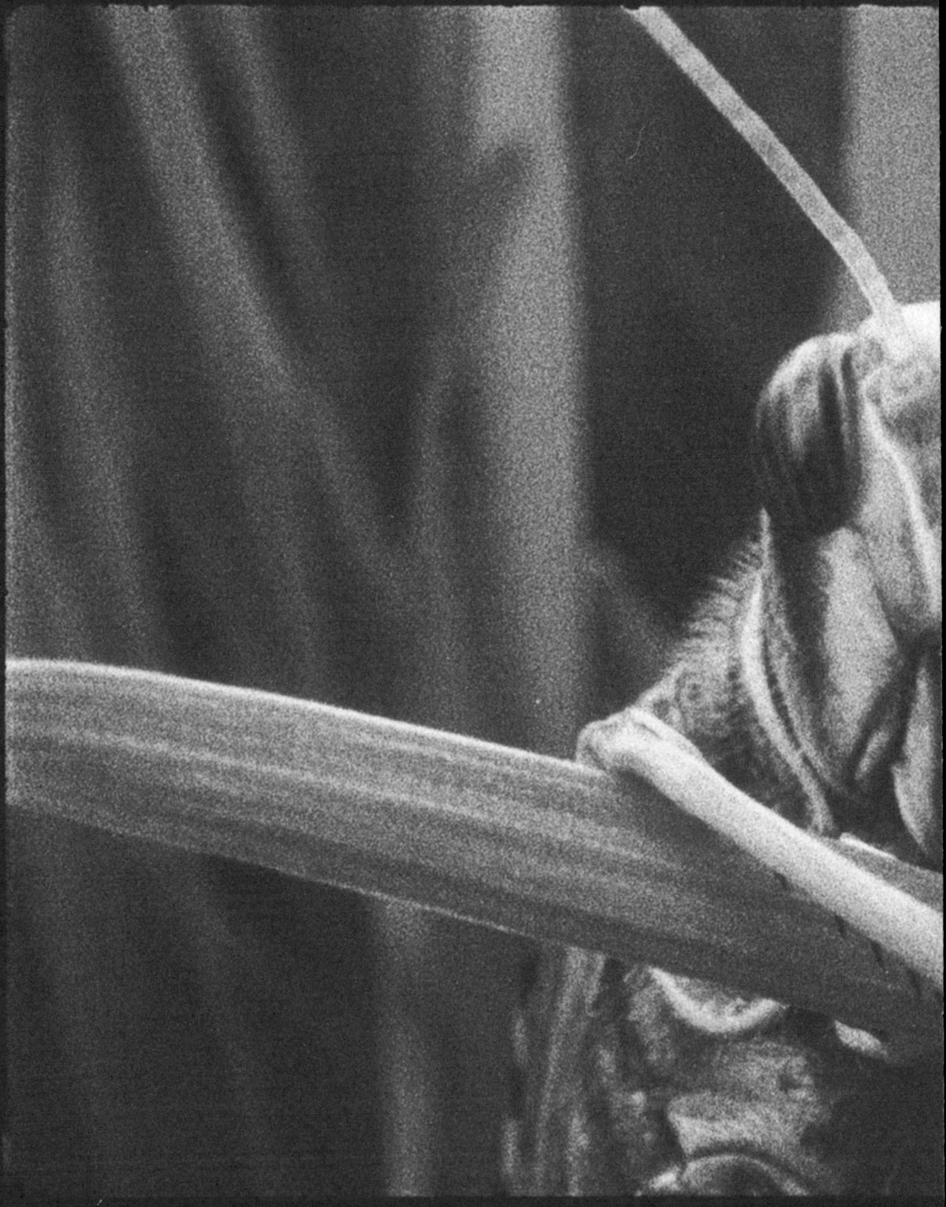

Michelle Williams Gamaker

Michelle Williams Gamaker,
The Bang Straws, 2021
film stills

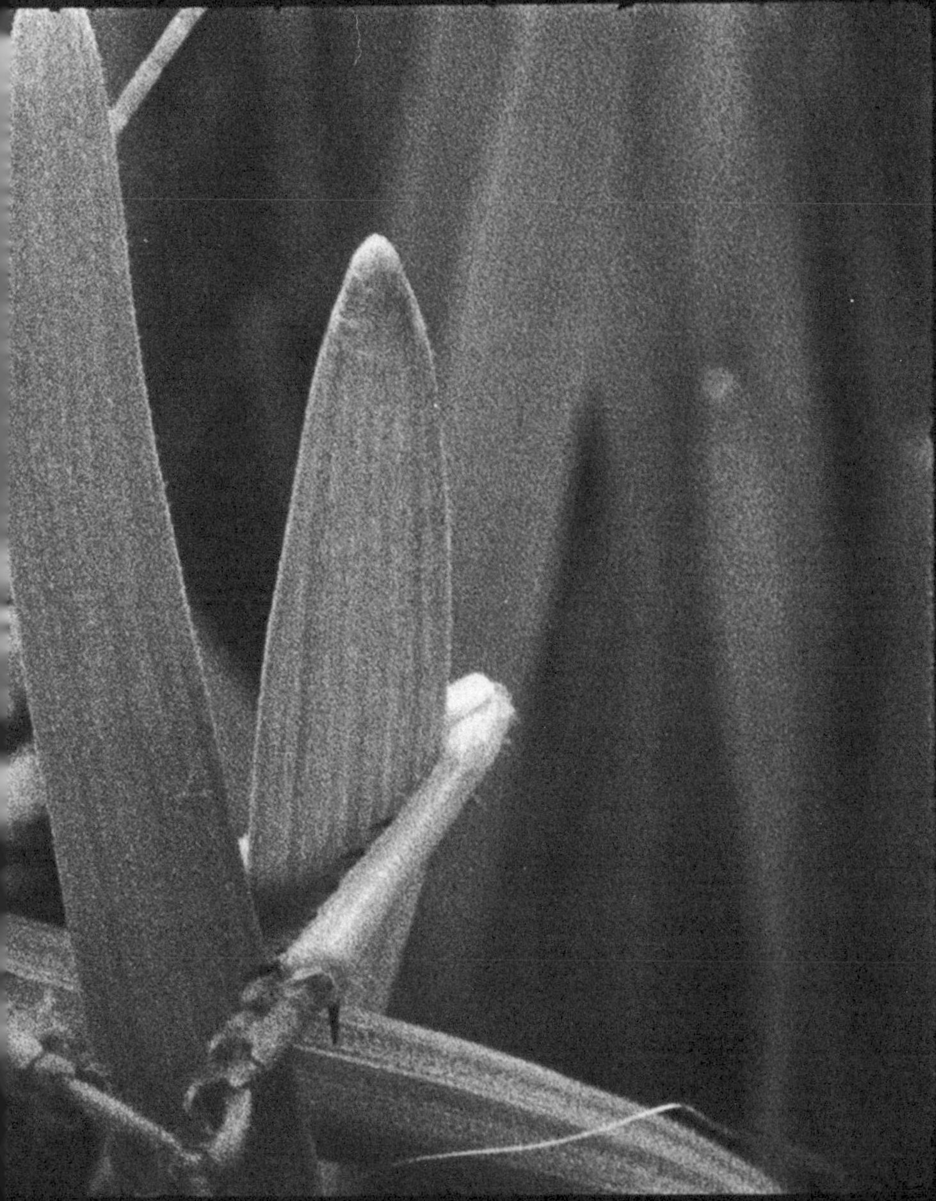

Archiving Memories

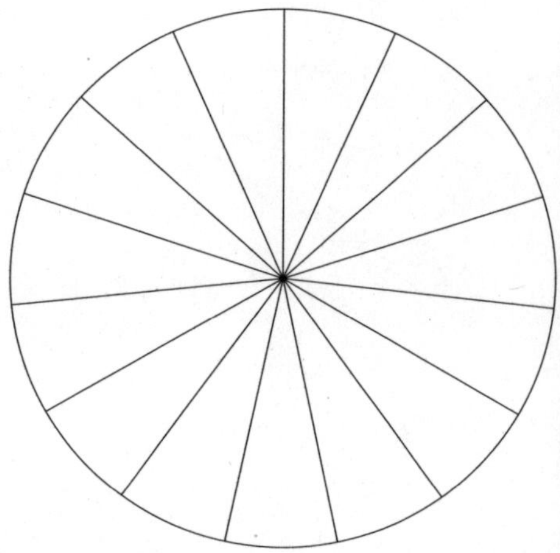

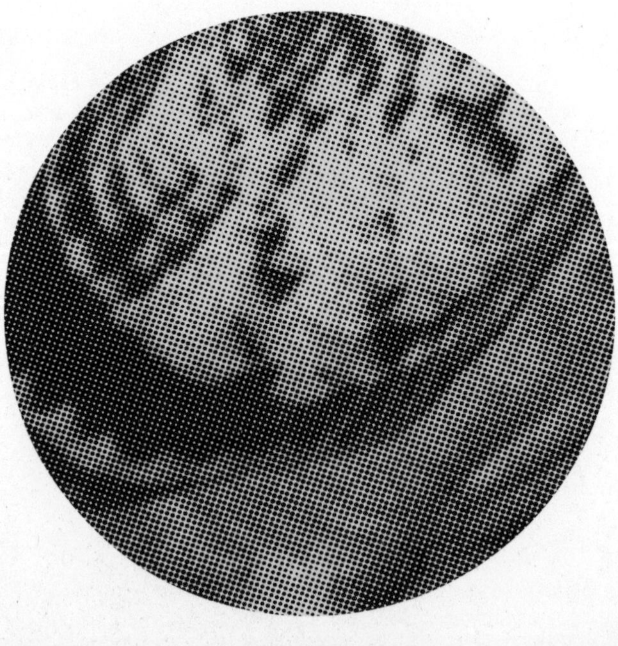

and Histories

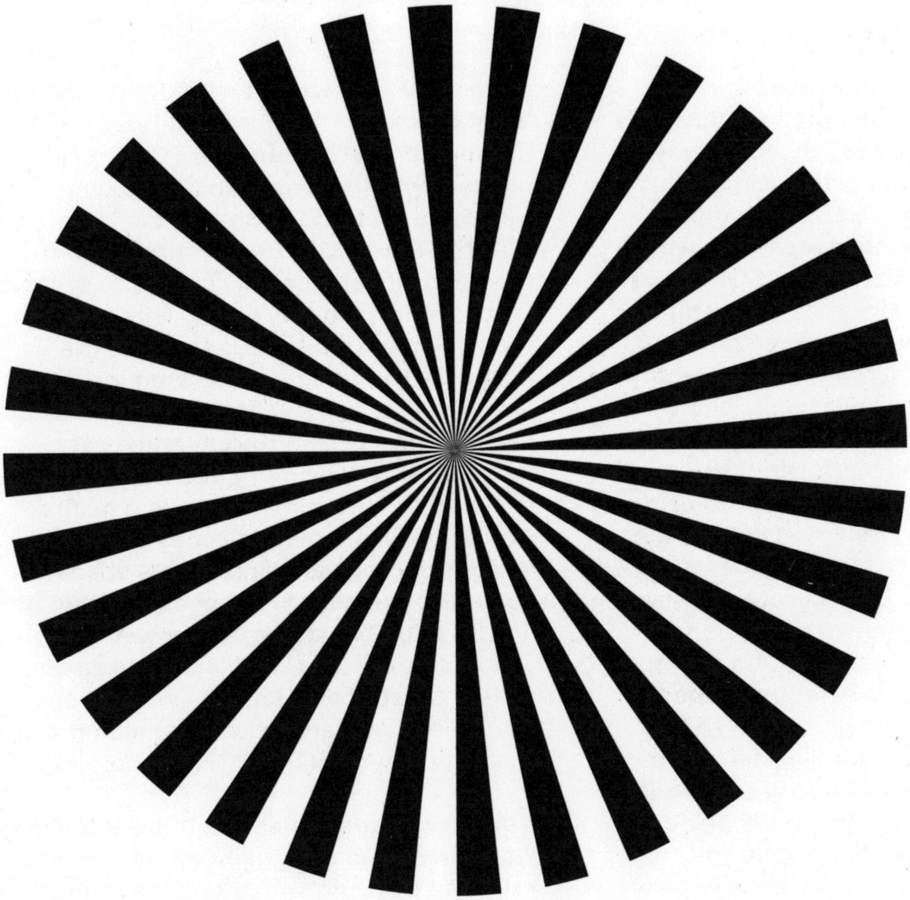

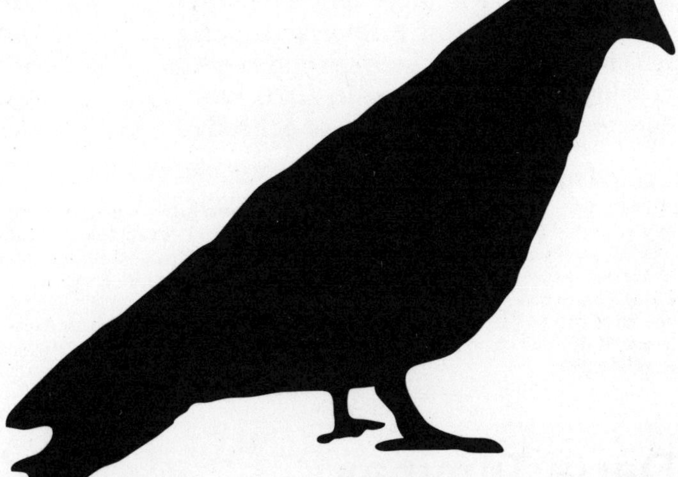

PASS IT ON Private Stories, Public Histories

What relations do artists build with photographic archival material? How can this material be defined? In which ways does it manifest itself within the artistic process? These are some of the questions that I confronted myself with while curating the exhibition 'Pass It On: Private Stories, Public Histories'[1] (27 November 2020–28 February 2021). The show brought together four ongoing projects rooted in the research of family photographic archives. It presented specifically works-in-progress in different stages of their development in an attempt to bring to the fore artistic processes behind the practices that are based on pre-existing imagery. One of my core curatorial drives was to create a framework in which, together with the artists and the audience, the reflection about the nature of these productions could be stimulated. In this text, I will expand, structure, and share several observations that may contribute to the space of meanings that is being shaped by the *Productive Archiving* publication.

Let me introduce the broader framework of the exhibition and the artists' works first. 'Pass It On' was hosted by FOTODOK, a photography exhibition space in Utrecht, the Netherlands, for which I curate. It focuses on one overarching theme each year. In 2020, we concentrated on the notion of collective memory. We kicked off with the exhibition 'Joint Memory: Photographic Fragments'[2] (November 2019–February 2020), proceeded with the show 'This Creaking Floor and All the Ceilings Below'[3] (March 2020–August 2020), and rounded up the theme in November 2020 with the project that I focus on in this essay. Throughout these three exhibitions, as well as the accompanying public programming, virtual tours, and publications, FOTODOK looked from three different angles at what collective memory and its relation to the photographic medium is. The first exhibition was a meta discussion on how various photographic platforms shape collective memory,[4] the second served as a self-reflective statement as well as an attempt to nurture the communal space: artists created site-specific work about the collective memory of the building and the area where FOTODOK is located.[5]

What we needed to add to this equation was something that followed rather naturally: the personal angle and the archive, without which the discourse about collective memory would not be complete. FOTODOK thus initiated 'Pass It On' and invited Inge Meijer (NL), Lebohang Kganye (ZA), Marianne Ingleby (US/NL), and Pablo Lerma (ES/NL) to prepare installations that would reveal the artistic methods they use while still working on the upcoming

1_The press release can be found at www.fotodok.org/en/exhibition-pass-it-on-private-stories-public-histories/ (accessed on 30 August 2021). The virtual tour can be visited at https://fotodok-pass-it-on.netlify.app/ (accessed on 30 August 2021).

2_www.fotodok.org/en/joint-memory/ Virtual tour: vrhouse.blob.core.windows.net/tours/fotodok-joint-memory/index.htm.

3_www.fotodok.org/en/this-creaking-floor-and-all-the-ceilings-below-opening-6-march/.

4_*Joint Memory: Photographic Fragments* brought together artists whose work reflected on how collective memory of historical events has been shaped through photography from the second half of the twentieth century until the present. The main purpose was to discuss the mediated and

Daria Tuminas

projects, which derive from 'found' photographic footage and question the notion of a 'family archive.' The exhibition path stretched through four rooms.

The first room, in which visitors would start their route, presented *Operation Detachment* (2016–ongoing) by Marianne Ingleby. After Ingleby's grandfather Bruce Elkus died, the artist's mother gave her a worn-out Kodak box filled with photographs he made as an official US army photographer during the Second World War. In March 1945, Elkus arrived at Iwo Jima. He joined the second half of Operation Detachment, which was to 'detach' the island from Japan, so it could be used as a springboard to the mainland. The operation was planned to last only a few days, but it turned into a long-lasting battle. Elkus documented the 147th Army regiment, whose task was to take out the Japanese resistance who were hiding in the extensive cave system and to clear the island of casualties. While on assignment, Bruce also documented a wide range of personal and controversial subjects. Next to aerial views of the island, photographs of military logistics, and battle scenes, there are images of daily routine, visits to the mainland and a local brothel. Only 28 photographs ended up in the National Archives, Maryland. The box apparently holds the 'army rejects' that didn't serve the military's purposes, and thus holds unique uncensored material. Ingleby has consulted with historians, travelled to Okinawa, and interviewed US war veterans. The material was digitized with the help of the Nederlands Fotomuseum and has temporarily found a home at the NIOD Institute for War, Holocaust and Genocide Studies, while Ingleby looks for its final destination. The installation included: at the beginning, a photograph of a military tent and a text next to it, telling the story of the single attempt of her grandfather to share with her the story of the war; a specially constructed table with all the images from the archive placed under different categories; a video work where the artist goes through a selection of images and poses questions to the archive and to her grandfather; two 150 × 150 cm photographs with views of the island (in a symbolic way, the cave from the crack of which we see the flames bursting, and the water with the strong fog above); an audio piece with extracts from the interviews with veterans; in front of it, an artefact—black volcanic sand from the island that was sent to Ingleby by one of the veterans.

The second room introduced *It Doesn't Stop at Images* (2020–ongoing) by Pablo Lerma. For the past three years, Lerma has been researching the concept of masculinity and investigating the lack of representation of gay men and queer

constructed nature of collective memory. Individual memories are shaped and preserved through narratives created by others. We wanted to investigate the specific role that photography plays in shaping collective memory through a variety of platforms such as books and newspapers, family archives, and online media.

5_In *This Creaking Floor and All the Ceilings Below*, FOTODOK found it important to look back at our own institution and research the collective memory in relation to our space. The building of Lange Nieuwstraat 7, Utrecht, was once a monastery, then a school for children with learning disabilities, and now is occupied by FOTODOK and Casco Art Institute: Working for the Commons, amongst others. We invited Bart Lunenburg to work on a site-specific installation, rooted in a year-long research of the history and the architecture of the place. Casco, with whom we collaborated on this event, introduced artefacts from site-specific projects that they had previously developed.

community throughout the history of photography. He has been focusing on vernacular and amateur imagery of the twentieth century, such as family pictures and snapshots. *It Doesn't Stop at Images*, initiated for the occasion of 'Pass It On' further developed these artistic interests of Lerma. He explored the IHLIA LGBTI Heritage collection's magazines from between the 1970s and the 1990s. The artist looked for printed matter that was connected to the places and times that shaped his own biography. Pablo was born in the 1980s in Spain, has lived in the USA for almost seven years, and in 2019 moved to the Netherlands. He realized his identity in the 1990s, and grew up surrounded by visually stereotypical representations of gay men in mass culture. Time has passed, but those stereotypes live on. Even the archives that are dedicated to queer legacy often lack alternatives. Take family pictures for example: the genre that bridges generations, creates a sense of belonging, and shapes collective memory; the gay community cannot find itself there. Lerma dedicates his practice to constructing a counter-history of gay men, gay (extended) families, and masculinity. He recontextualizes, re-edits, reframes 'cliché' images to propose new narratives. The artist asks: how and by whom have gay men been represented so far? Why do certain patterns reoccur? Is it possible to break through the heteronormative gaze?

For the exhibition, Lerma zoomed in on themes in magazines' illustrations discovered at IHLIA. He researched magazines from the Netherlands, Spain, and the USA. First, he presented the work based on *Homologie*'s material (a Dutch magazine that ran from 1978 until 1997).[6] Lerma divided the visual material into three separate themes, scanned photographs, reframed them, and presented them in the installation described by Drew Sawyer in his essay 'Postcards from the Archive: Pablo Lerma's Queer Poetics' as follows:

> The first [theme] consists of photographs of public figures, dissecting the construction of shared queer histories and heroes—featured amongst these images are portraits of historical figures as well as contemporary celebrities. The second group contains photographs that center on desire and representations of the body. Here, Lerma acknowledges the stereotypes of gay culture, pointing to its obsessions with dominant forms of masculinity and beauty. The third grouping contains photographs that show forms of relationships and community—there are images of gatherings and demonstrations, as well as couples embracing. Lerma presents these groupings in three vitrines that recall institutional forms of display. Spreads of the original publication often appear on top of a matte black board at the base of each case. Facsimiles of photographs hover above the magazines on the first sheet of glazing, while the second layer of glass not only protects the photographs below but also reflects the viewer's visage when looking from above. Together, the presentation creates a three-dimensional collage [...].'[7]

Next to these vitrines, the installation included three large prints, each representing one of the themes described

6_Lerma planned to change the installation twice throughout the duration of the show, using each time materials sourced from two more magazines. Due to the lockdown in the Netherlands that lasted from 15 December 2020 until 5 June 2021, the installation remained unchanged.

7_Drew Sawyer, 'Postcards from the Archive: Pablo Lerma's Queer Poetics,' in *Pass It On: Private Stories, Public Histories* (Utrecht: FOTODOK; Duivendrecht: METEØRØ EDITIONS, 2021), n.p.

above, and a standing glass vitrine, reminiscent of a school board, on which different references are collected, including the page with the text by David Wojnarowicz, 'Postcards from America: X-Rays from Hell', from which the title of Lerma's project, *It Doesn't Stop at Images*, is borrowed.

In *A Garden Revisioned* (2019–ongoing), which follows in the next room, Inge Meijer discovered hundreds of pre-wedding photographs and negatives at a six-story wedding hall in Gwangju (South Korea) which operated between 1988 and 2006, and stood vacant until it was demolished while the artist was in the country. In its prime years, it arranged around two hundred weddings a day, offering a full 'menu' of matrimonial services. In addition to officially registering their marriage, couples could rent their gowns, ceremonial rooms and restaurants, attend hair and beauty salons, as well as order pre-wedding photography sessions in the center's own indoor studio and outdoor 'photography garden.' This wedding palace had been abandoned for a few years, but its halls were intact, awaiting their fate. Weeks before the building was demolished, the artist discovered piles of contact sheets and negatives scattered on its floors. Meijer collected her findings just before the gigantic high-reaching arm of the excavator levelled the building to the ground. The site was purchased by an urban developer with plans to build 440 living quarters of 'officetels'—a problematic portmanteau of office, hotel, and housing. The installation was comprised of three 100 × 100 cm photographs of the wedding halls' interior (initially they were used to advertise the space); two monitors with videos of the demolition of the building and the 'photography garden;' a large lightbox table with a composition of negatives on top, as well as a system used by the artist in order to scan the negatives, including a camera and a monitor; and finally the so-called 'studies'—long rolls of paper (reminding of wallpaper) with a grid of images with close-ups from the scanned negatives—details of the body language, interior, props that interested Meijer.

The last space showcased the *Ho thubeha ha Lebone* (A Breakage of the Light) (2016–ongoing) by Lebohang Kganye. The artist dedicates her work to the research of her family's history. Kganye traveled throughout The Free State of South Africa in order to record her relatives' life stories and reproduce their family pictures, in both of which her grandfather Philemon Khanye reoccurred. Philemon was the first person in the family to move from The Orange Free State to Johannesburg. He did not want to be a farm laborer, and looked for a city job. Inspired by this move, others followed, temporarily staying in his house. Kganye's grandfather thus became the central figure of the family's mythology and of the artist's oeuvre. Kganye is interested in the discrepancy between the oral narratives she collected and what the domestic albums portray. Dressed in their best outfits, the figures seem like dreamy projections. Their truthful representation would have also shown the apartheid's socio-political context: the oppression, the patriarchal family structures, and the hard work at the factories. At the same time, these images were a way for Kganye's family to tell their own story. There were lots of photographs of black people taken by white people during this time. The family album became an independent platform for black people to pass memories onto other black people. At 'Pass It On' Kganye presented *Re Palame Tereneng e Fosahetseng* (We Took the Wrong Train) and *O Emetse Mohala* (She is Waiting for a Call). The first work told of the artist's aunt who used to take train rides with Philemon, when, due to his stubbornness and being new to the city, they would often end up taking the wrong route. The second is a reenactment of a photograph from Lebohang's grandmother Maria Magadeni Khanyi's family album, performed by Maria herself. At FOTODOK, Kganye presented for the first time her ongoing inquiry in translating the images into installations involving movement and light. *Re Palame Tereneng e Fosahetseng* was built as a stage occupying the whole room with moving figures of her grandfather, aunt, the train and the road sign. All the elements and lights were moving automatically.

At the foundation of all the exhibition's projects lay photographic materials as physical objects. Ingleby received a box with 425 10×15 B&W prints; 76 A4 sheets; 29 color and 112 B&W negatives (and also 88 letters). Lerma dealt with the photographic illustrations that he scanned from the magazine *Homologie*. Meijer's 'found footage' consisted of more than 200 envelopes with negatives, contact sheets, and VHS tapes. Kganye's source materials were photographs that she rephotographed or scanned during the visits from the family members in The Free State. Despite that, none of the artists used the original imagery within their presentations: they used reproductions instead.

Ingleby has been digitizing and conserving the archive with the Nederlands Fotomuseum, so we had all the images available in digital format. The purpose of the installation was to present the archive in its vastness and complexity, allowing visitors to browse through photographs placed in library-like boxes themselves. As we could not let the original photographs be part of an interactive setting, we chose to print the digital files. Lerma has been manipulating scanned images by cropping them, and we printed out those crops (a few copies of the *Homologie*'s issues were added). Meijer mostly had the negatives, and her installation included images that were scanned, post-produced, and printed, as well as negatives on the lightbox—which were 'fake' negatives, reproductions. Kganye transformed the original photographs into a staged setting, where the characters and elements got almost 'realistic' sizes, as well as depth. Moreover, these images are composites of a few different sources, which are never publicly revealed.

Artists reproduce (with an unavoidable degree of transformation), deconstruct and reconstruct original imagery, departing from photographs as objects and arriving at new objects. The artistic process suggests that they deal with the 'originals' in their daily practice. Paradoxically, in the context of 'Pass It On' sharing this process becomes possible only by using reproductions. Makers interpret and deconstruct the sets of original imagery, repositioning them within the contemporary moment. The physical presence of photographic materials and their objecthood could create a haunting allure—a mix of nostalgia and the attraction to the 'unknowable' quality of the vernacular material.[8] The absence of source photographic materials within installations[9] also allows to differentiate the archive as an entity on its own from the artistic transformative reading of it. Ingelby, Kganye, Lerma and Meijer do not merely provide the archive with the space to manifest itself but rather also use it as a case for exploring alternative historical narratives. They are interested in what Allan Sekula calls 'the semantic availability'[10] of pictures, the potential of the archival meaning to change over time and for history to be rewritten, perhaps, more than in presenting the objects' aura, their historiographic value, or emphasizing their material features. The groups of photographs the artists study are the sources of information and hidden narratives for them, however they are also interested in the archive-as-subject: its constitution, taxonomy, iconography, and usage.

It is interesting to look closer at how photographic materials are constituted as archives here. In 2014, for example, Marianne Ingleby received a box with various content that she had not known about earlier. It was a family 'heritage,' yet not the usual family archive—even though it represented a part of the lives of both her grandfather and grandmother, it told a much broader story. Ingleby had to first estimate the historical and artistic value of the materials and to consider them worth archiving, to proclaim them as an archive-to-be, and then start the formation of the archive (from scanning to finding a location for safekeeping). Eventually, the Bruce Elkus' documents have been shaped into an archive of the project *Operation Detachment* by Marianne Ingleby. Other artists of 'Pass It On' also had to initiate and produce an archive, before they could build on it. The archive initiation was caused either by a sudden discovery (like the one by Marianne Ingleby or Inge Meijer) or by starting a conscious search and gathering of imagery—Pablo Lerma created an archive within the institutional archive at IHLIA LGBTI Heritage and Labohang Kganye had to do 'field trips' in order to collects reproductions of photographs and oral narratives from her family members. In all scenarios, after choosing to engage into archivalization, the long and laborious process of producing an archive followed. Some of the elements such production included were: gathering, sorting, organizing, digitally reproducing, structuring of both the physical and digital elements, collecting commentary, and reflecting on the ownership or their own role in relation to the footage. All these steps have practical reasons, but at the same time they are artistic gestures in their own right.

The phase of the transformation of an archive into an artwork is rather curious. On the one hand, it continues the production of the archive, as it defines the form, architecture and context in which an archive presents itself to the world. On the other hand, the artists' main goal is not to purely represent the archive, but rather to create an artwork based on it. While being translated into the exhibition space and undergoing the artistic interpretation, the photographic materials can no longer be seen as purely an archive—the inventory, chronology, and categorization pave and free the way to narration. It is hard to establish a clear order of how exactly the 'preparation' of materials and shaping them into an archive shift

8_Kobena Mercer wrote about this 'haunting allure' in the essay 'Photography and the Global Conditions of Cross-cultural Modernity,' in *Unfixed: Photography and Postcolonial Perspectives in Contemporary Art*, ed. Sara Blokland and Asmara Pelupessy (Prinsenbeek: Jap Sam Books and UNFIXED Projects, 2012).

9_An exception would be a few copies of Homologie on view at Pablo Lerma's vitrines.

10_See Allan Sekula, 'Reading An Archive: Photography Between Labour and Capitalism' (1983), in *The Photography Reader*, ed. Liz Wells (New York: Routledge, 2003), pp. 443–52.

towards the 'realization' of the work. Is it possible to distinguish these processes? The artistic work derives from the archive (and in our case archive-in-progress, specifically), while the archive is being assembled in the first place due to the artistic intent and through artistic optics and tools. An attempt to construct an archive is counterbalanced by a simultaneous attempt to deconstruct it. The projects by Ingleby, Kganye, Lerma, and Meijer belong to the long-established tradition of archival art, which, as pointed out by Hal Foster in 'An Archival Impulse,'

> not only draws on informal archives but produces them as well, and does so in a way that underscores the nature of all archival materials as found yet constructed, factual yet fictive, public yet private.[11]

This in-betweenness is something characteristic of archival art in general. The works by the artists of 'Pass It On' are caught between the poles Foster mentions, but also between producing archives and producing art works, where one act feeds another.[12]

Producing archives and art works rooted in them means that there is a certain relation established between an artist and the footage. It starts with an idea of ownership. According to Allan Sekula, archives 'constitute a *territory of images*: the unity of an archive is first and foremost that imposed by ownership,'[13] while it may or may not coincide with authorship. For all the artists participating in the exhibition, the concept of ownership as defining their relation to the archive they build, is challenging.

Marianne Ingleby's archive might be legally owned by her, but from a wider ethical perspective photography has a shared ownership between the person who 'pressed the button,' people who are depicted, and a spectator. In *Operation Detachment*'s archive it is not only Bruce Elkus' photos that we see, but also multiple portraits of him, most likely made by other soldiers. People in front of the camera include not only American soldiers, but also Japanese who are in the images as either prisoners of war, as mutilated yet identifiable bodies, or as civilians at a brothel in Tokyo, which makes the whole system of ownership even more complex as it contains a power dynamics between a photographer and people he photographed. Ingleby in this context is not a solo owner of the photographic materials, but rather an engaged spectator who takes the responsibility of what she sees, and acts upon it.

In Pablo Lerma's *It Doesn't Stop at Images*, there is nothing to own. The artist is a reader between the (visual) lines of queer magazines. There are neither 'original' nor 'unseen' photographs he is interested in—they all have been available for the audience of the printed matter back at the time when they were published, and are currently available at the public archive or at private shelves. Even though Lerma has a few physical copies of the magazines himself, it can be hardly considered a 'unique' possession. The artist performs the gesture of gathering together the reproductions of some of the images that speak to him about the patterns of gay representation or

11_Hal Foster, 'An Archival Impulse,' *October* 110 (2004), p. 5.

12_The goal of the exhibition was to emphasize this fluid and interdependent mechanism, and to open it to the audience. Each week, during one of the days of the weekend, two of the artists were present at the space and available for a one-on-one conversation with the visitors, who could get to know the projects while they were still in the making and directly from the authors. The viewers were invited to become witnesses of the site of the archival art production, and to look at the process instead of at the product first. Another reason was to state a certain degree of transparency for both the artistic and archival practices, which both are usually complex chains of decision-making. While the approach of one-on-one meetings with artists at the exhibition space is a strategy partially caused by Covid-19 regulations measures and could also be useful for a wide range of artistic practices, we saw potential alternative histories they could constitute. He 'owns' the images no more than researchers 'own' quotes from books they study in order to implement them in their theory. Cat Lachowskyj suggests another metaphor of Lerma's role towards the materials he works with—'an excavator, meticulously unearthing our unnoticed narratives to re-root them in the foreground.'[14] Artists detect images that could resonate with the narratives they are building up, and while they're doing it.

In *A Garden Revisioned*, Inge Meijer saves the photographic materials from an actual 'excavator' that was demolishing the wedding hall, in which a pre-wedding photography studio was located. Being at an art residency, she did not plan to work on an archival project, and did not expect to come across any found (or rather lost?) footage. Meijer instinctively picked up all the negatives and contact sheets she could find left behind in a building to be demolished. The unanticipated nature of this finding as well as the full realization that it belongs to a context of a culture that she is not part of made Meijer actively search for self-identification: what am I to these images? The idea of an 'owner' seemed odd: photographs were in possession of the wedded couples and their families. It is quite an unusual situation in which probably most of the Gwangju citizens still preserve images as part of their family archives, while Meijer suddenly gets access to the imagery's sources and the possibility of multiplying them. The archive is built not on photographs that still actively function in society, but on negatives the value of which was dismissed by the wedding hall administration. Meijer builds the archive with at least three degrees of not-owning it: photographs (that she has not seen) belong to families; negatives were created and kept by the wedding hall workers; and she can't 'read' it in the same way as if she was part of the culture. While discussing this subject with Meijer in the early stages of preparing the exhibition, we concluded that we could see the materials she accumulated in line with Ariella Azoulay's thoughts about a photographic image that

> [...] can at most be entrusted to someone for certain time. It is a deposit, temporarily given over to whomever has it for safekeeping, but such persons are never its owner.[15]

Meijer's role then is a temporary caregiver for accidentally recovered photographic materials. As Natasha Christia points out in her essay 'On Inge Meijer's *A Garden Revisioned*,' 'caring as an action—as imposing care on somebody or something—is no less problematic, since it may also revolve around dynamics of oppression. But to gaze with care, to act with care—that is something entirely different. It is holding oneself accountable to these questions and the complex dynamics behind them.'[16] The writer also suggests alternative roles such as the provisional custodian or guardian of an orphaned assemblage. This vocabulary links to the idea of Joan Fontcuberta about image adoption: 'I think that now most artists adopt images because they don't pretend to be the biological parents, they just pick those images to make them

a necessity to use this approach in relation to archival art specifically as it creates sites for collective/dialogistic knowledge production.

13_Sekula, 'Reading an Archive,' p. 444.

14_Cat Lachowskyj, 'Pablo Lerma Uncovers candid queer histories within the international archive,' in *British Journal of Photography*, www.1854.photography/2021/02/pablo-lerma-queer-histories/ (accessed on 20 August 2021).

15_Ariella Azoulay, *The Civil Contract of Photography* (New York: Zone Books, 2012), p. 103.

16_Natasha Christia, 'On Inge Meijer's *A Garden Revisioned*,' in Trigger, fomu.be/trigger/articles/on-inge-meijers-a-garden-revisioned-or-on-claiming-space-for-an-ecology-of-dissident-migrations (accessed on 20 August 2021).

alive in another context. The importance is how we assign meaning.'[17]

Lebohang Kganye, like Lerma, has at her disposal only the reproductions she made on a field trip (and a small part of photographs that belonged to her branch of the family). There has been no corpus of images that existed before she initiated it. Kganye creates a meta-family album, in which stories and the copies of images are accumulated, and all of it is translated into spatial installations. The artist defines her approach as recalling, recollecting, restaging, and reconnecting. These strategies aid self-healing of the loss of her family members on a personal level, and 'collective healing of family from traumatic experiences associated with displacement and histories of partition.'[18] Kganye's artistic process, built upon thorough research into oral histories, is also defined by its experimentation with the form. While the images' components recur, their shapes are ever changing: from two-dimensional collages to animation. This principle mirrors how traditional oral narratives function—while the plot stays the same, how the story is delivered changes.

The paradigm in which all the artists relate to the footage they work with within 'Pass It On.' *Private Stories, Public Histories* can't be described as appropriation either. Artists manipulate images (take elements out by cropping or covering them) and recontextualize them to generate new meanings, and these are indeed features of appropriation art. However, the term itself described the work created in the few decades starting from the 1980s, where artists would declare the state of authority and apply subversive methods to the imagery they would use in order to reveal the mechanisms behind various social and cultural institutions. Ingleby, Lerma, Meijer and Kganye work in the opposite way—they dismantle their own authority, and while being critical to the practices that shaped the footage they address, they use it as a starting point for building alternative narratives.

The artists neither collect in the sense of how Jean Baudrillard defines collecting in *The System of Objects* as a project of possession, where 'just one object no longer suffices,' and the fulfilment 'always means a succession or even a complete series of objects.'[19] Here, artists don't attempt to continue the succession of items, nor strive for completeness, they accept the footage's random, arbitral, and fractional state; and they do not have the drive of possessing it, instead they search for triggers on the representational and informational levels that can be generative to the processes of knowledge production.

They initiate, make rules for, and produce archival situations in which they and the viewers can look directly at the line that separates what the footage shows and what it does not show. They locate themselves between what is represented and what can be retrieved or constructed. As Michel Foucault points out in *The Archaeology of Knowledge*, the discursive formation, such as an archive, emerges to the exclusion of what is not said, it is 'a distribution of gaps, voids, absence, limits, divisions'[20] that does not carry within it what it does not say, what it has not said yet or what it contradicts. The artists taking part in 'Pass It On.' *Private Stories, Public Histories* are specifically interested in these limits. As they

17_Shaun Pett, 'Mois de la Photo: Making Dense of the Photograph in the Web Era,' www.theguardian.com/artanddesign/2015/sep/15/mois-de-la-photo-making-sense-photography

18_Digital Wondering 04, f-stop-leipzig.de/en/digital-wondering-04/ (accessed on 20 August 2021)

19_Jean Baudrillard, *The System of Objects* (London: Verso, 1996), p. 86.

20_Michel Foucault, *The Archaeology of Knowledge* (New York: Routledge, 2002), p. 134.

are the initiators of the process of the archive and art work production (which are tightly interconnected if not indistinguishable), they build from within these gaps. They are aware that the materials do not contain what they exclude. And thus the artists bring in their points of view, methods, and tools to produce what has not been there.

THE ARCHIVE *ONETHIRTY*

OneThirty, one minute and thirty seconds, is the journalistic term for the average length of time allotted to a story in a news block to convey all the essential information about an event.

The work on the series *OneThirty* began in February 2011, after a stay in Athens for an exhibition at the Goethe Institute. Daily demonstrations took place on Syntagma Square in the Greek capital. The atmosphere was very tense and at the same time the news channels were full of reports of protests from North African countries. All this prompted a turning point in my artistic work and I started the project *OneThirty* which deals with the uprisings and unrests around the world. Since then, I have set up my camera in front of my television screen every day to take photos of news images and to use these as a basis for the hybrid photo series *OneThirty*, which eventually led to the idea for The Archive *OneThirty*.

The Production Process of the Photographs for *OneThirty*

Every day, television coverage presents us with drastic images of various protest movements, political events, violent attacks and civil war scenes, and every day they are put into new perspective by new images and new events. Every day for the past ten years, I have taken photos of the daily news, showing worldwide protests, reactions, and their consequences. I print these photos on a very porous, slightly toned drawing paper and rework each one with exclusively white and black water-soluble color. I paint over some parts to draw attention to the key scene; figures are traced and emerge from the blur. Sometimes I put the prints in a bathtub, so that the printer ink runs out and the photographed person/event is only rudimentarily visible and I have to rebuild the scene from scratch. The overpainting process traces and emphasizes the fleeting, instantaneous events. These reworked images are finally photographed again to convert the analog process back to a digital one.

All these artistic interventions are intended to bring the media images to a standstill, back to my consciousness and to make visible what can only be imprecisely identified in the speed and blur of reporting. Due to the lack of high quality of these media images the documented scenes appear indistinct, as if sedimented. People appear as interchangeable and lose their individuality. Human gestures seem to freeze into general ciphers of resistance, violence, power, failure and victory. The Archive *OneThirty* is not arranged hierarchically. Most of the people depicted in the media images are unknown—simply people on the street—but a few are familiar to the public. In the archive they are all rendered equal by the same artistic treatment (framing) and by consecutive numbering. I am interested in what emerges from the hundreds

Monika Huber

of still images qua repetition, blurring and reduction as image grammar and how media images are used to generate attention and engagement in politics.

The Material of The Archive *OneThirty*

In December 2010, the 'Jasmine Revolution' began with demonstrations in Tunisia. This was an enormously powerful impetus for many people in most North African countries to publicly express their displeasure with the existing regimes, and to demand democracy and human rights. The 'Arab Spring' seemed to offer hope for many people and the protests spread across the North African continent. In this situation, anyone who owned a cellphone could become a reporter, capturing events in quick, blurred images. TV stations and social media broadcast live these cellphone videos of the self-proclaimed reporters, so that every day there were new images of the uprisings, and the protests. It was a relentless media coverage and documentation of the moments of killing and dying. 24 hours a day, one revolution after another was broadcast in various countries—it seemed to go like wildfire throughout the world.

The way of reporting, the use of images whose blurriness implied authenticity and the speed of sharing the images on social networks had a surprising effect and was a new type of documentary image. The philosopher Judith Butler attaches particular importance to what constitutes the 'material' in the waging of war and 'whether cameras and their images can be counted as a part of the extended materiality of a war?'[1] This new visual reality, shared mainly on social media and in the news, had a great influence on the protest movements and drove them.

These media images drew me into events that were taking place far away. I saw protests, street fights, civil war-like scenes, thousands of people crowded on the streets and public squares: 'Tahrir,' 'Taksim,' 'Maidan' became the symbols of protest and resistance. The media images were omnipresent, haunting, disturbing, touching. Even I as a spectator was not spared. In reports about the Syrian civil war, some images were very brutal and disturbing. Susan Sontag writes in her book Regarding the pain of others: 'photos influence us in what disasters and crises we pay attention to, what we care about, and ultimately how we judge these conflicts.'[2] And also: photos 'haunt us and never let us go.'[3]

The Structure of The Archive *OneThirty*

The archive of the broadcasted media images currently comprises about 40,000 photos from which I selected 700 for The Archive *OneThirty*, as both hybrid

1_Tom Holert, *Image Counter Image* (Munich: Haus der Kunst, 2012), pp. 33, 35, quotes Judith Butler, *Frames of War. When is Life Grievable?* (London and New York: Verso, 2010).

2_Susan Sontag, *Das Leiden anderer betrachten* (Frankfurt a.M.: Fischer Taschenbuch Verlag, 2010), pp. 121–22.

3_Sontag, *Das Leiden anderer betrachten*, p. 104.

photographs and as source material for further videos and installations. The Archive *OneThirty* is intended as an artistic concept, as a long-term documentary to show global political and social change from the perspective of Western news media. It can be read like a walk through the politically motivated events of the last ten years.

The archive material—provided with an index (#worknumber_date) and stored in a digital database—functions as a 'toolbox.' All images can be linked and associated with search terms and further information. The contents in The Archive *OneThirty* include reworked media images in different editing versions, links to their sources, as well the date of shooting, the date of editing, the country in which they were photographed and important information about the event delivered on the day of shooting. Further deposited search terms include people, woman, man, country, protest, war, weapons, head, foot, arms up, smoke, blur, street, gestures, movement, text and so on. Particularly unusual search terms such as 'from above' and 'from behind,' which describe the camera's perspective, are also included. In this way, new connections can be found between images of different countries and times of recording. This allows new points of view to be revealed and combines artistic, aesthetic, historical, and political aspects.

Oliver Zyboc writes in his article 'Public Image' (2017) in the art magazine *Kunstforum International*, that medial experience means that different people in different places perceive the same thing at the same moment.

> This also exposes the experience that the difference between 'real' and 'fake,' 'true' and 'false,' between 'real' and 'unreal,' in short: between 'authenticity' and 'staging,' has been blurred by the media.[4]

Each new image added to the archive must be verified.

I am aware that archives are not static entities and sometimes need to be corrected. I am also aware that with every entry in the archive, the opposite opinion can also be added. It is very difficult to judge all this objectively, because the assessment always depends on the viewpoint of the person looking at it. While working on the archive, I have further noted gaps due to a lack of reporting. These occur, on the one hand, because certain events may not be reported for censorship reasons and on the other hand because I cannot document all events one hundred percent, despite the abundance of daily news material. Gaps notwithstanding, reporting and its archiving are absolutely necessary for capturing and remembering events, both to counteract the speed of reporting and to perceive connections.

4_Oliver Zyboc, 'Public Image,' *Kunstforum International* 246 (2017), p. 54.

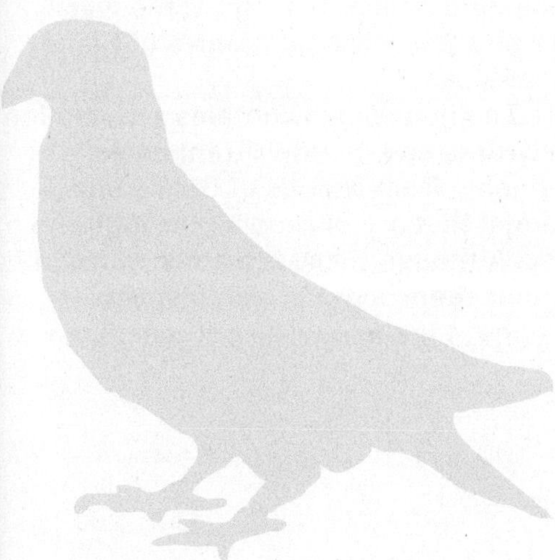

THE ARCHIVAL SPACE OF HERENGRACHT H401

Artistic Research as Productive Archiving

Introduction

Herengracht 401 (H401), until 2019 known as Castrum Peregrini, originates in a hermetic community of artists and scholars formed in Amsterdam in the years 1942–1945, during the German occupation of the Netherlands. Managed by a private foundation, over the past thirteen years the house was transformed into a cultural center with a hybrid structure of residency spaces, musealized interiors, a room for small events, and offices. Interwoven throughout the various spaces at Herengracht 401 is a cluster of archives and collections. There is first of all Gisèle's archive, which in itself is made up of many archival collections: a collection of letters she has received from her vast global network of friends. She stored them in a built-in fire-proof safe in her studio and sorted them alphabetically with type-writer-written lists pasted to the doors for a quick find. To navigate her studio there are the lists of drawings and paintings, numbers referring to drawers and boxes where to find them, with a floorplan to indicate their location. Her agendas and journals form a separate category. Photographs by and of Gisèle span her whole life and are neatly sorted on system cards with a rough categorization: friends, family, Greece, and so on. It gets a bit wilder when it comes to 'stuff' Gisèle deemed interesting—from newspaper clippings to exhibition folders and random notes on loose sheets of paper. These are kept in a separate storage room since after her death we opened up her studio space to public visits and simply needed to create space for that. The basement of H401 is also the archive of the Castrum Peregrini Press, spanning the period from 1950 to 2008. It is also the place where the Wolfgang Frommel archive used to be kept and it holds some unsorted archives in moving boxes or suitcases by individuals from the circle around Wolfgang Frommel. On the 3rd floor, with its original interior from the 1940s, is for instance the archive of hand writings and clandestine publications from the war years and the personal archive of Claus Victor Bock.

The house also contains a collection of artworks and (handwritten) books and poems from friends of Gisèle and Frommel that are spread all through the house. Although there is a small storage room for them, most are on display throughout the house, all of them listed

Lars Ebert

in a database. Very specific sub-collections such as the personal letters of her husband Arnold D'Ailly to Gisèle and the personal items she kept in memory of him are more or less consciously embedded in her interiors, as are those of the Dutch poet A. Roland Holst, the Dutch artist Joep Nicolas and others close to her. Displayed in the interiors you will also find other small collections of a specific nature, like the ethnographic collection of Gisèle's father or textiles and *objets trouvés* that refer to certain chapters in her life: the years on the Greek island of Paros, family paraphernalia from Austria, war-related 'shrines' or from specific travels, or interests such as circles of all kinds, a motif Gisèle was obsessed with.

At first sight, this dense cluster of smaller collections seems to have grown organically since 1942, but on reflection it was with the purpose of self-representation of a group and its individual members. The conventional purposes of an archive, functional archive and memory archive, can both be recognized in the various collections.[1] The collection of circles and circle images, for instance, had a functional purpose in the artistic work of Gisèle, for she used them in making her artworks, whereas family documents or letters from deceased friends were archived as a memory. They showcase the power of an archive in which those who are in charge decide, quite literally, what and who is included and what and who is excluded from it, who and what is represented in their memory-archive and how. The three upper floors at Herengracht 401 are historic ensembles with the above identified archives sometimes embedded in them. I therefore propose to see the house of Herengracht 401 in its totality as an 'archival space.'

The Histories of H401 in a Nutshell

In the autumn of 1999, I entered Herengracht 401 in Amsterdam for the first time. The labyrinth of rooms full of objects and stories fascinated me. At the time, the center of this hidden universe was undoubtedly the artist Gisèle (1912–2013), who loved to show visitors around and tell stories of a world of friendship and art. The way Gisèle looked at things was full of wonder, and she could spark a sense of amazement at the beauty of small things. I learned that Gisèle and

1_See Assmann's contribution in this book, 'The Archive as a Laboratory of the New,' p. 30–34.

two elderly men were living in the house at that time, Manuel Goldschmidt and Claus Bock, who were connected by their shared experience of war, persecution, and survival on one floor of the house during the German occupation of the Netherlands. The central figure in their stories from the past was the parlor scholar Wolfgang Frommel (1902–1986), whom they adored.

The stories about Frommel and Gisèle were all somehow glorious. Although they also told of hunger, police raids and loss in war and concentration camps, they always ended in the wondrous survival through friendship, reading or writing poetry and if the real story had not ended well, then at least that loss had not been in vain. The memory of someone who had not survived, such as Vincent Weyand (1921–1945), who died in the concentration camp Buchenwald, was celebrated like that of a saint. Trauma seemingly did not exist. The horrors of the past were instead sublimated in rituals of commemoration (e.g., poetry readings) and by awarding meaning to suffering and death (e.g., memory books). Similar to ancient Greek tragedies, there was no space for trauma, only for tragedy, pain and glory, gods and heroes, poetry and friendship. The post-war generation of friends around Frommel and Gisèle also internalized these stories, that functioned as a founding and binding mythology of their own community, as an alternative form of belonging in a post-war society of petty-bourgeois values, but also later, as an alternative to the alternatives that came forth from the student movement.

When the last Jewish person in hiding from the war, Claus Bock, died in January 2008, the literary magazine that was published by the survivors under the title *Castrum Peregrini* since 1951, ceased to exist. The foundation's director since 2004, Michael Defuster, had formulated the mission of turning the hermetic and anachronistic activities of a community that had dissolved (with the exception of a few individuals and Gisèle who had survived them all) into outward oriented activities that would make a relevant contribution to contemporary society. This did not go without a struggle against the remains of the old circle that perceived opening up as betrayal. But with patience and persistence and building up a new network of individuals and institutional collaborators, Defuster managed to transform H401, which I witnessed as a colleague and friend.

The first public interdisciplinary thematic year program took shape in 2009. The yearly programs of exhibitions, symposia, publications, theatre, and so on, tried to investigate areas such as fanaticism, freedom, friendship, and cultural memory. The activities reflected upon these themes on an abstract level so as to allow for discussions of broad relevance. The heroic history of the house provided narrative anchors toward topical issues. Its interiors, presented as a carefully curated narrative of deceased heroes, became conversation pieces by means of which social problems of today could be discussed.

The main source of this narrative were the few witnesses still alive or texts that had been published by the

2_Annet Mooij, *De eeuw van Gisèle: Mythe en werkelijkheid van een kunstenares* (Amsterdam: De Bezige Bij, 2018).

3_Wolfgang Frommel and Friedrich W. Buri, *Briefwechsel 1933–1984*, ed. Stephan Bischoff (Göttingen: Wallstein Verlag, 2017); Joke Haverkorn van Rijsewijk, *Entfernte Erinnerungen an W.* (Würzburg: Daniel Osthof Verlag, 2013); Marita Keilson-Lauritz, 'Die Liebe der Kentauren: Deutscher Widerstand in den besetzten Niederlanden im Umkreis des Castrum Peregrini,' in *Kentaurenliebe: Seitenwege der Männerliebe im 20. Jahrhundert*, ed. Marita Keilson-Lauritz (Hamburg: Männerschwarm Verlag, 2013); Frank Ligtvoet, *In de schaduw van de meester: Seksueel misbruik in de kring van Wolfgang Frommel*, www.vn.nl/in-de-schaduw-van-de-meester-seksueel-misbruik-in-de-kring-van-wolfgang-frommel/.

community in their magazine *Castrum Peregrini*. Therefore, we felt a growing need for a critically distanced understanding of H401 and in 2011 we took the initiative to have a biography written of Gisèle's life. Annet Mooij accepted the task, and in 2012 she began to scrutinize the existing archives and interview eye-witnesses. The biography was finally published in September 2018.[2] The long and intensive research period had a cathartic side effect. It served as a frame for the post-war generation in which they reflected on their own experiences. These ranged from a gay history perspective (Keilson-Lauritz, 2013), to a first critically distanced albeit empathic ego-document (Haverkorn, 2013), the editing of source material (Bischoff, 2017), to accounts of sexual abuse (Ligtvoet, 2017).[3] The biography of Mooij incorporated these accounts into the life story of Gisèle. The one-dimensional, heroic story, as it was told from within the Castrum Peregrini community before, has now grown into a multivocal complex of stories that ranges from heroic to traumatic.[4] We began to realize that the materiality of the house with its embedded archives represented the ambiguity of heroes, perpetrators, and victims next to one another, sometimes even in personal union. This newly discovered polyphony or even cacophony seemed to represent the *condition humaine* in all its consequences. It provided for a radically new and challenging frame for the cultural activities of H401.[5]

Ensemble, Collection, Storage: H401 as an Archival Space

Whoever has lived or worked with Gisèle knew her passion for archiving. She explained that with a story from her childhood, when, on her mother's family castle in Austria she loved to help her uncle in the family archive. When she visited the castle later in life, the library and the archive kept their magic attraction. In her home in Amsterdam she was no less of an archivist. This had only an indirect impact on her art and was in the first place motivated by the urge to keep memories alive through holding on to documents, books, artworks, and *objets trouvés*. As Gisèle was not at all a nostalgic person—what was gone was gone, who was dead was dead—it seems that she felt an obligation to keep appreciating the gifts of a life she was privileged to live. In that sense her obsession to keep things may have had a spiritual component, linked to her faith. But that is speculation. What we know is that she never threw anything away. Everything was kept, from a menu cart of a restaurant to a leaf found on the way to the restaurant and the letters of the dear person at the table. In preparation for an exhibition at the NIOD in 2008 we were surprised to find a clandestine note from the wartime that stated in red: destroy after reading. It was meticulously archived. In some cases her drive to archive traces of her life took more the form of paradigmatic collections, such as with stones, seashells, feathers, and dried leaves stored in baskets, boxes, and drawers: fisherman's cork with

4_The shocking accounts of sexual abuse triggered the constitution of an independent investigation commissioned by *Castrum Peregrini* and chaired by retired judge Frans Bauduin. It resulted in an extensive report published at h401.org/wp-content/uploads/CASTRUMONDERZOEK.pdf.

5_Please refer to Lars Ebert, www.roots-routes.org/the-moralistic-turn-working-through-trauma-in-a-climate-of-outrage-the-case-study-of-castrum-peregrini-by-lars-ebert/

fisherman's cork, colored glass with colored glass, and so on. But often these *objets trouvés* are grouped together as still lives on window sills or as furniture displays to tell a story.[6] Many visitors would agree that these 'collections are like works of art, because the function of a collection is not the restauration of the context of origin but the creation of a new context.'[7] Then there were those objects on lists: clothes, artist's supplies, letters received, letters to be written, and so on. Lists are omnipresent in Gisèle's belongings, put on top of boxes to describe their content, pasted on the inside of closet doors, collected in a binder with a list of all lists on top. There are also schematic lists, so to speak: floor plans of the rooms of the house, of the studio, for instance, with numbers on them and an index that lists where to find what. Looking for something specific can therefore feel like a scavenger hunt. As Georges Perec writes:

> My problem with classification is that they don't last; hardly have I finished putting things into an order before that order is obsolete. Like everyone else, I presume, I am sometimes seized by a mania for arranging things. The sheer number of things needing to be arranged and the near-impossibility of distributing them according to any truly satisfactory criteria mean that I never finally manage it, that the arrangements I end up with are temporary and vague, and hardly be any more effective than the original anarchy.[8]

This might as well have been written by Gisèle. She may have thought that there is triumph in trying and went on to rearrange the order of her paintings, documents, and objects: chronologically, alphabetically, thematically, sorted by technique or size. It kept changing and the present situation is nothing more than the state reached at the moment she deceased.

Gisèle was not the only inhabitant that left traces of archival fever at Herengracht 401. The other main figure in the history of Herengracht 401 was Wolfgang Frommel, who collected books and manuscripts during his extensive travels all over Europe. Often, they were meant for publication in the literary review Castrum Peregrini or to stock the Castrum Peregrini Archive (which is distinct to that of Gisèle), that focused on the lives of followers of Stefan George and Wolfgang Frommel.

The lifetime partner, assistant and later heir of Wolfgang Frommel, Manuel Goldschmidt focused his professional and personal efforts on this archive. It has been kept inaccessible for use by anyone else outside the inner circle around Wolfgang Frommel and later Manuel Goldschmidt and Claus Victor Bock. Ulrich Raulff for instance writes in his celebrated book *Kreis ohne Meister* in 2009 that due to the closed archive of Castrum Peregrini Press he was not able to add an important chapter of his book.[9] The archive had become an instrument of power to determine who can interpret history, and how. In the struggle between the new generation around Defuster and the founding generation around Goldschmidt the archive had become a sort of proxy war. Goldschmidt had taken the archive of Castrum Peregrini Press away from the foundation's premises as

6_On on paradigm and syntagma see Ernst van Alphen, *Staging the Archive: Art and Photography in the Age of New Media* (London: Reaktion Books, 2014), pp. 10–11.

7_Van Alphen, *Staging the Archive*, p. 60.

8_Georges Perec, 'Notes Concerning the Objects that Are on My Worktable' [1985], in *Species of Space and other Pieces*, ed. and trans. John Sturrock (London: Penguin, 1999), p. 146.

a reaction to the new direction in order to prevent the openness and thereby the perceived 'betrayal' of the hermetic group around Frommel that he feared. This resulted in a lawsuit of many years between the foundation Castrum Peregrini and the legal heir of Wolfgang Frommel, the former director Manuel Goldschmidt and, after his death, his legal heirs, the Wolf van Cassel Stichting. Today Gisèle and her friends from the wartime are all dead. I have described above how some of their archives are still embedded in the interiors in which they lived. These interiors have recently been recognized as 'meest bijzondere Interieur Ensembles' (most remarkable interior ensembles; LE) by the Rijksdienst voor het Cultureel Erfgoed (Cultural Heritage Agency) which declared the apartments designed by Gisèle in the 1940s, 1950s and 1960s as 'unique in the Netherlands.' They are unique because they tell a story, or rather because Gisèle tells us a story through them.

> The objects stored are the result of 'gathering together signs,' which means each object is not only stored because of its singularity, but because of what it means and does in relation to the other stored objects.[10]

It is because these interiors tell stories, that we can see them as an archival space. As this ensemble is motivated and structured as self-representation of their protagonists (on the one side Gisèle and her circle including Arnold D'Ailly, Joep Nicolas, Roland Holst, Max Beckmann and others, on the other side Wolfgang Frommel and his circle, including Manuel Goldschmidt and Claus Victor Bock) it cannot be used or read uncritically. We must always look at what is not there and why the things that are there are arranged in the way they are.In all its subjectivity this memory fabric, this syntax, is clearly constructed from an archival impulse, with archival methods and a struggle with these methods as well as a struggle between the urge for completeness (Gisèle throwing nothing away; Frommel collecting as much as possible) and the urge to be selective about what to highlight in one's own biography and what not. In Gisèle's case the latter is also a matter of what is on display on top of a cupboard or what stays in its drawers. Frommel and Goldschmidt had a more institutionalized view on the archive, which was by definition locked. Only they selected what would be published, by whom and how.

Herengracht 401 has always been seen as a house: a safe house, a publishing house, the house of Gisèle, and more recently as an unsafe house of sexual abuse. Today it is a house full of memories stored and collected in a historic 'ensemble,' including some real archives. In short, this house is an archival space in many respects. The challenge that faces us now is how does this archival space speak to us, how can we 'read' it and how can its archival contents be made productive?

How to Read the Archive from a Present-day Perspective

Ernst van Alphen writes: 'The archival collection can become self-enclosed, thanks to which its relation to the past is severed.'[11] This certainly is the case with

9_Ulrich Raulff, *Kreis ohne Meister: Das Nachleben Stefan Georges* (Munich: C.H. Beck, 2009), p. 24.

10_Van Alphen, *Staging the Archive*, p. 55.

11_Van Alphen, *Staging the Archive*, p. 60.

the archival collections of H401 that are staged and curated by its late inhabitants. To access the past that they represent, a certain knowledge of their collectors and their times, a certain experience or a method of deconstruction is needed. Or to speak with Walter Benjamin, a moment of recognition: 'Because the image of the past is lost in each new moment that does not recognize its presence as one of its own concerns.'[12] The relation between the original users, authors or readers of the collections at H401 in the past and us today is severed and prevents us from understanding it like 'there and then' and also from applying it 'here and now.' Unless we have the right set of semiotic tools, we may find this gap rather difficult to bridge. We need to piece together a puzzle of endless amounts of information to experience the world as it was back then. Unintendedly Gisèle had touched upon this problem when she noted in her diary:

> We all carry the Castrum story in us. It has settled in the corners of memory, taken various shapes that we bring to the surface from time to time, from this we can piece a puzzle. And then it will gain a face and others will look at it as one does at a portrait. But everyone will see something else.[13]

In the spirit of Benjamin, we could fail to see anything meaningful at all, other than an abstraction or an illusion as the understanding of an object from the past is fundamentally different today in the context of the world we live in. In addition to the difference between different temporalities, I also feel the gap between cultural realms when for instance reading a poem in the German tradition of George firmly rooted in Catholicism on the one side and the Dutch cultural realm rooted in Protestantism on the other side.

Making the Archive Productive through Artistic Research

In our ambition to maintain a productive space rather than a time capsule we kept working with artists to see how this severed relationship to the past could be bridged with artistic tools. This led us to look at the artist as a researcher and how creative inquiry might produce new knowledge and create currency in an archival space that otherwise seemed a container with the remains of a distant past. In addition to (art-)historical research—and that of other disciplines—we specifically looked at research through the practice of art. Bruno Latour makes a sharp distinction between research and science, which is helpful to understand the distinct role of the artist as a researcher:

> Science is certainty, research is uncertainty. Science is supposed to be cold, straight and detached, research is warm, involving and risky. Science puts an end to the vagaries of human disputes, research fuels controversies by more controversies. Science produces objectivity by escaping as much as possible from the shackles of ideology, passions and emotions, research feeds on all those as so many handles to render familiar new objects of enquiry.[14]

12_Walter Benjamin, *On the Concept of History*, www.sfu.ca/~andrewf/CONCEPT2.html.

13_Gisèle wrote her diary from Paros in English. Janina Pigaht (2016) quotes from it in 'Herengracht 401: Een van de jongens,' eenvandejongens.nl/projecten/herengracht-401/.

14_Bruno Latour, 'From the World of Science to that of Research?,' *Science* 280, no. 5361, pp. 208–09.

One could describe the specificities of artistic research as 'spasmic, interdisciplinary probes, haphazard cognitive investigations, dissipating interaction, and imaginary archiving.[15] A view that Henk Slager acknowledges when he writes:

> That form of research cannot be channelled through rigid academic-scientific guidelines dealing with generalisation, duplication and quantification, since it engages in the unique, the qualitative, the particular, and the local.[16]

In other words: artistic research, or better, research based on the practice of art, does not assume a fixed set of questions but develops its method in relation to a specific situation or a specific context under scrutiny. If these situations and contexts are archives, then a mindset free of predetermined assumptions—stemming for instance from the moral consensus of the contemporary art world—is as important for the artist as it is for the spectator in order to prevent a self-directed appreciation of theory or cultural critique to confirm one's own truth. As an alternative concept to truth-seeking morality and theory-based practices, artistic research that works with archival matter, form and fiction can produce new knowledge, and hence unexpected access to the past. If this creative research is open-ended and autonomous, reading the archival fabric of places such as H401 can overcome the limited understanding of the historically distant spectator and become productive. It creates new perspectives and the possibility for contemporaries to relate to something that would otherwise be incomprehensible in its complexity caused by historical and cultural distance and its ambiguity: being this and that.

The projects of artistic research which I will discuss below support the thesis of Robert Pfaller that the material work of the art—notwithstanding its conceptual backbones—is the only instrument of artists that makes it possible to discover something that they did not know or did not intend at the outset of the process of creative inquiry and consequently create knowledge through making art.[17]

Artists that have worked at H401 and have used its archival space for their inquiries and works have made the archive productive through their artistic research. They critically work with references so that images and objects become something 'other.' They do not restore an original meaning, but rather add meaning or alter it in hindsight.

Three Projects of Artistic Research at H401

As Ernst van Alphen writes:

> Contemporary art practices modelled on the archive tend to make use of either one of two media, art forms or genres in order to investigate the principles and effects of the archive. The first one is the medium of installation, the second one the artist's book.[18]

Amie Dicke's work at Herengracht 401 will exemplify the book, and the work of Ronit Porat will exemplify the medium of installation she uses. The third example, of Renée Turner's work, will add a

15_Sarat Maharaj, 'Unfinishable Sketch of "An Object in 4D: Scenes of Artistic Research,"' *Artistic Research*, ed. A.W. Balkema and H. Slager (Amsterdam and New York, 2004), p. 50.

16_Henk Slager, *The Pleasure of Research* (Ostfildern: Hatje Cantz, 2015), p. 29.

17_Robert Pfaller, *Die blitzenden Waffen: Über die Macht der Form* (Frankfurt a.M., 2020).

18_Van Alphen, *Staging the Archive*, p. 18.

medium that Van Alphen does not mention explicitly: the online artwork in which the archival tool of a database is combined with fiction. All three examples depend on the use of photography.

Photography occupies a central place in this discussion. Many contemporary archival installations are installations of photographs and many of the artist's books consist of collections of photographs. This preference for photographic archives in either book form or in the form of an installation can be understood as informed by the intimate mutual relation between the archival medium and the medium of photography.[19]

It seems that these artists have used photography to leave aside their own viewpoint, their own personal filter, which blurs the view on the object. Engaging a photographer to isolate an image from its context enables them to establish a mediated relationship that makes it possible for them to 'own' the object for a genuine creative act: for breaking, for bending, for blending. This 'intimacy' with photography is a crucial step towards the creation of something new that transcends the archival context.

Amie Dicke

Amie Dicke's participation in the first exhibition at H401 (then still Castrum Peregrini), AURA, curated by Michiel van Iersel, marked the beginning of a six-year-long artistic engagement with the stories and the material heritage at Herengracht 401. Dicke was fascinated by what disappeared through material decay, by that which is hidden in plain sight in interiors and archives or that which reveals itself through being erased by her own hands. Dicke herself used the term the 'unmade,' which integrates two interconnected opposites and can be understood with the image of a palimpsest: by adding a layer, another one disappears, by erasing a layer an unexpected one appears (Dicke 2011).

Her first work for the AURA exhibition was the site-specific *Claustrophobic*. The exhibition marked a rite of passage from the 'old' and inward-looking Castrum Peregrini, mainly a publishing house, to the newly defined cultural activities that were directed toward the world. Van Iersel had asked a group of artists to reflect on what it means to transform a place into something new and whether the aura that was felt there would pertain when 're-produced,' with a reference to Walter Benjamin.[20] Dicke was fascinated by the apartment in which Claus Victor Bock had died in 2008. The last Jewish survivor from the wartime period of Castrum Peregrini had come to live at Herengracht 401 again after retiring. Before the apartment was about to be dismantled, Dicke set out to cast a death mask over the interior before it disappeared by applying a layer of agricultural plastic

19_Van Alphen, *Staging the Archive*, p. 19.

20_In his essay *Das Kunstwerk im Zeitalter seiner technischen Reproduzierbarkeit*, first published in Paris in 1936, Walter Benjamin argues that an artwork loses its aura once reproduced.

over the furniture, covering and wrapping everything in the room. Only then was the apartment emptied and left a transparent plastic shape of what was no longer there, reflecting the essence or aura of a place, an 'unmade' space.

Later Dicke investigated the former hiding apartment, which today still is largely unchanged from what it was during the years of occupation. The last inhabitant of the apartment was Manuel Goldschmidt, the life-time companion of Frommel. Dicke started to wrap furniture, books and objects in golden emergency blankets so as to safe them, just like victims of an accident are saved by emergency blankets from the destructive influences of weather or environment. She soon undid this wrapping exercise as the 'poetics' of the space had helped her understand the actual possibility for her creative intervention, the cracks and the in-between spaces of the historic interior. There was no need for drawing attention to any kind of emergency or to the decay, the threatening loss of matter. Instead, the overlooked little slots between carpet and wall, the cracks in the furniture and plaster of the ceiling, the wormholes in a table, those were the overlooked parts of the interior, maybe the ones that held the genuine being and uniqueness of the space. Dicke meticulously and with utter care filled those mostly tiny spaces with gold foil. Upon entering the apartment, nothing was visible. But just like eyes have to adjust to darkness, they had to adjust to this subtle grid of golden fault lines that

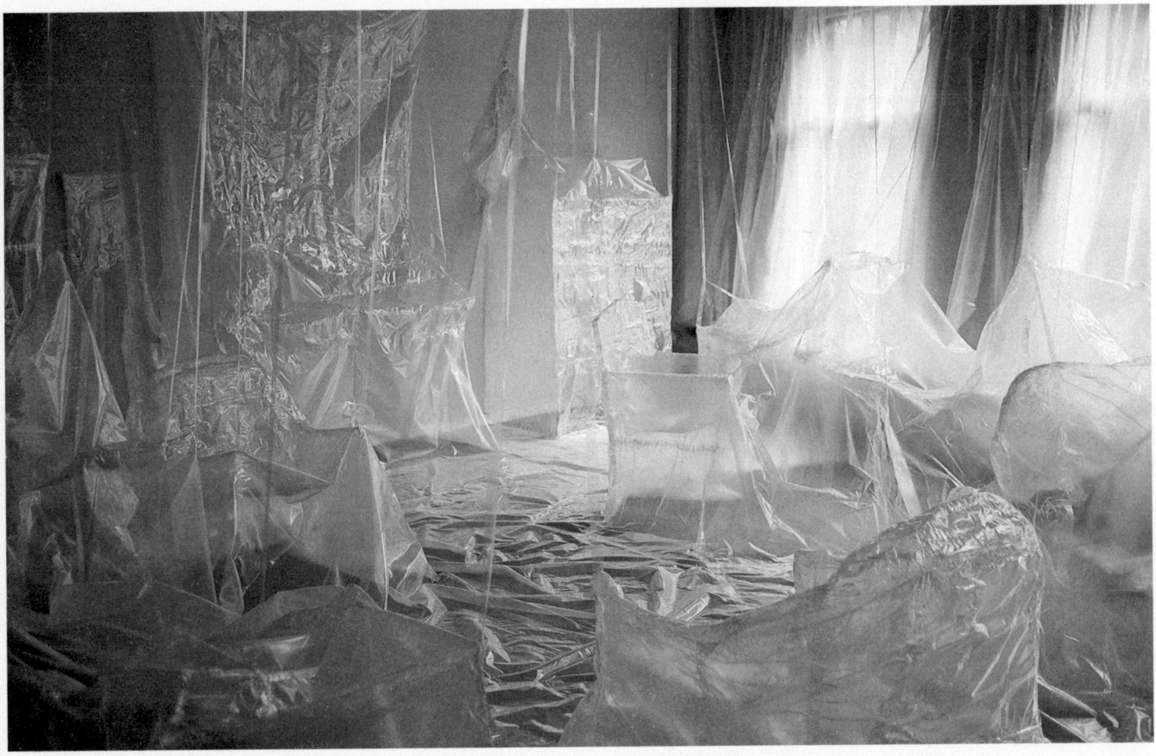

Amie Dicke, *Claustrophobic*, 2009

defined the space anew and showed the substance matter of overlooked absence.

These works were set out as a material and spatial investigation. In a third stage they led to Dicke's engagement with the house from an archival perspective, now in the apartment and the studio of Gisèle. Supported by the Mondrian Fund she worked there for a year. Like an archaeologist she engaged a professional photographer to document details of the interiors that revealed original colors, when for instance frames were removed from their place on the wall. Dust functioned like the color of a silk print, revealing the artwork when the screen is taken off the paper. She collected images from various archives throughout the house, by having them photographed in the same way she did with the material structures of the furniture, the curtains, tapestry, upholstery, books and the

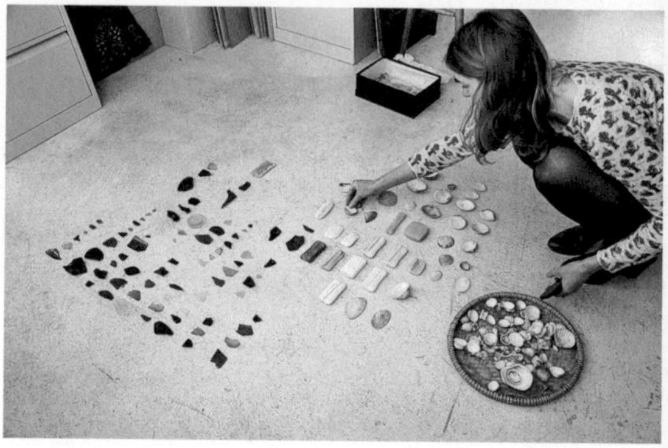

Amie Dicke, piecing together objects from the studio of Gisèle's studio

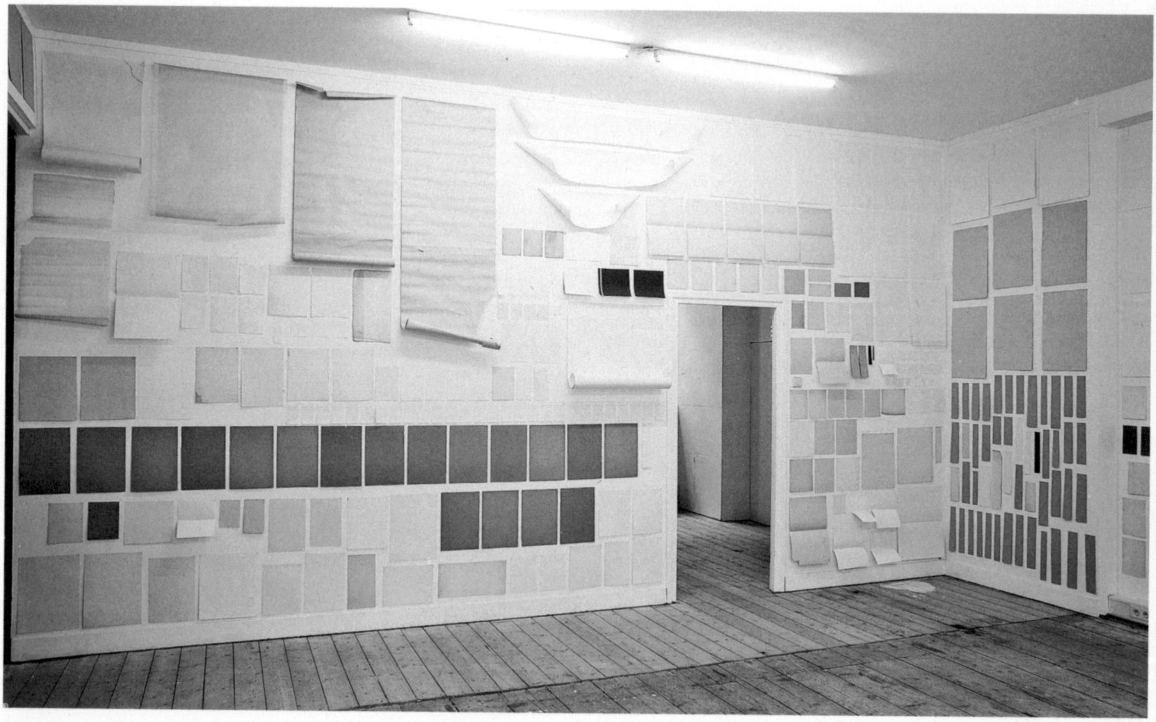

Amie Dicke, *Inbetween*, 2009, photo: Sander Tiedema

endless numbers of *objets trouvés*. A special focus lay on the little notes that Gisèle had used more and more the older she got to compensate for the loss of her own memory and for labelling all kinds of objects, such as an empty video tape with the words 'nothing to see here.' It is exactly where we commonly assume that nothing is to be seen that Dicke's art makes us see. She established a photographic account on a website and ultimately made a final selection for an artist's book, arranging her finds like an archivist but using an ordering system that only reveals itself by engaging in its flow of images. Henk Slager writes about this approach:

> Against the Foucauldian perspective where a clear connection is made between an archiving rhetoric and the dispositive of power, artistic archiving adds the perspective of desirology: thinking in terms of new orders of affective associations, of fluid taxonomies, and above all a thinking in terms of intellectual and artistic pleasure linked to derange the symbolic order.[21]

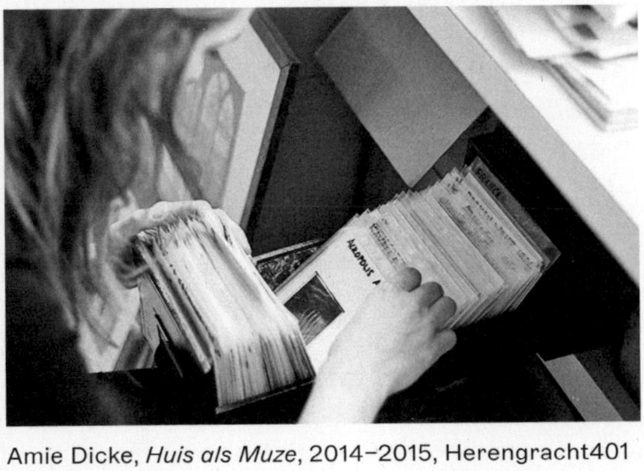

Amie Dicke, *Huis als Muze*, 2014–2015, Herengracht401

21_Henk Slager, *The Pleasure of Research*, p. 83.

In this dynamic Dicke's work could be seen as that of an 'archivist of decay' like an ancient muse bringing forgetfulness by visualizing the erasure of memory and thereby creating access to something that would have otherwise not been visible: new possibilities and meaning.

Dicke's art has brought us new insights into the value of decay. Her work illustrates that there is a case to be made for and against preservation, that each object, each space and context requires a new negotiation of its status as to be protected or as to be left to vanish or as to be used for new creations. The artworks of Dicke make me see what was always there but out of sight. For H401 they brought about a sharp perspective on the change that is needed to experience material traces of the past as 'auratic,' authentic, speaking to us today. The value of the heritage in question may best be served by wandering off the beaten track, for instance by taking the backside of a photograph as serious as its front, by removing it and putting it into a new context, and then investigating the empty spot it leaves. In this sense Dicke's work had a liberating effect for us: material heritage now not only represented the need of protection but also the possibility of something new.

Ronit Porat

Ronit Porat too committed to a long-term engagement with the historic and archival matter of the house. First during a residency in which she created new work for the H401 exhibition 'In Search of Lost Time,' curated by Ronit Eden in 2014 and later as a one-year resident of the Transhistorical Coalition between Oude Kerk, Van Loon Museum, Reinwardt Academie and H401, which hosts an artist in residence every year. Porat is a photographer by training and a tireless auto-biographer or rather an 'auto-fiction-ist.' Porat grew up in a kibbutz in the north of Israel, did her military service and studied photography. In her whole being and work she represents the tensions that come with such a background, combining deep affection for her home country with critical reflection on its violence and exclusion, suffering herself from the isolation so many of her peers feel. Her upbringing in a kibbutz, including small traumatic anecdotes, like an accident her brother had, return in her work. More broadly, Porat is interested in biographies and histories that constitute collective identities. With her own radically independent life she frees herself from those collectives that have deeply formed her and with which she still feels an empathic bond. In her work she digs into archives, brings histories and biographies to the fore in which she always inserts her own presence, and thereby breaks the plain photographic documentation with counter images, creating collages that exude an absurdist or surreal quality. Porat's work responds to Benjamin's problem of the 'aura of an artwork in times of technical reproduction' by inserting the aura from her own genuine story, her own worries, sorrows, pains, joys and her own fantasy in the aura-less archival material whose original meaning is cut off or blurred by the passing of time.

Hal Foster speaks about the content of an archive as 'found yet constructed, factual yet fictive, public yet private.'[22] In analogy with what Foster argues, Porat develops her own artistic practice on the basis of archives. During her residency at H401 she dug deep into the histories of the wartime community in hiding and into the books of Frommel and photographs from the archive, as if to free some of the biographies in them from the corset of the heroic narrative that Frommel and his circle assigned to them posthumously. In his book *Archive Fever* Derrida argues that archives demonstrate an intrinsic link between narrative and power. The word archive comes from *Arkheion*, the seat of the rulers in ancient Athens, and it is this residence of the powerful where also documents were stored.[23] This archive preserved the stories of the winners and made these stories a historical reality or scientific truth. Where the Castrum Peregrini archive preserved the truth of Frommel and his disciples, Porat intuitively focused among others on Liselotte von Gandersheim, who drowned in the North Sea just after the war had ended and on Vincent Weyand, who died in extermination camp Buchenwald. She liberated them from the corset of a hero by taking their tragicness, their vulnerability and their human smallness seriously. The collages that she produced were arranged spatially in combination with objects from the archive, text fragments from Frommel's library and some handwritten reflections of Porat

22_Hal Foster, '*An Archival Impulse,*' *October 110* (2004), pp. 3–22.

23_Jacques Derrida and Eric Prenowitz, 'Archive Fever: A Freudian Impression,' *Diacritics* 25, no. 2 (1995), pp. 9–10.

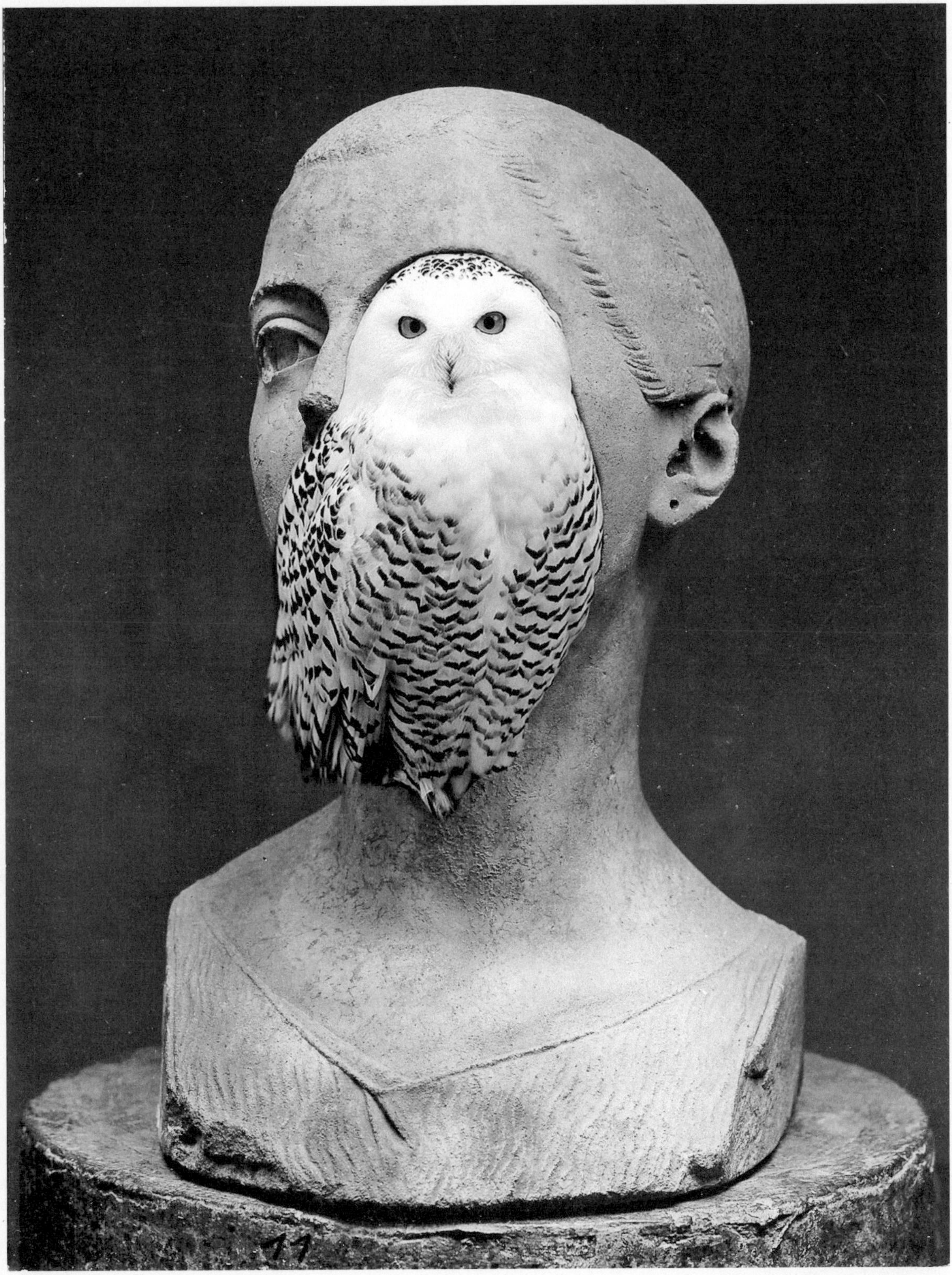

Ronit Porat, *Owl Woman*, 2012–2013

that connected them to her own life experience. Through this installation she brought to the surface unacknowledged and up till then hidden aspects of the stories told about the past of the place. Liselotte von Gandersheim, for instance, used to be seen as one of the 'founding heroes' of the wartime community. In October 1945, just months after the liberation, she tragically drowned in the North Sea. Gisèle kept an impressive commemoration landscape in black ink by her hand in a central place in her salon and a black-and-white photograph of Liselotte with a framed curl of her hair next to her bed. The first publication that publicly used the code name Castrum Peregrini after the war was a memory book for those who had not survived: Vincent Weyand, Percy Gothein and Liselotte von Gandersheim. Porat started to investigate Von Gandersheim and her death. Later, a piece published by Christiane Kuby suggested that Frommel, who took Gandersheim on the swim, trespassed military wiring, took the danger of possible mines that were not cleared yet and also that of the well-known lethal undercurrents at that part of the shore.[24] Porat herself never asked the question about what really happened or about responsibilities, but clearly brought to the surface the mechanism of turning a tragic death into a constructed and heroic narrative and thus away from a traumatic experience toward one that gave meaning to the group. It would even, much later, also be used for attempts to set up a Castrum Peregrini women's poetry reading circle in analogy to the hermetic male circle around Frommel. Porat's work amplifies that tension between the purposefully unanswered question of what has really happened and the consequences for the group that lived on with a constructed and authoritative story.

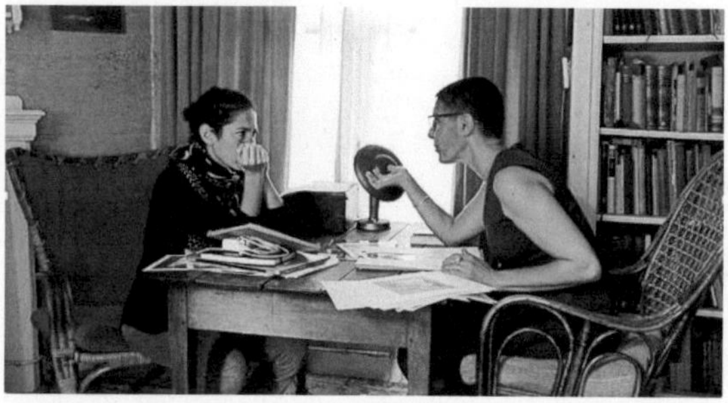

Ronit Porat with curator Ronit Eden during her residency at Herengracht 401

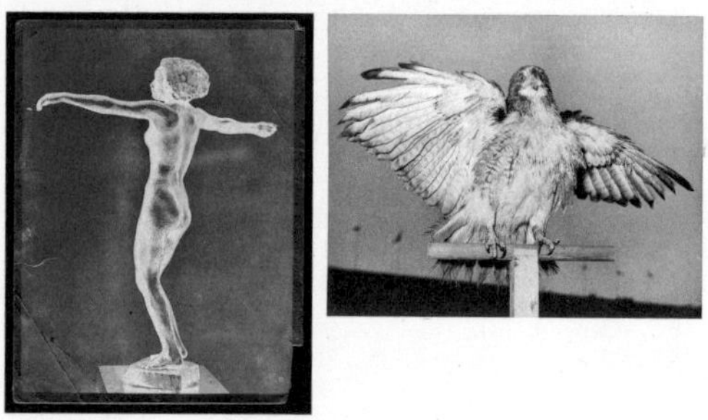

Ronit Porat, *Diptych*, 2012–2013

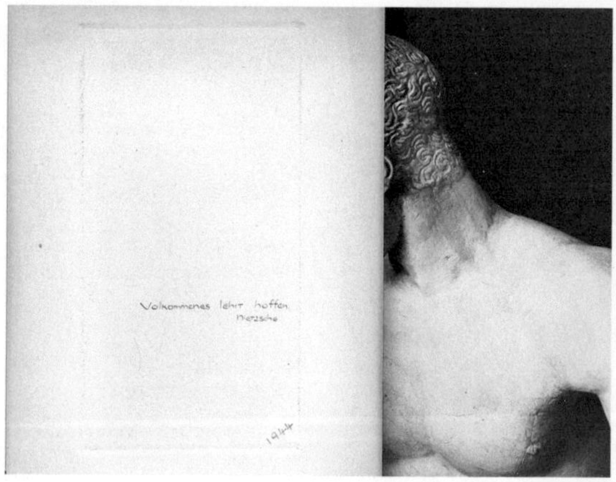

Ronit Porat, *Vollkommenes lehrt hoffen (Nietzsche)*, 2014

24_Christiane Kuby, *Mein Kind Liselotte* (2018), www.faz.net/aktuell/feuilleton/buecher/themen/als-frau-im-george-kreis-unfall-oder-fahrlaessige-toetung-15755649.html.

Porat shows that meaning-making has shaped and blurred the memory of Liselotte in a certain way. In her installation she used archival material and handwritten texts with reflections on traumatic memories from her own life. We learn how this constructed memory works through in Porat's own constructions. They make a historic social group dynamic visible by researching and showing that very dynamic in her own life and work.

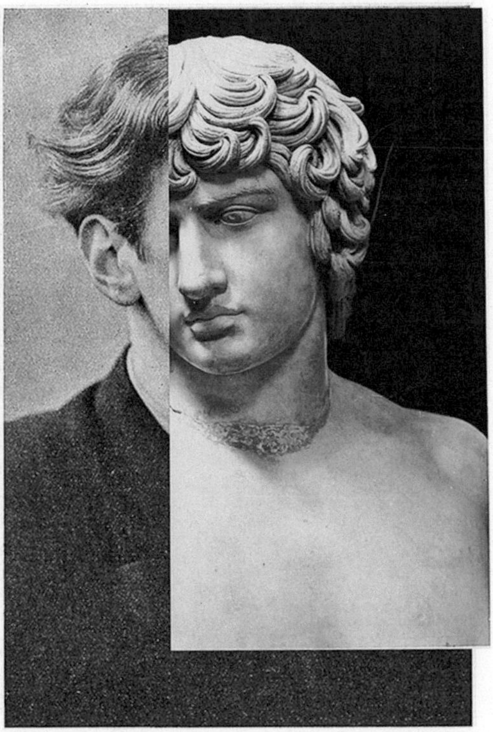

Ronit Porat, *Untitled (Antonius)*, 2014

Renée Turner

The Rotterdam-based artist, teacher and researcher Renée Turner has developed a collaborative practice since her time in the cross-disciplinary art collective Geuzen. In her work at H401 she combines various visual forms of research with online writing to explore female identity, narratives of the archive, media ecologies, and spaces of co-learning. The project *Warp and Weft of Memory* maps the wardrobe of Gisèle d'Ailly-van Waterschoot van der Gracht, as the most intimate remains of her as a person, that which was literally closest to her very being, her skin and body.[25] Fashion is treated as the medium that situated Gisèle in the world. Turner developed a digital archive of Gisèle's wardrobe as a means to reflect on her life, work, and various histories. She builds a bridge to the past by setting up an alternative archive.

Gisèle had left her wardrobe, like other collections in her apartments, in a meticulous order, with lists, labelled and categorized.

Storage is based on the accumulation of objects. Those objects are each

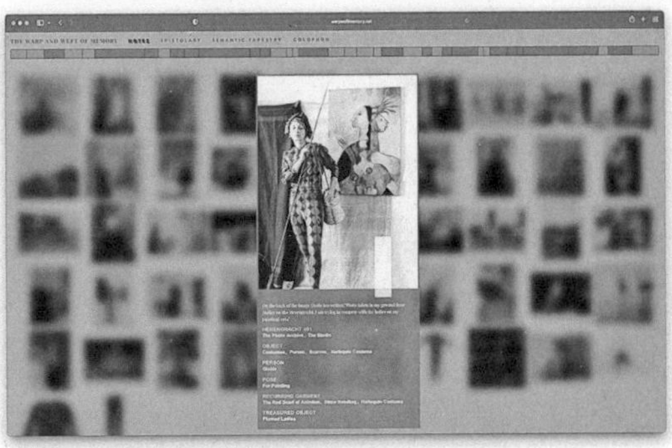

Renée Turner, www.warpweftmemory.net

25_Renée Turner, *The Warp and Weft of Memory* (2017), warpweftmemory.net/#/foreword.

complete in themselves. Objects that are part of a collection do not have that completeness. They only have significance in relation to each other; each object is different form the other objects in the collection as well as representative of the collection as such. Because each element is representative of the collection it is part of, the principle of organization of a collection is inherent to it.[26]

The web-based archive was developed on the existing structure left by Gisèle herself. Porat worked with a team of programmers, photographers, and a graphic designer who created an online database with various entry points, including Turner's own notes, which offer a very personal view on the artist's encounter with a person she meets only through her wardrobe as well as through correspondences of Turner with third persons about her project. One possibility of access for the user is the *Semantic Tapestry*, an archive of photographs sorted in interrelated taxonomies that provide an order and at the same time a possibility to become lost and wander around.

Turner's own background can be raced in the twofold approach to her project. It shows her practical impulse of putting things in order, stemming from her own roots in the DIY movement. But it also is clearly driven by her academic

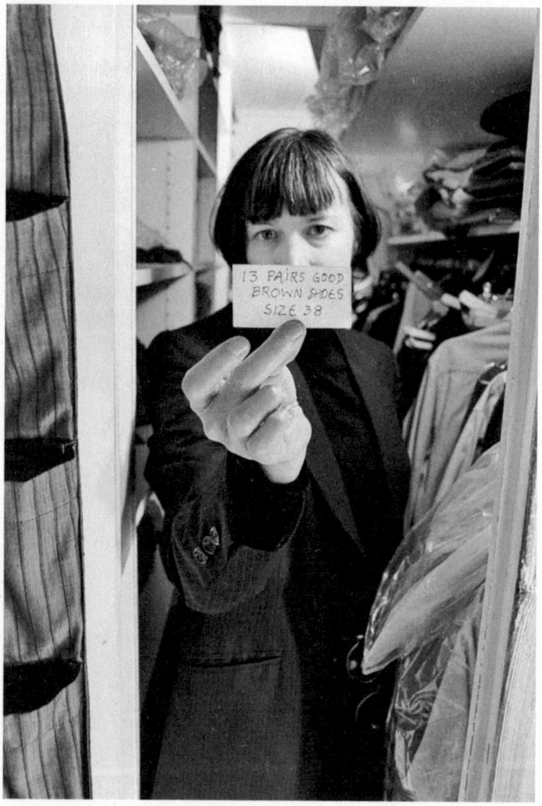

Renée Turner, *Warp Weft Memory,* photo: Cristina Cochior

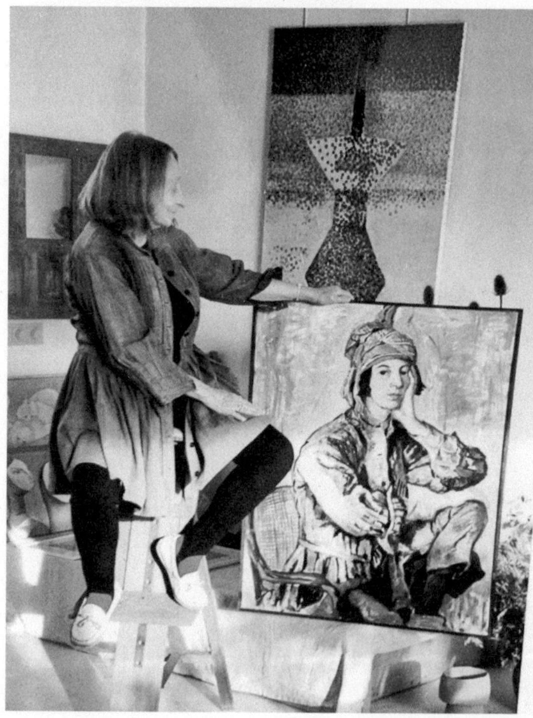
Renée Turner, *Warp Weft Memory,* photo: Cristina Cochior

26_Van Alphen, *Staging the Archive*, p. 91.

grounding in a theoretic discourse that provides a framework of references for critical reflection and for rooting out her project in a broader discourse. The latter translates in her pedagogic endeavors of creating spaces of dialogues for students, artists, and scholars during her research period in the house. These dialogues were an essential part of her method. The added value for us as an organization was the insights resulting from these conversations. It reassured us of the function of the archival space as a space of dialogue, with this dialogue being an intrinsic part of a creative process.

By building a database of Gisèle's wardrobe and including photographs from her archive in which she wears the garments—and which often display other friends from her life or a relation to her art at the same time—Turner links the very personal, the wardrobe, to the social fabric in which Gisèle was embedded and to her own productivity as an artist. With the additional dimension of Turners own reflections, she questions her own productivity and artistic practice by engaging her own life with the realities of Gisèle's past.

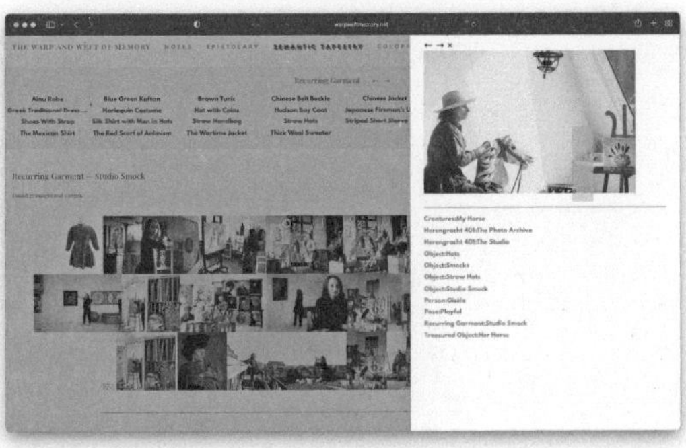

Renée Turner, www.warpweftmemory.net

> You left a tag on a pair of pants which read: 'These pants are good, but too short.' They were listed in one of your 'To repair' inventories. Just to let you know, I took them home, let the hem out by a centimeter and a half, and then returned them to your closet. Judging by the length of the rest of your trousers I think they would now fit.[27]

I have described Gisèle's intense urge for order, how she meticulously archived everything her life produced. Turner's work can be read as a poetic and yet scholarly attempt to pay tribute to this life endeavor. And yet, the methodological rigor of Turner's approach is motivated by artistic experiment, bringing to the surface connections with her 'Semantic Tapestry' and add associative connections in her 'Notes,' both creating rhizomatic assemblages that also bring together the seemingly unrelated. Turner's view that 'an archivist's work inevitably ends without a sense of closure' may have been true also for Gisèle's work. It has certainly helped me to understand her life a bit better. Still, we are left without a sense of closure. But this open-endedness becomes part of Turner's art. She gives it a value in itself and shows a dimension that is difficult to grasp: the factuality of matters such as wardrobe pieces relates to the relational reality of Gisèle's life, which knows many viewpoints. Bringing together these aspects in one online work shows us how the various collections and smaller archives in the house gain an added value in their interconnectedness in the common archival space of Herengracht 401.

27_Turner, 'Epistolary: The Unreceived Note,' *The Warp and Weft of Memory*, warpweftmemory.net/#/foreword

Conclusion

Artistic research produces new knowledge and insights for the archival institution. In the case of H401 it concerns an institution with a public program, with guided tours and projects in which the artistic works reach a broader audience. For visitors, the artworks offer a mode of access to complex historical matter. Artistic knowledge production in an artistic language offers a contemporary view with relevance for today on a historic object.

Amie Dicke's work draws from the archive and becomes in turn part of the archive, with her artist's book, with the framing of archival material that becomes part of her art which she then leaves in the archival context of H401. Dicke has challenged us to evaluate decay and loss, which in her work go hand in hand with creating something new.

Ronit Porat worked in the library of Frommel, which is in a fragile state. The return of new knowledge and insights in the end outweighed the potential loss through material decay. Her work has challenged the narrative of the institutional founding figures and has shown us that heroes may have been tragic figures of meaningless loss, and at the same time her work engages in the constructions of new meaning.

The project of Renée Turner has brought us as an institution toward a continuous investigation of the tension between forgetting and remembering, which according to Assmann stimulates our archival impulses. Turner built an archive as an artwork itself. She has put the archival impulse into the form of a database in which she could invest her own interests and concerns. Her work shows us how we can insert our own life in an archival space, to enter into a conversation with it and let it speak to us.

As an institution we have learned to value the ongoing conversation with artists to negotiate the balance between the responsibility for the historical material and the mission to produce something new and meaningful for today. It is a field of tension that makes the archival space a productive space.

HIDDEN MAP OF THE CITY OF BUENOS AIRES

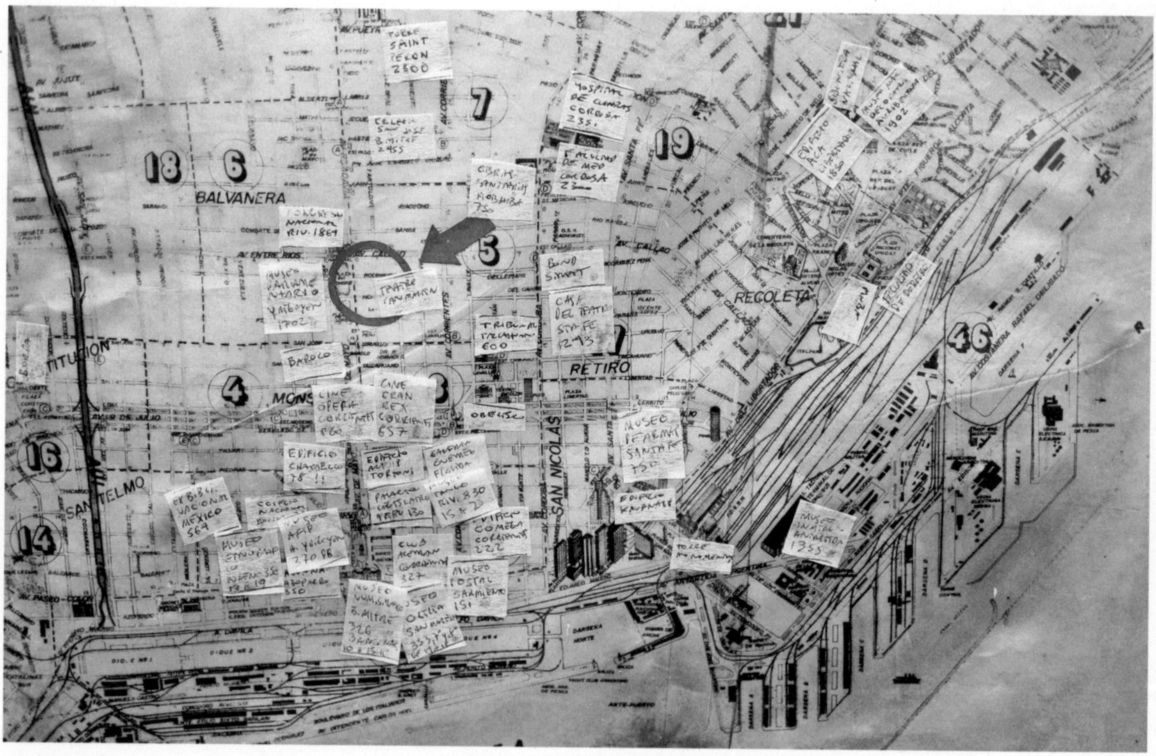

Sebastián Díaz Morales, *Hidden Map of the City of Buenos Aires*, 2012

Sebastián Díaz Morales

go out the door of the stall of one of the bathrooms at the Faculty of Medicine. walk through it. open the door to the exit that leads to the central corridor of the first floor. go down the corridor and turn right following the sign that indicates the Main Lecture Hall for Anatomy. open the small door, probably of a storeroom, that leads to the first basement of niches of the Chacarita Cemetery. cross the large pavilion of staircases that connects the basements. go through the door next to the staircase that leads to the ground floor. find the exit through the door on the left side of the pulpit of the Metropolitan Cathedral of Buenos Aires (of the Holy Trinity). go down the entire length of the central nave in the direction of the exit. in the narthex, turn left and climb the six steps that lead to a carved wooden door. open it to enter a room in the former ESMA (Naval School of Mechanics), *a clandestine detention, torture, and extermination center during the last civil-military dictatorship (1976-1983).* this room is lined with wood, with small cupboards fixed to the wall. the floor creaks. go across it and immediately climb the three steps that lead to the interior of a locksmith's shop crammed with handles, padlocks, bolts, keys and where two men go about their business behind a counter. walk past of them without drawing their attention. go to the other end of the room and turn into the corridor lined with shelves on the left. at the end of the corridor there is a man at a makeshift desk and behind him is a door. open it to enter a landing in the staircase on the first floor of the Bernardino Rivadavia natural science museum. go by the display case dedicated to the classification of Argentinean birds and enter the narrow, tall door to the room One Million Years Ago. this door leads to the rooms of the Juan José Naon Anatomy Museum at the Faculty of Medicine of Buenos Aires. go by the shelves with the flasks of lower and upper limbs of the human body in formalin. turn left into a corridor and go past the display case with the dissected body between the two staircases leading to the balcony of the room. turn right after passing through the series of shelves in the Splanchnology gallery. go to the door with the inscription Antarctica Argentina. **do not enter it**. find the exit from the museum with the glazed doors. go to it and open it to enter the galleries onto the courtyard of an old tenement house on Rivadavia or Hipólito Yrigoyen and Libertad streets. enter the men's room between the two lifts on the first floor. the entrance leads to the Argenchino Chinese supermarket. cross the yerba mate shelves and go to the refrigerator behind the cold meats and dairy counter. this entrance leads to the passageway under the Roverano arcades of the building on Perú and Avenida de Mayo that connects to the underground station Perú. *the A underground line was the first in Latin America. the line maintained, until Friday January 11 2013, its old Belgian La Brugeoise cars, built by La Brugeoise et Nivelles during the 1910s. unfortunately, these were replaced by Chinese trains*. go through the small door at the end of the passageway near the entrance to the platforms that is flanked by two other doors, one of them with bars. this entrance connects to one of the classrooms in the neo-Gothic building of the Buenos Aires Faculty of Engineering on Avenida Las Heras. at the time you enter, the room will not be occupied. exit the classroom and go through the small Science and Technology museum in the entrance of the building. on the same ground floor, probably to the left of the entrance of the building, there is a common room with a map of Argentina. go through it. open the small door, a meter and a half wide, that leads down a flight of stairs. go down them to come out again on the corridor on the first floor of the Faculty of Medicine. turn right towards the doors of the Juan José Naon Anatomy Museum. open them and you will find the underground passageway Obelisco Sur, which crosses 9 de Julio Avenue. at its entrance there was a reproduction of the Mona Lisa. today, the whole passage has been remodeled, eliminating the original architectural design and mysticism. go through the gallery of display cases of this corridor until you again reach the basement of the Chacarita cemetery. near the stairs the corridor turns into the public baths of the cemetery. the place has always been very abandoned and dirty and the mere thought that this space is in the cemetery makes you want to leave immediately. the bathroom door leads to the lateral balcony of the central room of the Casacuberta hall of the San Martín Cultural Centre. go down the stairs and across the hall. Look at the high allegorical relief by the sculptor Carlos de la Cárcova, and the round, glazed table in the center of the hall, if it is still there. toward the end of the hall you will find the tenth and last floor of the building, where you will discover the mythical Lugones cinema. open the leather-covered double doors that lead back to one of the corridors of the Faculty of Medicine. this corridor is out of use and on the ninth or tenth floor. walk towards the entrance to the bathroom besides a monument that is missing a bust or relief. on entering, immediately leave one of the stalls of the bathroom. the bathroom is crammed with chairs. enter the next stall on the left. this leads to a common space in the Cervantes restaurant at 1883 on Pres. Tte. Gral. Juan Domingo Perón street. the daily fixed menu here is very cheap and two or even three people can eat from one plate thanks to the abundant food. stop in front of the blue door with a poster of Chaplin in the movie The Kid. open it and go out of the bathroom into the dining room of the pizzeria las Cuartetas, probably at lunch time. the curious thing is that you don't hear the diners talking. you can only hear the sound of the cutlery on the plates. the waiters wear bow ties. the end of this pizzeria connects again with the dining room of the Cervantes restaurant. head back towards the toilets. the glass door will turn into one of the giant gates of the Bernardino Rivadavia Museum of Natural Sciences. it is worth mentioning the detail of the mirrored, wrought-iron gates with two spiders in their respective webs. enter the museum again and cross directly to the fascinating Geology room. fortunately, this room has not been refurbished, as so many other rooms in the museum, regrettably, with infographics and dividing walls that have nothing to do with the original design of the museum. cross through the Palaeontology room and enter the present-day mammals room, where there is a huge bone structure of a fin whale in the center. turn left in the center of the corridor to enter the Comparative Osteology room. open one of the double door panels next to the fire extinguisher and the poster of what might be a Siberian brown bear. this leads to a hall in the Almagro Boxing Club, or ABC, which is probably full of men jumping rope at the time. *this is the oldest boxing club in the city, founded in 1923.* enter the blue metal door that on the lintel declares: 'You are about to enter history.' exit through one of the stalls of the public restroom of an old building on the property of the former ESMA. the second door of the bathroom from the left connects with the video club El Master. exit behind the desk of the manager, who in the past studied theatre and belonged to the Military and Artistic Resistance TIT (Theatre Research Workshop). cross the space towards the exit door that when opened connects with the public

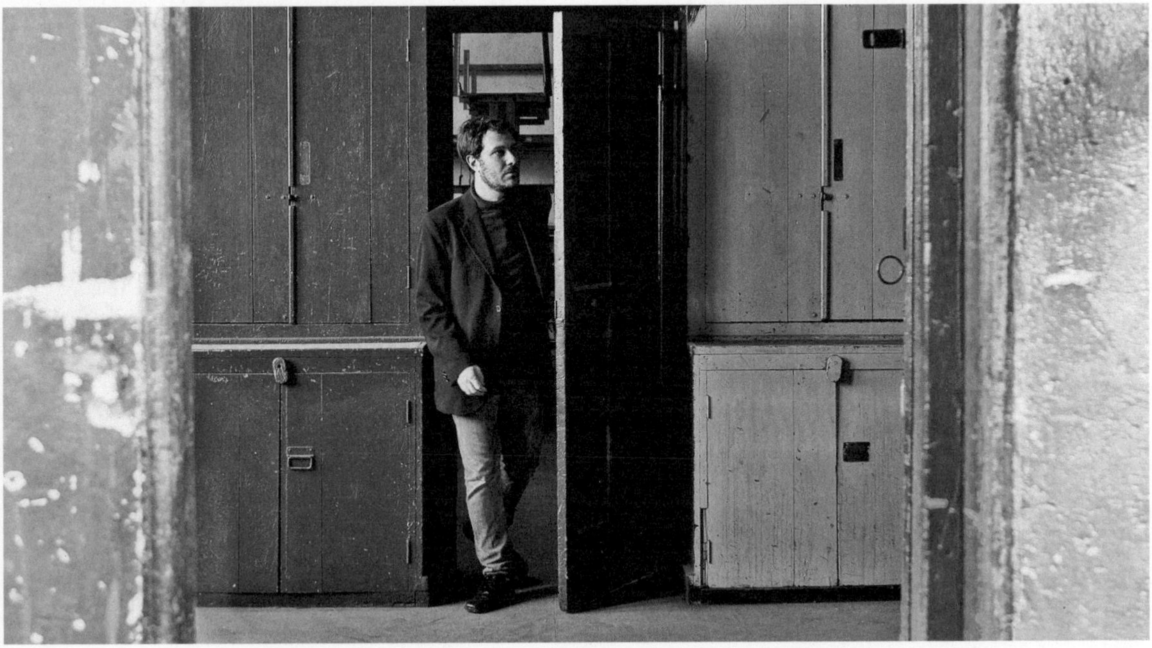

Sebastián Díaz Morales, *Pasajes I*, 2012, film still

restrooms of another building of the former ESMA, today the CONTI Cultural Space. the bathrooms have been remodeled and do not resemble the original ones at all. enter one of the stalls, the second one from the entrance. it leads to another room of the former ESMA, paneled with wood painted green. go cross the room and go down a small slope to reach a large, high space of about 100 square meters. this space was formerly occupied by a power station or similar factory. natural light enters through the skylights in the ceiling and everything is in a state of abandonment and deterioration. find a pair of three-meter-high doors. open them to see the only exit to the outside on this entire route. on the other side you see men working on the foundations of a new building. **do not enter here**. close the doors and continue on your way. walk a little crookedly in the direction of a door at the end of a long white wall. enter and recognize a small space that resembles a kitchen. when leaving this, turn right to find a door in its frame, erected in the middle of the space and devoid of a wall. when crossing the doorway the space does not change. these last rooms of the Centro Cultural San Martín are in a state of abandonment. leave through the wooden door. once again enter one of the many spaces of the former ESMA. go through two rooms and walk towards a door that could lead to a storeroom. A small transition through the Chacarita Cemetery leads back to a large, naturally lit hall of the former ESMA. the floor is made of erratically laid bricks. at the end of this space find another small wooden door with frosted glass at the top. this is my favorite space, for no particular reason. open the door and enter the waiting room at the space of the FM radio La Tribu. the room is small and poorly lit. find the exit easily. this door connects to another space, once again in the former ESMA. access it through the door with a painting of South America upside down, the opposite of how it is normally represented. cross this space and arrive at another room inhabited by sculptures of people in everyday situations in what would appear to be on a street, at a street demonstration, a square. cross this space and enter again a common room of the Faculty of Engineering. open a high door with two panels that leads to the interior of a flat in the Congreso neighborhood at Bartolome Mitre 1676, block 2, second floor, flat 8. cross it briefly to open another door that connects to the stall of a bathroom X. exit through the Lugones hall in the San Martín Cultural Centre. go down once again, but in the opposite direction, the red carpet to get to the door of a small cleaning supplies closet in the Faculty of Engineering. open it and exit through the toilets of the Chacarita Cemetery. cross a room of niches to arrive at a gallery near the stairs. the spaces begin to repeat themselves more frequently. the last or first door of this route is in a space with paint on the ceiling that is peeling, the walls with small square green tiles.

vimeo.com/49541840
Password: preview

Translation from Spanish
by David Sánchez Cano

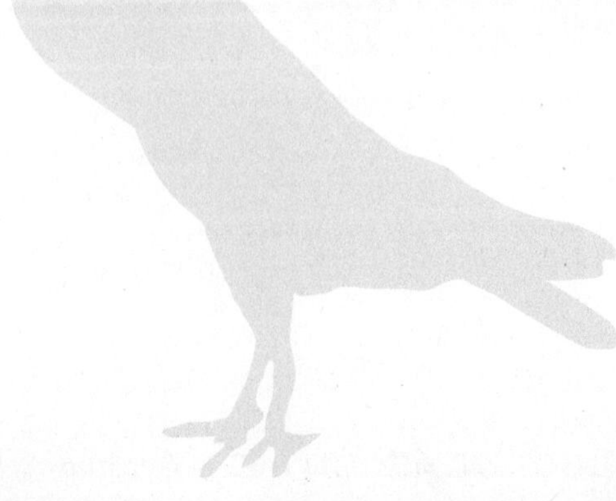

THE FINE LINE OF MEMORY

The Passages in the Work of Díaz Morales

'I do not know. It's like you're on an escalator to a cloud with him, you never know where that ladder goes.'

> Justin Theroux's statement on David Lynch while filming *Mulholland Drive*..

Meke Paradela, 'Cine: Veinte años de Mulholland Drive: El gran misterio de David Lynch,' *La Izquierda Diario*, October 12, 2021

The fiction is already there. The writer's task is to invent reality (prologue to *Crash*, 1979)

Ana Paula Saab

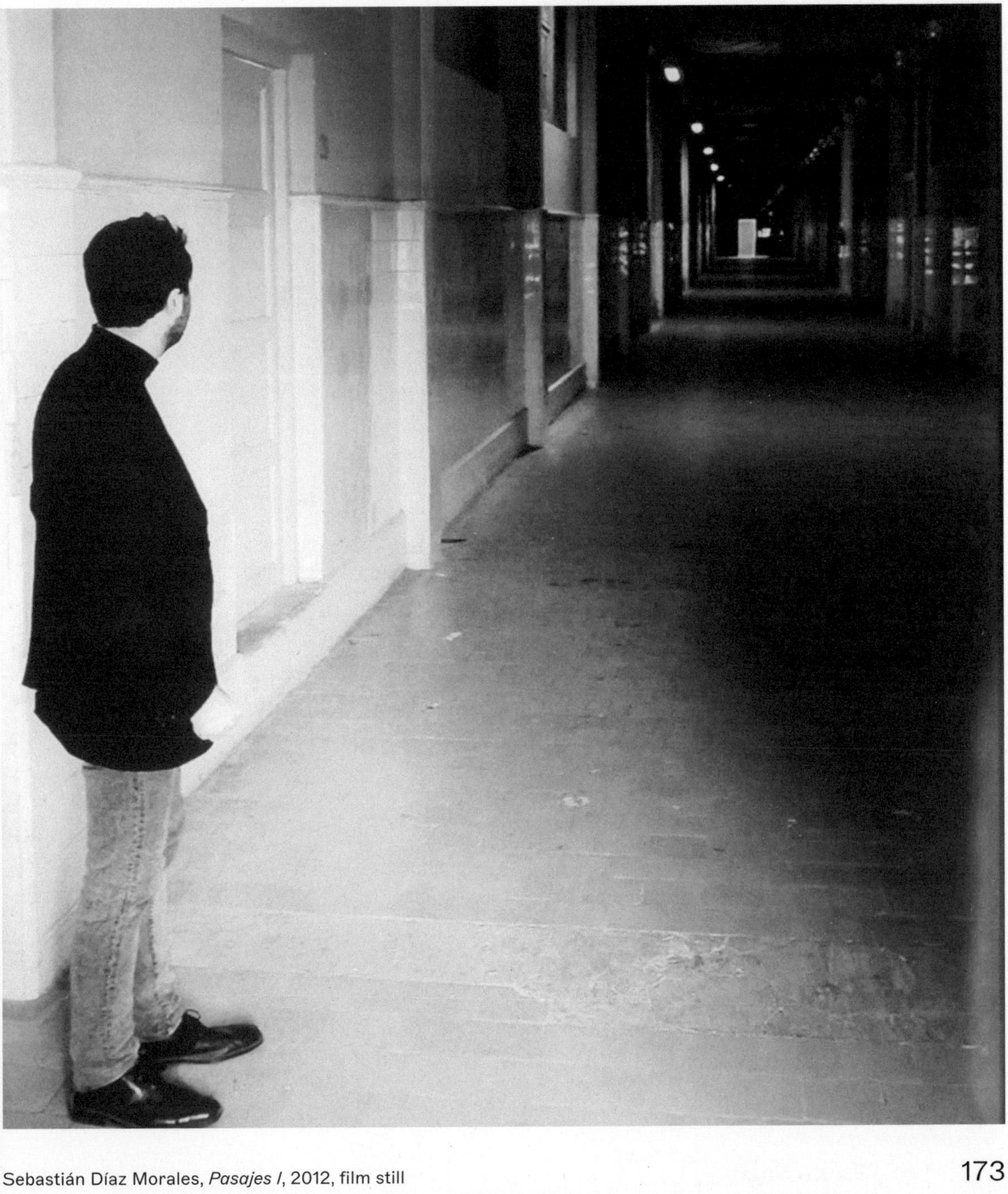

Sebastián Díaz Morales, *Pasajes I*, 2012, film still

Passages I and *Passages I/II*, by the artist Sebastían Díaz Morales (2012 and 2013) essentially show a path. In the first passage, an individual goes through rooms, halls, empty classrooms, corridors, and over abundant and endless stairs in the second. We do not see the beginning of this journey, nor its end. We know nothing about the character or his objective. He is an individual in motion, someone who moves forward without ever going back, but we do not know the motor or the logic behind this endless displacement, from which

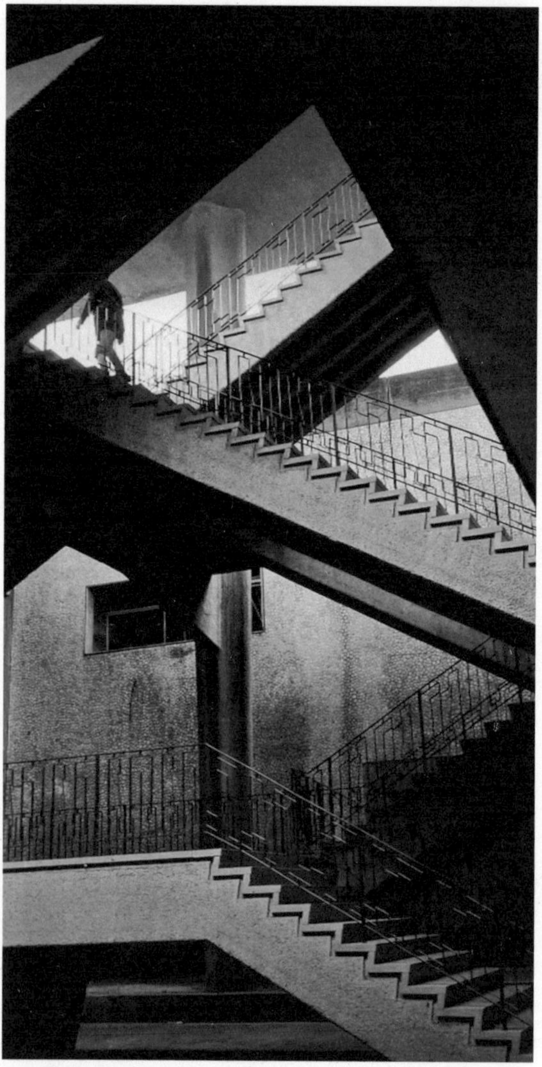

Sebastián Díaz Morales, *Pasajes II*, 2013, film still

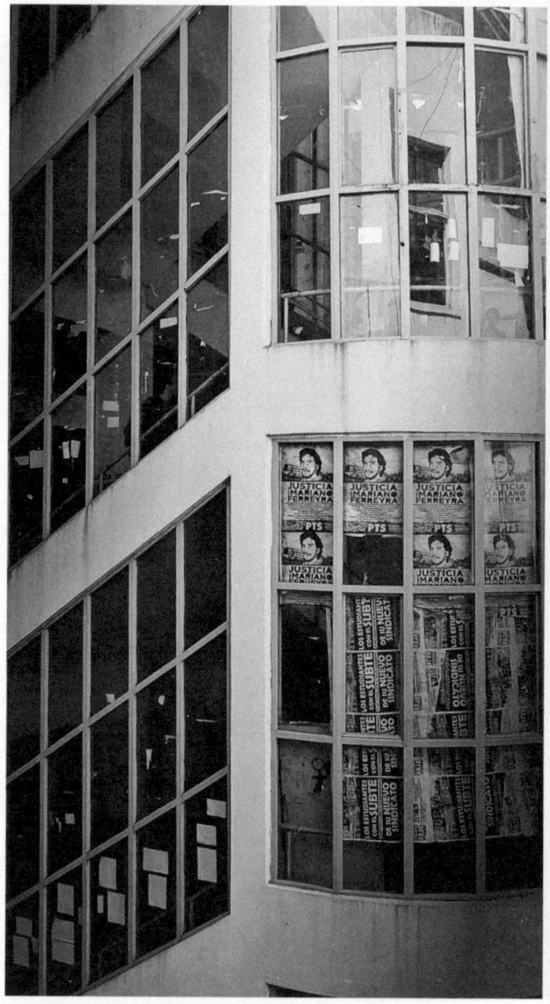

In this passage are the posters with the face of Mariano Ferreira, a university leader assassinated in 2010 by the railway union bureaucracy during a demand for better working conditions for railway workers.

all concatenation between causes and consequences has been elided or simply does not exist. Nor does it appear to have a starting or ending point. The images of heterogeneous spaces follow one another, having as a common thread the subject that walks through them and the regular sound of his steps.

The man who walks is not a kind of *flâneur* or a tourist, he is not strolling or visiting these buildings. The apparent determination and directionality of his walk, and the fact that he does not stop anywhere, suggests that he is indeed heading somewhere. This turns the spaces crossed into obstacles, the passage never becoming a place, where one could dwell or linger, not even to rest. The spaces crossed are mere transit passages. However, the arrival that would give this wandering or transit a meaning seems to be infinitely delayed. It is about a journey that emancipates itself from its instrumentality, just as waiting strips off its object in *Waiting for Godot*, thus dissolving its eventual meaning. Something that, on the other hand, does not seem to demoralize the lonely walker we meet in the middle of his march and leave in the same situation. The rooms he passes through appear to be public places, stations, banks, college corridors, classrooms, lofts, and offices. The interspersed ellipsis produces the feeling that all of them, all these spaces, are contiguous. The few people who cross his path seem to be possessed by the same spirit of transit that inhabits the walking subject. If the first passage is marked by the doors that are crossed, the second has its sign on the stairs. The variety of staircases—which in their intricacy remind us of the magical continuities of the Möbius strip, or of Escher's geometrically vertiginous figures, and even, sometimes, of Piranesi's speculative architecture—also appear in a succession of fragments, linked by the path of the walker. As in the Möbius strip, what looks like an ascent is altered by the perspective of the camera that rotates and inverts the planes, transforming all ascent into a simulacrum and all descent into an inverted ascent.

The spaces that we walk through with the protagonist are visibly degraded by time, by use, and by lack of maintenance. Some fleeting signs that we distinguish in his path inform us of a transcendent geographical location. The map on the wall of a school, the recognizable facade of the ESMA, a poster protesting the murder of Mariano Ferreira, are signs that give away Buenos Aires. But it is a purely interior Buenos Aires, the dilapidated interior of the great and once pretentious public buildings built in the early twentieth century. They are buildings that bear the traces of a 'glorious' past and now seem to vegetate in decadence or relative abandonment that makes the passage of time tangible. The city is then reduced to its interiors, because its eventual exteriors, its streets and squares, its urban agitation, have been elided. It is the disturbing geography of a labyrinth without an outside, an infinite labyrinth, full of possibilities (doors, corners, corridors, stairs, passages), but they lead nowhere, and above all to no exterior. At times, we suppose that this man is looking in vain not for a specific place of arrival, but simply for an exit door. This turns his tiring wandering into a nightmare. Wherever the subject goes, he will find new rooms or new stairs that at the same time impel him to march on. Morales seems to have resorted to the narrative resource of infinite postponement that characterized many stories by Franz Kafka (and in Latin America by Jorge Luis Borges or Mario Levrero). Walter Benjamin called it 'the epic of Scheherazade.' There is always one more story, after the story, there will always be a room beyond this room, and another corridor at the end of the hall. As in the paradox of Achilles and the tortoise that so fascinated Borges, the finite set that is a city contains an infinite interior. But Kafka's messenger (carrying the message of a dead man), or Mario Levrero's lost traveler in *El lugar*, even Scheharazade, have a discernible purpose, something our wayfarer seems to lack. Infinite postponement has always functioned as a metaphor for the implosion of meaning.

It is possible to understand this wandering as the conscious search for a memory by the walking subject. In that case, the subject, his own search, as unsuccessful as it is incessant, would be shaping the rooms, which would allude to the performative nature of memory. But if the walk of this passer-by has no cause, neither formal nor efficient, nor, consequently, a destination, what shapes or channels its perpetual movement, is space itself. When the space of memory or memories is not organized by a story (and every story is nothing but a journey), the subject loses consistency, remains lost in the labyrinth of memories. He remains a prisoner of drives, which are like doors that open or stairs that invite you to climb. These interiors of infinite possibilities and infinite concatenations could constitute a metaphor for the past as it is preserved in memory: more like an accumulation

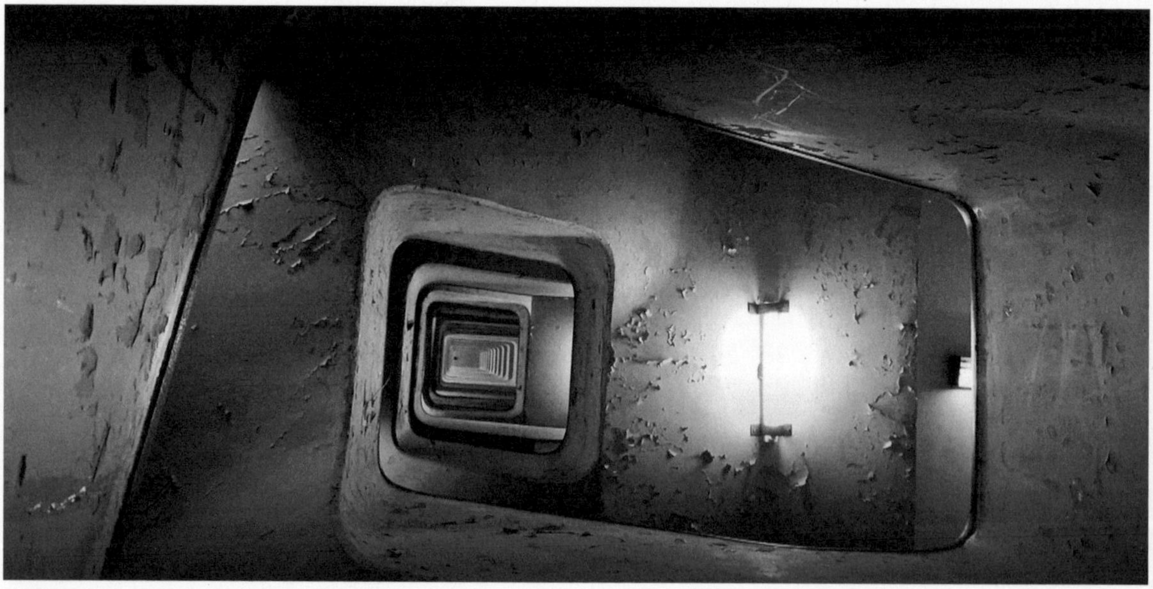

Sebastián Díaz Morales, *Pasajes I*, 2012, film still

of sediments of varying intensities than as a map that adequately represents the logic of its twists and turns. Temporal indiscernibility refers to a personal appreciation of time, that is, it reproduces how the subject perceives the temporal dimension while remembering. The logic that governs the mnemonic act is not the classic narrative logic (because the past is always recovered from the present and distortions, hesitations or forgetfulness are common). One memory leads us to another, or an image leads us to another image, without a solution of continuity, in the same way that a room takes us to another room without the association process being able to effectively resolve itself into a coherent story or journey. Before the rooms can be transformed into a meaningful whole, if only by the well-known surrealist procedure of chaotic articulation, the walker (and with him the camera that follows him) has already left them without exploring them. It is as if we can only realize its infinite multiplicity.

Even so, these rooms claim meaning, the arrangement of their furniture, their posters, the pictures and signs that we see fleetingly, propose or simulate an order. We would like to 'suspend the step'—this step that marks time with the sound precision of a compass—of the walker and say that history passed by as an old sign says on one of the doors that are crossed: 'you are about to enter history' (minute 8). It would not be so much about personal memory, but rather the heteroclite landscape of a shared oblivion, the warehouse where the ruins of a national past accumulate. We feel that somewhere in this labyrinth, there is an image of the past that awaits us. A room, an image, that corresponds to us. A fragment of the past in which the present can be recognized.

References

_Samuel Beckett, *Waiting for Godot*, 1955
_Walter Benjamin, 'Franz Kafka: On the Tenth Anniversary of his Death,' 1934
_Jorge Luis Borges, *Obras completas*, 4 vols. (Barcelona: Emecé, 1996)
_Franz Kafka, 'An Imperial Message,' 1919
_Mario Levrero, *La trilogía involuntaria* (Madrid: Punto de lectura, Debolsillo, 2016)

Pasajes I

Sebastián Diáz Morales

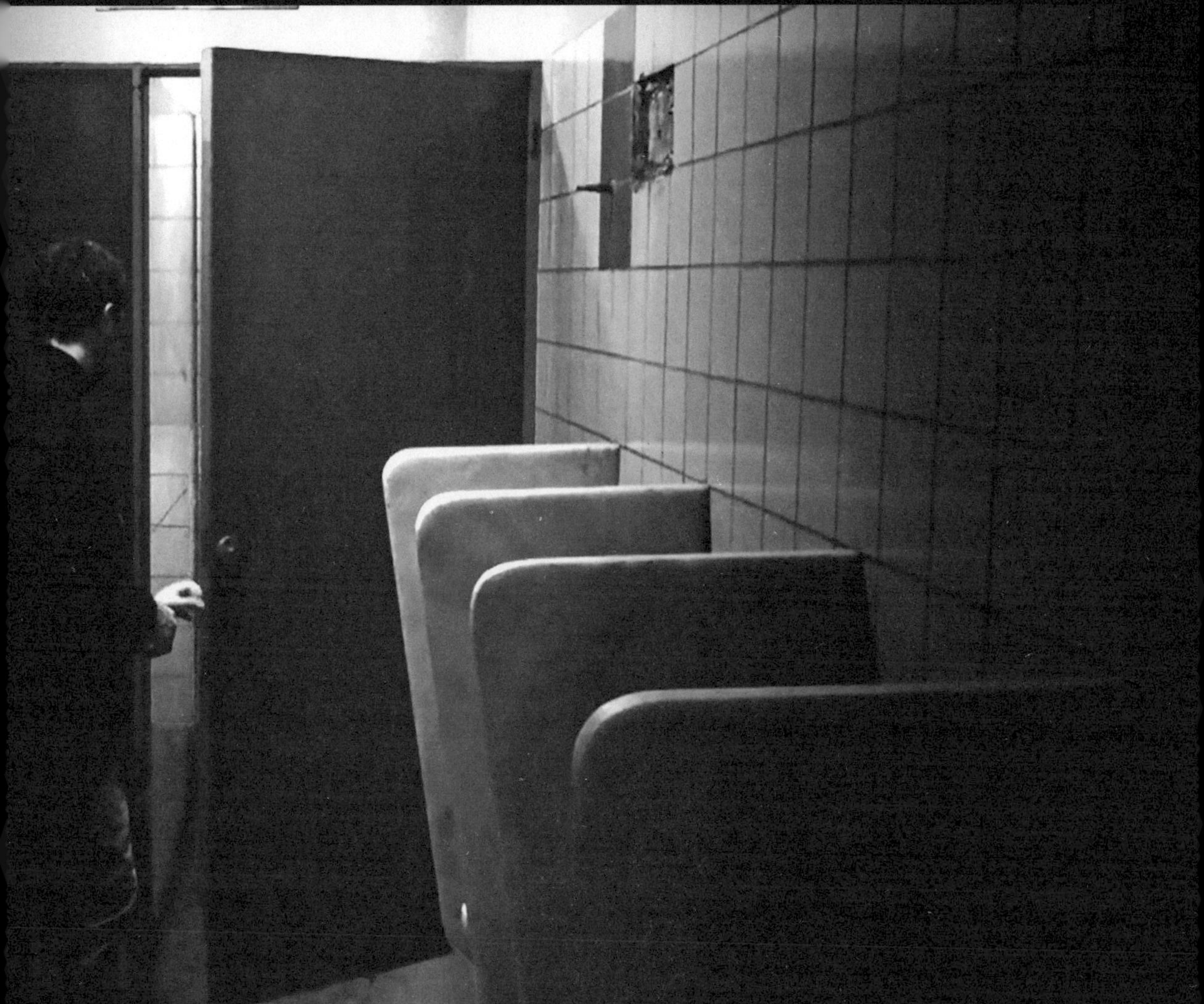

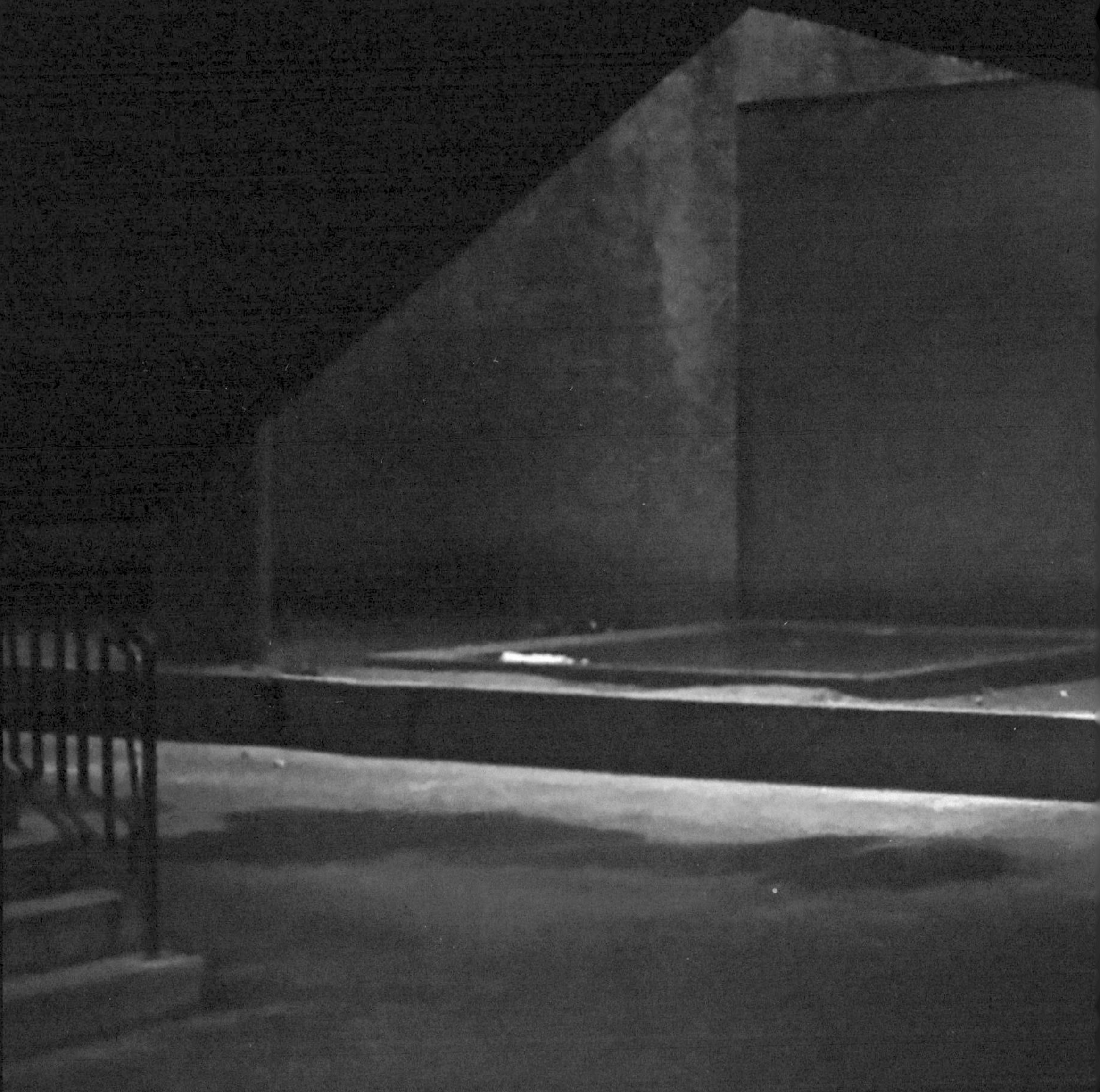

Sebastián Diáz Morales

Sebastián Diáz Morales,
Pasajes I, 2012
32 stills, digital video /
HD format / 12'30

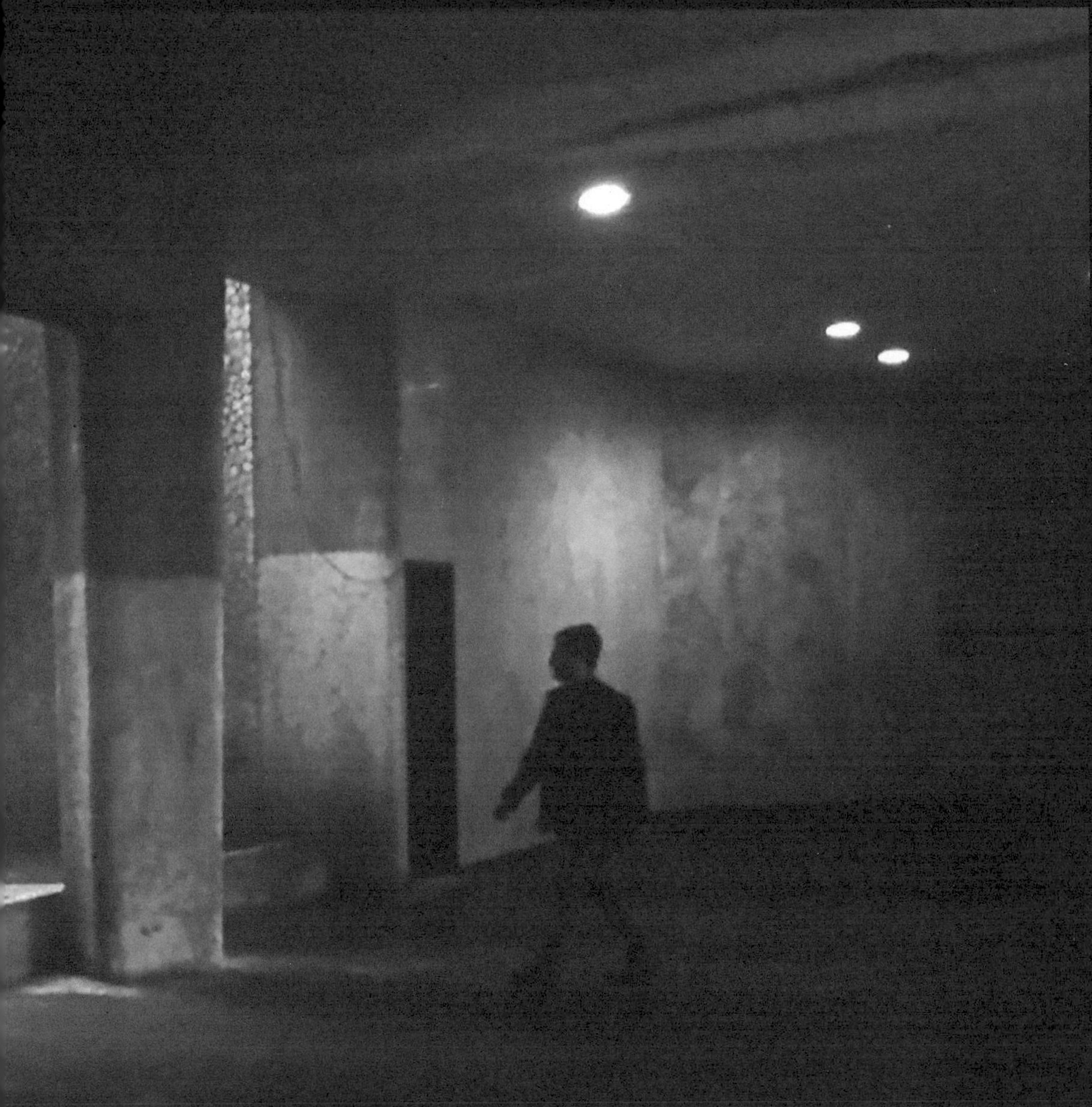

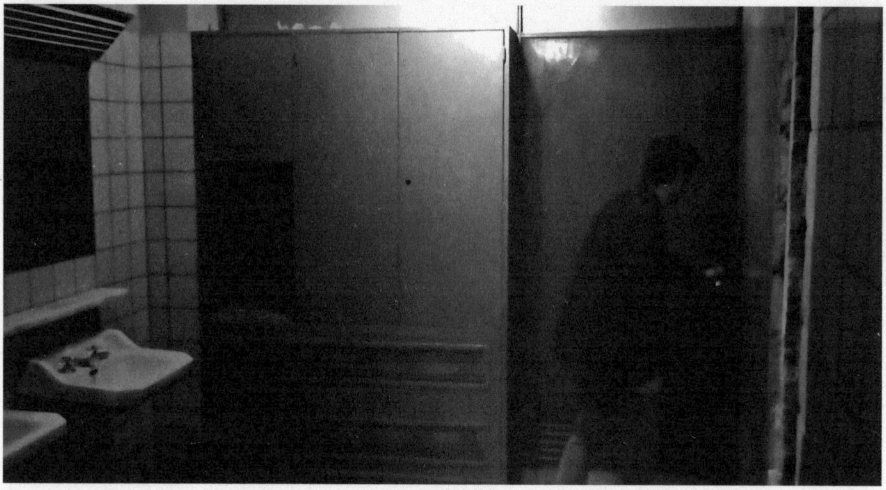

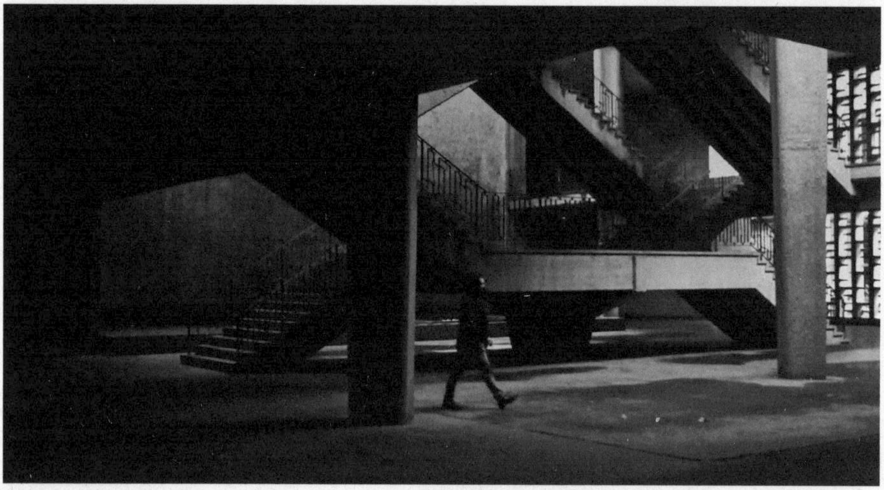

Sebastián Diáz Morales

Sebastián Diáz Morales,
Pasajes I, 2012
32 stills, digital video /
HD format / 12'30

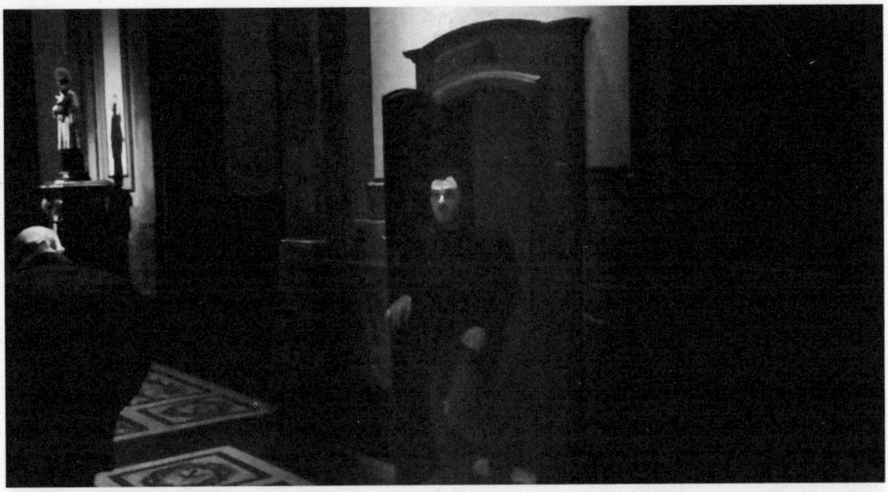

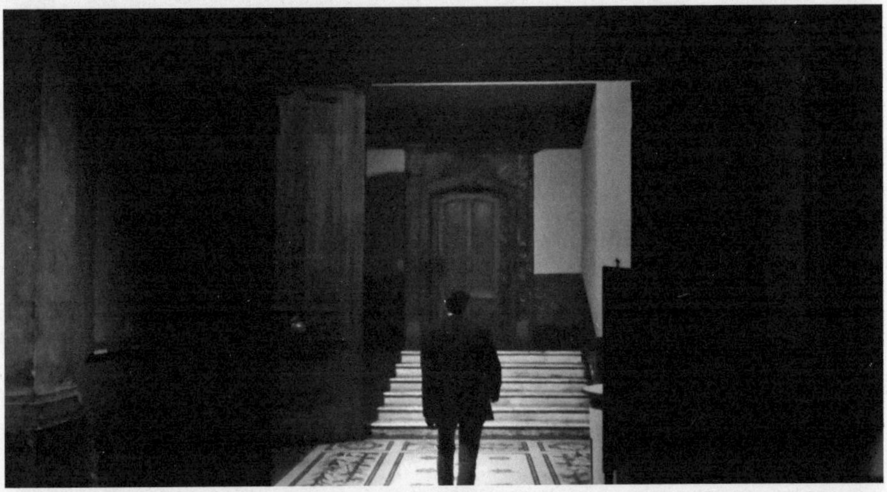

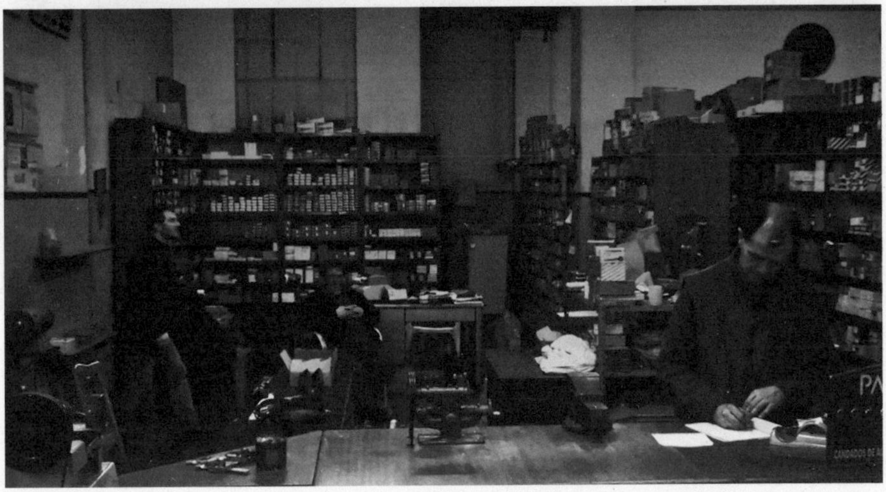

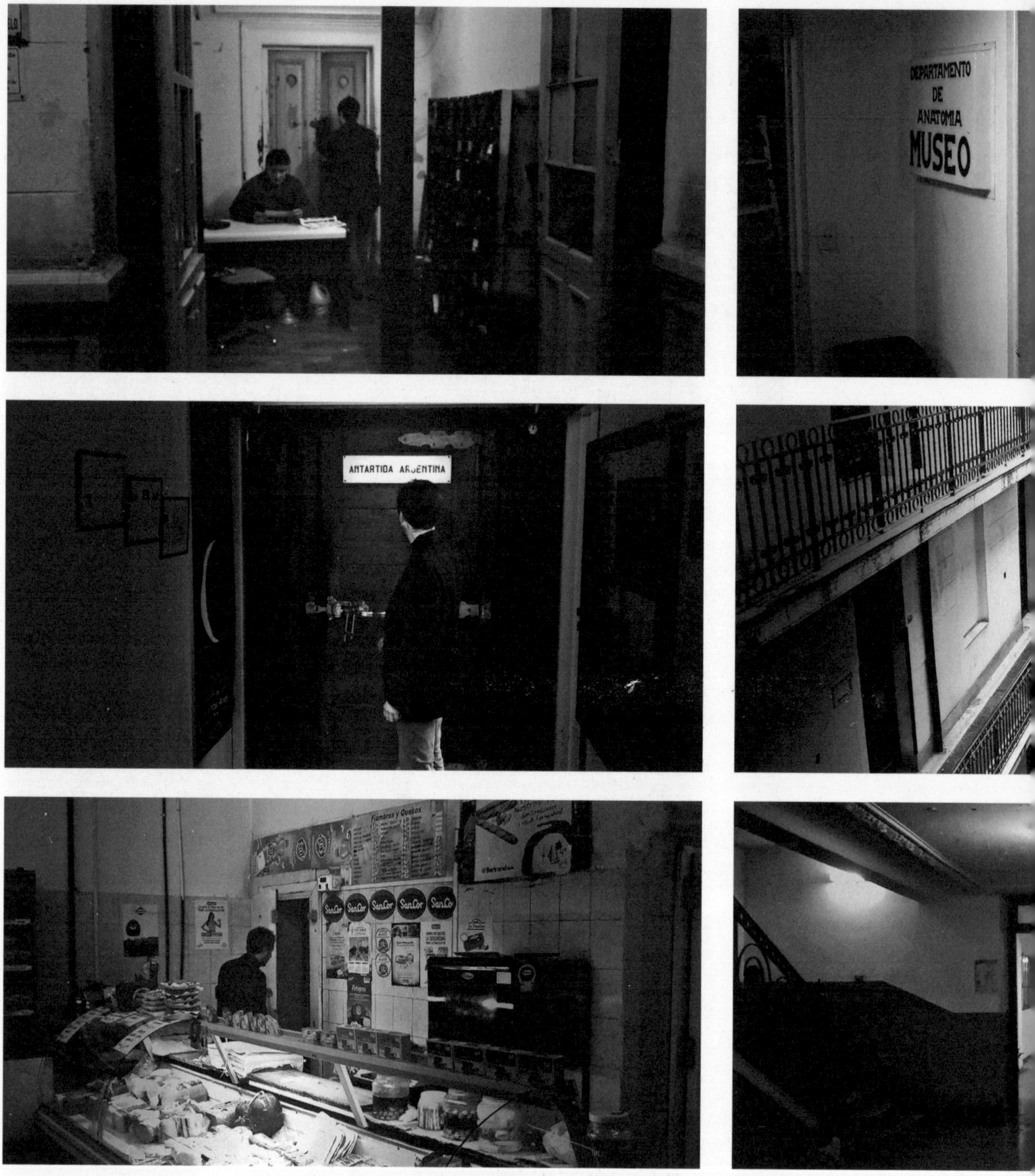

Sebastián Diáz Morales

Sebastián Diáz Morales,
Pasajes I, 2012
32 stills, digital video /
HD format / 12'30

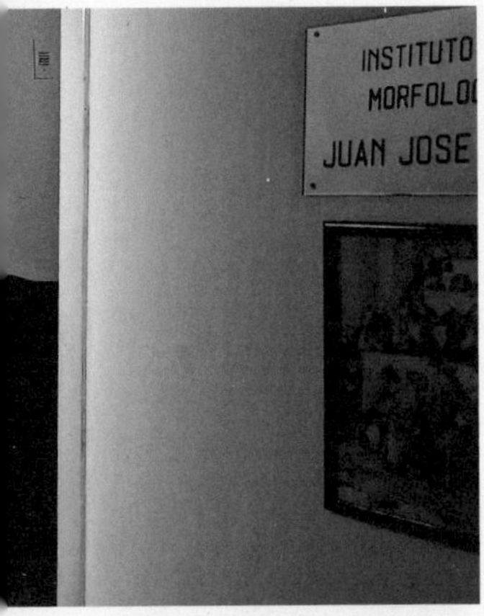
INSTITUTO
MORFOLO
JUAN JOSE

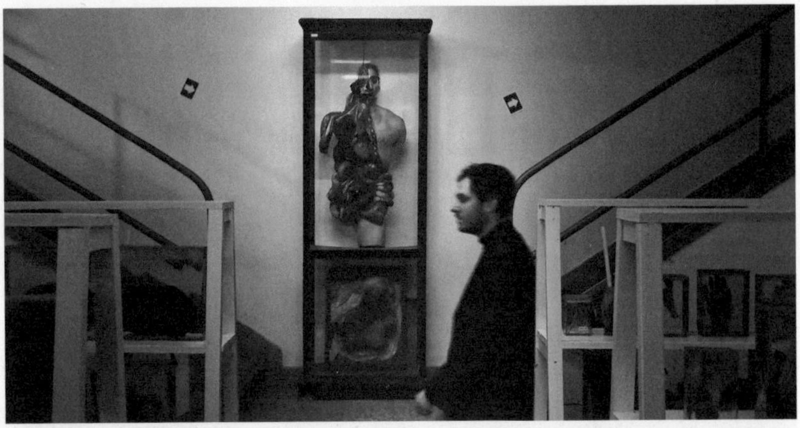

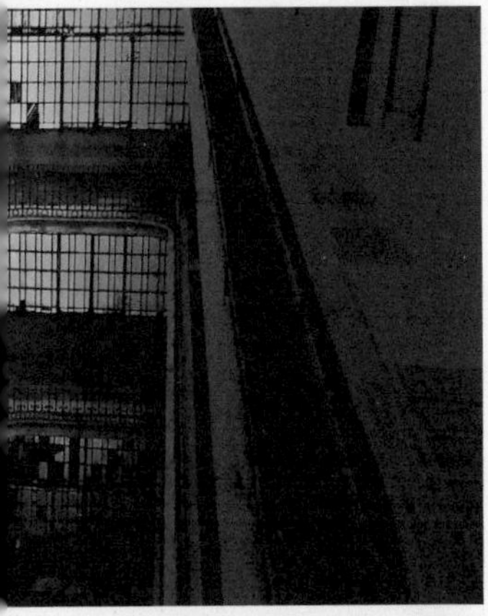

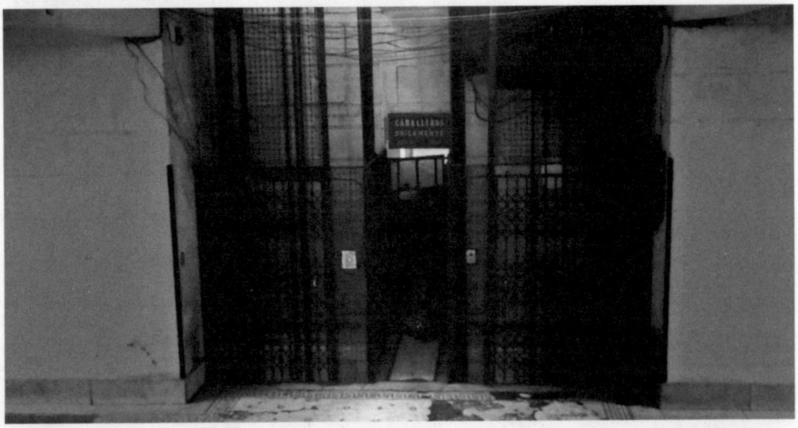

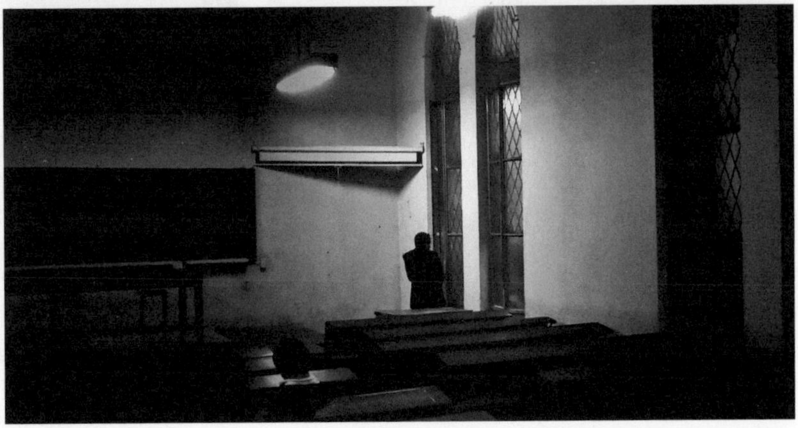

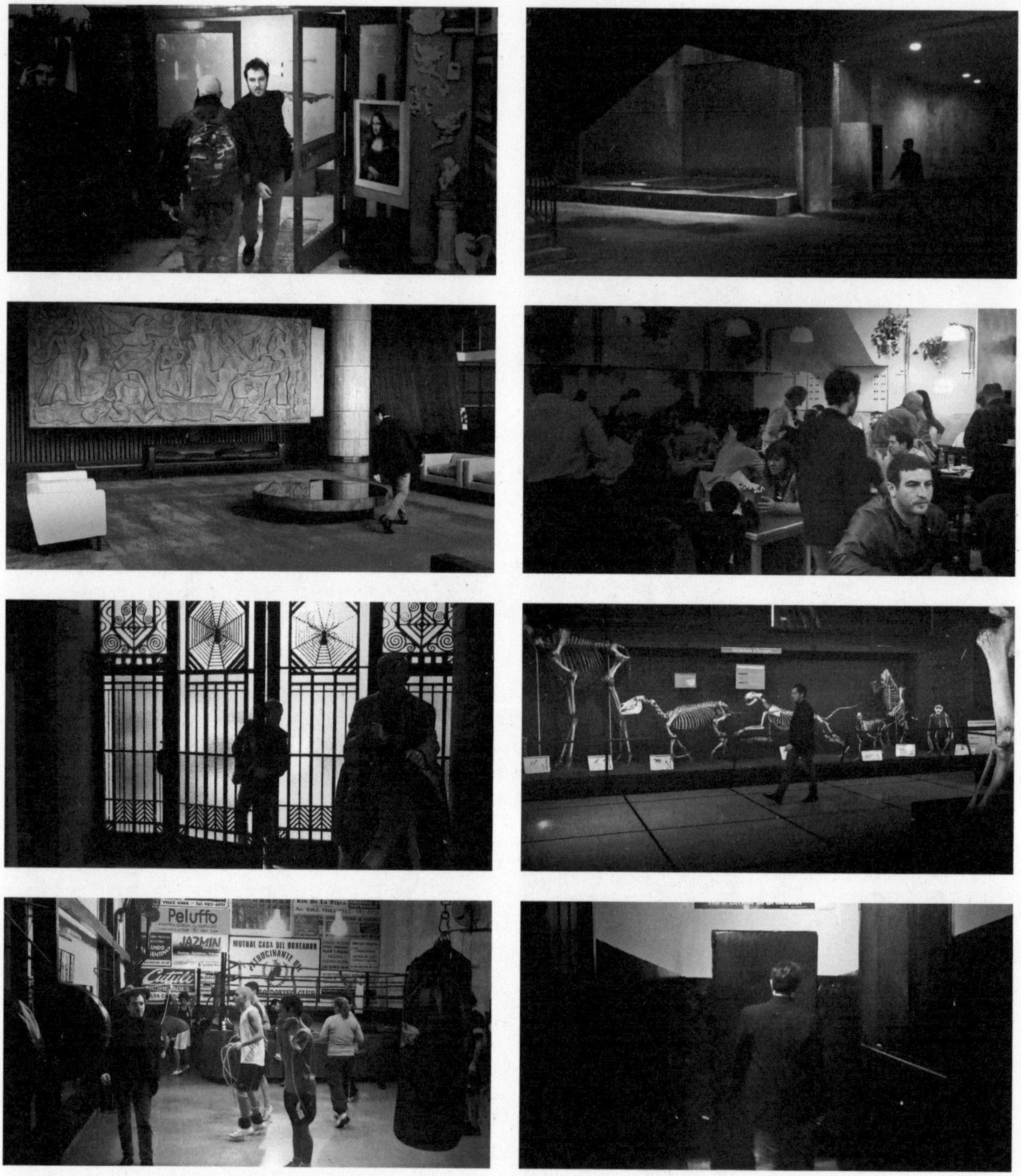

Sebastián Diáz Morales,
Pasajes I, 2012
32 stills, digital video /
HD format / 12'30

Sebastián Diáz Morales

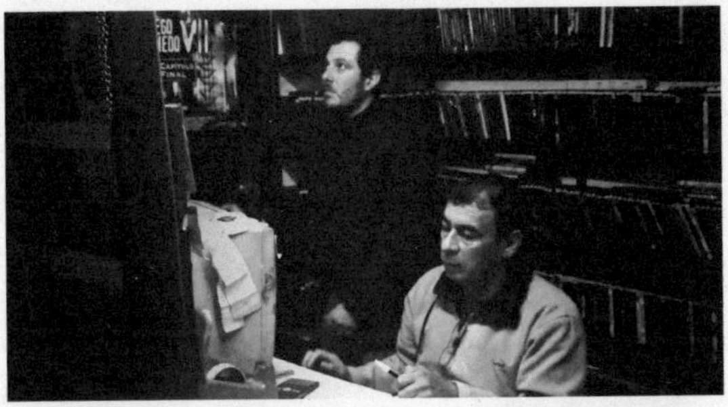
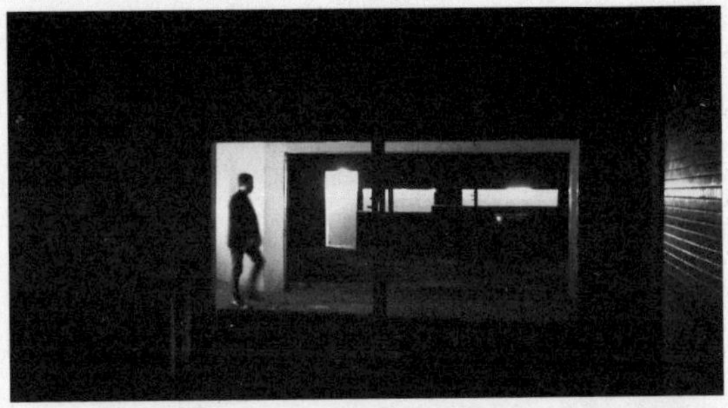
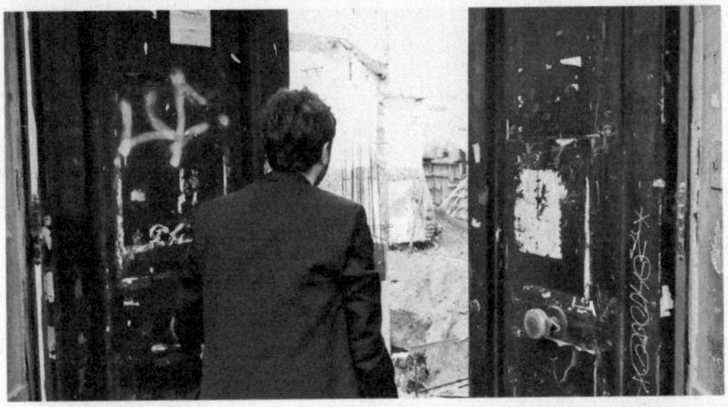
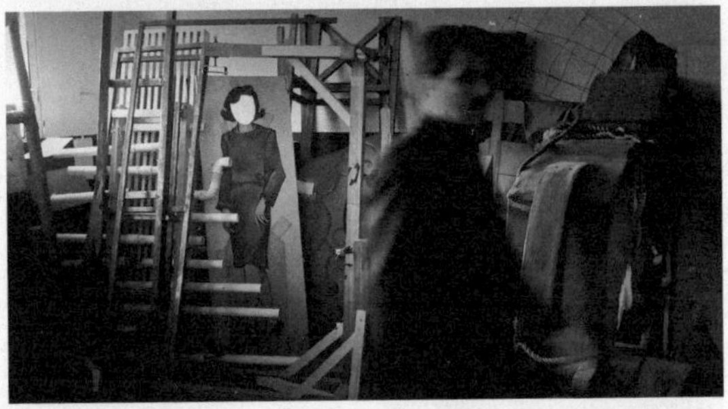
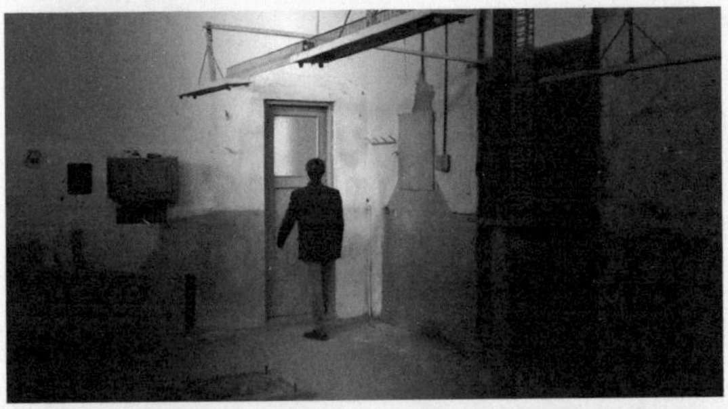
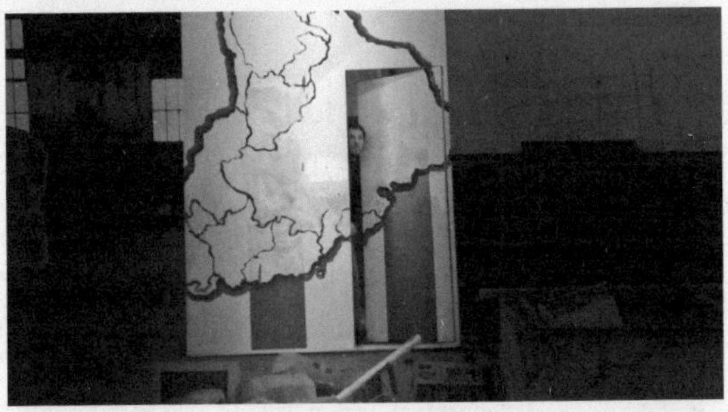
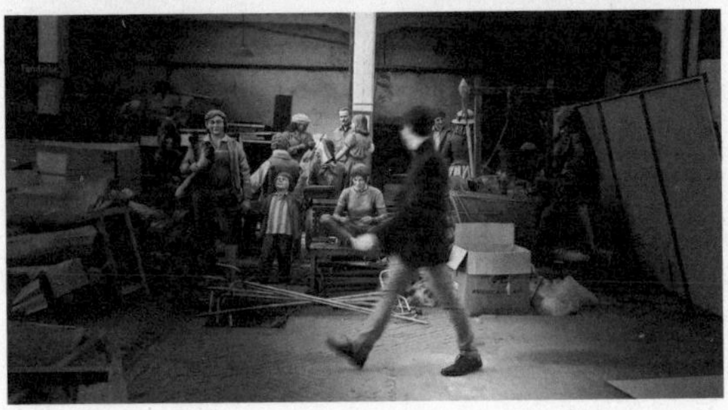
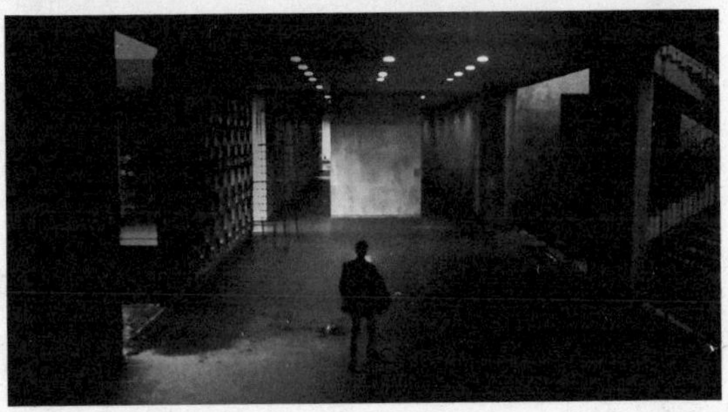

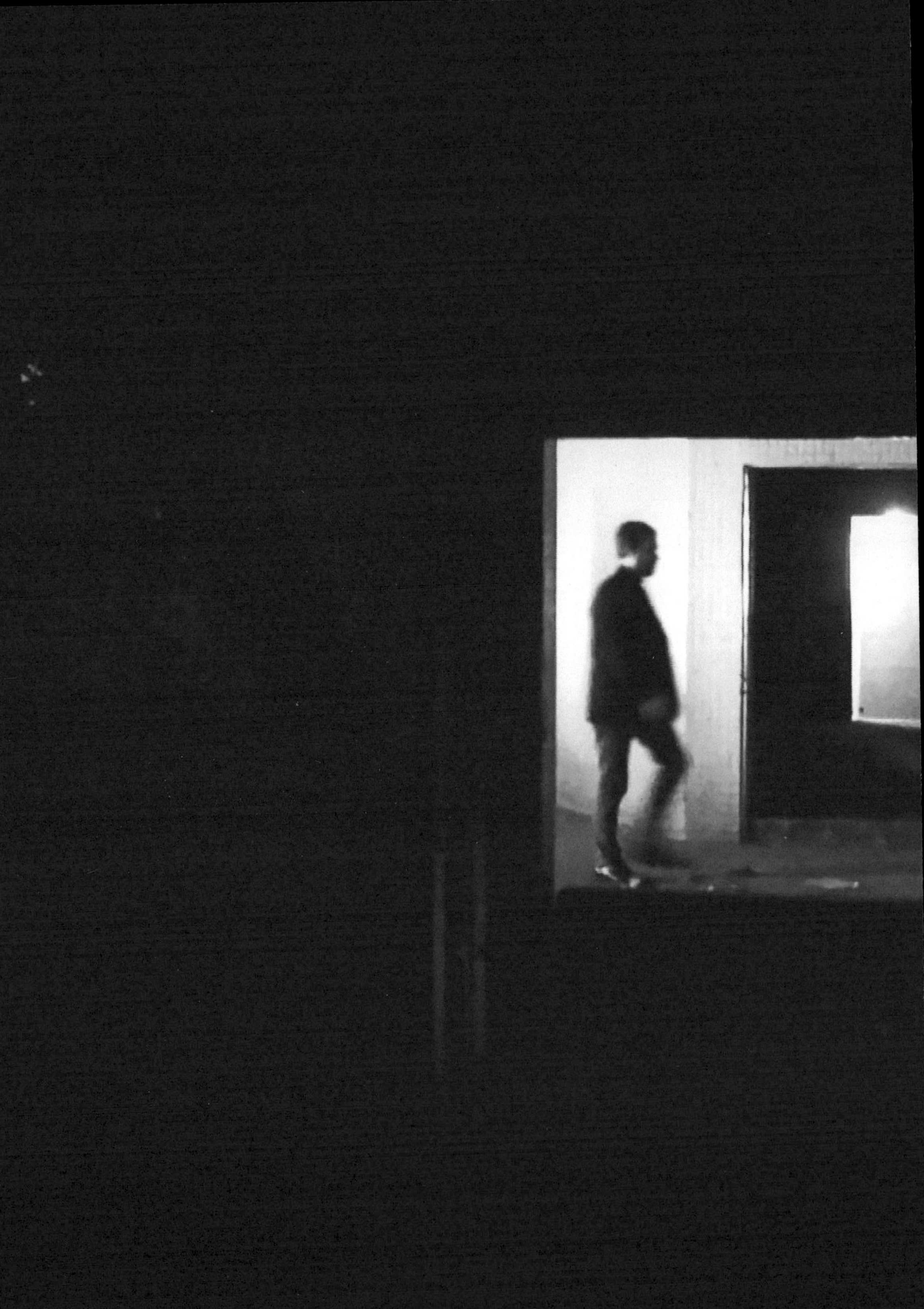

Sebastián Diáz Morales

Sebastián Diáz Morales,
Pasajes I, 2012
32 stills, digital video /
HD format / 12'30

Waiting for the Sibyl

William Kentridge

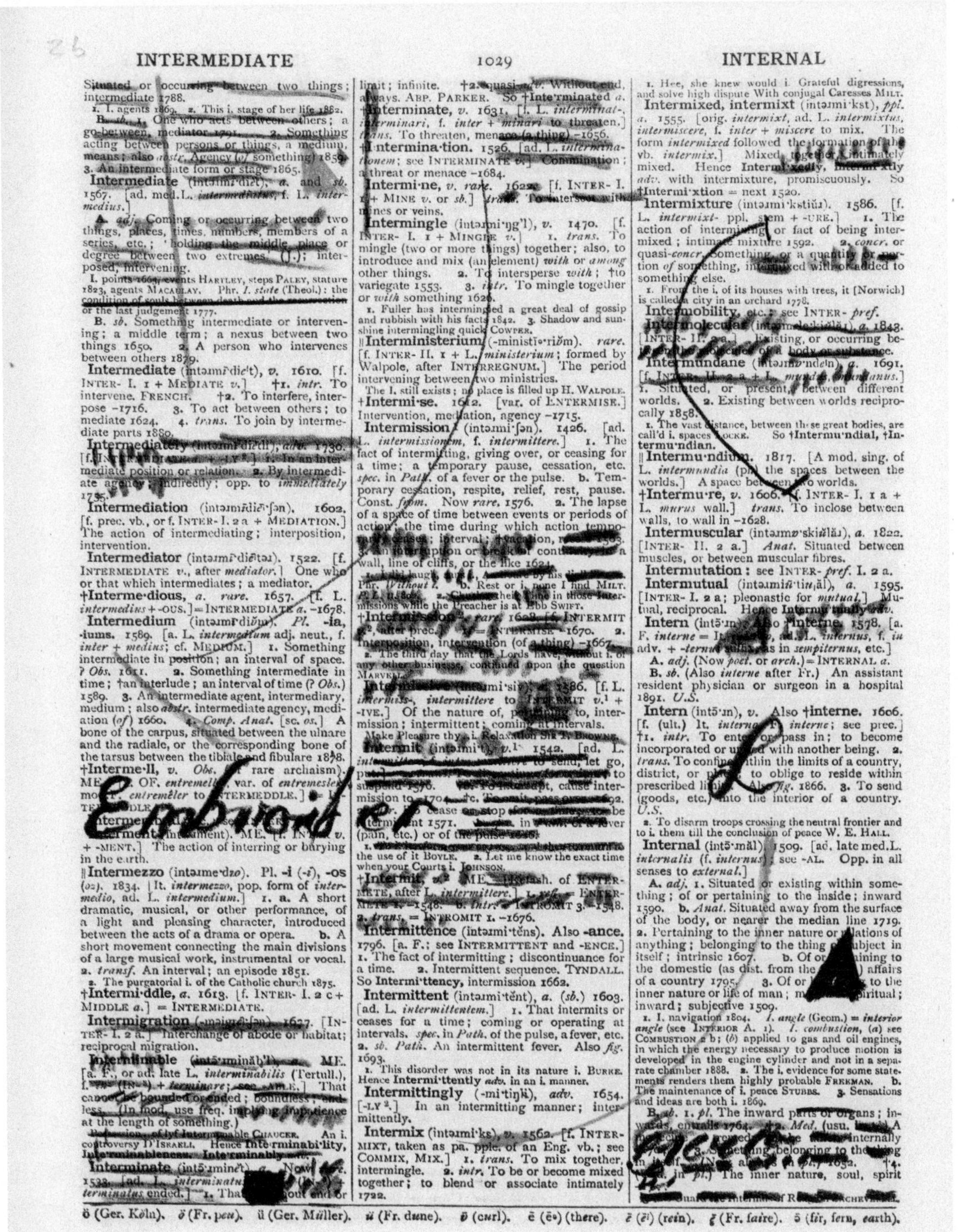
INTERMEDIATE
1029
INTERNAL
Embroider
15

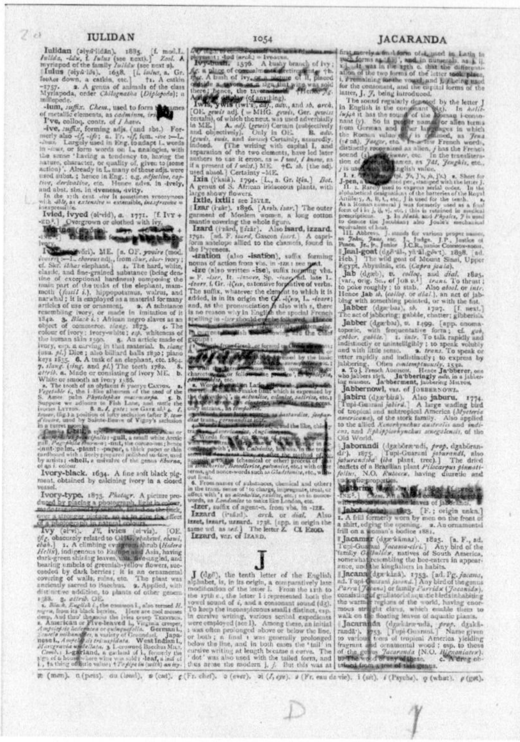

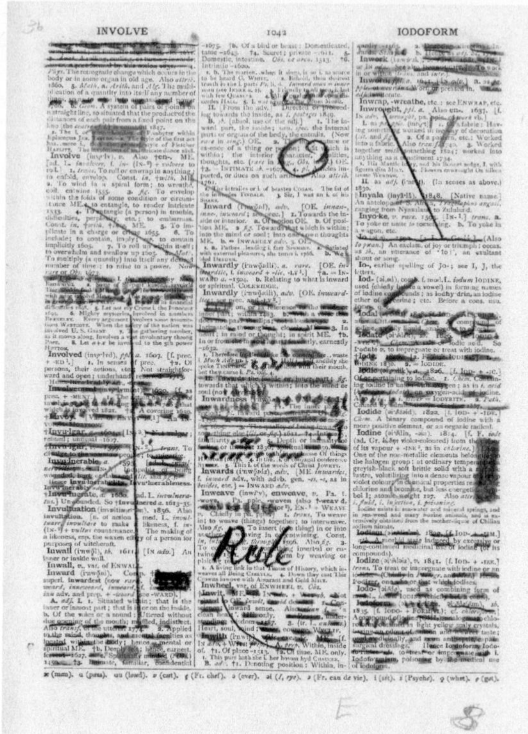

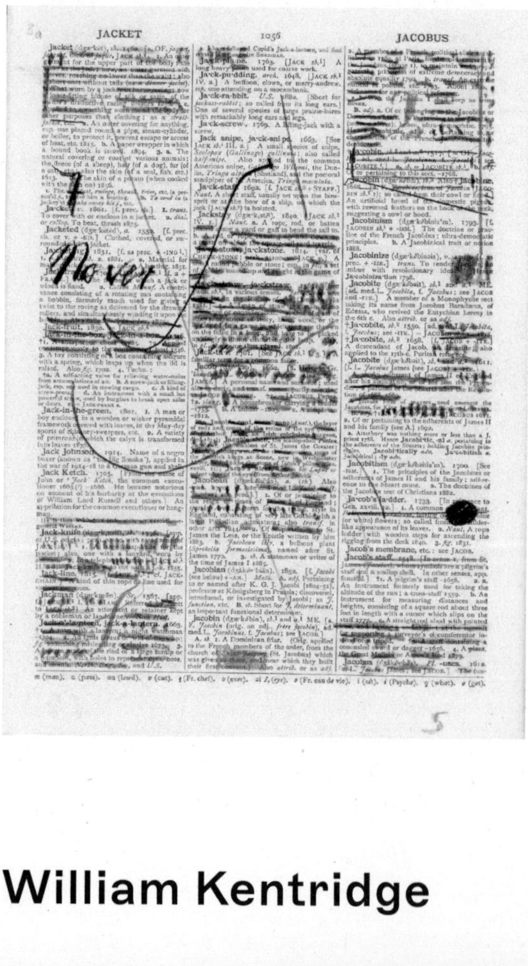

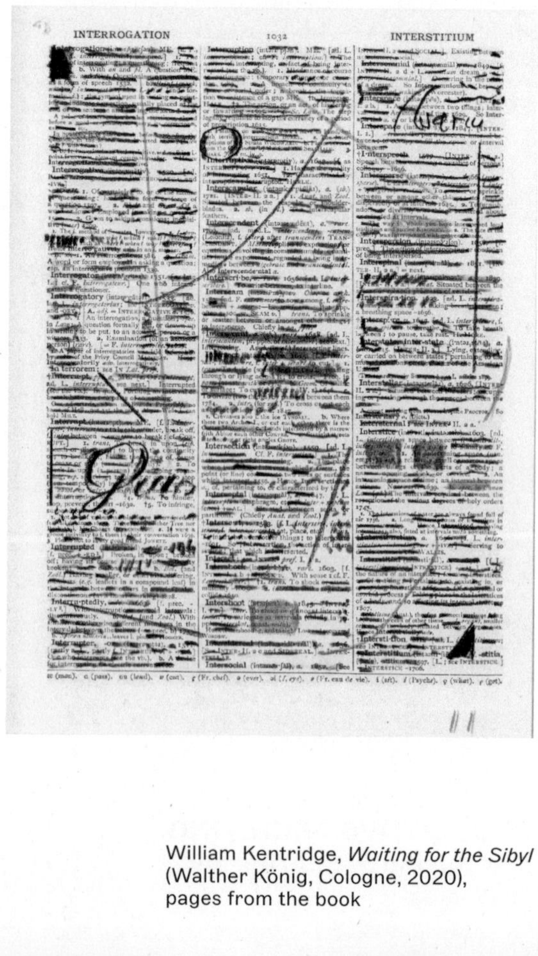

William Kentridge

William Kentridge, *Waiting for the Sibyl* (Walther König, Cologne, 2020), pages from the book

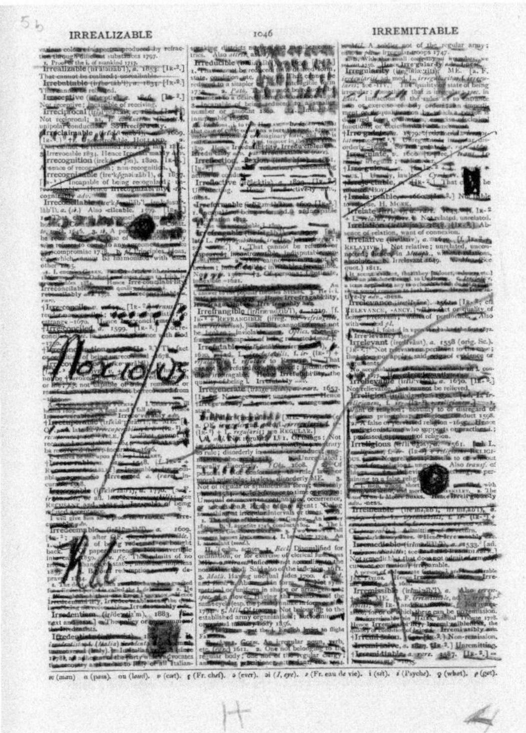
IRREALIZABLE
1046
IRREMITTABLE

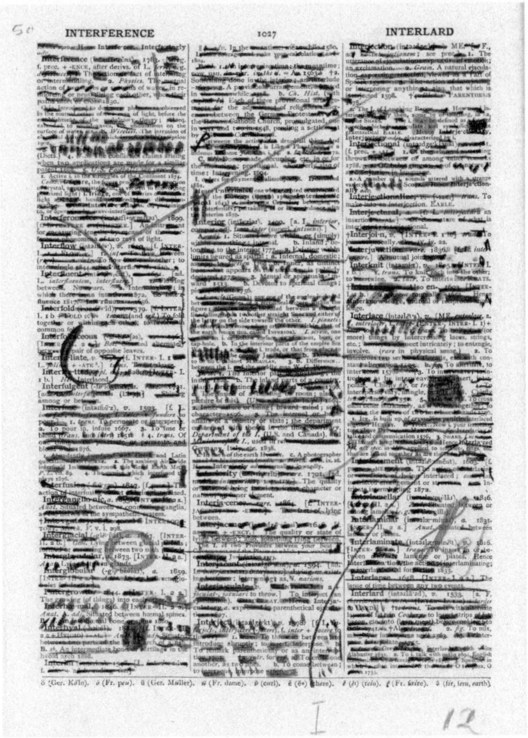
INTERFERENCE
1027
INTERLARD

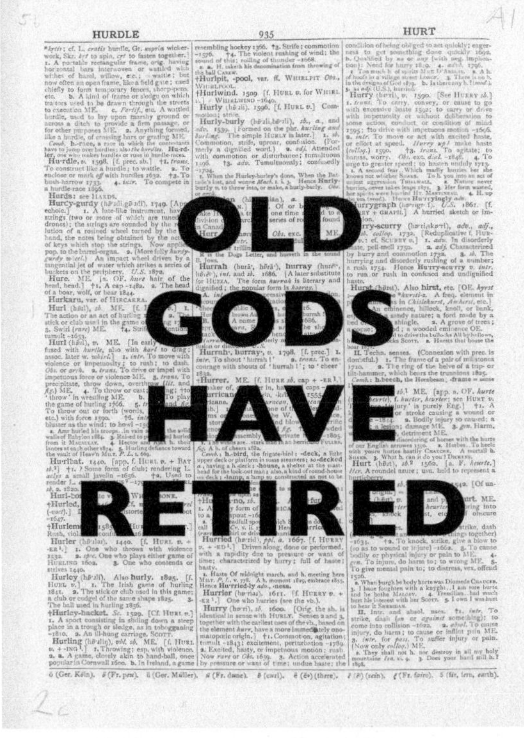
HURDLE
935
HURT
OLD
GODS
HAVE
RETIRED

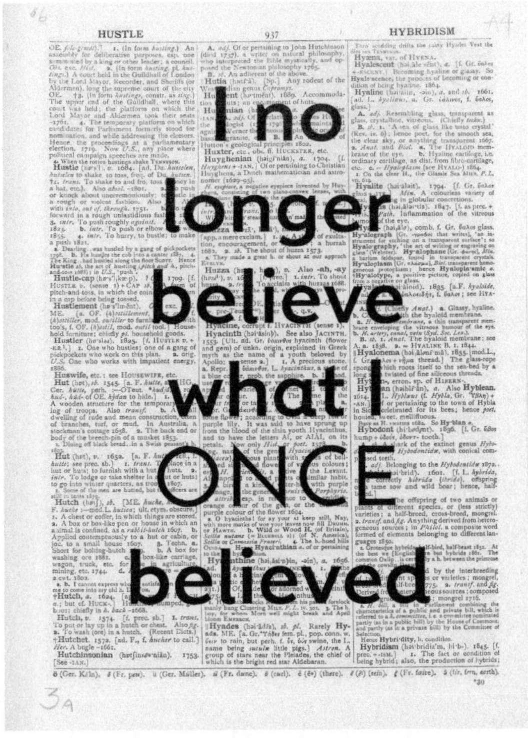
HUSTLE
937
HYBRIDISM
I no
longer
believe
what I
ONCE
believed

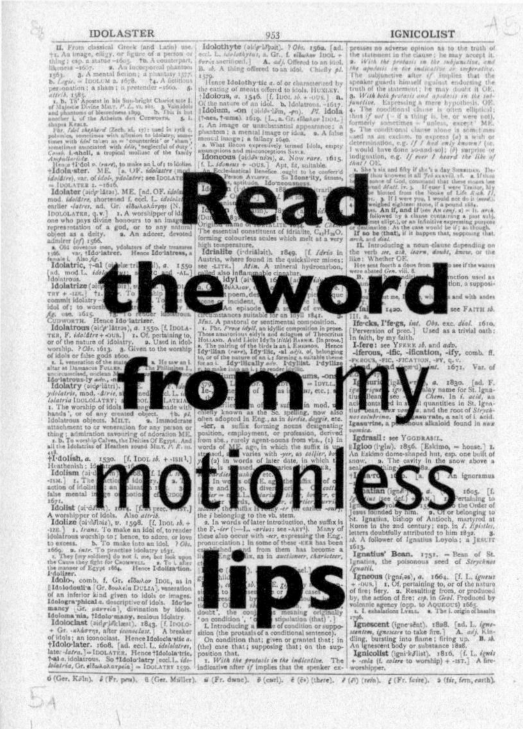

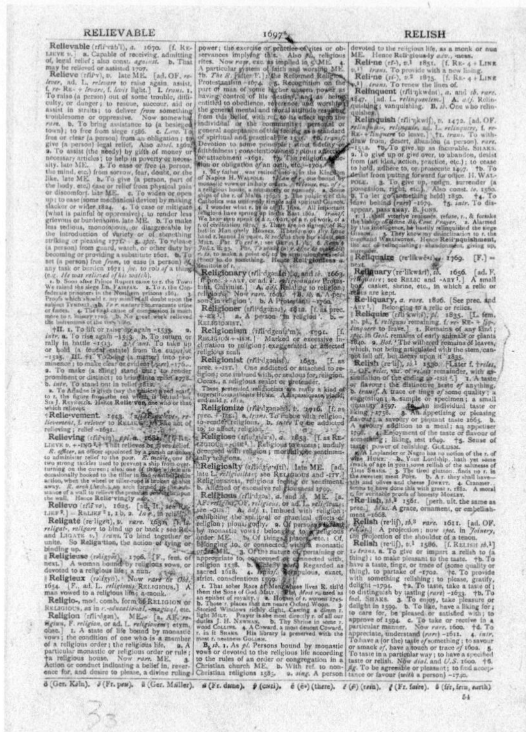

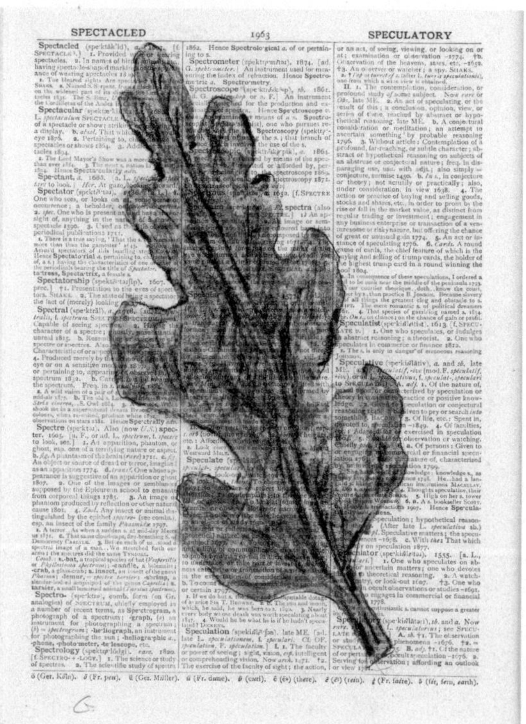

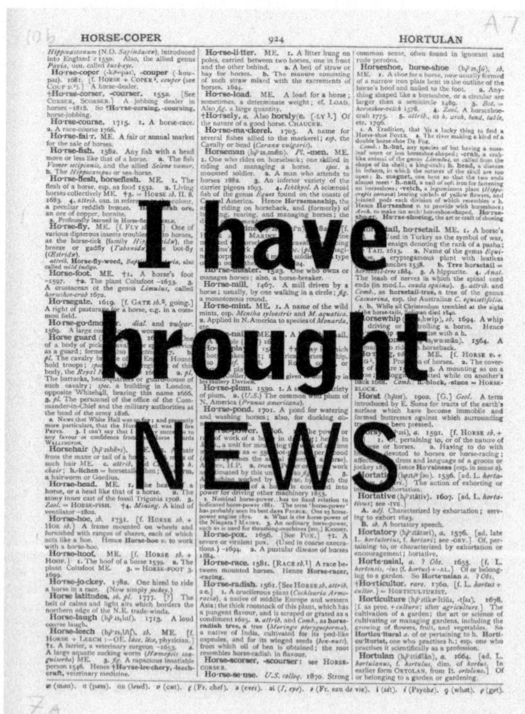

William Kentridge, *Waiting for the Sibyl* (Walther König, Cologne, 2020), pages from the book

William Kentridge

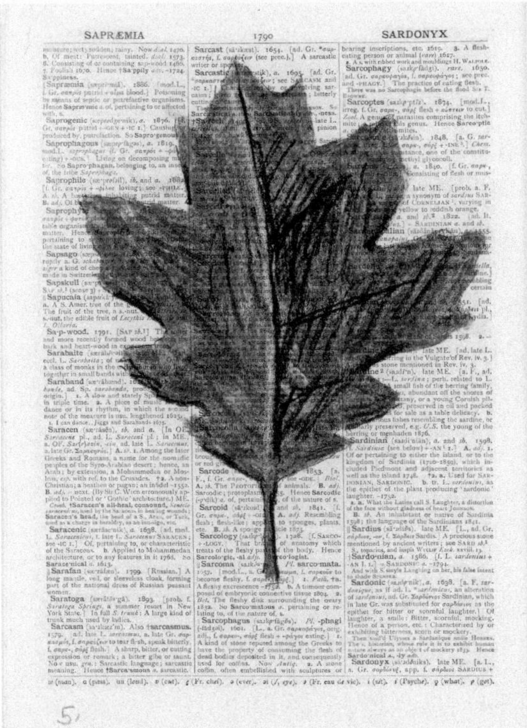
SAPRÆMIA 1790 SARDONYX

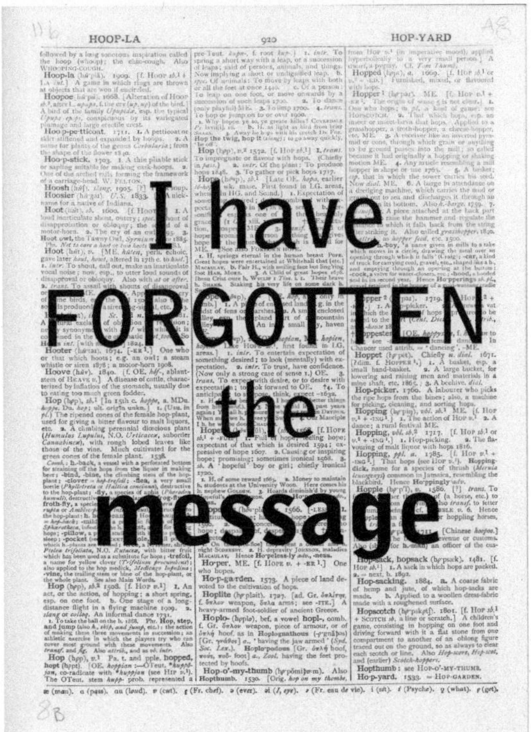
HOOP-LA 920 HOP-YARD
I have
FORGOTTEN
the
message

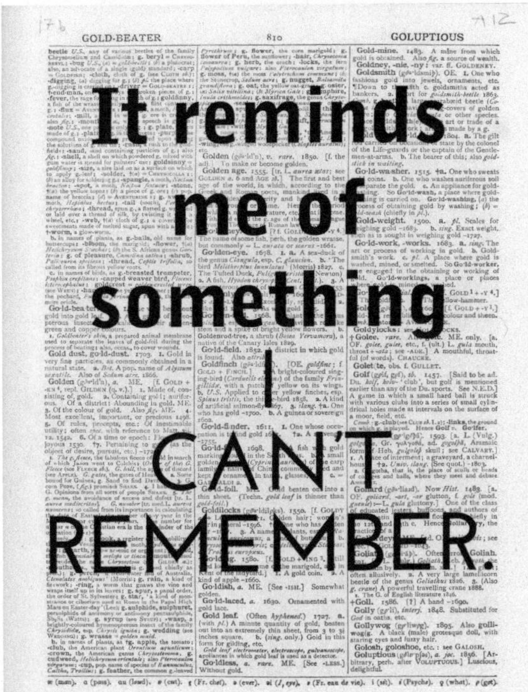
GOLD-BEATER 810 GOLUPTIOUS
It reminds
me of
something
I
CAN'T
REMEMBER.

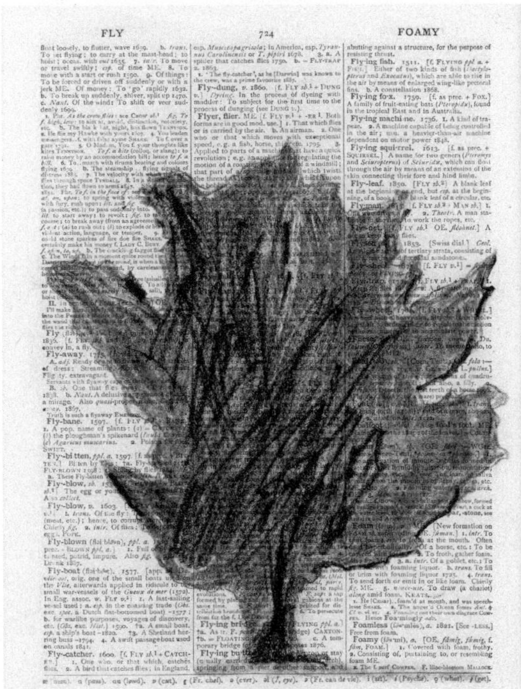
FLY 724 FOAMY

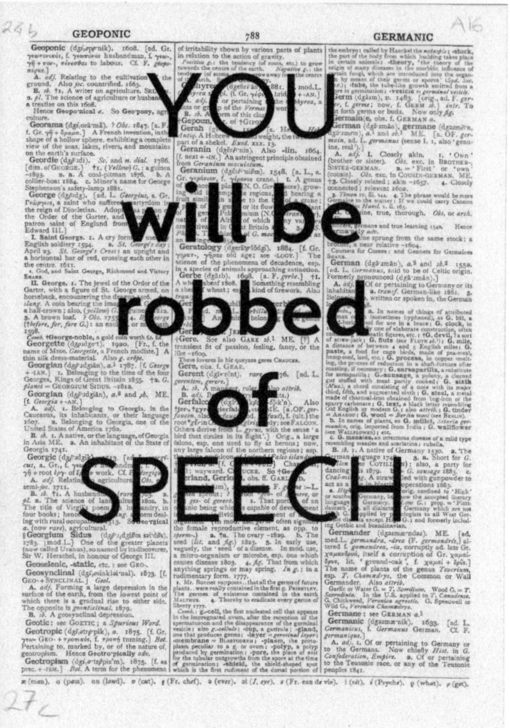

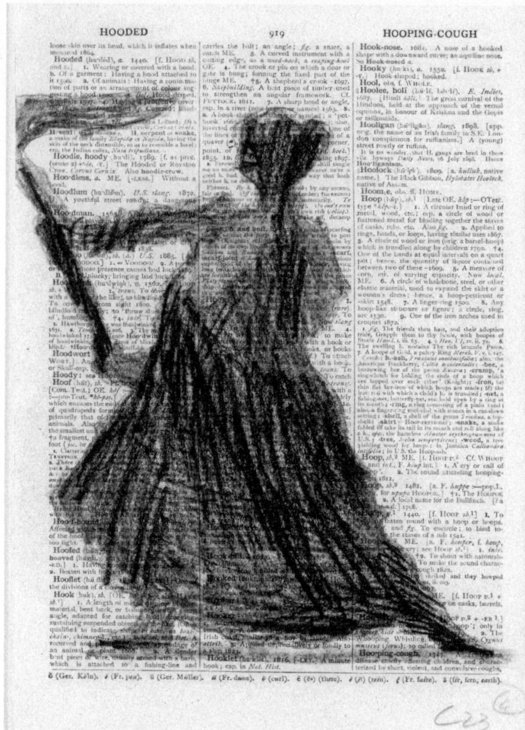

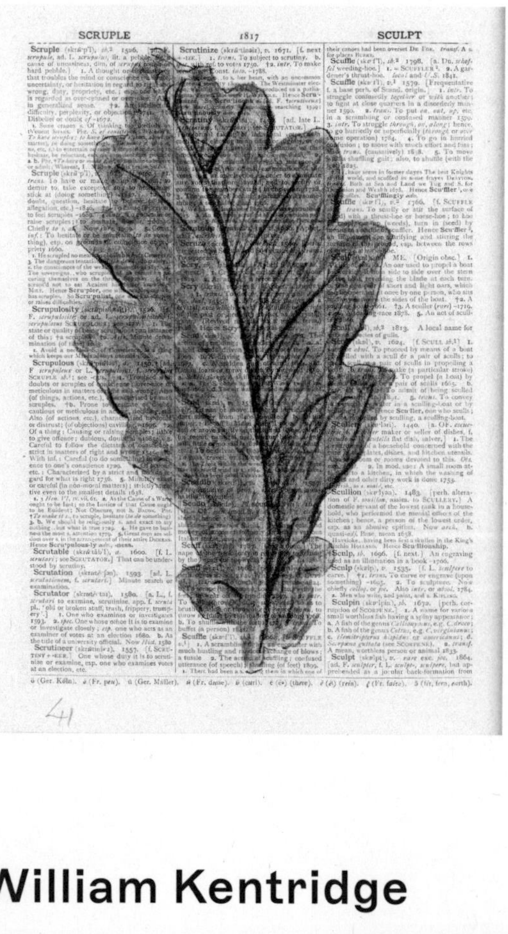

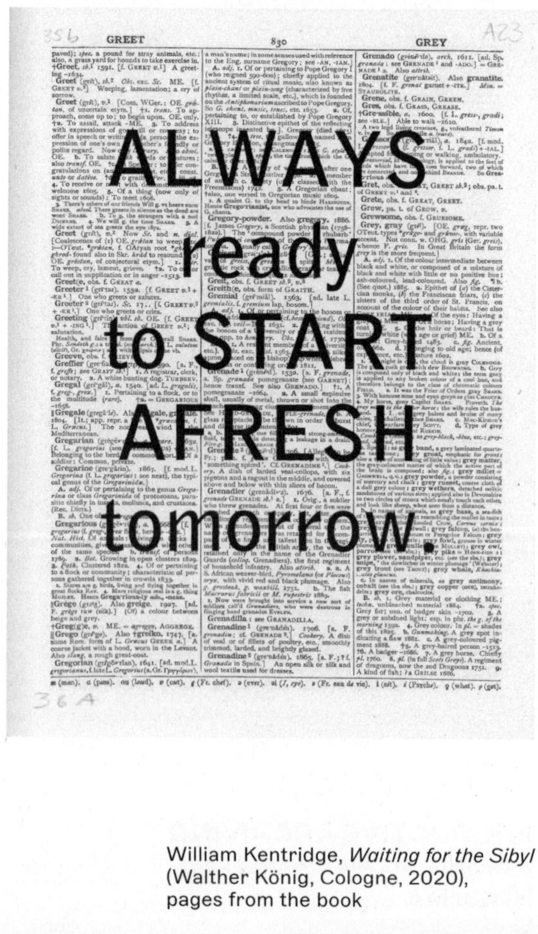

William Kentridge

William Kentridge, *Waiting for the Sibyl* (Walther König, Cologne, 2020), pages from the book

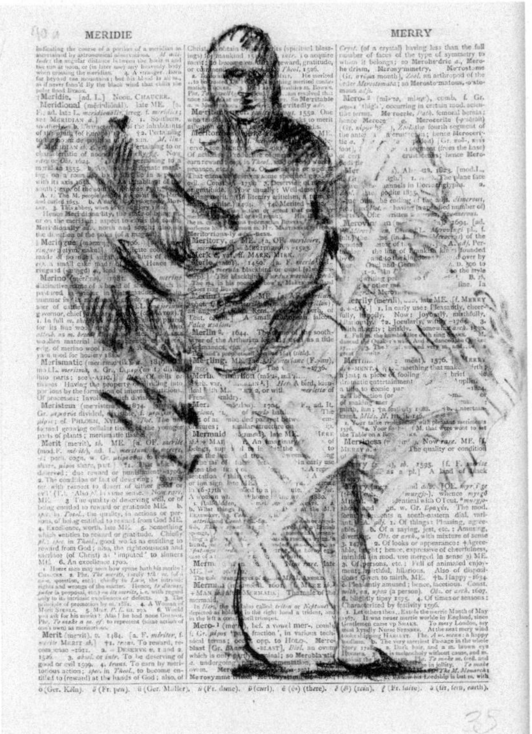

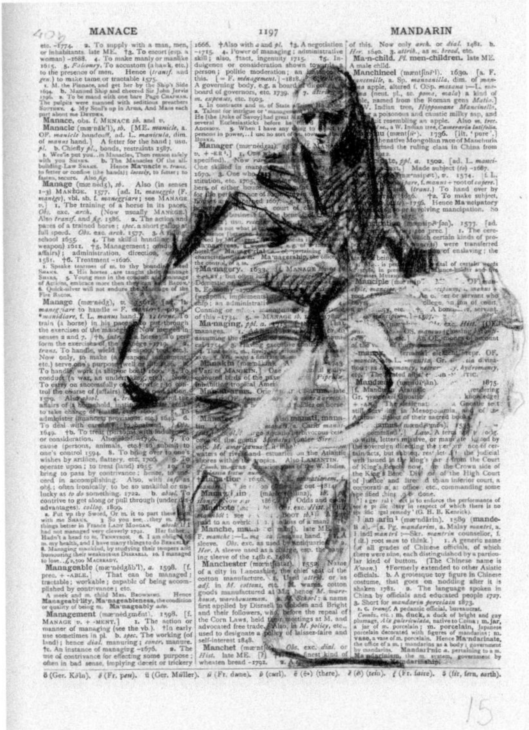

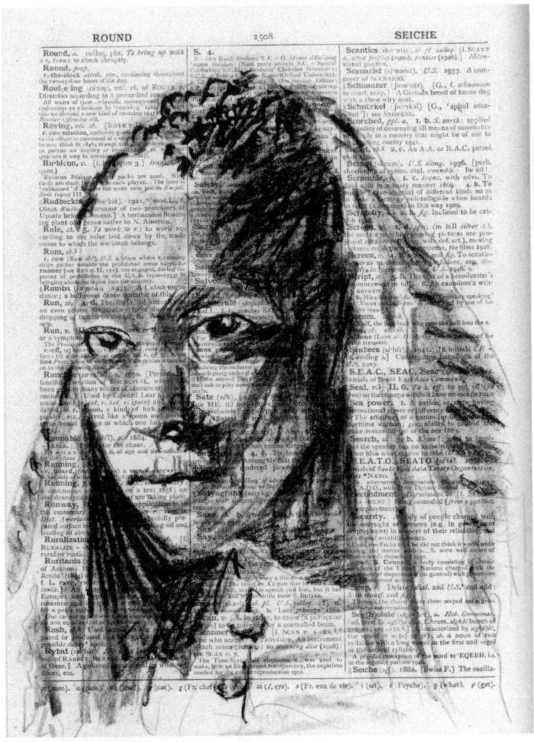

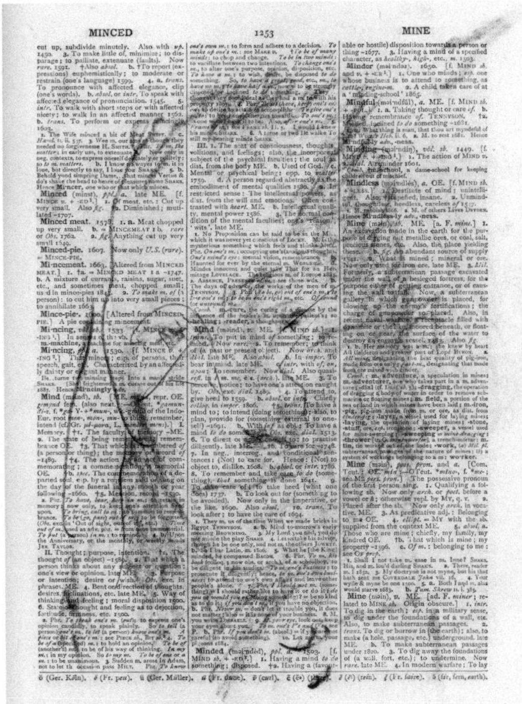

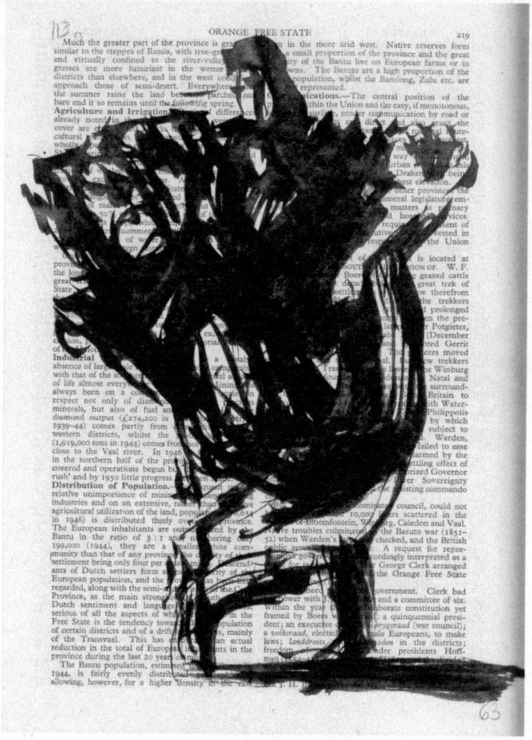

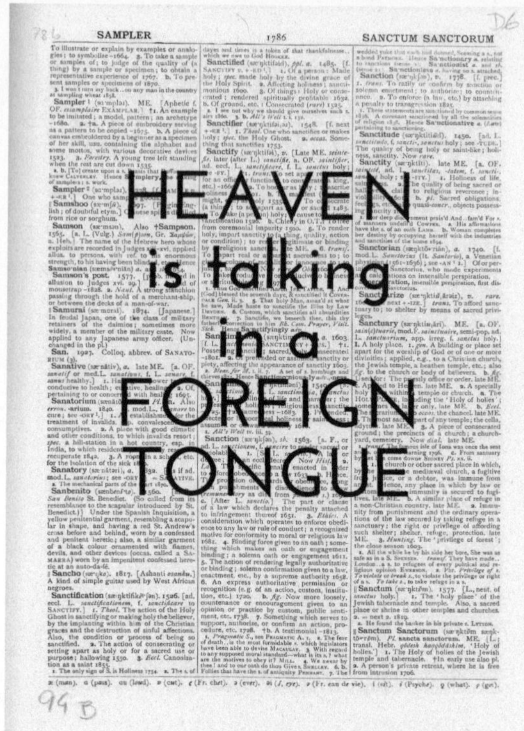

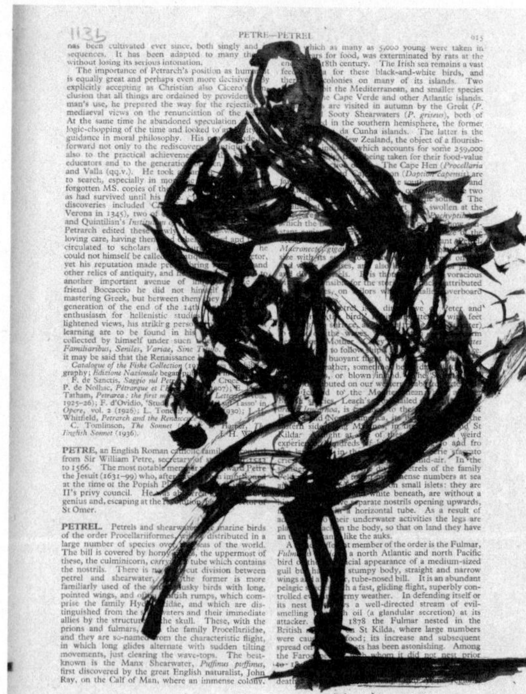

William Kentridge, *Waiting for the Sibyl* (Walther König, Cologne, 2020), pages from the book

William Kentridge

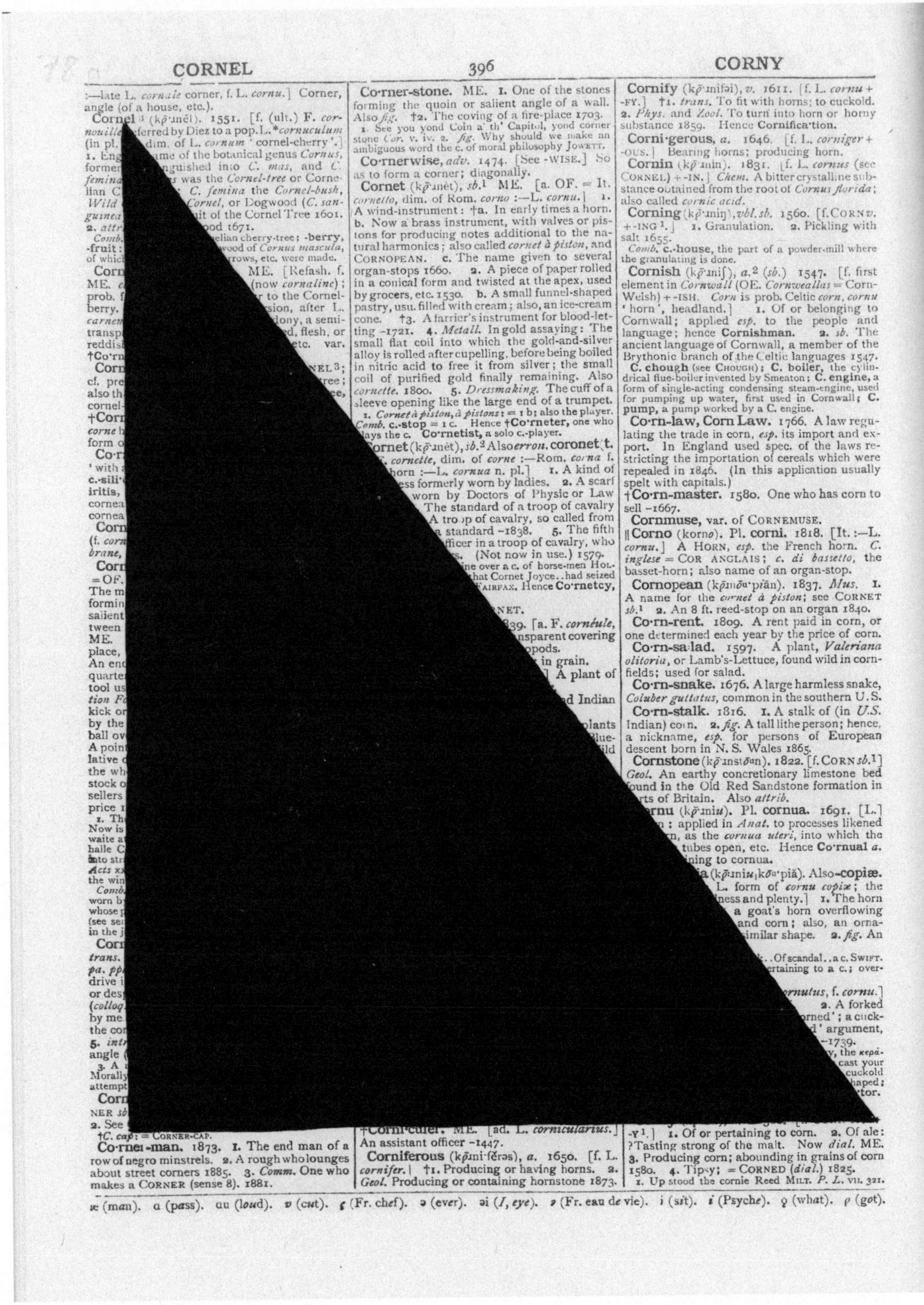

CORNEL 396 CORNY

:—late L. *cornale* corner, f. L. *cornu.*] Corner, angle (of a house, etc.).

Cornel ³ (kǭ·ɹnĕl). 1551. [f. (ult.) F. *cornouille* ... ferred by Diez to a pop.L.**cornuculum* (in pl., ... dim. of L. *cornum* 'cornel-cherry'.]

Co·rner-stone. ME. **1.** One of the stones forming the quoin or salient angle of a wall. Also *fig.* †**2.** The coving of a fire-place 1703. **1.** See you yond Coin a' th' Capitol, yond corner stone *Cor.* v. iv. 2. *fig.* Why should we make an ambiguous word the c. of moral philosophy JOWETT.

Co·rnerwise, *adv.* 1474. [See -WISE.] So as to form a corner; diagonally.

Cornet (kǭ·ɹnĕt), *sb.*¹ ME. [a. OF. = It. *cornetto*, dim. of Rom. *corno* :—L. *cornu.*] **1.** A wind-instrument: †**a.** In early times a horn. **b.** Now a brass instrument, with valves or pistons for producing notes additional to the natural harmonics; also called *cornet à piston*, and CORNOPEAN. **c.** The name given to several organ-stops 1660. **2.** A piece of paper rolled in a conical form and twisted at the apex, used by grocers, etc. 1530. **b.** A small funnel-shaped pastry, usu. filled with cream; also, an ice-cream cone. †**3.** A farrier's instrument for blood-letting -1721. **4.** *Metall.* In gold assaying: The small flat coil into which the gold-and-silver alloy is rolled after cupelling, before being boiled in nitric acid to free it from silver; the small coil of purified gold finally remaining. Also *cornette.* 1800. **5.** *Dressmaking.* The cuff of a sleeve opening like the large end of a trumpet. **1.** *Cornet à piston, à pistons*: = 1 b; also the player. *Comb.* **c.-stop** = 1 c. Hence †**Co·rneter,** one who plays the c. **Co·rnetist,** a solo c.-player.

...ornet (kǭ·ɹnĕt), *sb.*² Also *erron.* **coronet**... *cornette*, dim. of *corne* :—Rom. *corna* f. ... horn :—L. *cornua* n. pl.] **1.** A kind of ... ess formerly worn by ladies. **2.** A scarf ... worn by Doctors of Physic or Law ... The standard of a troop of cavalry ... A troop of cavalry, so called from ... a standard -1838. **5.** The fifth ... fficer in a troop of cavalry, who ... (Not now in use.) 1579. ... ne over a c. of horse-men HOL... hat Cornet Joyce..had seized ... FAIRFAX. Hence **Co·rnetcy,**

†**Corni·culer.** ME. [ad. L. *cornicularius.*] An assistant officer -1447.

Corniferous (kǭɹni·fĕrəs), *a.* 1650. [f. L. *cornifer.*] †**1.** Producing or having horns. **2.** *Geol.* Producing or containing hornstone 1873.

Cornify (kǭ·ɹnifəi), *v.* 1611. [f. L. *cornu* + -FY.] †**1.** *trans.* To fit with horns; to cuckold. **2.** *Phys.* and *Zool.* To turn into horn or horny substance 1859. Hence **Cornifica·tion.**

Corni·gerous, *a.* 1646. [f. L. *corniger* + -OUS.] Bearing horns; producing horn.

Cornin (kǭ·ɹnin). 1831. [f. L. *cornus* (see CORNEL) + -IN.] *Chem.* A bitter crystalline substance obtained from the root of *Cornus florida*; also called *cornic acid.*

Corning (kǭ·ɹniŋ), *vbl. sb.* 1560. [f. CORN *v.* + -ING ¹.] **1.** Granulation. **2.** Pickling with salt 1655. *Comb.* **c.-house,** the part of a powder-mill where the granulating is done.

Cornish (kǭ·ɹniʃ), *a.*² (*sb.*) 1547. [f. first element in *Cornwall* (OE. *Cornwealas* = Corn-Welsh) + -ISH. *Corn* is prob. Celtic *corn, cornu* 'horn', headland.] **1.** Of or belonging to Cornwall; applied *esp.* to the people and language; hence **Cornishman. 2.** *sb.* The ancient language of Cornwall, a member of the Brythonic branch of the Celtic languages 1547. **C. chough** (see CHOUGH); **C. boiler,** the cylindrical flue-boiler invented by Smeaton; **C. engine,** a form of single-acting condensing steam-engine, used for pumping up water, first used in Cornwall; **C. pump,** a pump worked by a C. engine.

Co·rn-law, Corn Law. 1766. A law regulating the trade in corn, *esp.* its import and export. In England used spec. of the laws restricting the importation of cereals which were repealed in 1846. (In this application usually spelt with capitals.)

†**Co·rn-master.** 1580. One who has corn to sell -1667.

Cornmuse, var. of CORNEMUSE.

‖**Corno** (korno). Pl. **corni.** 1818. [It. :—L. *cornu.*] A HORN, *esp.* the French horn. *C. inglese* = COR ANGLAIS; *c. di bassetto,* the basset-horn; also name of an organ-stop.

Cornopean (kǭɹnōᵘ·piăn). 1837. *Mus.* **1.** A name for the *cornet à piston*; see CORNET *sb.*¹ **2.** An 8 ft. reed-stop on an organ 1840.

Co·rn-rent. 1809. A rent paid in corn, or one determined each year by the price of corn.

Co·rn-sa·lad. 1597. A plant, *Valeriana olitoria*, or Lamb's-Lettuce, found wild in corn-fields; used for salad.

Co·rn-snake. 1676. A large harmless snake, *Coluber guttatus*, common in the southern U.S.

Co·rn-stalk. 1816. **1.** A stalk of (in *U.S.* Indian) corn. **2.** *fig.* A tall lithe person; hence, a nickname, *esp.* for persons of European descent born in N. S. Wales 1865.

Cornstone (kǭ·ɹnstōᵘn). 1822. [f. CORN *sb.*¹] *Geol.* An earthy concretionary limestone bed found in the Old Red Sandstone formation in ...rts of Britain. Also *attrib.*

...rnu (kǭ·ɹniu). Pl. **cornua.** 1691. [L.] ... : applied in *Anat.* to processes likened ..., as the *cornua uteri*, into which the ... tubes open, etc. Hence **Co·rnual** *a.* ... ning to cornua.

...a (kǭɹniu,kōᵘ·piă). Also **-copiæ.** ... L. form of *cornu copiæ*; the ... ness and plenty.] **1.** The horn ... a goat's horn overflowing ... and corn; also, an orna... imilar shape. **2.** *fig.* An

Co·rner-man. 1873. **1.** The end man of a row of negro minstrels. **2.** A rough who lounges about street corners 1885. **3.** *Comm.* One who makes a CORNER (sense 8). 1881.

...-Y ¹.] **1.** Of or pertaining to corn. **2.** Of ale: ?Tasting strong of the malt. Now *dial.* ME. **3.** Producing corn; abounding in grains of corn 1580. **4.** Tipsy; = CORNED (*dial.*) 1825. **1.** Up stood the cornie Reed MILT. *P. L.* VII. 321.

æ (man). ɑ (pass). au (loud). ʋ (cut). ȝ (Fr. chef). ə (ever). əi (*I, eye*). ə (Fr. eau de vie). i (sit). ɨ (Psyche). ǫ (what). ϱ (got).

THE ARCHIVE ONETHIRTY

Monika Huber

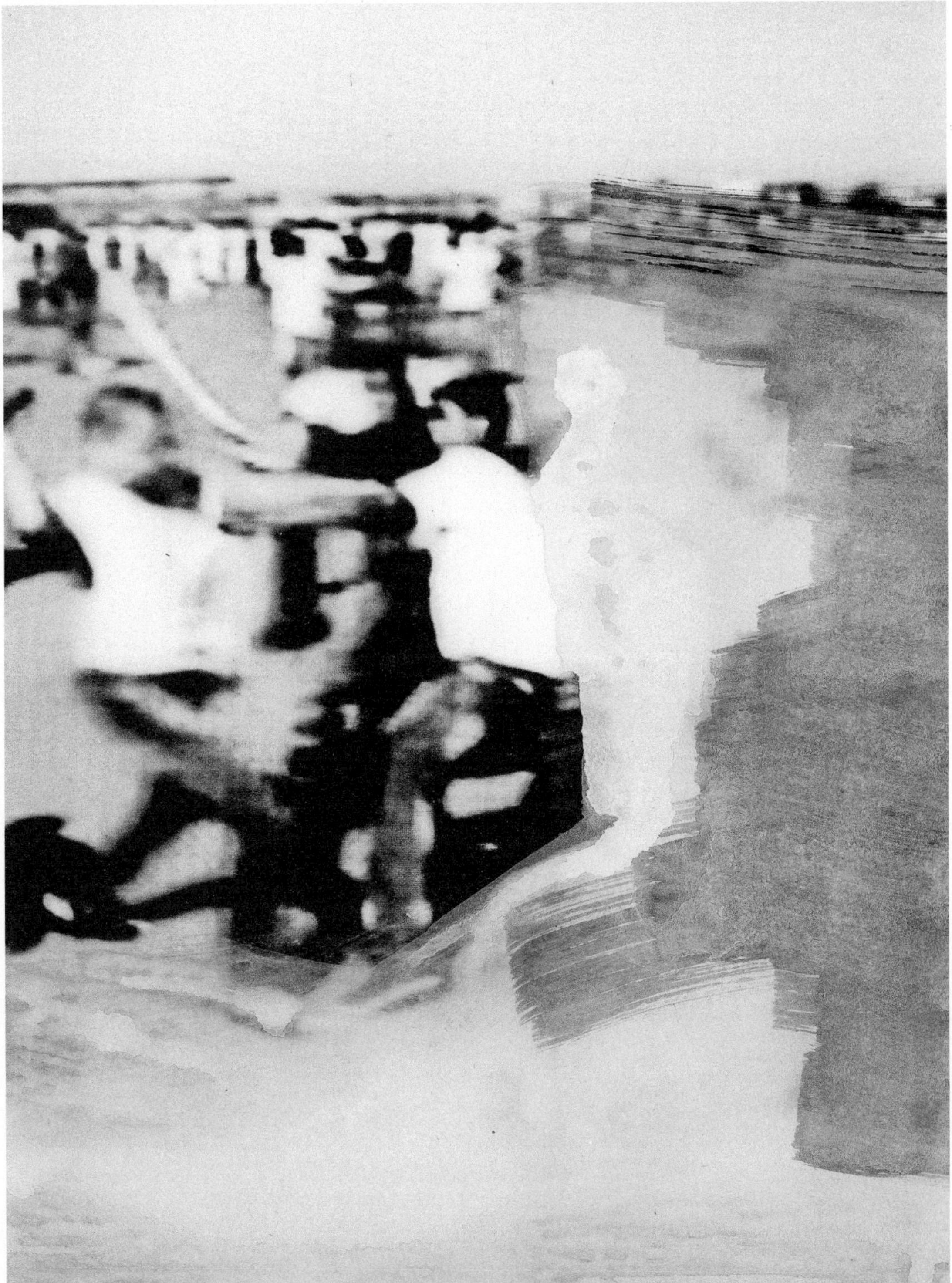

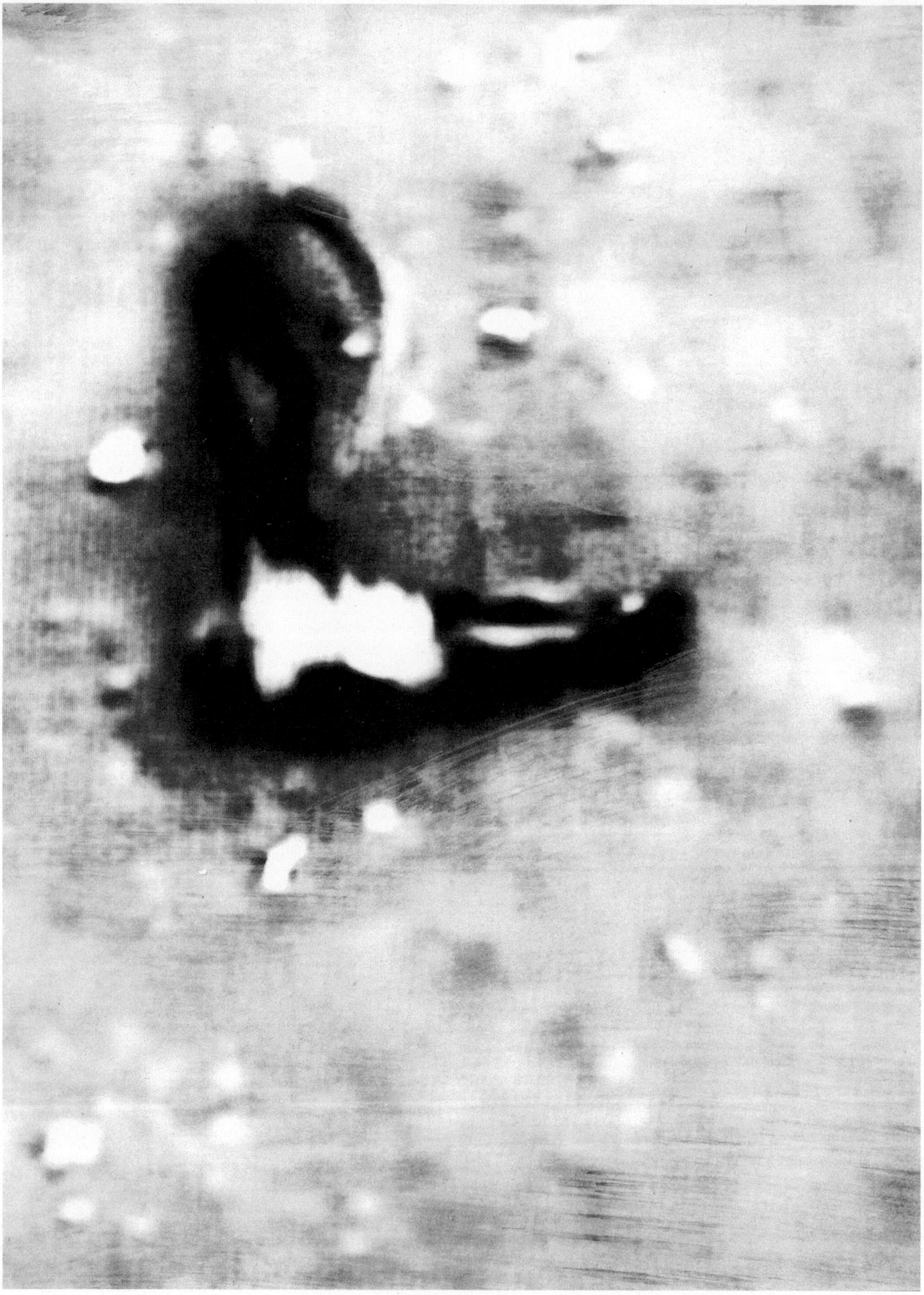

Monika Huber

Monika Huber,
The Archive *OneThirty*, 2011

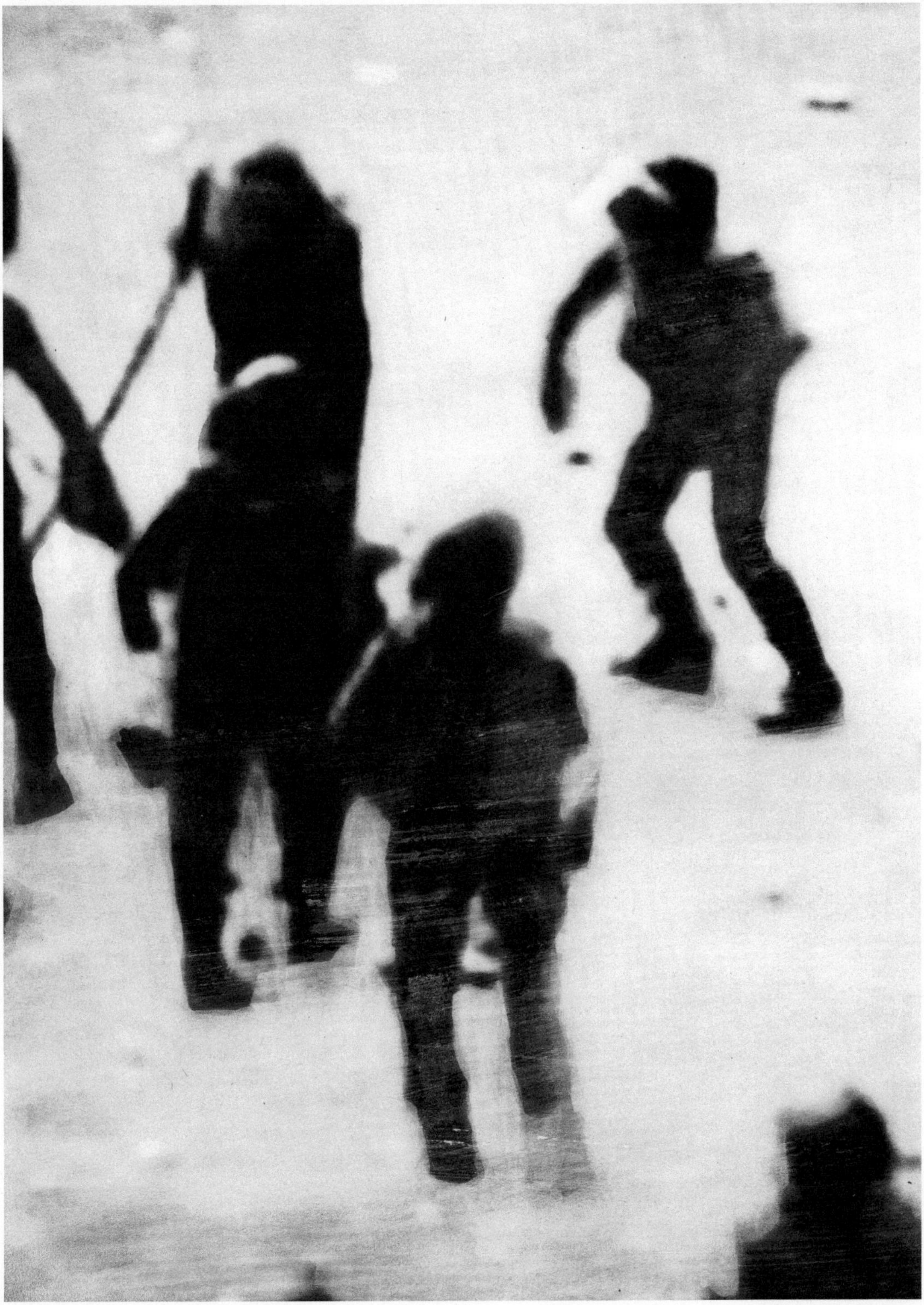

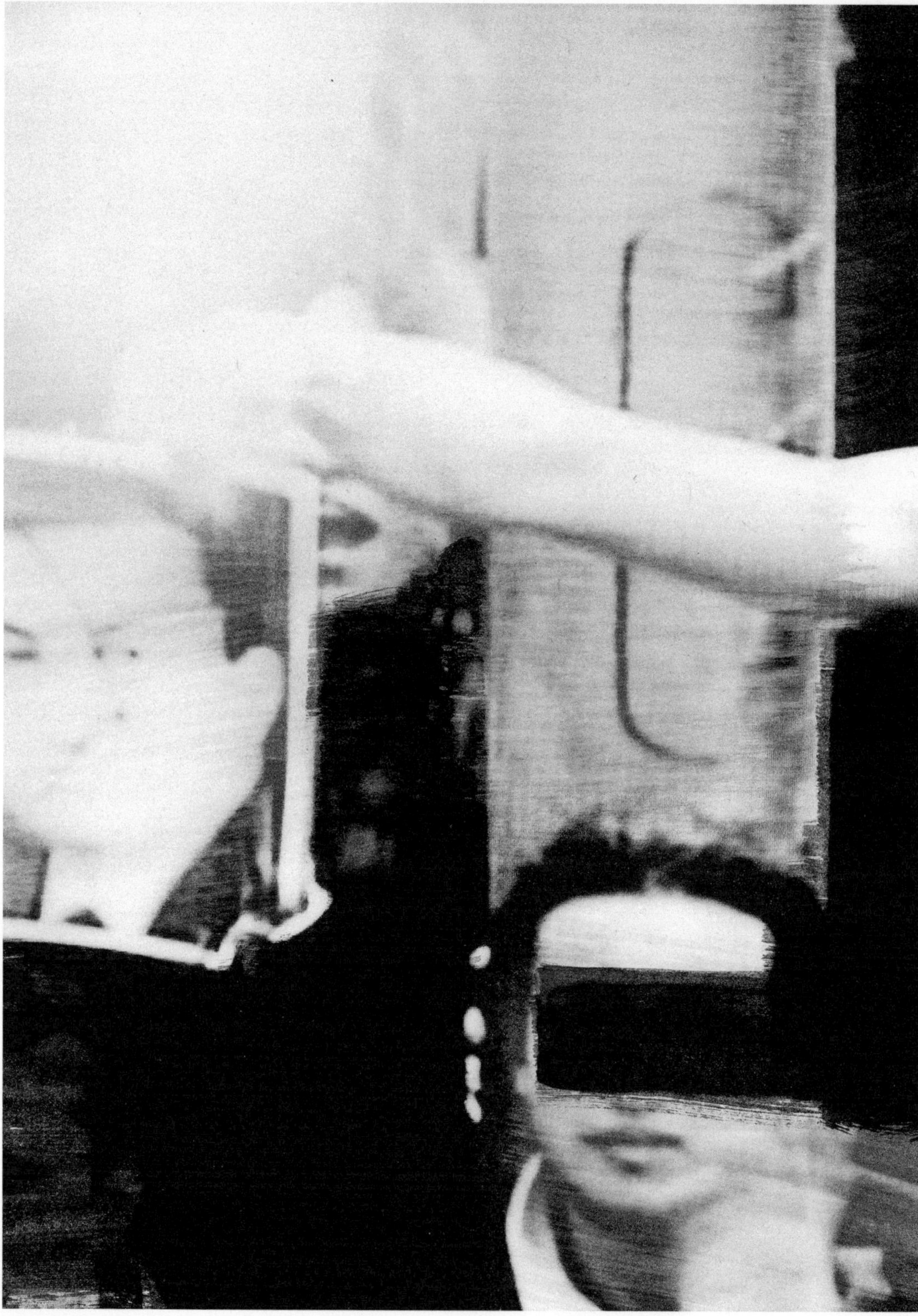

Monika Huber

Monika Huber,
The Archive *OneThirty*, 2011

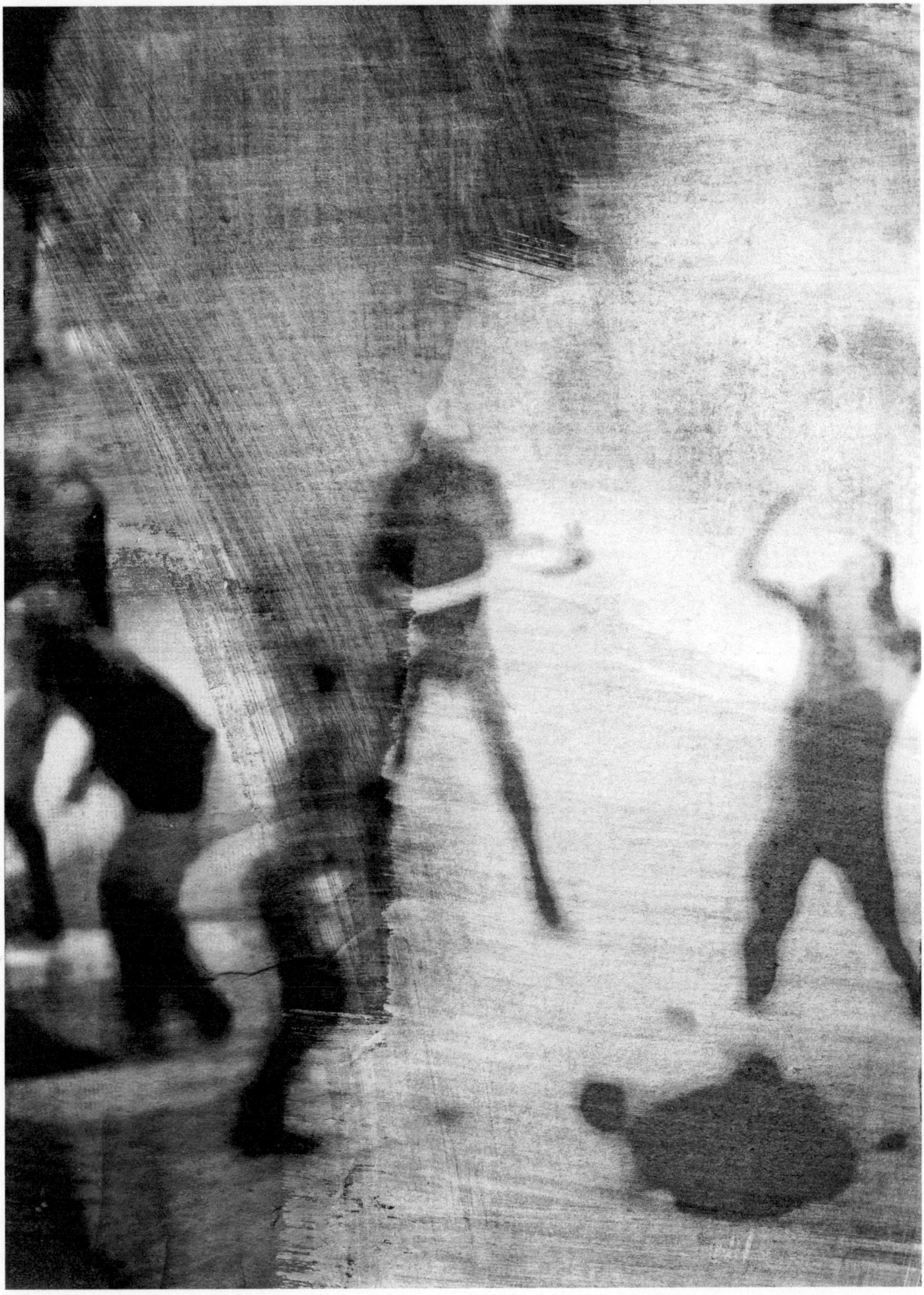

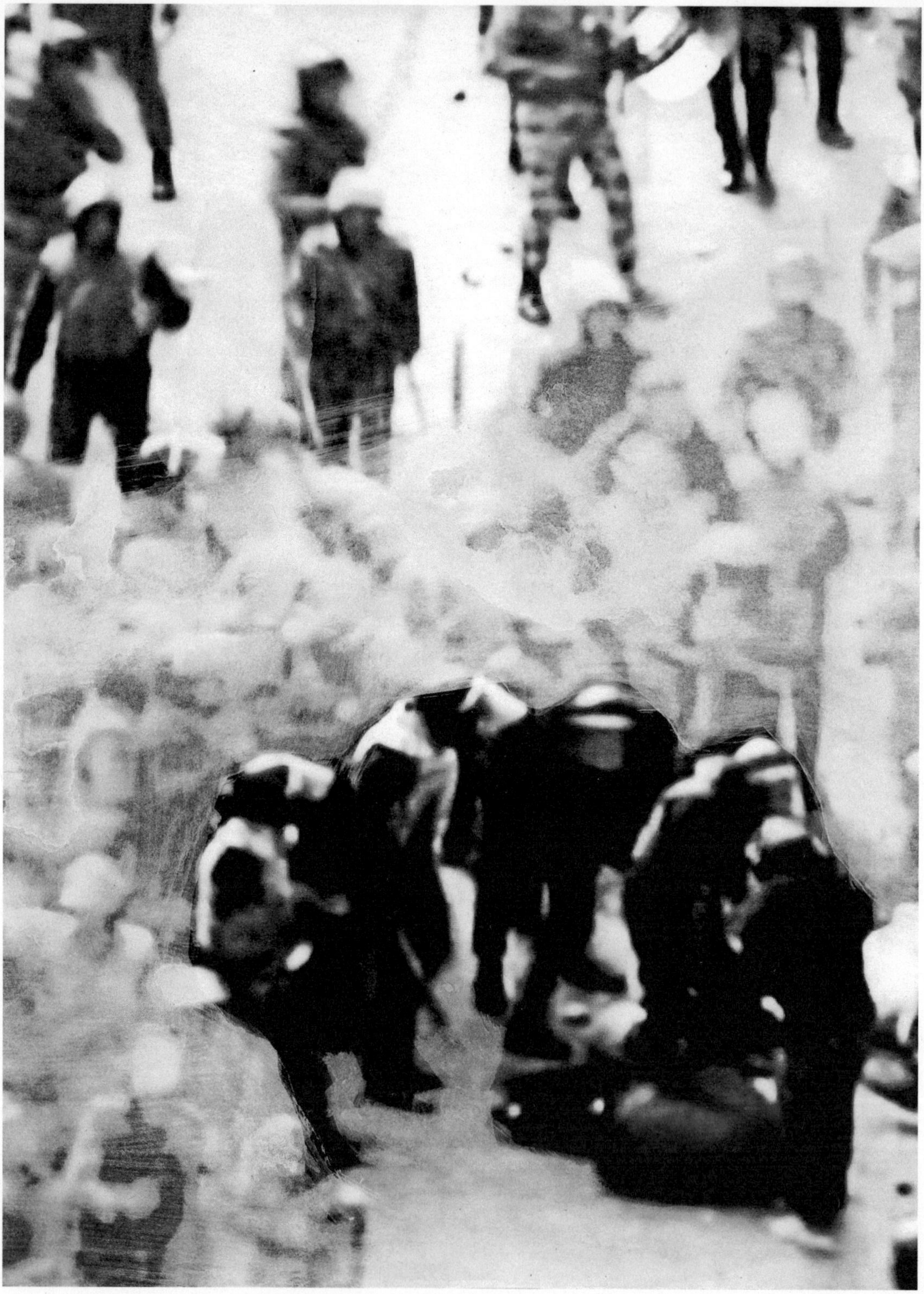

Monika Huber

Monika Huber,
The Archive *OneThirty*, 2011

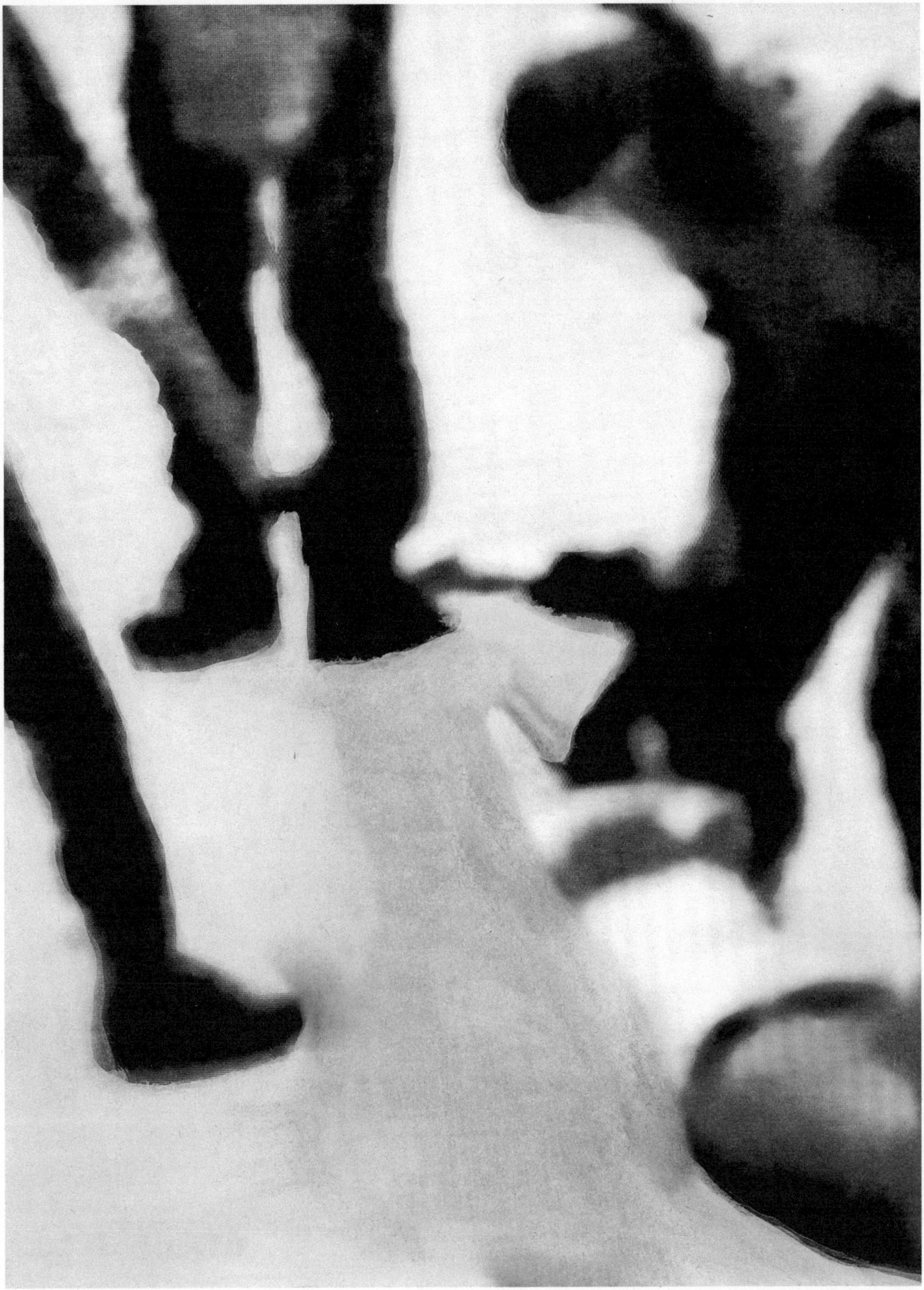

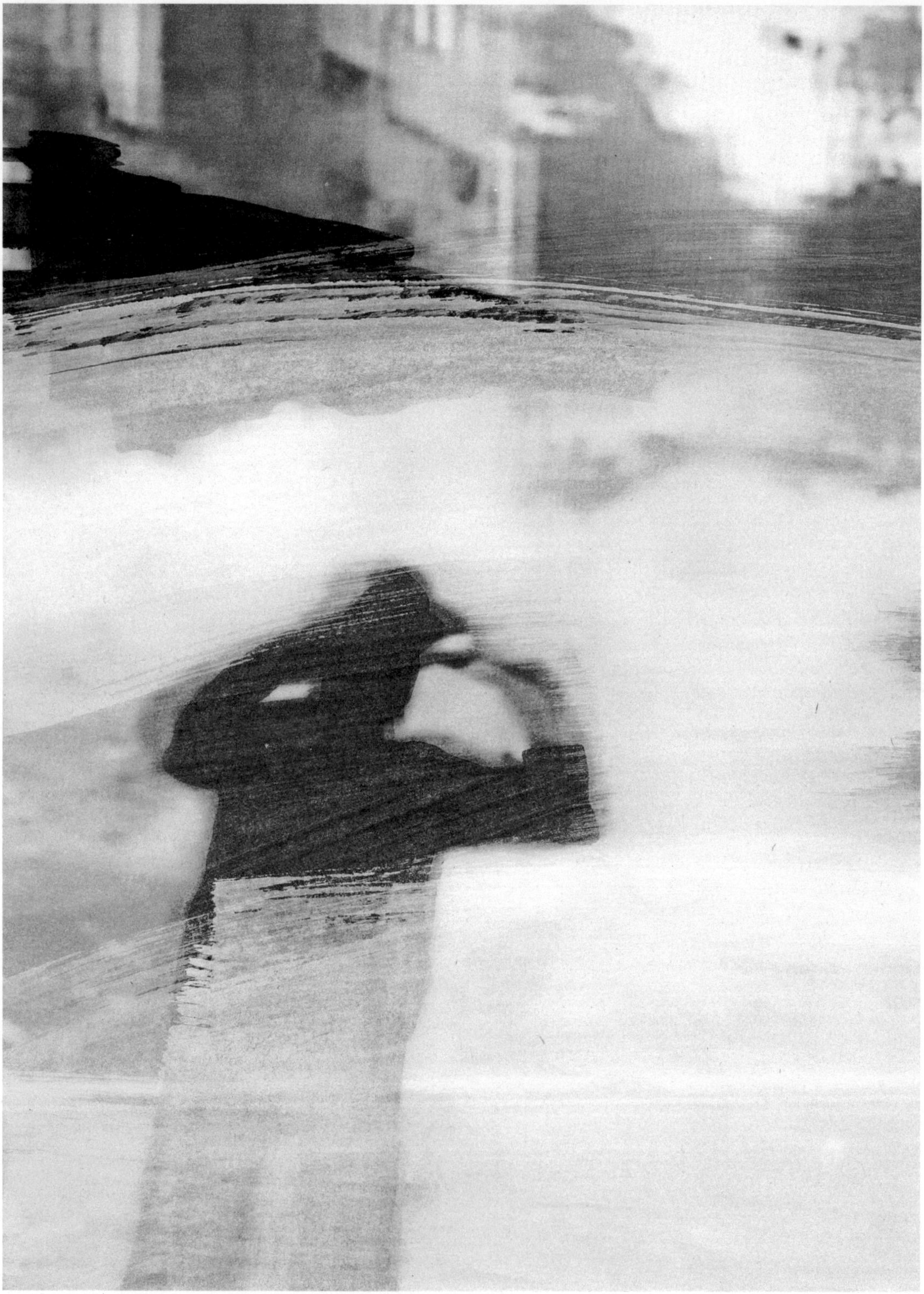

Monika Huber

Monika Huber,
The Archive *OneThirty*, 2011

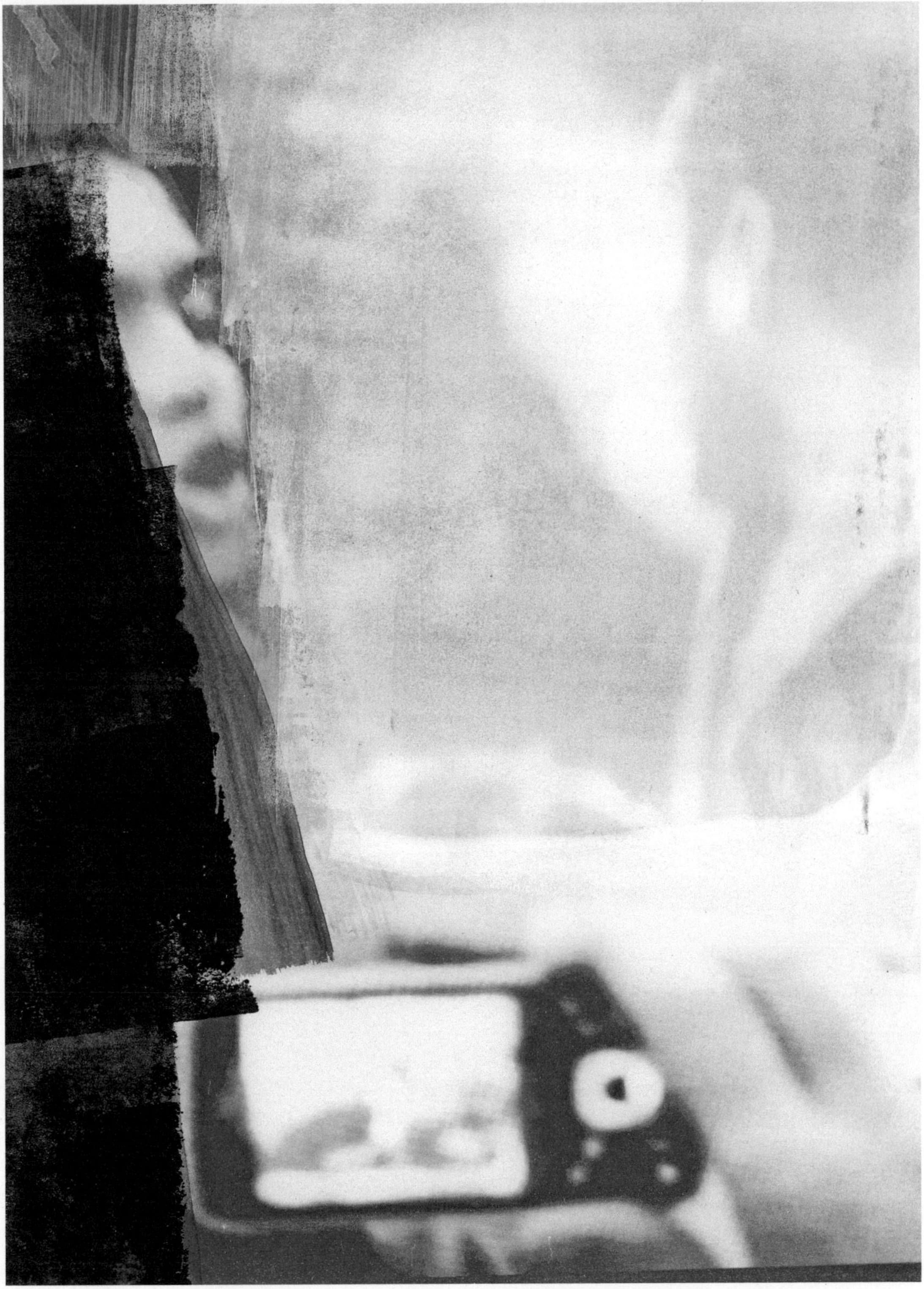

Archiving Objects

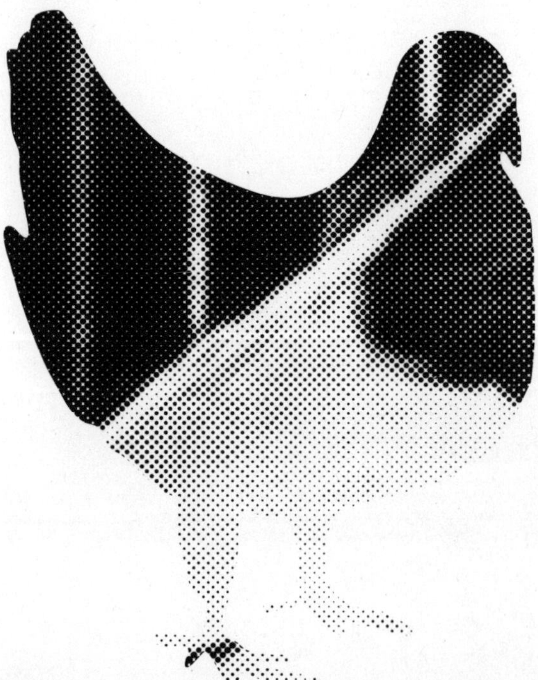

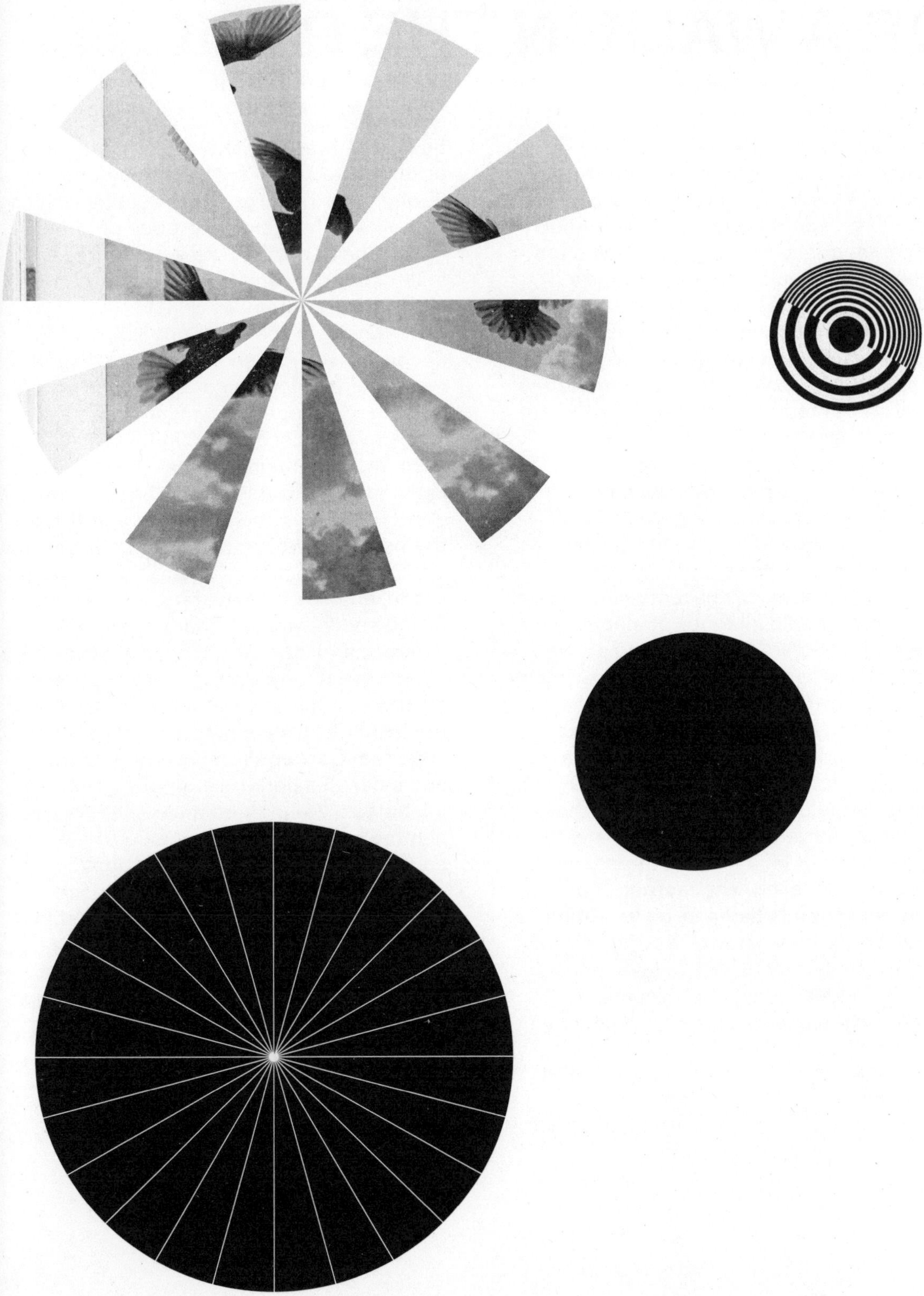

ARCHIVAL ABSURDITY, OR A WALK IN THE PARK

I grew up in a small village. We lived in an old converted farm in the middle of the town with a large but narrow garden in the back, about 4 meters wide and 30 meters long. The garden had three plum trees: Reine Claude, Prunus 'Victoria' and 'Marjorie's Seedling.' At the far end were shrubs bearing redcurrants and blackcurrants, and one gooseberry, never my favorite. At the height of summer, I spent many moments stuffing myself with the soft sweet fruits. A line of various types of trees separated us from the neighbors on the left, and a low fence on the right demarcated our garden from that of my aunt and uncle. Our garden was all grass, no flowerbeds, no herbs, and no vegetables. My parents had a shop in which they sold all types of electrical goods, and had little time to tend gardens. I loved the grass. The soft and sometimes prickly or moist blades of grass beneath my feet always felt like summer. There was an additional perk: mowing the lawn was rewarded with a few cents to buy ice cream. Some of my friends lived in the nearby countryside on small farms with large swaths of land around them where we never got bored. The mother of one of my best friends had a large vegetable patch where they grew most of their own food. Come harvest time, strawberries, cherries, elderflower, redcurrants, blackcurrants, gooseberries, raspberries, blackberries, plums, grapes, apples, pears, tomatoes, onions and cucumbers would be sorted, washed, and cooked into jams or fermented in jars. The hissing and bubbling of the large glass demijohn filled with slowly fermenting grapes or plums is still one of my favorite sounds. Yes, I am still tempted by any fresh fruit, but I never got into gardening.

Living in the inner city didn't help of course: with fresh groceries available next door and looking out over one of the most picturesque Amsterdam canals, it never even crossed my mind. After having lived in city centers for over thirty years I moved to the outskirts, and now I own a garden. Lacking the experience or drive, the first year we simply tossed out the overgrown blackberries and the abundant nettle, and sowing several packages of mixed seeds saw to it that we enjoyed a summer amidst a field of wild flowers. The bees were happy, and so were the weeds, nettles and horsetail that quickly engulfed the 'wild' yet fragile annuals. The second year, the 'Garden Women' lent a hand and cleared a path through the green mishmash. We planted a tree, the freshly planted perennials kept most of the weeds back, and the bees were still happy.

Over the years several friends had asked me if I might be interested in setting up a small vegetable garden, a green enclosure on the outskirts of the city, a place to relax or do some weeding, but most of all to enjoy the freshness of home-grown greens. I never really felt the urge. Despite having been raised in

Annet Dekker

the countryside I'm not keen on growing my own food, perhaps because I had experienced—or rather, witnessed from a distance—the hard work, the disappointment of losing a crop, and the frustration of lice, ants, snails, caterpillars, grubs and leaf miners, to name but a few. I love nature, I love animals in nature, green and blue are my favorite colors, but despite my outdoor heritage I am disinclined to turn nature to my liking—well, at least not in the sense that it requires continuous labor.

Then Covid happened. Forced to stay put and work from home I started noticing the garden, and before I knew it, I was hooked. I began looking at (other people's) plants, spent countless hours online looking for a specific flowering type, read about garden design, more flowers, bushes, trees, climbers, ground coverers, cat attracters, snail lovers or repellents, how to line up a (mini) herb garden without it being infested by unwanted insects, about various textures, leaf shapes and different shades of green. I bought second-hand gardening books, especially rare ones that were hard to obtain and contained a wealth of insights and possibilities. I even discussed gardening with fellow green-lovers. I finally understood why people over the years had tried to lure me into the delights of an allotment.

In 2010 Dutch photographer Anne Geene published *No. 235/Encyclopaedia of an Allotment*.[1] Geene is a keen observer, with a great sense of curiosity and an idiosyncratic way of looking at nature. She studies and extracts information about animal and plant life from literature and science. She collects and prepares leaves, small critters, and flowers to document, delineate, and categorize, and finally makes her findings known to the world in a publication. Unlike many other taxonomic works, she doesn't focus on the conventional aspects of plant and animal life such as garden plants, mammals or insects; instead, she tries to provide a complete visual overview of a specific location, in this case, allotment garden no. 235, which is part of the allotment garden association 'Eigen Hof' (Own Garden) in Rotterdam.

In her investigation she looks for all kinds of patterns and phenomena, and depending on the situation she creates alternative categories to classify her observations. *No. 235* is divided into three parts: part 1 provides a geographical delineation of Google Earth photos, a map of the 'Eigen Hof' terrain, and a photographic montage of the plot including its four topographical borders, as well as an overview of the impact of the different seasons on the garden, the highest living species, a black-backed gull, and the lowest living species, a Death's-head hawk moth cocoon, and finally the most widespread plant: the seven-leaf, and the most common animal: the woodlouse.

1_Anne Geene, *No 235: Encyclopedia of an Allotment* (Rotterdam: De Hef Publishers, 2010).

Part 2 consists of observations, including the species in order of observation, prepared specimens, forms, colors, patterns, behavior, traces (from animals to garden tiles), clouds/skies, various water surfaces (e.g., on and below the surface of a pond), multiple puddles, and types of rain. Part 3 contains all kinds of measurements, such as the effects of sunlight on leaves, and their transparency, the group behavior of snails, the speed of swimming ducks, the camouflage of frogs, the variety of pigeon silhouettes when observed in flight, and the impact of sunlight on earthworms. Geene's approach is akin to that of a scientific biologist, yet her science is based purely on visual similarities, patterns or contrasts. At times idiotic and absurd, the conclusions are also insightful and surprising. Delving into her world shows the results of the meticulousness and fastidiousness of human intervention in nature that can be perceived in the microcosmos of the allotment, albeit that the human influence is obscurely represented through animals, plants, behaviors, forms, colors, patterns, traces, and other topological features. Her depiction of this world presents a space where all kinds of species live, yet—and befitting the encyclopedic method—seemingly function independent of each other.

After observation comes documentation, followed by organization, interpretation and finally categorization. This is how Geene depicts the world around her. In the preface to *No. 235* Geene states that it is not her intention to provide a complete determination of plant or animal species, something that is abundantly present in other works; rather, her work is a detailed visual study of the plant and animal kingdom on a human observable scale. While she is interested in objectivity and categorization, she primarily explores and shows the different meanings an image can convey. As she mentions, 'you can move with contexts and information.

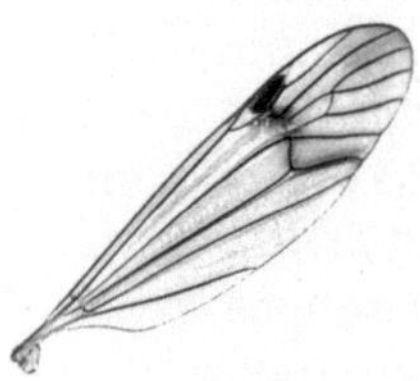

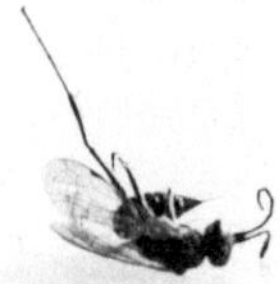

Anne Geene, *Insecten van de vensterbank* (Insects from the windowsill), 2010

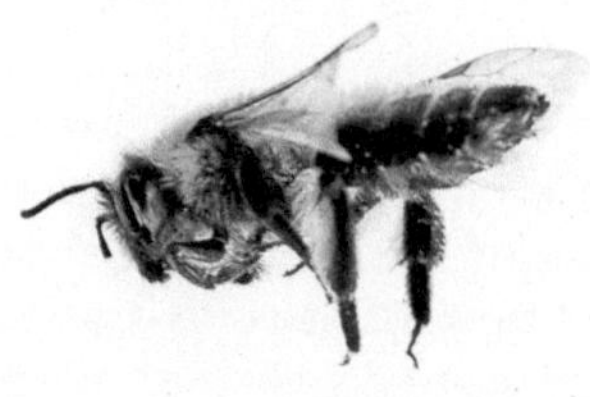

These images appeared in: Anne Geene, *Perceel Nr. 235. Encyclopedie van een volkstuin*. Rotterdam: Uitgeverij de HEF publishers, 2010). (1.) p. 79 and (2.) p. 122

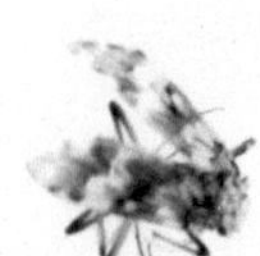

I see photography mainly as an information carrier with which different stories can be told.'[2] Photography in this sense is an archive. In addition to being a documentation device, the apparatus—the framing, the camera position, the way the light enters the aperture—is an archival medium. Rather than 'archive fever'—Jacques Derrida's claim that people have an uncontrollable urge to collect—in her observations and consequent encyclopedic efforts Geene wants to invert perception. She shows that it is possible to capture a world in images, texts or sounds, but she asks, what does such a record actually represent? In other words, while using universal strategies of categorization and standardization, Geene also denies the existence of objectivity, or at least she questions it. Her focus and ways of classifying seem absurd: how important is it to know about the impact of the different intensities of sunrays on earthworms, or the group behavior of various species of snails? However, her idiotic system transcends logic and opens up the imaginable, confronting readers with their own thinking. Observing the image of snails forming a networked trail forced me to reconsider snails not as loathsome enemies who are after my precious lettuce, but as interesting nodes in a community that perhaps move according to certain unknown (at least to me) rules. The irregular, disturbing or abnormal are key in a heterotopic, and while this works well in an art project, how can a system that is based on absurdity be implemented into 'regular' archiving? Moreover, when following 'archival absurdity' could such a method also become a way to (re) structure the world, similar to how by structuring a world, archival practice can also sometimes have the effect that a world starts to behave like the archives that are maintained of it?

Allotments are busy places teeming with living creatures trying to do the thing they are best at: growing and multiplying. The battle of the fittest is often disturbed by human interference. Bushes are trimmed, hedges tamed, weeds eradicated and flowers picked before their seeds or roots can disperse to conquer new soil. Pesticides minimize the damage caused by unwanted bugs, and after fruits and vegetables are harvested and eaten, their precious seeds and pips are carelessly tossed into the garbage. From a human perspective maintaining a garden is about creating a thriving ecology. Brightly colored marigold flowers add zest to green salads, but when planted in a vegetable garden also ensure that ants, whiteflies and other vermin avoid young vegetable sprouts. If marigold plants sense the presence of microscopic worms known as nematodes, they release a toxin into the soil and any of the devouring-root-worms that are too close perish.

The dynamics of gardening is a good example of how artists and archivists could start to think together, since for a gardener, the challenge is paying attention to sudden changes: an unexpected turn in the weather may ruin crops. Similarly, for an archivist, the challenge is noticing that there are always other factors, both human and non-human, which—sometimes at unanticipated moments—may influence the record-keeping process. The call for generalizations can hinder an archivist's attention for the particularities of change and process or their ability to hear other

2_www.mondriaanfonds.nl/en/pcprofile/anne-geene/.

voices. For an artist, the challenge is observing the minute details and finding a way to translate them in such a way that they appeal to the imagination. What the three share is a first step toward the 'arts of noticing,' which, as explained by anthropologist Anna Tsing, means that rather than merely looking and seeing, sniffing and smelling, touching and feeling, or listening and hearing, implies a subtle shift: to notice is also to realize there is a change, that the past is different from the present.[3]

Similar to Geene, Tsing uses a metaphor to describe society at large. For Geene it is the microcosm of her allotment, and for Tsing it is the significance of the *matsutake*, an expensive mushroom and Japanese delicacy, which due to its root system and symbiotic relationship with certain types of pine trees cannot be cultivated. By tracing the various sources of the *matsutake* Tsing reveals the human, fungal and arboreal relationships and how they are entangled with global social and economic processes. So, what happens when using the concept of noticing as a model of creating and fostering ecologies in which humans and non-human alike may thrive?

As a speculative thought experiment, let's take another allotment adventure. This time in a perhaps unexpected place: Finland. Thinking of Finland and allotments may seem contradictory; the country's large expanses of forest, numerous lakes and sparsely populated countryside seem at odds with the need for an allotment garden. However, the first Finnish allotment garden dates back to the time before the country's independence. As elsewhere, city people found their moments of relaxation in these small plots of land. The oldest and still thriving allotment association can be found in Helsinki's Central Park:

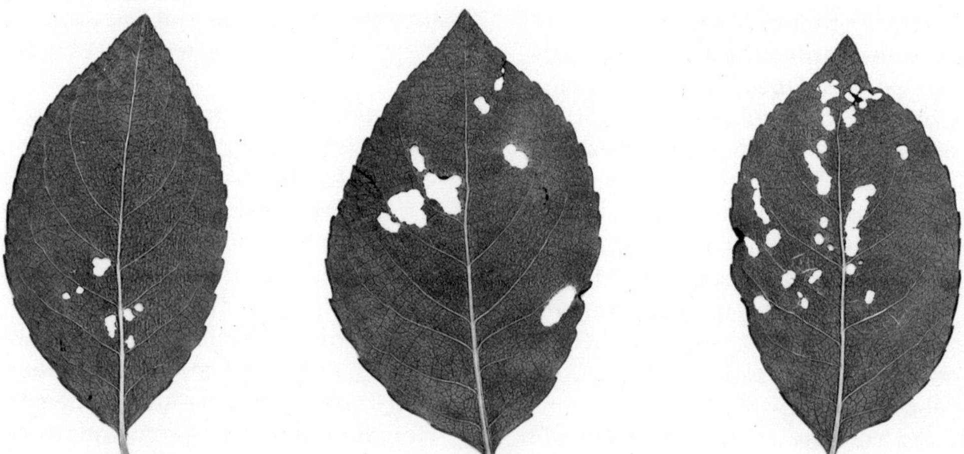

Anne Geene, *Vraat* (Damage), 2021

3_Anna Tsing, 'Arts of Inclusion, or How to Love a Mushroom,' *Manoa* 22, no. 2 (2010), pp. 191–203. Similarly, Stengers makes a plea for a slow science which she characterizes as 'the demanding operation that would *reclaim* the art of dealing with, and learning from, what scientists too often consider messy, that is, what escapes general, so-called objective, categories.' Isabelle Stengers, *Another Science is Possible: A Manifesto for Slow Science*, trans. Stephen Muecke (Cambridge: Polity Press, 2013 [2018]), p. 120.

Ruskeasuon siirtolapuutarha (Brunakärr koloniträdgård), founded in 1918. Just a few years earlier, in 1911, as a unique piece of urban forest Helsinki's Central Park was established and developed as a public park. Central Park is 10 kilometers long and extends from the city center at Töölönlahti Bay up to the northern city limit, crossing many of the city's districts.

Central Park has a significant value for Helsinkians. It provides space for daily exercise, nature observation and all kinds of other recreational activities. Its vastness can be witnessed in the abundance of wildlife: from elks, badgers, foxes, arctic hares, brown hares, weasels, raccoon dogs, and muskrats to the rare flying squirrels, as well as various species of birds, such as the black woodpecker, gold crest, Eurasian jay, tits, dunnock, garden warbler, wood warbler, and red-breasted flycatcher. And of course, it is now also home to several allotment associations, which are designated open and free recreational areas. The season starts around the end of May, by which time any fallow, uncultivated or deserted allotments will be redistributed to new gardeners. However, parts of the green center of the city are under threat, this time not from negligent caretakers but from the bureaucratic establishment, which is plotting new housing and an urban boulevard that will replace some of the green meadows, bushes, and flower fields. To defend the park, a group of alarmed users of the park emerges and wants to connect the multiplicity of lived experiences, micro-histories, struggles, changes and future visions of the park. The group, under the name Project Archives,[4] is driven by the fear that the bureaucrats will appropriate parts of the park to further their agenda of housing and urban development, to circulate capital within their institutional networks, and to rationalize environmental policies, without considering local needs, dependencies, or wishes. In an attempt to change the direction and highlight the ethical tensions between the different parties, Project Archives wants to emphasize a more emancipatory way of working by focusing on layered narratives and the language of advocacy that might in the end enable a discussion between different stakeholders.

The final goal of Project Archives is to create a commons of shared archives and a set of sustainable archiving practices around the park, in close cooperation with local communities and individual users. This idea is based on federative and grassroots archives whose contents are created, shared and networked via online open data infrastructures. In this way the project wants to focus on facilitating plural and decentralized forms of knowing and making that knowledge accessible. The notion of 'conceptus' becomes leading, as it emphasizes a consensus-based concept in which everyone can represent their own trajectory.[5] With Project Archives two different perspectives that are common in similar situations are interesting to highlight: the 'artist-activist' and the 'federative-archivist' approach.

Without much training or mentoring an artist-activist is keen to explore the multiple facets of the park: the community, neighborhood, suburb, forest,

4_While Project Archives may share some similarities to the existing project Central Park Archives (a M-cult project presented in the context of Gathering for Rehearsing Hospitalities 2020: www.m-cult.org), any direct resemblance is coincidental. However, in exploring the speculative thought experiment around Project Archives, I am indebted to conversations with Minna Tarkka, Susanna Ånäs and Ali Akbar Mehta whose preliminary experience and ideas have inspired this imaginative Project Archives.

5_Conceptus literally means an embryo with all its surrounding tissues, but Minna Tarkka used the term to describe the alignment of various interests into a conceptual consensus in the early phases of a collaborative process.

park, site-of-redevelopment, site-of-disrepute and space-in-flux, with the aim of transforming the conventional structures into platforms for dialogue. Although the intention is to work closely with the residents living around the park, due to specific circumstances it is impossible to have close or intimate contact, resulting in a slow and intermittent process of data collecting. In time, the understanding of the project and the comfort level among the residents to partake increase. The data from the residents are retrieved or copied and digitized. Some have large historic photo collections that show the changes in the park, others made recordings of various types of birds, there are also videos of rare species such as the flying squirrels who have chosen the park's spruce trees as their westernmost habitat on the globe (a development that could well be used to advance political causes), as well as documentation of the demonstrations and struggles against the proposed changes to the park. At the same time, methods with a low participatory threshold are considered to make more residents enthusiastic about the project. All the data are merged, overlaid and combined with existing city planning documents, zoning maps, and other cartographic data in an open-source map on a dedicated website that everyone involved can access and maintain.

For an artist-activist, the aesthetic vision and framework are secondary to the conceptual framework of commoning and the notion of conceptus. Archiving turns into a process of co-learning and co-developing, and thus co-archiving. The one-way stream of information gathering and data collecting, with participants providing information without receiving much in return, is now proliferating, but information moves in every direction. While everyone retains their own data and experience, once all is submitted, viewed or experienced collectively, the data defragments, it starts to grow, multiply and diversify and at times is brought together again. Narratives emerge through various ways of access: overlapping stories, micro and macro stories tumble one over the other, yet each is distinct. A reciprocity emerges in which the artist-activist becomes, if only for a moment, also an archivist-creator-participant. Yet, regardless of the name, the core of this practice is a process of relation making that may lead to endless multiplication. As described by philosopher Isabelle Stengers, such

> subtle interlocking of disparate remnants witnessing and taking their consistency the one from the other, contributes not only to more knowledge but also to apprenticeships in new ways of narrating various pasts.[6]

The federative-archivist treads the data carefully, being fully aware of the impossibility of completeness—the suggestion alone could raise anxieties and hamper the goals—while trying out different ways to organize the data, the residents, the communities, the locations, the times, the themes, and the media. Perhaps the specific opportunities for discovery, exploration and experiencing are more mechanically perused. A shared interface for access to co-curated materials is developed and peer-learning workshops on co-archiving are organized to collaboratively fill the holes and plant the seeds

6_Stengers, *Another Science is Possible*, p. 69.

for future enquiries. Existing documents, formal records from city archives and informally created documentation through interviews, soundscapes, historical imagery and imagination, provide a mesh of information extending the scope of investigation. Yet all are testimonies of the residents' relations with the nature in the neighborhood. The archive tells the stories of these relations between nature and residents; as such, archiving becomes the co-creation of a script, or of multiple narratives, held together by the system and structures in place, which have their own stories to tell. This time rather than a project website, the choice is for a Wiki system.

Finding a coherent and structured way to organize and control data and its revisions is at the core of archival practices. The use of a Wiki matches the goals, as it has several advantages: it provides a collaborative working method, the open structure can be created by multiple users, and it is based on a simple version control system, which means that any change to the site can be retraced by anyone in the site's 'history.' Moreover, combined with Wikidata and/or Wikidocumentaries[7] it can become a federated Wikibase in which data from different Wikis is synced. Such a structure, also known as the portmanteau 'fediverse' (a combination of 'federation' and 'universe'), allows different levels of decentralization and interoperability in terms of network architectures and data circulation. As mentioned by researchers/artists Aymeric Mansoux and Roel Roscam Abbing: '[...] federation is a concept derived from political theory in which various actors that constitute a

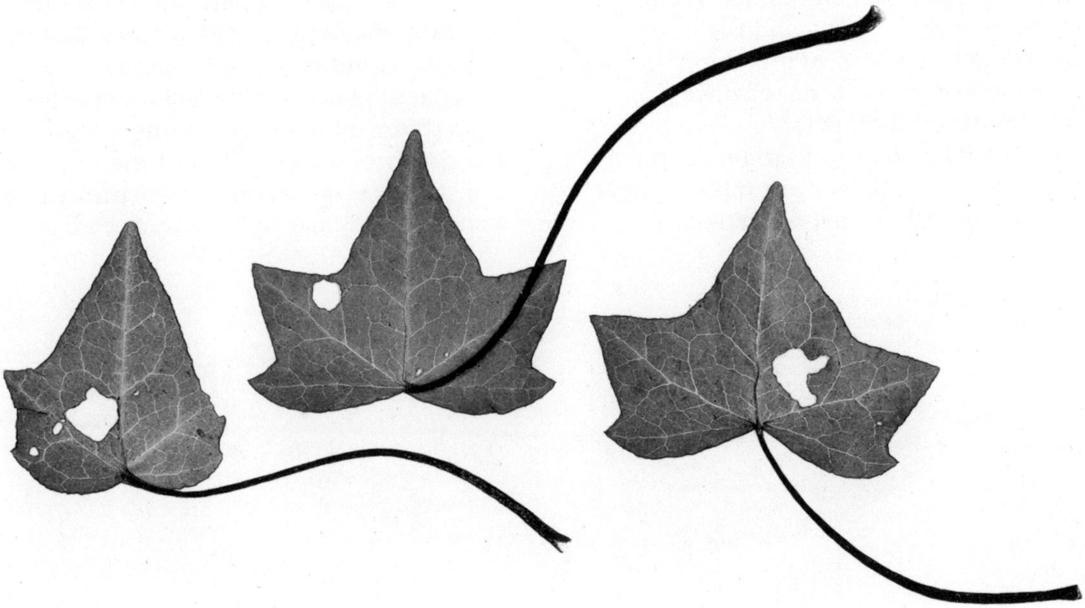

Anne Geene, *Vraat* (Damage), 2021

7_Initiated in 2018 by Susanna Ånäs, the Wikidocumentaries platform builds a bridge between micro historical materials and the open infrastructures of global cultural heritage. wikidocumentaries-demo.wmflabs.org/.

network decide to cooperate collectively. Power and responsibility are distributed as they do so.'[8] As such, and perhaps in addition to an archive, a fediverse connects disparate efforts and converges diverse projects into a shared network in which the participants share some similar goals. In other words, it develops and amplifies different perspectives while working towards conceptus. Without having to be partisan or privileging certain stories over others, a fediverse-archivist recovers agency through the structures that are developed and enacted. While 'wiki' means quick in Hawaiian, a name chosen to reflect the need to facilitate quick and easy communication between software developers, here the quickness is countered by the slowness of negotiation, meetings and endless revisions that are at the heart of Wiki. Such slowing down means 'becoming capable of learning again, becoming acquainted with things again, reweaving the bounds of interdependency. It means thinking and imagining, and in the process creating relationships with other[s].'[9]

It could also be said to be performative, wherein the agency of the different users (residents, archivists, artists) collides with the system; moreover, they define each other and their prosperity determines the progress. Obviously, such a process does not happen without friction or conflict. For one, Wikis are notorious for their rules and regulations as well as their attention to detail, creating a dense 'history,' which to many archivists may seem utterly absurd. In this case, absurdity can be traced in the content of uploaded data as well as in the system that sustains it.

The forms of archiving I have explored in this essay are diverse, perhaps even contradictory. Despite the fact that Anne Geene and Project Archives are both concerned with accessing and opening perspectives, their methods differ. Project Archives uses the potential of vernacular science, encouraged by the participation of those who enjoy the park. They collaborate directly with the residents to liberate knowledge creation and dissemination from the rule of experts. For Geene, the human connection operates on a different level: while interested in human intervention, it's not the creator she's interested in but rather the resulting process and how her encyclopedic

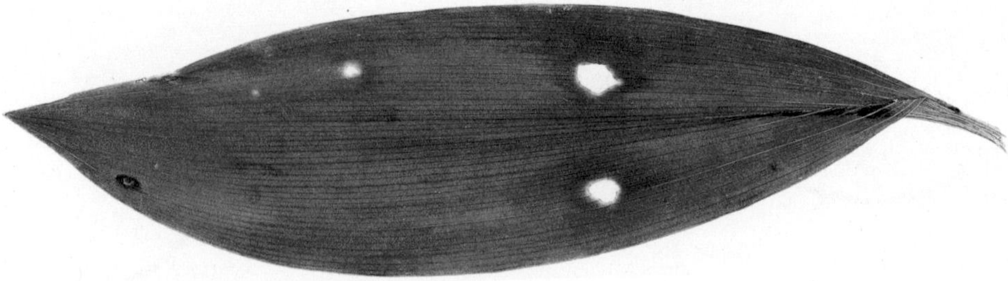

Anne Geene, *Vraat* (Damage), 2021

8_Aymeric Mansoux and Roel Roscam Abbing, 'Seven Theses on the Fediverse and the Becoming of FLOSS,' in *The Eternal Network: The Ends and Becomings of Network Culture*, ed. Kristoffer Gansing and Inga Luchs (Amsterdam and Berlin: The Institute of Network Cultures/ transmediale e.V., 2020), pp. 124–42 (p. 125).

9_Stengers, *Another Science is Possible*, p. 81.

rendition offers the chance to provide more insight into human/nature ecologies. For her, the efforts to re-sculpt, as happens in an ordinary allotment, provide a metaphor to also make a broader statement about the evolving processes of humans and nature. In the end her proposition may lead to a better understanding between the two.

Both interventions contrast with the hegemonic, plant/animal/nature science, as well as archival practice, which both strive towards generalizations, universal categorizations and standardization. In their aim to control human and nonhuman landscapes, archival science, and for that matter most other sciences, certainly the bio-sciences, specialists, managers, directors and researchers make the decisions: what is included and what is excluded, which system is used and which is not, and so on. While providing access to their decisions is one of the top priorities for any archive, its users are hardly ever consulted. If they are, it's mostly to confirm the standard, not to create a new system, or even to expand existing categories and develop other ways of working. Such interference is less appreciated. Indeed, as mentioned by Tsing, in most cases, 'love does not flow between expert and knowledge-object.'[10] In contrast, I have tried to emphasize how advocacy for nature can lead to subversive archival projects, while at times it may also lead to archival absurdity. It's a passion for gardening, even if only recently discovered, and socio-natural ecologies more generally, that makes these projects possible. At the same time, the examples show how the act of noticing encourages passionate immersion in and with the subjects under study. Using collaborative tools and opening up the imagination may lead to layered ways of archiving, but rather than merely critiquing conventional methods they cultivate a critical reflexivity and a learning with others as well as acknowledging such accumulated knowledge.

10_Tsing, 'Arts of Inclusion, or How to Love a Mushroom,' p. 201.

REDUCTION AND ANACHRONISM IN THE ARCHIVE

The *Small Systems* of Gianfranco Baruchello

My objective in the pages that follow is to probe the complex system underlying Gianfranco Baruchello's work. I do so from a particular perspective of a long process of research that, over several years, has led me to examine hundreds of archival documents. But these documents are more than documents in the artist's archive; they should be considered as works by the artist modelled on the archive. Many of these include schematic notes on the production of books, archives of different topics, museums for personal use, and do-it-yourself encyclopedias: the *Libro dei libri* and the *Libro nerissimo* (literally, 'Very Black Book,' in which Baruchello wrote the text in such tiny characters and so close together that it appeared almost entirely black and impossible to read[1]) both of which form part of an archival file on the subject of 'Book-how to make;' the *Grande Enciclopedia del sensibile umano* (G.E.D.S.U.); *Archivio delle ossessioni* (which fed into the *Archivio dei cinque cuori*), the *Museo* (the idea of a museum 'not as a space but as the transferred definition of Anthology or encyclopedia'), the *Archivio degli archivi*.

One such project, the *Archivio dei cinque cuori* has remained untouched. It was located in Rome in the artist's studio at 23 Via Monte Senario from the end of the sixties, and since 1973 in his home/studio on Via di Santa Cornelia. It comprises more than a hundred suspension files arranged alphabetically by subject in metal Olivetti filing cabinets. Ways of conceiving archives and archives as real repositories of materials for his work thus blend together in the spaces in which Baruchello has lived and worked. On more than one occasion, over the

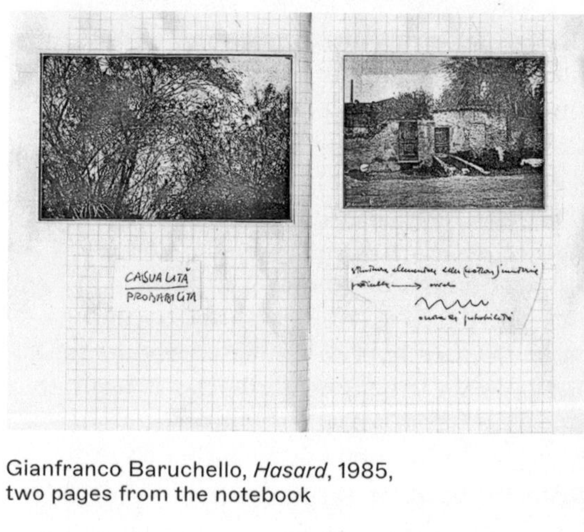

Gianfranco Baruchello, *Hasard*, 1985, two pages from the notebook

1_Interestingly, in 1976, Frank Zappa composed a piece called *The Black Page*. Its sheet music is so dense with writing it's almost illegible.

Carla Subrizi

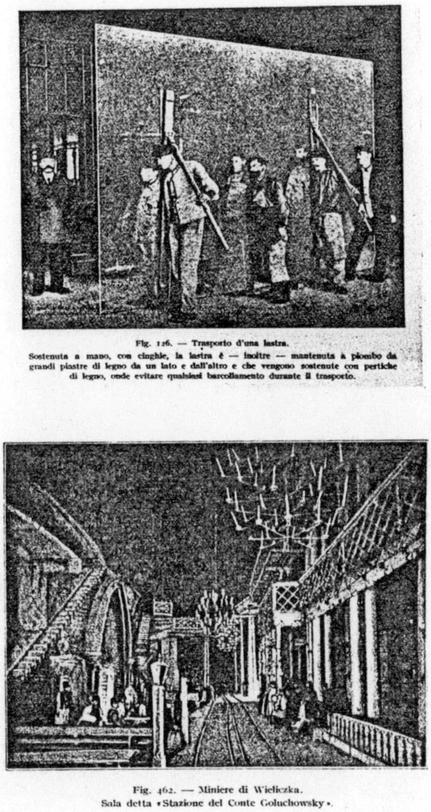

Gianfranco Baruchello, *La Stazione del Conte Goluchowsky*, 1978, two pages from the book, Centro Rank Xerox, Bolognathe notebook

years, the materials in his archives have been the starting point for projects in their own right. Some examples are the film *Ars memoriae* (2008–2009), *Hasard* (1985), and the book *La stazione del Conte Goluchowsky* (1978). He writes in an unpublished note: 'I am surrounded by archives—I have every possible type of lists and storage and boxes and drawers—and each one of them really represents something that resembles a document in a file.'

Appropriation, disassemblage and assemblage, observation and the capturing of images, accumulation and above all lists in the form of words, numbers, photographs and images, are therefore all part of the process underlying all of Baruchello's work. Storage is a constant practice. The artist used lists, alphabets, dictionaries, and archives, collage and montage, since his early works.

In 1962 Desmond Morris' book *The Biology of Art* was published in English and French.[2] The book is about experiments with animals who learn to paint and draw. Gianfranco Baruchello was intrigued by this experiment. He bought

2_Desmond Morris, *The Biology of Art: A Study of the Picture-Making Behaviour of the Great Apes and Its Relationship to Human Art* (New York: Knopf, 1962); Desmond Morris, *La biologie de l'art: Étude de la creation artistiques de grandes signes et de ses rapports avec l'art humain* (Paris: 1962).

the book (the French edition) and cut out some pictures showing the 10-year-old gorilla Sophie drawing, assisted by her tutor Chris Baris. This cut-out, together with others of the same type, were glued onto a wooden board and in the year that the book had been published became a work entitled *Abstract-Expressionism-Zoologique*. It is not just a collage. The collage is present but the conceptual idea behind this kind of work is to subtract images from different contexts and then ask how to reassemble them in different systems of juxtaposition. The work presents a montage of seven cut images of drawings made by a gorilla (two cuttings) and by other kinds of monkeys (two cuttings). There is also an image illustrating 'des gestes aberrants [...] observables quand l'application se relâche,' another the 'prise primitive du pinceau avec le pouce dirigé vers le bas.' The last image is a montage within the montage, a painting juxtaposed with three words taken from a text of Emilio Villa dedicated in 1961 to Cy Twombly.

The two images that relate to the gorilla Sophie, who was the object of great interest in 1958 after being observed drawing at the Rotterdam Zoo Blijdorp, are captioned: 'Planche no. 9. Sophie en train de peindre sous le regard de son gardien Baris' and 'Planche no. 7. Sophie, gorille adulte du Zoo de Rotterdam, se concentrant sur un dessin.' The irony of the juxtaposition of abstract expressionist art and a scientific experiment occurs frequently in Baruchello's work.

In the same couple of years, Baruchello produced other works that included clippings of letters, documents (such as his first pay cheque, see *Primo Stipendio*) and photographs. These works are neither simply a collage nor a photomontage, and even if they were in part, the idea is to make found materials somehow part of the same visual thought. Indeed, a disposition for producing little 'archives' was already evident. This union

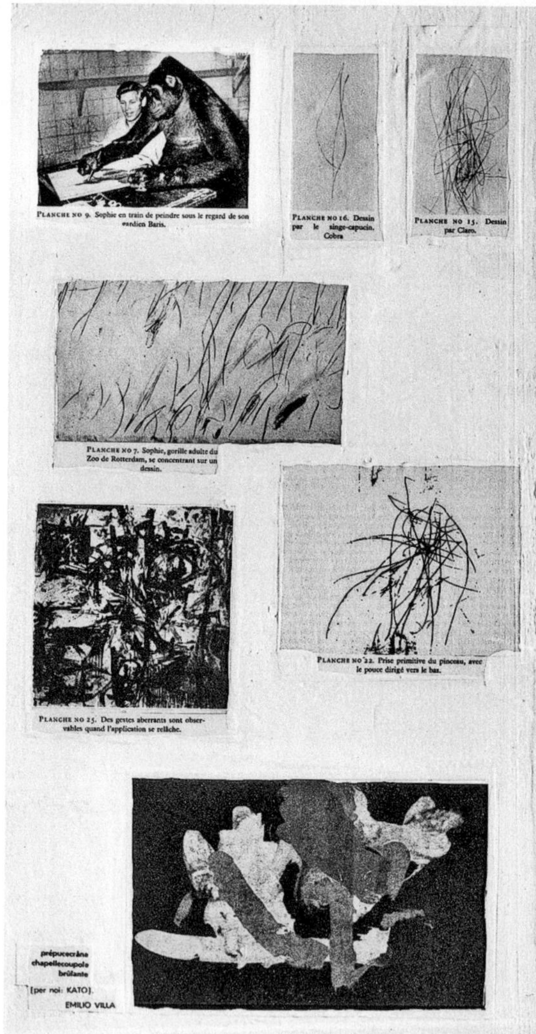

Gianfranco Baruchello, *Abstract Expressionism Zoologique*, 1962, photo: Ezio Gosti

of existing pictures and the visual offers a key to reading works of this nature.

In *Una lettera* (1961), cuttings from a letter are recombined with photographic images of the artist himself, of an elderly man (his father, lower right) and a part of his boat. Here, again, the arrangement of the images is rather simple: they constitute a line, reading from left to right as suggested by the letter itself. The letter is cut out in such a way that the written text is illegible. We find a similar assemblage of images, but in this case including elements of actual brushwork, in *Errata corrige* (1962), while in *L'Asia, crogiolo di razze* (1962), the same scheme is used for the arrangement of flat boxes (for razor blades), cut-out photographs and documents. As such, these examples produce a peculiar, discursive ordering of systems for classifying different categories. However, the distinct elements that underlie this type of work is their difference in respect to conventional systems. Classification indexes things and brings them together on a basis of similarities, of typologies of different things. The underlying principle in Baruchello's work, and specifically his montage-like 'pages,' is articulated both in the alignment of elements, which contrasts with the free and subjective choice of an assemblage driven by specific impulses and motivations, and in the cutting out of found materials which serve as images with which to radically rethink the act of painting. In the same way, the use of cut-out illustrations and photographs contextualizes the use of the medium (photographs) within painting, just as the written word is used as an image (thus removing from painting its gestural content—i.e., the brushstroke—color and the very materiality of the paint).

It is indeed in painting and drawing that Baruchello employs the same conceptual way of working: the images are reduced and concentrated in visual nuclei that pulverize in their juxtapositions the possibility of proceeding in one narrative direction. In a work exemplary of this way of proceeding titled *La turbulence de l'intelligence est une* (1965), small images and letters of the alphabet, freed from any form of narrative connectedness, trace a circular form on a white surface with an empty space in the center. The circular progression embodies the paradox of a vision that can no longer

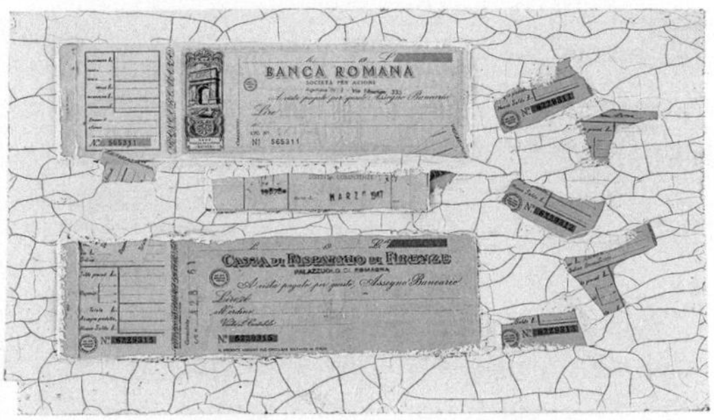

Gianfranco Baruchello, *Primo stipendio BPD inizi di carriera nel capitale*, 1962, photo: Claudio Abate

Gianfranco Baruchello, *La turbulence de l'intelligence est une*, 1965, photo: Ezio Gosti

seek a hub, a center from which to set off: the center is nullified and it is instead from various points in the margins that a visual itinerary might begin. A space that is non-hierarchical, that is not organized in relation to a center, where the edges become as important as any other point on the surface: this is the kind of space that Baruchello conceives in his painting from the early sixties. Seen from afar, it appears monochrome, but it is not; up close it is clear that the surface is crisscrossed by images so small that they are hard to make out. It is a space that dematerializes any form of narration, which can also be understood as a prelinguistic space, in the sense that, not abandoning either the iconic or the anti-iconic—with a nod to Duchamp[3]—it returns to the primal elements of language. The instructions as how to orient oneself in this distribution of elements, which constructs multiple linguistic chains within the same (pictorial) space, are varied. They invite one to view simultaneity rather than single aspects, to overturn spatial stereotypes (above may become below, right may become left, and so on), to move without coordinates of time, putting to the test a juxtaposition of events that take place while one works, and for which the surface/picture comes to serve as a sort of blotting paper. This kind of surface or space that blocks a narrative reading of the space as such, has the structure of an archive. A great diversity of elements is assembled in it in such a way that the relationships between the elements is not explicated by an underlying system or narrative.

What connects the practice of archiving and this way of painting—which conceptualizes the same impulse—is the need to work on a single element decontextualized from the predefined semantic and linguistic codes that connote it. This does not mean that an element is isolated from its context and leaving it as such. Baruchello assembles, looking for the short-circuit and the contradiction. His archives, objects, and paintings are dynamic devices that do not collect in order to be deposited but to have materials available that can provoke each other. The archive is thus a device: works as archives but also archives that solicit works. So, the question arises: how and why does Baruchello assemble so many materials and media in the most different forms?

Reduction

The archive is a way of reducing. But what does it reduce? Or what does it help reduce?

In a text from 1981, later partly revised for the Italian edition of *La pittura del segreto nell'epoca postmoderna, Baruchello*,[4] Jean-François Lyotard introduces the concept of the 'monogram.' The text is composed of several paragraphs ('Historiette,' 'Minima moralia,' 'Rebus,' 'Interminable,' 'Kóan,' 'Réserve,' 'Clair,' 'Celer,' 'Camarade peintre,' 'Un nom chaque matin') and was written on the occasion of the exhibition 'Baruchello. Loin du doux,' at the Galerie Le Dessin, in Paris, in 1982.

> In Santa Cornelia,[5] between the window and the shutter, the space is stuffed with vegetable stalks. While clearing them with a brush, G.B. finds a shivering fledgling. He speaks

3_Marcel Duchamp, *Duchamp du signe: Écrits* (Paris: Flammarion, 1994), p. 48.

4_Jean-François Lyotard, *La pittura del segreto nell'epoca postmoderna, Baruchello* (Milan: Feltrinelli, 1982), also published in *Jean-François Lyotard: Écrits sur l'art contemporain et les artiste/Writings on Contemporary Art and Artists*, ed. Herman Parret (Leuven: University Press, 2012), vol. II, pp. 164–251.

5_Baruchello lived in via di Santa Cornelia from 1973 to 1998. It was also the place of the activity *Agricola Cornelia S.p.A. 1973–1981*. From 1998 this house and studio became the Fondazione Baruchello.

to it: you are not yet big, *poverino, povero uccellino*, etc...[6] He lays it down outside, in sight of its mother. Will this small adventure crystallize itself in a monogram? Kant calls monograms the ideals of sensibility. [...] The little images disseminated into G.B.'s surfaces or boxes are these monograms They have no didactic function. They do not dictate anything about the activity of painting. [...] They are deposits of narrative energy. Little mothers of fantasy. They call for other possible monograms, at the cost of unique stories. One has to make rather than rediscover. Take a painting, a box, a book by G.B. These are large stores of invisible little stories that are hardly audible, emerging in the visual and indicating themselves incomprehensibly within it through monograms.[7]

The idea of the monogram helps us to reflect on the process of reduction that crosses objects, images, spaces and forms of temporality. We will speak of an anachronistic dimension that results from this reduction of every temporal form to its character of event or mental happening. Lyotard articulates in this text, the monogram as a decontextualized piece that is tending to find different forms of relationship with other pieces: the 'deposits of narrative energy.' In the words of Lyotard:

> *Kóan*. [...] What does GB do? Very little, as little as possible. Let yourself be awakened by the event, put it to sleep in a monogram, a figurine, a word, pass it on for other awakenings. What was awakened asleep, was not thought of, seen or heard. Everything that is present on the surfaces, in the boxes, in the films, sleeps, as the thread of ordinary life sleeps. Myriads of events. Each of them can be an occasion for awakening. [...]
>
> *Clair*. [...] Consider all the works of G.B. with their various supports stuffed with monograms where the possible awakening sleeps. It is the clear mirror of all that there is, passed by the archive.[8]

It is this passage that seems to me fundamental for understanding the process of reduction that takes place in the archive that the artist uses as a 'deposit' of narrative energy in progress. Reduction occurs not only in the arrangement of words and images within these 'deposits.' The contraction crosses both space and time, the geographies and forms of temporality. In Baruchello's montage systems it is both spatial and temporal simultaneity that defines spatial directions or the densification of information nuclei. While an event happens, something else happens simultaneously. Very often the nuclei of images are accompanied by words such as 'meanwhile,' 'elsewhere.' These terms denote the coexistence of different events or facts, sometimes temporally distant from each other and, at the same time, offer multiple visual orientations. The contracted system breaks the very syntax of a 'system.' Asystemicity is the paradigm behind reduction and assembly, fragmentation and apparent order (lists, lists) between different subjects. Small systems are transformative systems that generate change in both pre-existing materials and structure. The syntax between a before and an after

6_English translation: 'poor, poor little bird.'

7_Jean-François Lyotard, 'Baruchello: Loin du doux,' in exh. cat. Galerie Le Dessin (Paris, 1982).

8_Lyotard, 'Baruchello.'

or between a cause and a consequence loses this unique possibility of articulation. The syntax fragments and 'reduces' the measures and temporal passages to facts that once again bring into play their own possibility of meaning.

Like painting, different elements and materials can find a place and coexist in Baruchello's work. Little photographs (Baruchello's *Foto picolossime*), photocopied photographs, cut-outs accumulate by placing them next to each other. By appropriating these elements and leaving them to rest in the potential place that is the archive, the documents are transformed. Narrative structures are broken up and each element becomes once again a singularity available for new connections. For example, Baruchello lets the objects settle around him. Perhaps similar to his obsession with collecting and archiving, there is a fear of getting rid of something that has been used. Baruchello does not throw anything away. He accumulates sheets, clippings, fragments of any newspaper or photocopy of text that is interesting to him. Before making a work, he 'studies,' reads and takes notes of what he finds in the form of cards or lists of topics to be explored. Clippings or other pieces of paper he has already taken from somewhere are often taped to the wall. In this way, these isolated fragments begin to become elements that become part of a list, an inventory or inserted into a work to become part of a dialogue with other elements, find their own new capacity to tell something. Reduction is thus the process that interrupts syntactic and semantic chains. Each element of the archive is dynamic and activates (produces) new forms of relationship. The same element in the archive can be inserted into different dossiers, depending on the perspective that the artist has chosen to use at a certain moment.

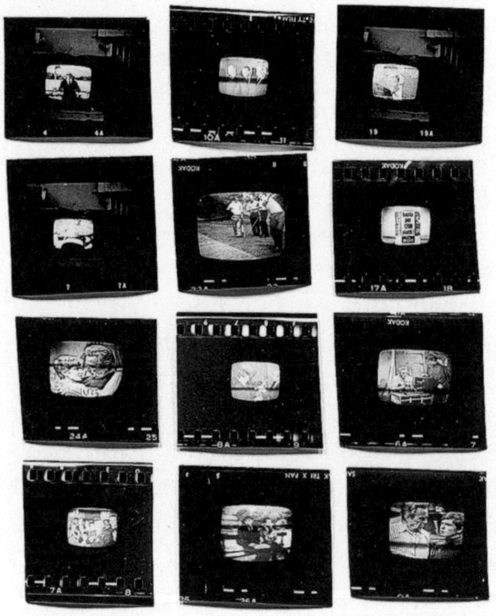

Gianfranco Baruchello, *Foto piccolissime*, 1967

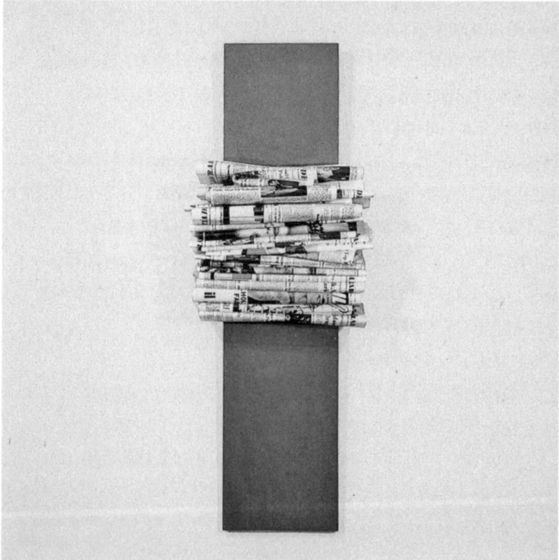

Gianfranco Baruchello, *Awareness II*, 1962

The past and the present are annulled in an anachronistic dimension that is not 'timeless' but rather the possibility of locating itself in the dynamic simultaneity of the temporal short-circuit. The event is this singularity that awaits the short-circuit capable of making it active again.

This is the case, for example, with works created from the accumulation of materials in the studio. With *Awareness II* (1962) Baruchello took part in an exhibition that charted some of the trends of that period and also some historical ones on the use of objects: the exhibition 'New Realists' at the Sidney Janis Gallery. *Awareness II*, which identified the need for 'awareness' in the world of information and opinions, froze a stack of daily newspapers using vinavil glue to a wooden table that was painted in red lead. The newspaper and the book were ordinary objects. They were current, everyday objects. These books and newspapers were placed one on top of the other without any claim to inventing or creating order or disorder of any type. There was an absence of any 'creative' impulse in these objects

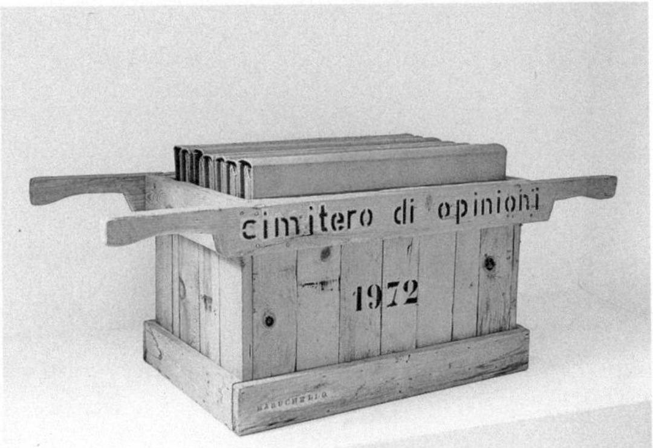

Gianfranco Baruchello, *Cimitero di opinioni (per Feltrinelli)*, 1972, photo: Claudio Abate

on the part of the artist, who decided to simply 'assemble' the newspapers one on top of the other. He created a kind of archive for a week's worth of newspapers, sometimes a month's worth. Other times he chose newspapers that had dealt with the same topic for a certain period of time or a collection of newspapers, arranged without being folded in microfiber folders, to make a large *Cemetery of Opinions* (1972): an archive of the newspaper dedicated to the death of Giangiacomo Feltrinelli but also to the period before and after this death.[9] Feltrinelli (1926–1972) was a publisher and activist. The daily newspapers are bound in six large volumes. This work therefore constitutes one of the most important archives on political activism and militancy in the extra-parliamentary left.

I think it is interesting at this point to consider, albeit briefly, another aspect of Baruchello's way of working: the writing. Baruchello's writing proceeds by accumulation, using juxtaposition as a system of adjacency of ideas, thoughts and images rendered by words. The accumulation of newspapers that we have just mentioned, archived documents and the way of constructing a text present quite a few analogies. For example, in the text *Ioiomiss*, a sort of manifesto, written and published in the catalogue of a 1966 exhibition at the Schwarz Gallery in Milan.[10] *Ioiomiss* is a name Baruchello takes from James Joyce's *Finnegans Wake*, yet makes it his own word. In Italian '*Ioiomiss*' carries within it the double repetition of the first-person singular pronoun 'I.' 'I,' thus doubled, and 'miss' play on a critical presence and absence of the self. In the catalogue Baruchello 'tells' two stories

9_*Cemetery of Opinions* (1972) is part of the collection of the ZKM Museum in Karlsruhe from 2014.

10_Gianfranco Baruchello, *Ioiomiss*, exh. cat. Galleria Schwarz (Milano, 1966), n.p.

using this manifesto ('ideas, moods, expectations and preambles') and seven pages of drawings: on the one hand is his research into the first 'alphabets' of images which started in the late 1950s; on the other the phases that a more comprehensive history of art and culture went through to research new linguistic and cognitive horizons with, nevertheless, a full awareness of the post-Auschwitz period.

The manifesto is devoid of punctuation and written in capitals. The flow of words and 'ideas' in it takes on the agrammatic flow of a set of words whose consequentiality is not in the articulated sentence of the discourse but in the neutralized succession of fragments of thought. Baruchello seems to collect and place thoughts, hypotheses, and images on the same level. The proceeding by fragments of speech that do not end and that follow one another without any apparent connection between them, make this manifesto a sort of inventory of ideas taken from different levels of consciousness and woven on the page as details of a discourse to come. Cataloguing is a way to select and decontextualize images, make repertories, 'dictionaries of culture': the 'rhyming book' and the *archives* that Baruchello said he had 'set up,' made of 'objects men books hypotheses aetiologies fables techniques scores electrical household appliances' also include the 'lullabies after Auschwitz' for his sons, to which 'monstrous illustrations, men with one head two arms two legs' whose 'testament is already made' must be added. A 'post-Auschwitz' vocabulary of the traumatic conditions in which the World War II postwar period began could not but introduce fear, hostile elements and error in a new way.[11]

Time already adopts a critical role because it translates what is a real fact into a happening in the mind.

In this mode of writing one can find a common principle that is the premise

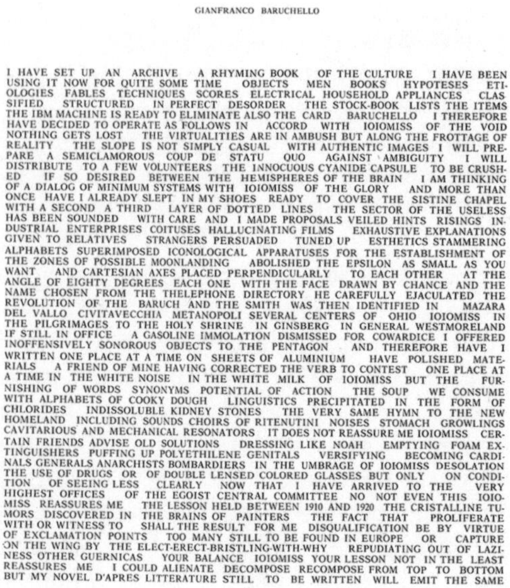

GIANFRANCO BARUCHELLO

I HAVE SET UP AN ARCHIVE A RHYMING BOOK OF THE CULTURE I HAVE BEEN USING IT NOW FOR QUITE SOME TIME OBJECTS MEN BOOKS HYPOTESES ETIOLOGIES FABLES TECHNIQUES SCORES ELECTRICAL HOUSEHOLD APPLIANCES CLASSIFIED STRUCTURED IN PERFECT DESORDER THE STOCK-BOOK LISTS THE ITEMS THE IBM MACHINE IS READY TO ELIMINATE ALSO THE CARD BARUCHELLO I THEREFORE HAVE DECIDED TO OPERATE AS FOLLOWS IN ACCORD WITH IOIOMISS OF THE VOID NOTHING GETS LOST THE VIRTUALITIES ARE IN AMBUSH BUT ALONG THE FROTTAGE OF REALITY THE SLOPE IS NOT SIMPLY CASUAL WITH AUTHENTIC IMAGES I WILL PREPARE A SEMICLAMOROUS COUP DE STATU QUO AGAINST AMBIGUITY I WILL DISTRIBUTE TO A FEW VOLUNTEERS THE INNOCUOUS CYANIDE CAPSULE TO BE CRUSHED IF SO DESIRED BETWEEN THE HEMISPHERES OF THE BRAIN I AM THINKING OF A DIALOG OF MINIMUM SYSTEMS WITH IOIOMISS OF THE GLORY AND MORE THAN ONCE HAVE I ALREADY SLEPT IN MY SHOES READY TO COVER THE SISTINE CHAPEL WITH A SECOND A THIRD LAYER OF DOTTED LINES THE SECTOR OF THE USELESS HAS BEEN SOUNDED WITH CARE AND I MADE PROPOSALS VEILED HINTS RISINGS INDUSTRIAL ENTERPRISES COITUSES HALLUCINATING FILMS EXHAUSTIVE EXPLANATIONS GIVEN TO RELATIVES STRANGERS PERSUADED TUNED UP ESTHETICS STAMMERING ALPHABETS SUPERIMPOSED ICONOLOGICAL APPARATUSES FOR THE ESTABLISHMENT OF THE ZONES OF POSSIBLE MOONLANDING ABOLISHED THE EPSILON AS SMALL AS YOU WANT AND CARTESIAN AXES PLACED PERPENDICULARLY TO EACH OTHER AT THE ANGLE OF EIGHTY DEGREES EACH ONE WITH THE FACE DRAWN BY CHANCE AND THE NAME CHOSEN FROM THE THELEPHONE DIRECTORY HE CAREFULLY EJACULATED THE REVOLUTION OF THE BARUCH AND THE SMITH WAS THEN IDENTIFIED IN MAZARA DEL VALLO CIVITAVECCHIA METANOPOLI SEVERAL CENTERS OF OHIO IOIOMISS IN THE PILGRIMAGES TO THE HOLY SHRINE IN GINSBERG IN GENERAL WESTMORELAND IF STILL IN OFFICE A GASOLINE IMMOLATION DISMISSED FOR COWARDICE I OFFERED INOFFENSIVELY SONOROUS OBJECTS TO THE PENTAGON AND THEREFORE HAVE I WRITTEN ONE PLACE AT A TIME ON SHEETS OF ALUMINIUM HAVE POLISHED MATERIALS A FRIEND OF MINE HAVING CORRECTED THE VERB TO CONTEST ONE PLACE AT A TIME IN THE WHITE NOISE IN THE WHITE MILK OF IOIOMISS BUT THE FURNISHING OF WORDS SYNONYMS POTENTIAL OF ACTION THE SOUP WE CONSUME WITH ALPHABETS OF COOKY DOUGH LINGUISTICS PRECIPITATED IN THE FORM OF CHLORIDES INDISSOLUBLE KIDNEY STONES THE VERY SAME HYMN TO THE NEW HOMELAND INCLUDING SOUNDS CHOIRS OF RITENUTINI NOISES STOMACH GROWLINGS CAVITARIOUS AND MECHANICAL RESONATORS IT DOES NOT REASSURE ME IOIOMISS CERTAIN FRIENDS ADVISE OLD SOLUTIONS DRESSING LIKE NOAH EMPTYING FOAM EXTINGUISHERS PUFFING UP POLYETHILENE GENITALS VERSIFYING BECOMING CARDINALS GENERALS ANARCHISTS BOMBARDIERS IN THE UMBRAGE OF IOIOMISS DESOLATION THE USE OF DRUGS OR OF DOUBLE LENSED COLORED GLASSES BUT ONLY ON CONDITION OF SEEING LESS CLEARLY NOW THAT I HAVE ARRIVED TO THE VERY HIGHEST OFFICES OF THE EGOIST CENTRAL COMMITTEE NO NOT EVEN THIS IOIOMISS REASSURES ME THE LESSON HELD BETWEEN 1910 AND 1920 THE CRISTALLINE TUMORS DISCOVERED IN THE BRAINS OF PAINTERS THE FACT THAT PROLIFERATE WITH OR WITNESS TO SHALL THE RESULT FOR ME DISQUALIFICATION BE BY VIRTUE OF EXCLAMATION POINTS TOO MANY STILL TO BE FOUND IN EUROPE OR CAPTURE ON THE WING BY THE ELECT-ERECT-BRISTLING-WITH-WHY REPUDIATING OUT OF LAZINESS OTHER GUERNICAS YOUR BALANCE IOIOMISS YOUR LESSON NOT IN THE LEAST REASSURES ME I COULD ALIENATE DECOMPOSE RECOMPOSE FROM TOP TO BOTTOM BUT MY NOVEL D'APRES LITTERATURE STILL TO BE WRITTEN WILL EMIT THE SAME

Gianfranco Baruchello, *Ioiomiss*, 1966, first page of the text from the catalogue of the solo show, Galleria Schwarz, Milan

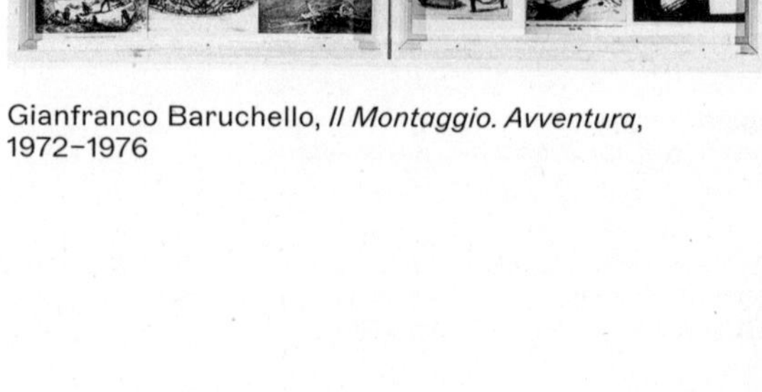

Gianfranco Baruchello, *Il Montaggio. Avventura*, 1972–1976

11_All the quotations are from Baruchello, *Ioiomiss*.

of all of Baruchello's work. Reduction in this case intervenes to free the discourse from elements of linkage, connection, grammatical rule. The words move like fragments of thought and it is not the subject-predicate form that constructs a sequence but the search for relations, resonances, and cross-references. The transversality of the language and techniques used by Baruchello, from painting to the object to writing, as we have seen, help us to seek a red line, not in the content but in the method that moves between words and images, between different types of material, with the same urgency to understand, accumulate information, cataloguing and testing different systems of relationships and connections.

Loss of Quality

Reduction and loss of quality are deeply connected. In an undated note but probably written after 1972, Baruchello focuses on the loss of quality produced by a process he repeatedly used:

> The photo-of-photo (or photograph of a photograph) is a technical-philosophical, technical-conceptual expedient for producing photographs that encompass the idea of a loss of quality. The photo-of-photo contributes to the loss of quality of the photographed subject when it is presented in the form of a photograph. The loss of quality is not to be seen as the introduction of something negative, an affront to the photo, nor does it diminish its conceptual content. Loss refers to a depletion of the qualities of appearance, aesthetics, and presentation; it decontextualises the photo from a particular context (thus making it lose its point of reference).[12]

Il Montaggio—which comprises ten double 'pages' in hinged frames of wood and glass (each page c. 90 × 90 cm)—was conceived precisely as an archive of photos-of-photos on ten themes (Woman, Water, Adventure, War, Food, Death, Money, Dream, Painting, Mind, with a finale double page to serve as an 'Index'). The images were taken from a wide range of sources, including magazines, military vehicle catalogues, cookery books and encyclopedias, for instance the children's encyclopedia *Genti e Paesi*.

The poor quality of the images, caused by the fact they are copies of cuttings that were photographed and then scanned (the loss of quality in each phase being used deliberately), contributes to our perceiving the event differently to how we might have seen it in some newspaper or other kind of publication. The low quality presents the event in an altered state, removed from the immediacy with which it would be received in the original print: the event reaches the consciousness as though it were remembered.

It is this reduction of quality that produces a shared 'sense of family' among images taken from different sources. It is almost impossible to reconstruct their provenance philologically, but this should not obstruct the search for a potential

12_This note is contained in the folder 'Fotografia per la pittura—Progetti fotografici—Foto di lavoro—Foto di Foto—(Montaggio)—Fotocopia,' in *Archivio dei cinque cuori* (Rome: Fondazione Baruchello, 1969– in progress). A recent work conceived as a big volume, *Psicoenciclopedia possibile* (Roma, 2020) reactivated all these photographic archives, together with the archives of writings (from 1947 to the present) to produce an encyclopaedia conceived as the fragmentation, montage, alphabetical order, and complex system of links between 'entries' and 'tables of images,' of all these materials. The *Archivio dei cinque cuori* was recently published (Rome, 2017–2018): each folder became a volume of 'photocopies' of the documents contained within it. The overall project involved 200 single-copy volumes. *Archivio dei cinque cuori* (Arbor Editions) was exhibited during the 'Gianfranco Baruchello' exhibition, curated by Nicolas Bourriaud, Villa Arson, Nice, 2018 and in the same year at the Fondazione Baruchello within the exhibition 'Archivio dei cinque cuori ed altri archivi'.

historiographic-critical approach. Indeed, in this process of excision—the forgetting of the contexts from which the images were taken—the author is aware that it is memory that he is soliciting. When we observe the image of a man who is sitting on a pot to defecate, probably in prison, while two other men (one is Giovanni Agnelli, an Italian industrialist) seem to be watching him, while soldiers are running to climb a staircase, and at the bottom, a man is being blindfolded who is about to be killed, what will be the resulting perceptional situation? It is not a case of finding a meaning that unites or makes their proximity more plausible.

Contamination translates the unsaid; the hybrid mixing of subjects and themes restores the dark side: the removed (or deleted) part of the image. What comes about, in this manner, through a paradoxical adjacency that subverts habituation, even in the face of images of great horror, is the need to look more attentively at the very place where it seemed everything was already familiar. Looking becomes synonymous with investigating, and thus with knowledge. The difference between the images is irreducible, and remains so. Archiving and producing loss of quality are part of a multi-step appropriation process: selection of images, manipulation of images through the use of photocopying or photography of the photograph, cataloguing, montage. Reduced, the same images may become part of objects or paintings. This kind of manipulation is thus aimed at producing a different physiognomy of the pre-existing material.

In the 1970s Baruchello experimented with the use of parallel logics: the dream and contradiction were not just practicable, but their results and premises could be shown through experiment. Thus, the three-part film *Tre lettere a Raymond Roussel. Limbosigne, A Little More Paranoid, La degringolade*,[13] had also been a recording and subsequent manipulation of dreams; the film had then turned blue, and was accompanied by a soundtrack obtained from recordings, upon waking, of dreams, also in successive phases. Barely comprehensible, these recordings were the film's soundtrack: voices that recount night-time experience, without having to follow plots but seeking to communicate (in the film, a man and woman tell each other their dreams). For Baruchello, the dream was an important source from which to draw images, on the basis of the paradoxical dynamics of association. But transcriptions of dreams have also been the starting point for archives of dreams that have become books (such as *Avventure nell'armadio di plexiglass* in 1968) or films such as *Tre lettere a Raymond Roussel*.

The film's images are like flashes of dreams, vague memories of tales emerging with no comprehensible logic. The dream determined a 'loss' of legibility of the image, forcing its meaning and determining other meanings. Subjecting the image to alteration, through the mechanism of the dream, but also through mechanisms of association or through the use of simple technologies (photocopying), produced transformations of meanings at the outset. In 1968, in *More News in a Moment*,[14] Baruchello had already given rise to a loss of 'legibility' through the use of the 'very small photograph.' He had photographed images from the television screen until making them tiny and,

13_The film *Three Letters to Raymond Roussel* is divided into three parts: *Limbosigne*, *A Little More Paranoid*, *La degringolade* (1969, film, 16 mm, color, sound, 8'49", 6'50", 12'). In this film, television material is edited (found footage) as in *Verification Uncertain*, although in the latter film he had edited 1950s film material, reduced to fragments and glued together with scotch tape.

14_This was a project (reduced photographs and captions) which then became the cover of the catalogue for Baruchello's exhibition 'Supericonoscopio' at Galleria Schwarz (Milan, 1968).

consequently, illegible. A 'non-sense' was achieved through the warping of sense or the very impossibility of reading.

Some of the books that Baruchello did in the late 1970s were a work on the 'loss of quality,' understood as an element accelerating the birth of new meanings. The images of books, photocopies from photographs (from books, not his own), and mounted on captions in *La stazione del Conte Goluchowsky*, 1978, or arranged alongside notes and drawings as in 1979's *L'Altra casa* in addition to telling other stories, if compared to the contexts from which the starting images had been taken, produced a 'loss' of legibility; however, in the measure of this loss, the images (and words) became the vehicle of memory, of intimacy, or secrets. The captions or notes, in this montage operation, did not function to provide explanations or indications. Instead, they were additional disorienting elements, autonomous, and set beside one another to cause a short-circuit.

The loss that alludes to 'a mechanism of continuous substitution' is born from the decontextualization (of images and words from their original 'text') and then becomes another, through forms of adjacency and juxtaposition in the archiving practice. The loss to which Baruchello refers alludes to processes of demystification and of subtraction of importance, to put into practice, we have seen, a conceptual reduction of the original meanings. This procedure of loss was another one that Baruchello used to reduce, subtract, and delete; as he made the images lose quality, they became illegible just as he had done with the tiny photographs, or as he did ever since he had introduced the use of the small image.

Interestingly, these tiny images captured from printed materials from different sources often become images in his paintings. Indeed, the archives of photographs, of photos-of-photos, are therefore thought of as materials to be reactivated, not only in the various projects we are mentioning here, but also in painting.

The loss of quality when it occurs, as we have seen, in cinema or in the use of video, is a way to challenge and counter all the rules of definition, of high quality, of the outcomes of increasingly sophisticated equipment. To this as well, Baruchello responds by subtracting quality from the image, making it complementary to this subtraction, the daily experiment to seek beyond the definition of an individual detail, the complex confusion that is generated if the dream mixes with reality, the fable, the cartoon, politics, and history. It is not just a postmodern practice, but a thought that moves between boundaries, an archival practice that seeks, in the folds of the archival categories themselves, a way to produce other possible narrative systems, without cause and effect, focusing on the infinite resource of juxtaposition and montage.

Anachronism

Time is a particularly conspicuous theme in these processes of reduction and archiving; it is also more widely a constant object of reflection in his objects and paintings. History and memory are both concerned with time, but the differences between them are profound. Whereas history deals with chronological time, with dates and events that are the result of causes and effects, transitions, ruptures, and progressions, the time of memory is one of amnesia or, to paraphrase once again Jean-François Lyotard (2000), a time that squeezes itself into the gaps, into that which is repressed. Memory thus draws on a different, discontinuous, anachronistic form of time, a time without chronology.[15]

The idea of a system that is small and fragile is the idea to combine together, in the non-monumental space of the experiment, differences and similarities, in order to produce infinite solutions that may arise. The 'cuttings' of the world are no longer the world but the starting point for imagining worlds to come. The archive, in this sense, is not about the past, but the ungrammatical hypothesis about a time to come.

Quoting Sigmund Freud, we could now connect a concept that can be linked to an anachronistic dimension of time. Where facts lose their most common connections and fragment into a horizontal dimension, where the very criteria that determine the importance of a fact are lost, the production of unseen relations becomes possible. Instead of hindering a form of narration that has to give something up in order to be articulated, the short-circuit and the contradiction become the activators of unprecedented perceptions and memory. 'The uncanny is that species of the frightening that goes back to what was once well known and had long been familiar' observes Sigmund Freud.[16] It is in this way that the uncanny offers a point of departure for another reflection that will take us along another itinerary through Baruchello' archival system.

A system is not an order or a construction. Far from this common meaning, we can observe a particular adjacency, at this point, between a storage and a perspective that reactivates it. Hierarchy is absent; instead, there is a sort of horizontality that has been conceived as the unfolding of a story, a story that repositions itself, returning the materiality of time, in short frames, to a state of physicality in which even that which has been repressed can re-emerge.

In 2008, Baruchello conceived a work that comprised a long process of writing and the production of a sort of catalogue of pages. The final phase took the form of a video. He titled it *Ars memoriae*. The idea was to elicit memories taking as a starting point a number of personal photographs. The first phase was dedicated to a sort of cataloguing, in the form of a series of pages (c. 29 × 21 cm) on which he glued a range of photographs selected from his personal albums and arranged non-chronologically. In total, he assembled sixty-two of these pages.

> Recollect to make lists, or rather remember in order to archive. [...] The memory has to be able to become fragmentary, and even if it has a reference to time, to the past moment, it has to possess some characteristic that can be linked with the present of the person who is remembering it with the intention of making it into an (entirely personal) archivable component. But it is in disorder that these fragments, these memories, inhabit our mind, and as such, to progress, the archive must not put things in order but simply suggest nexuses (of chance, but also of analogy) with other memories in

15_Jean-François Lyotard, *Misère de la philosophie* (Paris: Galilée, 2000).

16_Sigmund Freud, *The Uncanny* (London, [1919], 2003).

> a succession that brings to mind the vanishing point. An archive conceived in this way takes shape like a landscape, a rememberable horizon. There has to be a border with the past, beyond which one cannot venture/remember. [...] The archive should not be a story, but an act (or tool?) that inverts the sign of what is forgotten, so that it becomes what is remembered.[17]

As these lines from the sub-entry *Ars memoriae* reveal, the exploration of 'remembering' is central to the project. The final choice of oblivion, of a 'personal amnesia' before the lens of the fixed video camera posed the question of the complex relationship between time, archive, and memory.

What is important to underline is that the film *Ars memoriae* starts from the archive to produce archive cards. Let us dwell on the process. Baruchello makes around sixty cards into which he glues a series of photographs taken from his albums of the past. He wants to undergo an exercise: to look at the photographs and remember, starting from each one, as many stories and facts as possible, including the names of the people photographed. By placing the photos on the cards, he also produces a kind of 'disarray' in the original album. He selects the photos and places them next to each other through memory flashes as he looks at them.

Once the cards have been produced, he starts to write memories on them, names, facts that slowly come to light. He then mounts the film, which is divided into four screens: in one Baruchello himself reads a text in which he tells the genesis of this project; in the second, he mounts some pieces of films made by his father, in which we see Baruchello as a child; in the third, he passes the photographs around individually; in the fourth, we see Baruchello's hand flipping through the cards and showing them one by one. At the end, the four screens disappear and in a single video we see Baruchello throwing the cards one by one into the fire of a fireplace until they are totally burnt.
The different levels, the 'strata' in which interiors and exteriors, intimacy and history, personal and collective memory meet in the film *Ars memoriae*, trace the

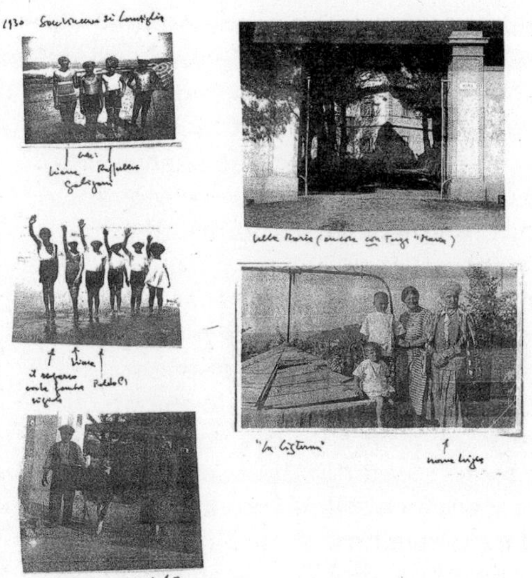

Gianfranco Baruchello, *Ars Memoriae*, 2008–2009, photocopy from the original, burnt card

17_English translation of the Italian text that Baruchello reads in the film *Ars memoriae*.

image's possibilities of being a carrier and translation of experiences illegible or invisible elsewhere.

It is not only memories that re-emerge, through curiosity that prompts us to select forgotten images or episodes. Remembering becomes a multi-layered action: it reassures, enables association, strikes and disturbs. If a photograph in the album was kept close to other photographs of the same period or perhaps of the same people, in the file it reactivates all its potential to solicit and perhaps even disturb. Baruchello's film in fact proceeds by cataloguing, compiling, and eliminating cards. What slowly emerges in this long exercise of 'memory' is a combination that brings to the surface what had been removed with those images: what one did not want to remember. This awareness led to the decision to burn the cards and to reduce a few months' work to 'ashes.' Here, the 'powers of the image' are situated in making the time of history, the time of the individual fact, into a fragment of a more complex temporality, which also makes the viewing more complicated. The simultaneity of adjacencies, the function that the image produces alongside another image, and the montage that is built between the individual aspects are transformed into an uncustomary function.

In a 2018 work titled *L'archivio ci guarda* [literally, 'The archive is watching us'], a number of photographs (photos-of-photos) from the early 1970s are shown in a video in two series, which are organized according to a simple criterion: individual gazes and group gazes. The visitors witness a projection, at ground level, onto two sides of a square base. The element of mirroring is re-evoked in the gaze of the visitors who watch both sides of the base at the same time. Around the time of this project, Baruchello spoke of the adverbial function of the image, by which he meant the function that an image has if placed alongside another image. Adjacency is transformed into a generator of 'time,' a space that is not 'dead' between one image and another, but an active zone. In this zone, in which the interval between one sequence and another, between one frame and the next, becomes a micro-temporality perceivable in the simultaneity produced by the adjacencies, as occurs in the 'archives' where Baruchello arranges materials, images, words, or frames of film through thematic, alphabetic, and temporal juxtapositions, time is transformed into the time of memory.

It is the montage and the archive that assign the image the power of saying what history or experience on their own cannot say: they render legible and visible that which in history and experience always remain outside of it. These are the 'voids' or the sensitive spaces that Baruchello has investigated, reasoning about the physicality of time, about painting as 'stop-image,' or about the film frame as an 'adverb' that precedes what follows: history is reconstructed beyond linear time— made of causes and mechanical effects—in the point where the desire (to remember) and the fact meet, or in the complex game that transforms time into sensitive time, and sensitive time in turn into memory. The practice of montage and archiving is building the hypothesis of different ways of having a number of things exist together: *small systems* are also these projects, starting from the most simple experience, from facts that everyone knows, in order to bring out of all this what neither experience nor fact can communicate on their own.

In this way, the archive can be considered as a work that is concerned with history and its temporal dimensions, but history and the events of history have not yet been written down. If the telling of history strips an event of its time and reduces it to an emblem of a political, historical or cultural event that belongs to a particular epoch or period, Baruchello helps us to consider that it is in the apparent contradiction of the materials itself that a different record of time and history can be produced. Anachronism occurs in what remains outside of real events: it arises in the encounter or in the short-circuit and in small events; it is between the wonder and the anticipation that disconcerts us—because we were not expecting this or that combination—that the unexpected reveals a temporal dimension that does not come before or after but is positioned in the apparently neutral horizontality of what can become something else.

TAKING CARE OF IMAGES

The Collecting and Archiving of Inge Meijer

After a centuries-long dominance of the linguistic and the medium of the book, the second half of the twentieth century was instead dominated by a pictorial turn and the predominance of the visual image. But that period, in which the image became the most important symbolic mode, has come to an end in our computer age. In the words of new media theorist Laura Marks, writing around the turn of the century: 'The period of visual culture is over,' and '[i]t is ironic that all these programs in visual culture are starting up, just at the point where information culture, which is invisible, is becoming the dominant mode.'[1] This assessment of our age suggests that visual images have become dated—that they belong to the past, although a still-recent one—and that one has to take care of images before they become antiquarian or even disappear.

Some artistic practices are fueled by the urge to take care of images. A good example is the Lebanese artist Akram Zaatari who co-founded the Arab Image Foundation (AIF) in 1997. Based in Beirut, this archival foundation has collected thousands of photographs and negatives from countries in the Middle East and North Africa. Zaatari himself has conducted research in photographic practices in Lebanon, Egypt, Jordan, and Syria, and has collected images from those countries. He envisions his collecting of images as an intervention in the social life of waning photographic images. Because of the conflicts in the Middle East, it is a matter of urgency to preserve these images from destruction. In Beirut, for instance, most commercial photo studios, which were located in the downtown area, were ruined in the Lebanese Civil War (1975–1990), and the only remnants of their productions are prints collected from Beirut families. Throughout the Middle East, studios' collections have been threatened as part of their commercial decline. Many of them have sold off their negatives because of the value of their silver content. Preserving these images from annihilation is not enough for Zaatari; being buried in an archive is another form of disappearance. He has reanimated the archive of photographs through a variety of practices, such as making documentaries about specific photographers and photography studios and making selections of images based on a specific category, including studio clients posing with recently acquired cars, for example.[2]

Inge Meijer's work can be seen in the same line—as an artistic practice that takes care of images. In her recent work *A Garden Revisioned* (2019–ongoing) she literally and materially takes care of the collection of negatives and contact sheets

1_Laura Marks quoted in James Elkins, *Visual Studies: A Skeptical Introduction* (New York and London: Routledge, 2007), p. 136.

2_For a discussion of the harmful effects of archiving, but also of productive practices of archiving, see my book *Staging the Archive: Art and Photography in the Age of New Media* (London: Reaktion Books, 2014).

Ernst van Alphen

of an abandoned photo studio she found in a building in the South-Korean city of Gwangju. This building stood behind the hostel where she was staying during a three-month residency in 2019; it was empty and awaiting demolition. It had been a 'wedding palace,' which had functioned between 1988 and 2006 as a place that offered a whole list of matrimonial functions such as officially registering the marriage, renting gowns, providing ceremony rooms and restaurants, hairstyling, and beauty salons. There also were spaces where 'pre-wedding photographs' could be taken, not only at an indoor studio, but also an outdoor garden. It was in the indoor studio that Meijer found these rolls of negatives and contact sheets. Wedding halls went out of fashion in the twenty-first century, and the photographic genre of the pre-wedding photograph, taken a few days before the official ceremony took place, became obsolete.

The wedding images were meant for the family album, or the wedding album as sub-genre of the family album. Within that context we look at dear family members on the so-called most beautiful day of their lives. But within the context of the archive of a photo studio, we look differently. We do not see individual people or details, but rather the conventionality of the wedding image, of the poses of the couples, of their rented

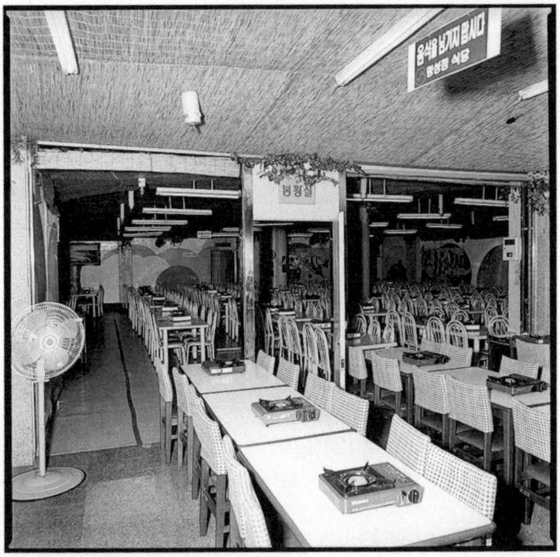

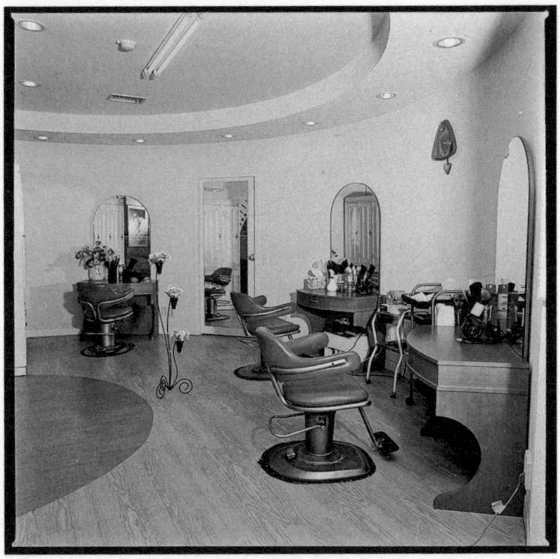

Inge Meijer, *The Wedding Collection*, 2019–ongoing

clothing (there are two kinds of outfits: a suggestive 'Western' style, meaning a long white dress for the woman and black tails for the men, or the eclectic 'Western' gowns referencing the eighteenth-nineteenth centuries; and 'Korean' style, the generalized idea of the traditional). Our viewing is reduced to recognition—of a pattern, or of a specific category or convention. A remarkable and at first sight arbitrary pattern is, for instance, the fact that the brides never show their feet, whereas the grooms do.

The special context of the family album, and the mode of looking activated by that archival context, was foregrounded in 1991 by Dutch artist Armando when he published his artist book *Sans-Souci*.[3] In this book he presented the photographs he had collected at flea markets in German cities throughout the 1980s. All of these images had one thing in common: they showed Nazis and German soldiers in uniform, always in a family context. These images all came from family albums, and so the book Armando designed to show this collection of images resembled a family album itself. All the pages were, for instance, separated by a sheet of cobweb paper. When one sees Nazis in uniform, one expects to see devils incarnate. But in the archival context of the family album, it is difficult to see evil; one only sees caring fathers and loving partners.[4]

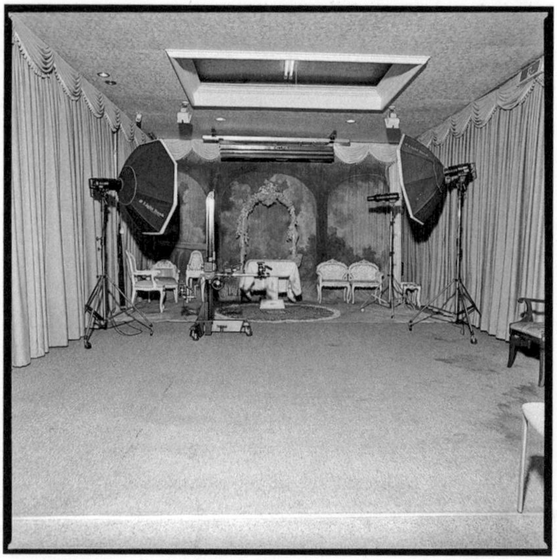

Inge Meijer, *The Wedding Collection*, 2019–ongoing

A Garden Revisioned, which Meijer exhibited at FOTODOK, consists of much more than the found archive. She made her own archive by adding all kinds of other documents, made by herself, to the found materials. The artist's collection of items consists of more than two hundred envelopes with negatives, VHS tapes, interviews, video documentation of the demolition of the building, and photographs of the studio's showroom. The installation presents a selection of the negatives on a massive lightbox; a monitor shows the demolition of the building; and another one depicts the outdoor garden where pre-wedding photos were also made. A third element in the installation are photographs of the building produced originally in order to promote the services of the hall. And finally, there are images Meijer made herself, the so-called 'studies,' which highlight details (gestures, props and so on) in the found pre-wedding photographs.

The installation is not presented as a finished object—it is an ongoing research project. Throughout the run of the exhibition Meijer has continued systematizing the materials; researching the images, places, and contexts in which they were taken and found; and updating the presentation. In short, what we see

3_Armando, *Sans-Souci* (Frankfurt am Main: Portikus; Cologne: Walther König, 1991).

4_For an analysis of Armando's work see my book *Caught by History: Holocaust Effects in Contemporary Art, Literature, and Theory* (Stanford: Stanford University Press, 1997).

is not a finished archive, but the process and activity of productive archiving. But how precisely should the last element of the installation, the details of the pre-wedding photographs, be understood in terms of taking care of images and of productive archiving? Meijer's detailing should not be seen as appropriation of the found photographs. Instead, we can consider it as a practice that does not only take care of the image in the material sense, but rather transforms the modality of looking. When we study the original photographs, we do not really see what is visually present in the image; our gaze is based on recognition. We recognize similarity or even sameness between images,

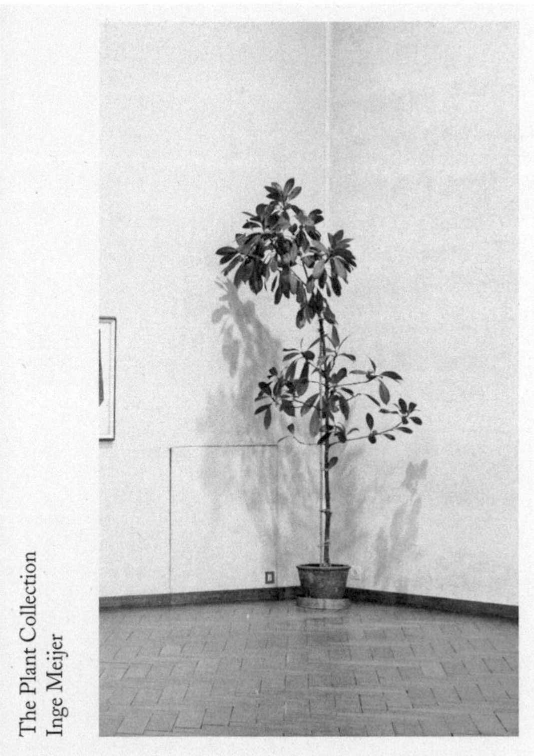

Inge Meijer, *The Plant Collection*, 2016–ongoing

we recognize the conventionality of these images, as well of the outfits and poses of the brides and grooms.

Meijer's addition of her own 'studies' to the archive alters our mode of looking: we suddenly see details that are overlooked in the original, 'authentic' contexts of these images. I write contexts in plural, because as mentioned earlier, there are two original contexts of these pre-wedding photographs: the archive of the family album or the wedding album; and the photo studio's archive where they were found. The details on which Meijer zoomed in show beautifully baroque curves as part of the wedding gowns. In terms of the specificity and individuality of wedding images, this attention for baroque curvature and lining seems rather arbitrary. But when we consider all of Meijer's additions together, again, a form of recognition rather than a seeing and looking carefully, seems to be activated, because we note similar curves across all of the images. However, this is the first time that we pay attention to these details, as our mode of looking has been changed. Meijer's way of archiving by adding images to the archive demonstrates that taking care of images should not just be understood in the literal, material sense of the expression, as preserving, but also as transforming our mode of looking at images. Meijer's images do not specifically care for baroque curves, but for the way we look at them, by transforming recognition into a way of witnessing the overlooked.

Meijer has done something similar in her previous archival project that is titled *The Plant Collection* (2019). She researched the archives of the Stedelijk Museum, Amsterdam and discovered something remarkable. Many of the images that documented the exhibitions after the Second World War showed plants as part of the exhibition. It was typographer and curator Willem Sandberg, the newly appointed director of the Stedelijk Museum, who placed a monstera next to a Piet Mondrian painting in 1946, at an exhibition organized in honor of the artist. For Sandberg, the aesthetic placement of a plant within the museum made a statement. No longer would the Stedelijk Museum be an elite temple for art; rather, he wanted the public to become accustomed to contemporary art in a familiar, domestic environment. Meijer investigated the vanished and subsequently forgotten vegetation in the museum during the period between 1945-1983. It turned out that Sandberg had started a new kind of museum display, which was continued by the directors who succeeded him. One of the guards was given the special responsibility of taking care of the Stedelijk Museum's plant collection, and former director (1963–1985) Edy de Wilde wrote letters of gratitude to people who had donated their plants to the museum. In the late 1980s, this practice gradually came to an end. Just like the zoomed-in elements of pre-wedding photographs in *A Garden Revisioned*, the images of plants Meijer brings together in *The Plant Collection* are crops—in this case from the official exhibitions' installations documentation. In both cases what we see is not just insignificant details, but ones that point to a buried history.

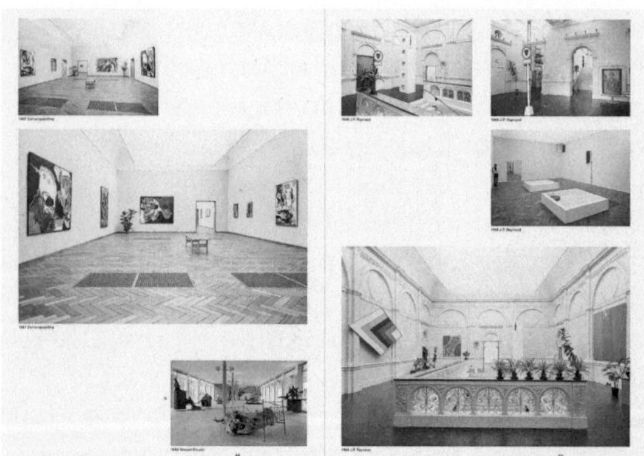

Inge Meijer, *The Plant Collection*, 2016–ongoing

From our present perspective, the notion of the museum as a domestic environment is remarkable. We are used to an idea of the museum and the gallery as 'neutral' spaces, or 'white boxes,' although even this conception is now dated. From the perspective of the archive, on the other hand, it is remarkable that the

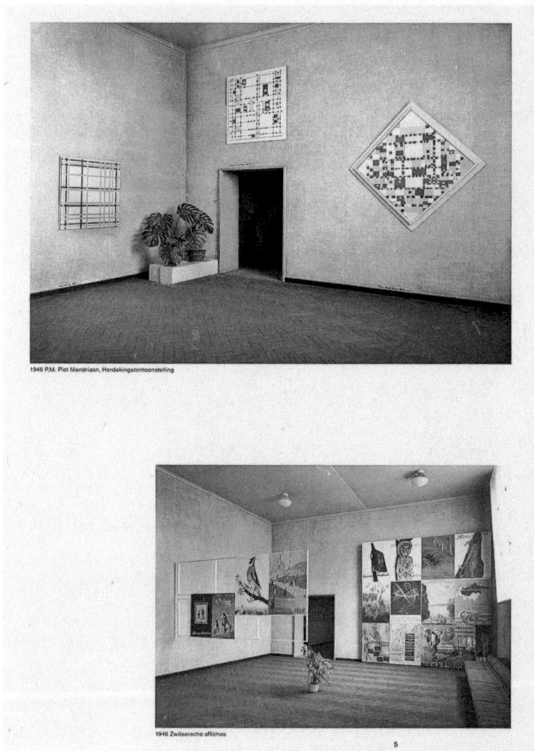

plants were present in all the documentation of exhibitions that took place during that period, yet, they were overlooked. Nobody noticed them, because later notions of museum display had no room nor attention for plants. To be included in the archive does not equate to being visible. The archive frames objects and documents in a very specific way, and in the case of the Stedelijk Museum, its archives frame exhibitions in such a manner that all attention goes to the artworks, and not to the parallel, traditionally domestic objects that alter the museum space itself. It could be said, that through this process of taking care, Meijer has modified the way we look at this archive's images, allowing us to see what was overlooked for decades.

The Plant Collection is archival in a double sense: it is based on the archives of the Stedelijk Museum, and it presents in book form the results of the research conducted in that archive. The book is a very appropriate medium for archiving. The presentation of lists and collections often takes place in book form. Not only are encyclopedias, dictionaries, and catalogues archival books, but the artist's book is often also the medium for archival projects. The books of artists Anna Atkins, Ed Ruscha, Sophie Calle, Christian Boltanski, and Annette Messager are often archives in book form. Meijer's interest in taking care of images and of the archive is not only expressed in the above projects; this sensibility also appears in her film work, which could just as easily be considered archival in nature.

Meijer's film *Carrousel* (2014) collects the different uses of one specific place—a room that was originally used as theatre as well as a gym. But the same location is now also used for dancing lessons, for playing bridge and bingo, doing aerobics, for henna parties, and for celebrating *Sinterklaas* (a Dutch winter festival). Meijer has collected different images that are all from the same space, and all footage is shot from the same camera position. By doing this she has created a specific image category, and as result, we recognize the space that holds the category together as a through line. But of course, this image category is rather bizarre or arbitrary; as a category it is less common than the wedding photograph. One could say that it is unique, rather than conventional or common. Usually, it is conventionality that enables and motivates categories. In *Carrousel*, Meijer challenges the distinction between two different modes of looking: one of recognition, and one of really seeing what is specific to the footage. Through this categorization, Meijer, as with *The Plant Collection*, again converts recognition into seeing what is specific.

Another of Meijer's films is named after a children's song: *If you go down to the woods today* (2016). It was filmed in the woods of Gilze en Rijen, and shows a man in the center of the image walking with an animal, approaching the camera. At first, our seeing is based on recognition: we recognize the familiar image of a man walking his dog. But when the man comes closer to the camera, we see something rather special: this man is walking with a leashed bear. We learn that the man used to train animals to perform in films or television, but because this is now forbidden, all he can do with his bear is take it for walks in the woods, not far from where he lives. The central camera position—filmed as if this is commonplace—frames the scene as being as normal as a man walking a dog. As in the examples above, with *If you go down to the woods today*, Meijer complicates the relationship between the *recognition* of conventionality and *seeing* what is specific. These modalities form the central problem of archiving: how do we use and structure the archive. Because of this, *If you go down to the woods today* could be seen as an archival film. Its structure is not based on listing or collecting—it just shows the very simple narrative of a man walking his bear. But how this narrative is presented to us again alters recognition into seeing. It is exactly this transformation that characterizes Meijer's *A Garden Revisited*. Meijer changes the surface conventionality of the pre-wedding photograph into a deeper representation by highlighting details of the found images and adding those to the archive. In both projects the viewers are exposed to images they usually do not get to see.

Meijer's artistic practice seems to be based on collecting and archiving images that have something in common. Her films, as well as her more outspoken archival projects, share that practice. But the archive as a medium can be very unproductive, because images, documents, and items become buried in the archive itself. They are lost in the archive because of their reduction into the category under which they are archived. Hence, the archive discourages the modality of looking that discerns what is unique. The pre-wedding photographs, within the context of the Gwanju photo studio's archive, demonstrate that effect of archiving strictly by category. But Meijer does not accept the confining, reductive effects of the archival medium—she liberates the images caught in an archival context by taking care of them. She shifts the viewing process activated by the archive into one that is able to unearth and rediscover what is particular to these images.

Meijer's short film *Maple Tree* (2017) shows a tree moving through a Dutch landscape, as if by magic—a rather strange image, I would say. This image does not belong to a conventional image category. Of course, this cannot be real, and after some time we learn that the tree is being transported atop a trailer hitched to a car. Before she made this film, Meijer had been collecting images and taking photographs of people transporting plants. When one decides to start paying attention to people transporting plants, you suddenly see them everywhere. This too is not a conventional category of images, but the moment you start collecting them they become a category. Although *Maple Tree* is a film that stands on its own, it is clear that it came out of Meijer's archival project of establishing the image category of 'people transporting plants.' But this archival project also challenges the expected effects of archiving, like her other works and projects do. The created category is not really common and conventional, because in Meijer's case it activates a mode of looking that does not recognize, but sees the uniqueness of the category. This paradoxical practice of looking that liberates the image from the confining context of the archive, is the primary way on which Meijer takes care of images.

The Tree Collection

Archive felling permits

A tree cannot move itself and that can be fatal, especially in the city, where space is limited. Your trunk may have become too big, too crooked, too long or too thick. Your roots disrupt stones, flower boxes and facades. Although in most cases you have not planted yourself, you are still charged if you are in the wrong place.

The tree owners give a reason for felling a tree. Some are very functional and short. Others are a bit more extensive and then you see a glimpse of the injustice that a tree can do: it can take away (sun) light, spread leaves, provide housing for birds that defecate in the tree owner's garden and damage all kinds of valuables.

Collecting these photographed trees is a way of narrowing them down. Together they form a group of fellow sufferers, a series of portraits of the last moment before they are felled. Sometimes the resistance or justice of the impending act can already be seen in photography. Half portrayed, captured without too much attention.

Some tree owners' requests for felling permits

Anna Paulowna tree
(Paulownia tomentosa)

Cutting down a tree in the garden because it threatens to damage the foundation of the adjacent building and therefore also grows crooked and can possibly fall over.

Black alder tree
(Alnus glutinosa)

There is a tree in the back garden and we would like to remove it. There is only 1 large tree in the entire courtyard of all the gardens within our building and it's in our garden. We would like to remove the tree because it's very large and the roots are close to running into the foundation of the building, half of the three has already been cut down and is dead, we get all the leaves in our garden, it blocks the sunlight.

Maple tree I
(Acer)

In the garden is a (blown) maple of about 10 meters high. This tree causes nuisance: neighbours' gutters become clogged and lead to things such as flooding, the honeydew secretions make everything sticky and cause insect pests, fluff from flowers, helicopters and a lot of leaf fall. Tree is too big, and space too tight. We want to cut down this tree so that the cause of the nuisance and (future) damage is solved.

Conifer
(Coniferae)

Application for felling a tree in the register 8116. The conifer has become much too large, in disproportion to the neighboring house that is 1 metre away. The tree causes damp and damage problems in walls and basement (roots). In addition, a lot of nuisances from nests of pigeons and starlings that have discovered the tree and leave behind a thick layer of excrement and a pungent stench.

Inge Meijer

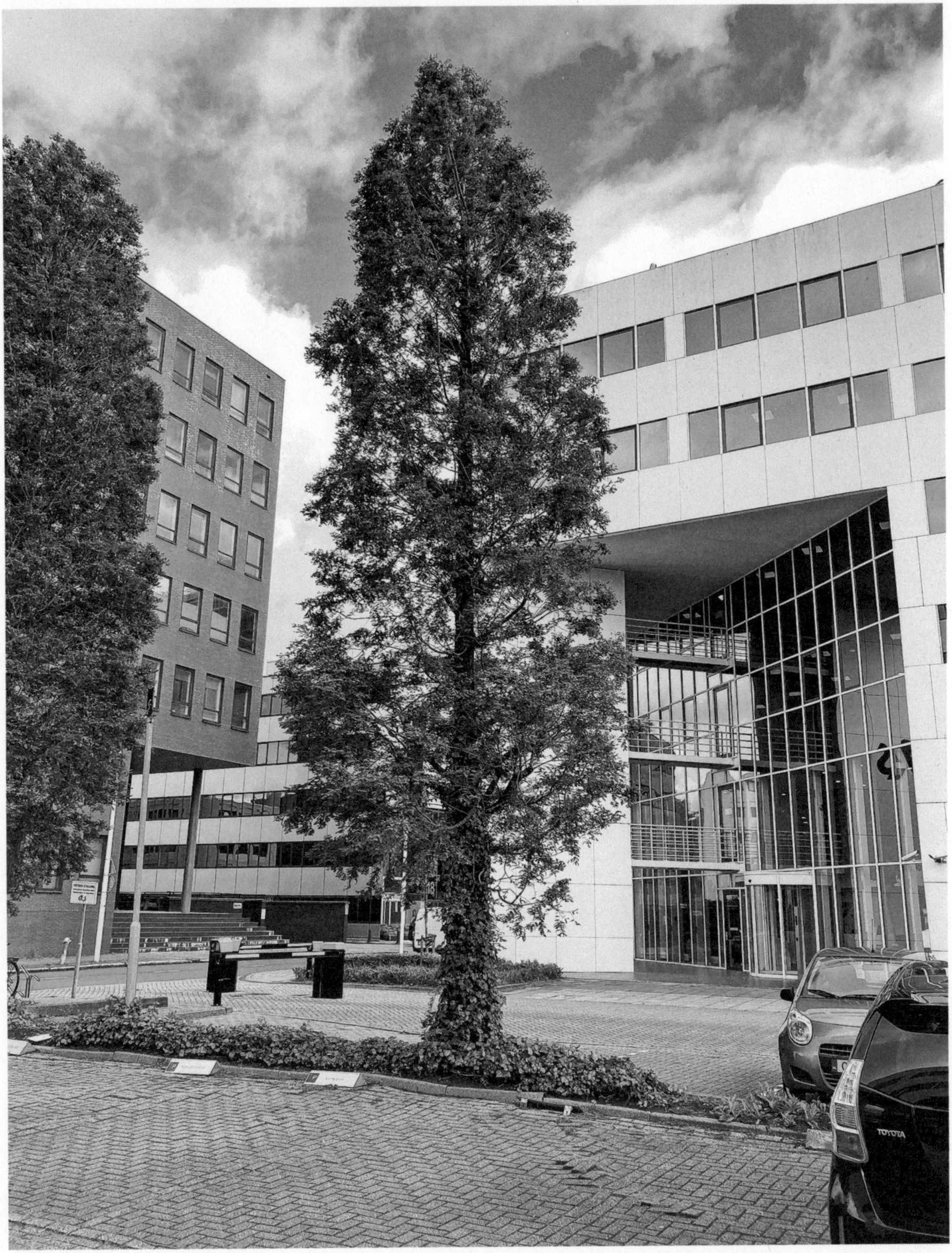

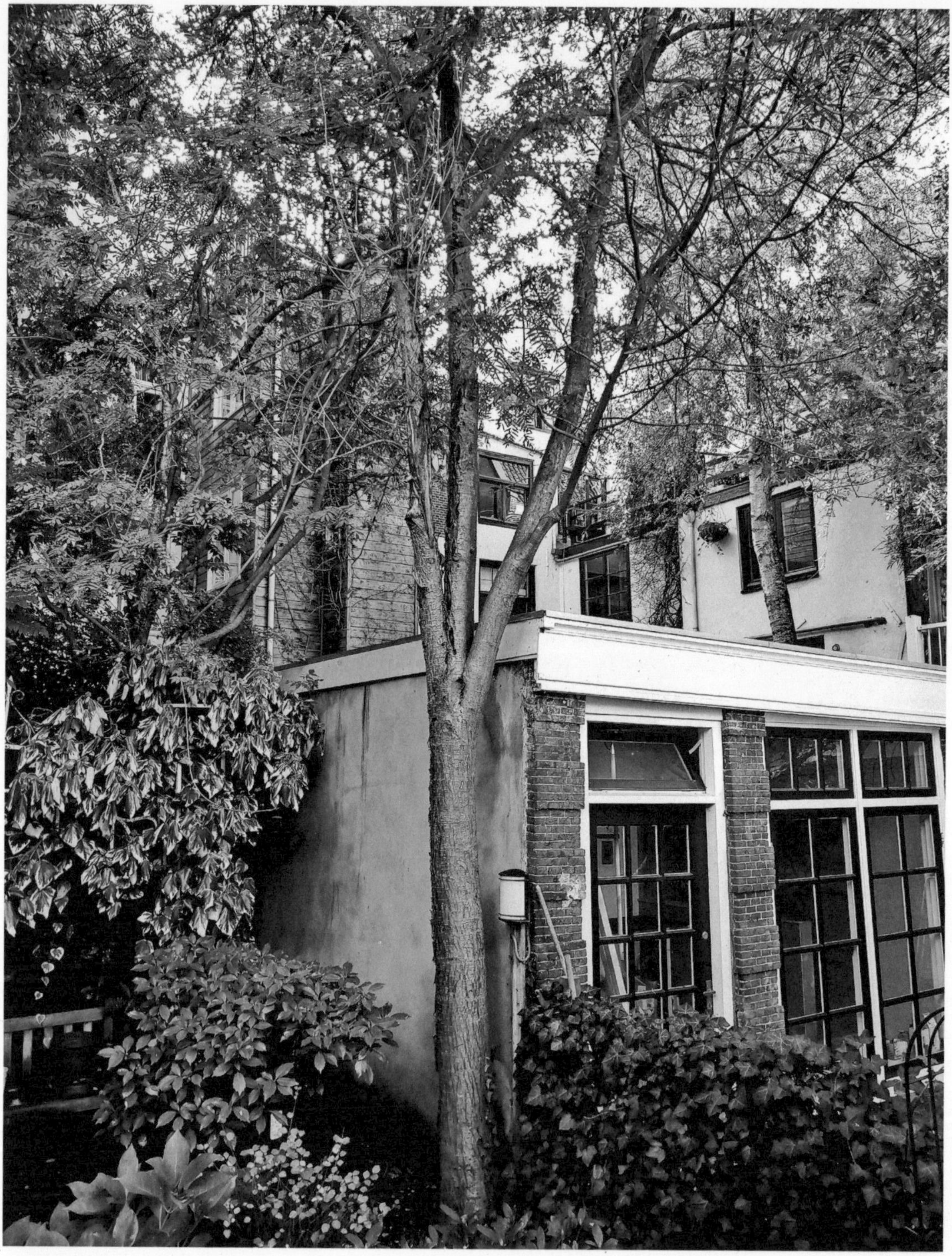

Inge Meijer

Inge Meijer,
The Three Collection, 2020–ongoing
color photography

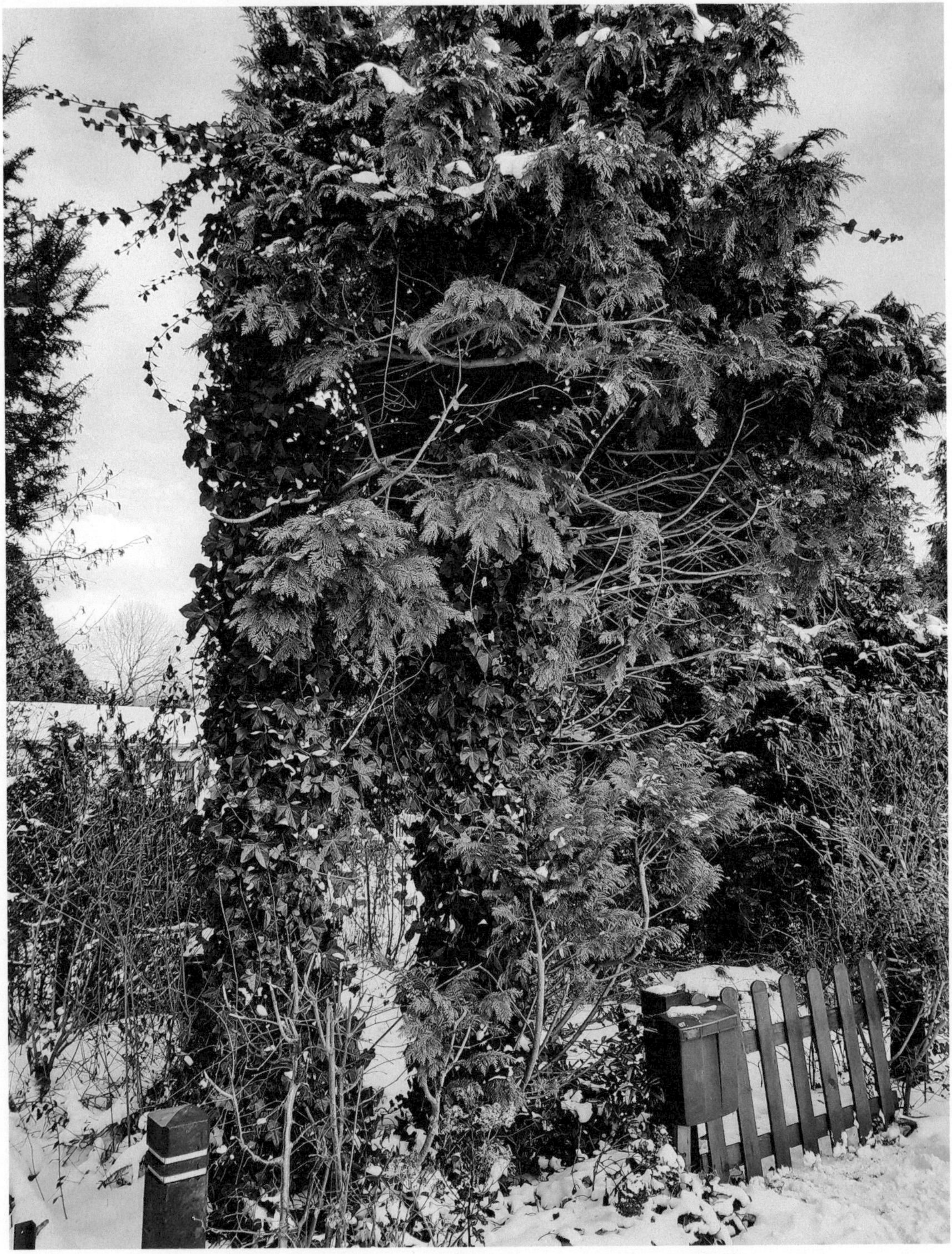

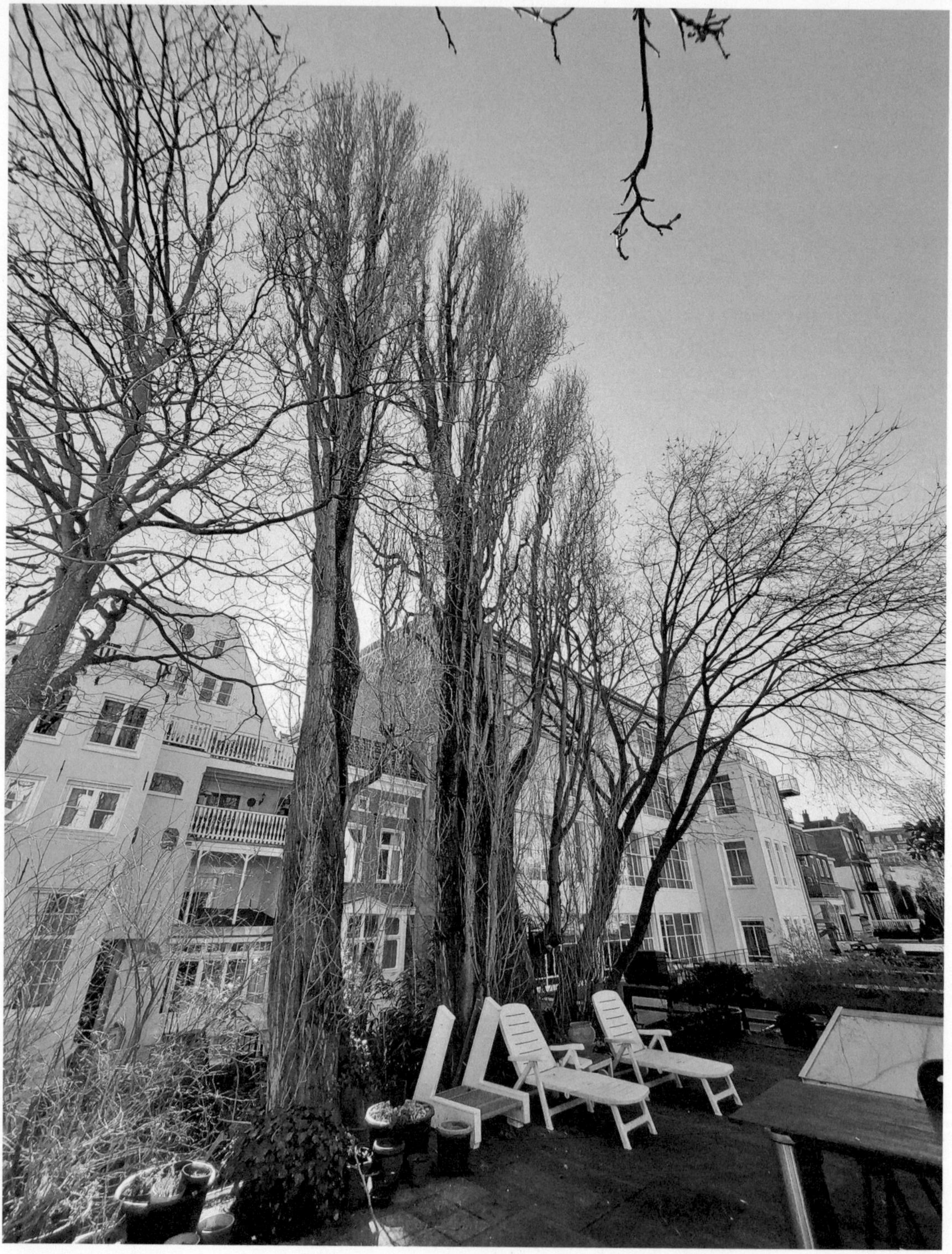

Inge Meijer

Inge Meijer,
The Three Collection, 2020–ongoing
color photography

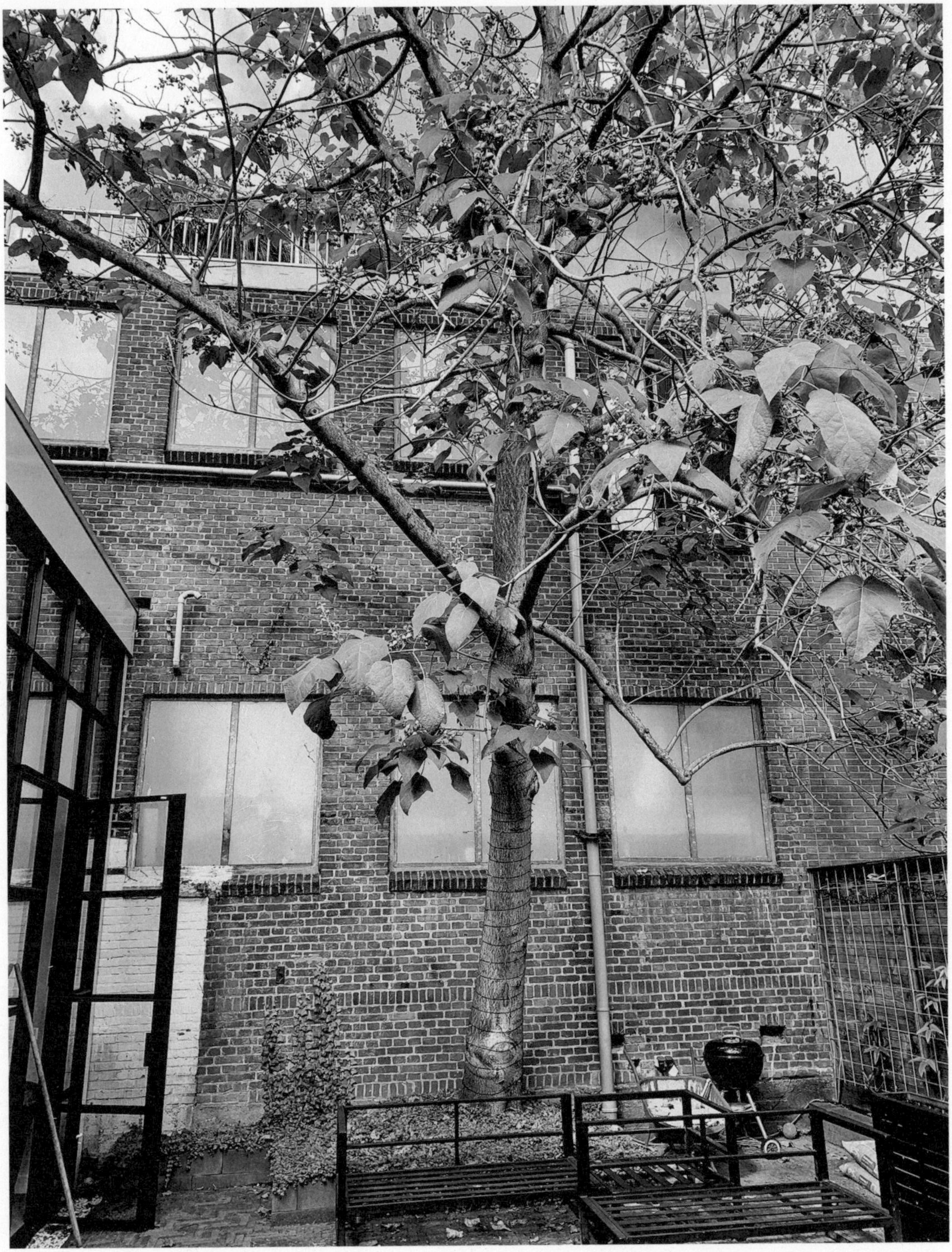

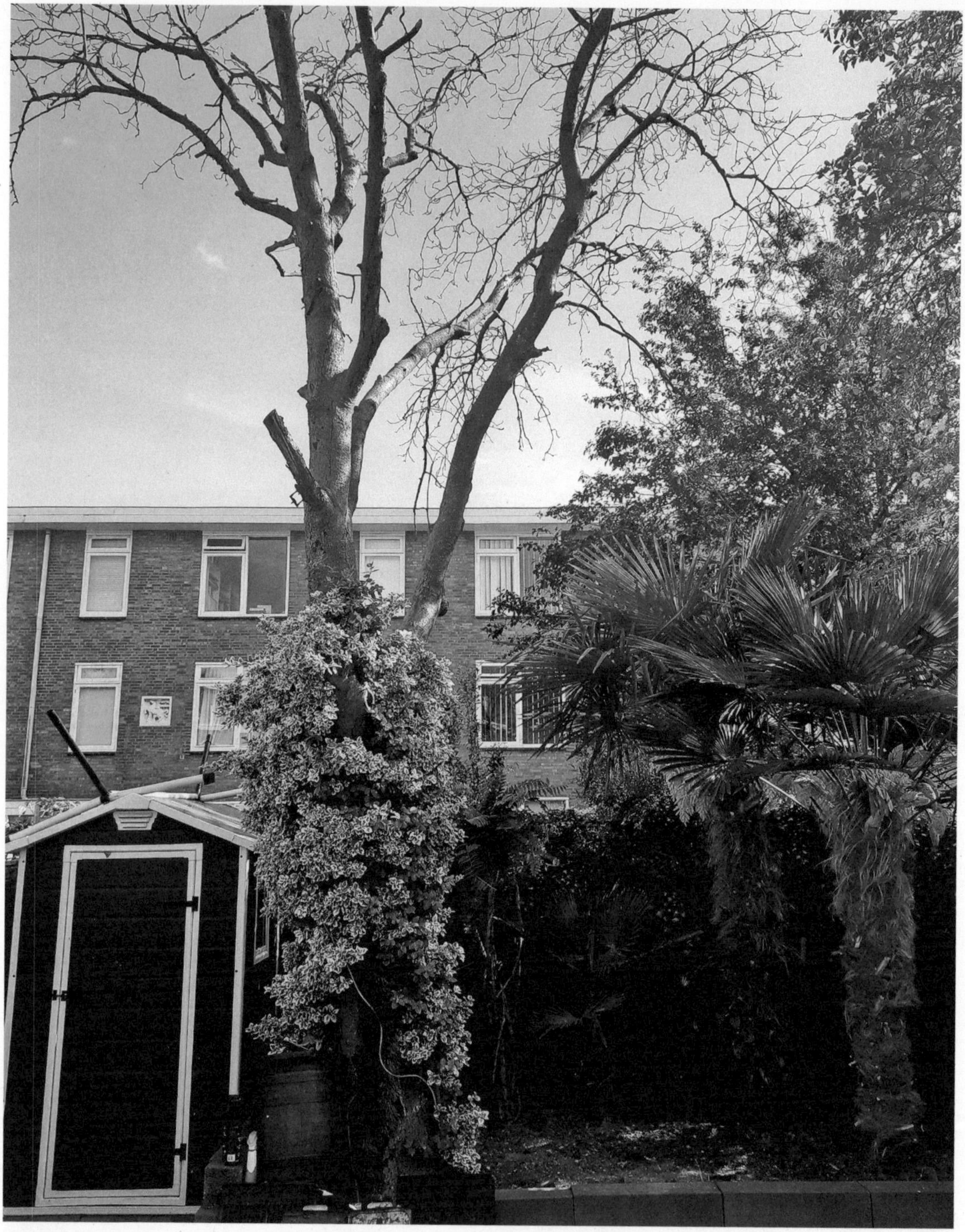

Inge Meijer

Inge Meijer,
The Three Collection, 2020–ongoing
color photography

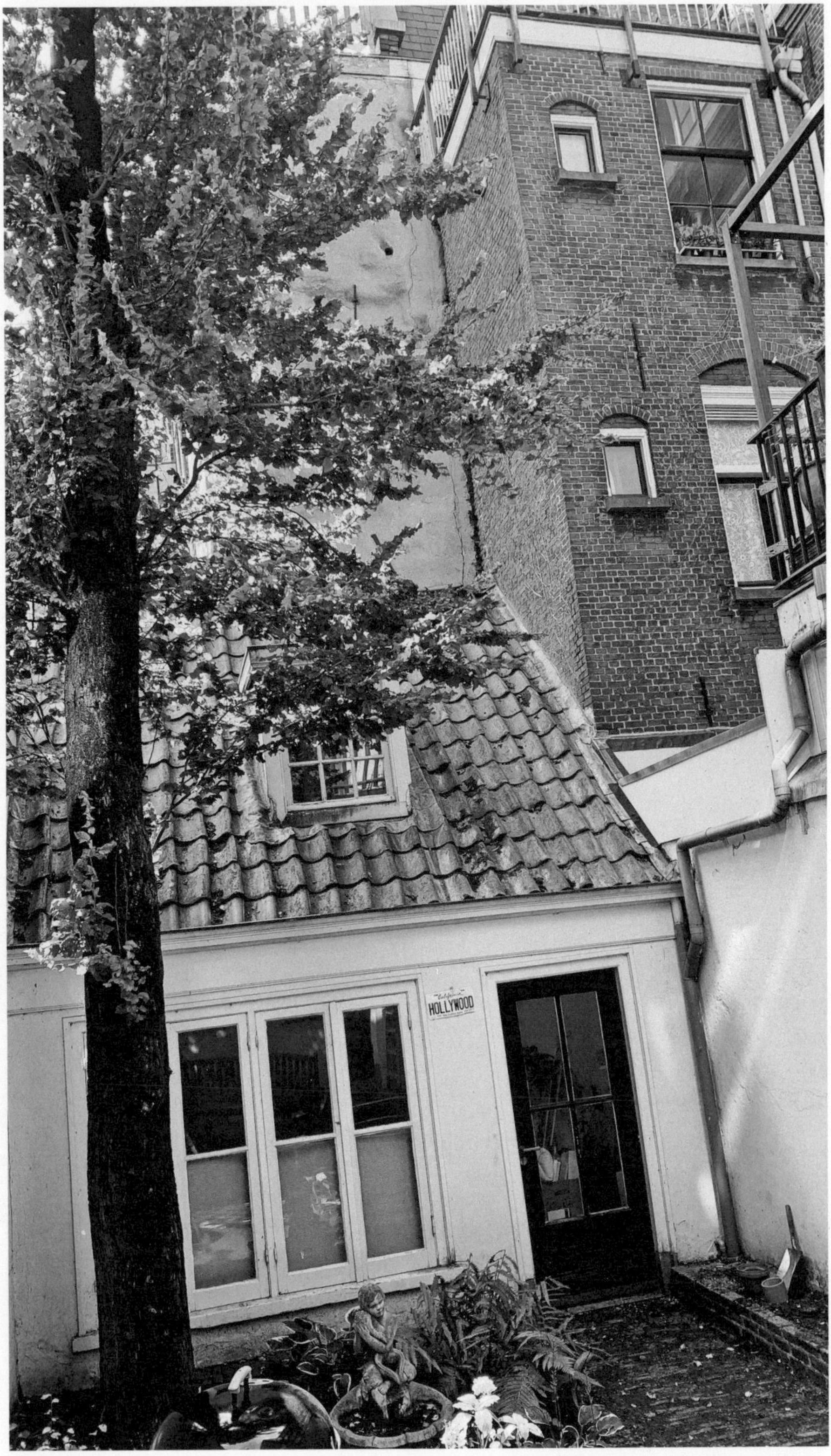
HOLLYWOOD

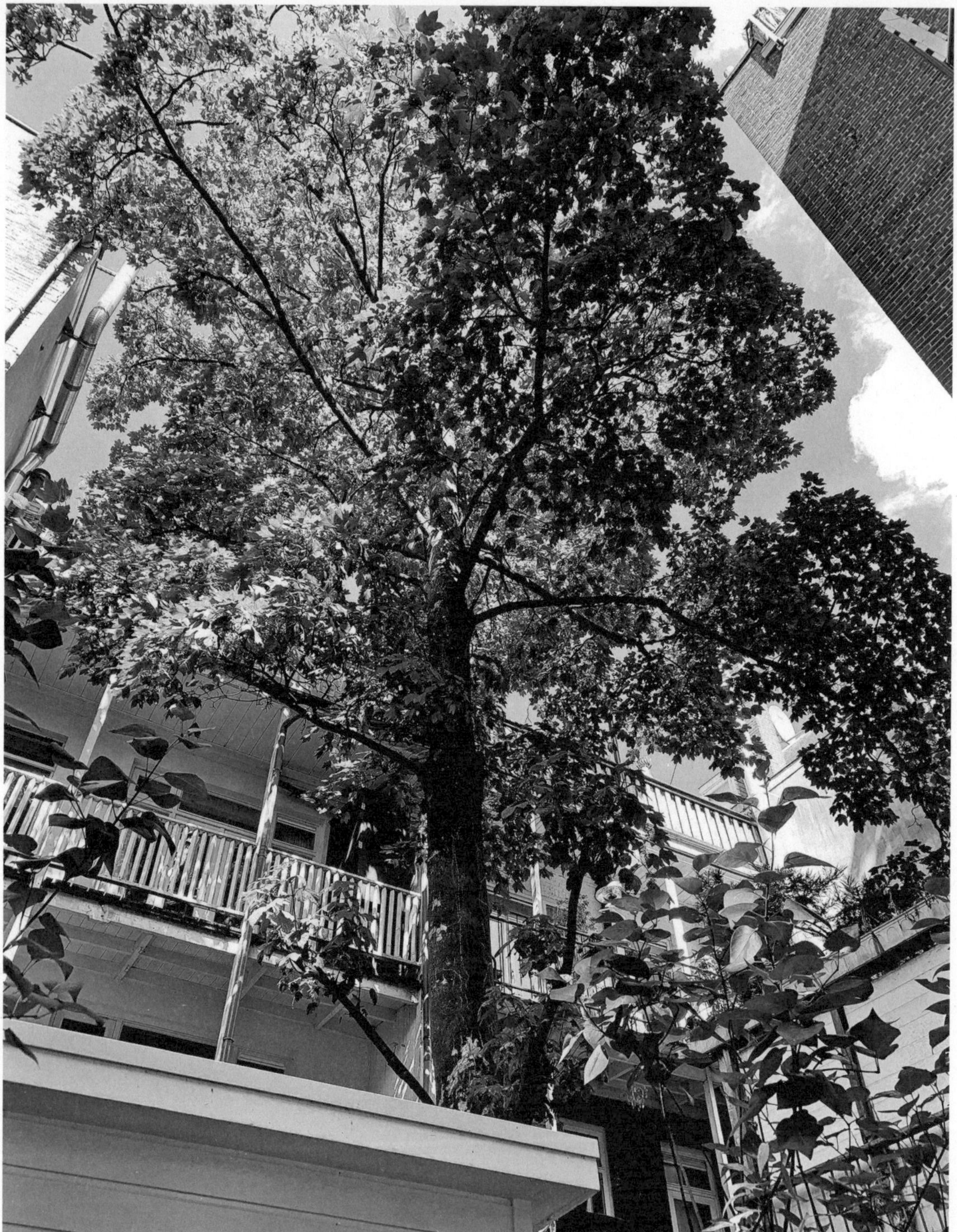

Inge Meijer,
The Three Collection, 2020–ongoing
color photography

Inge Meijer

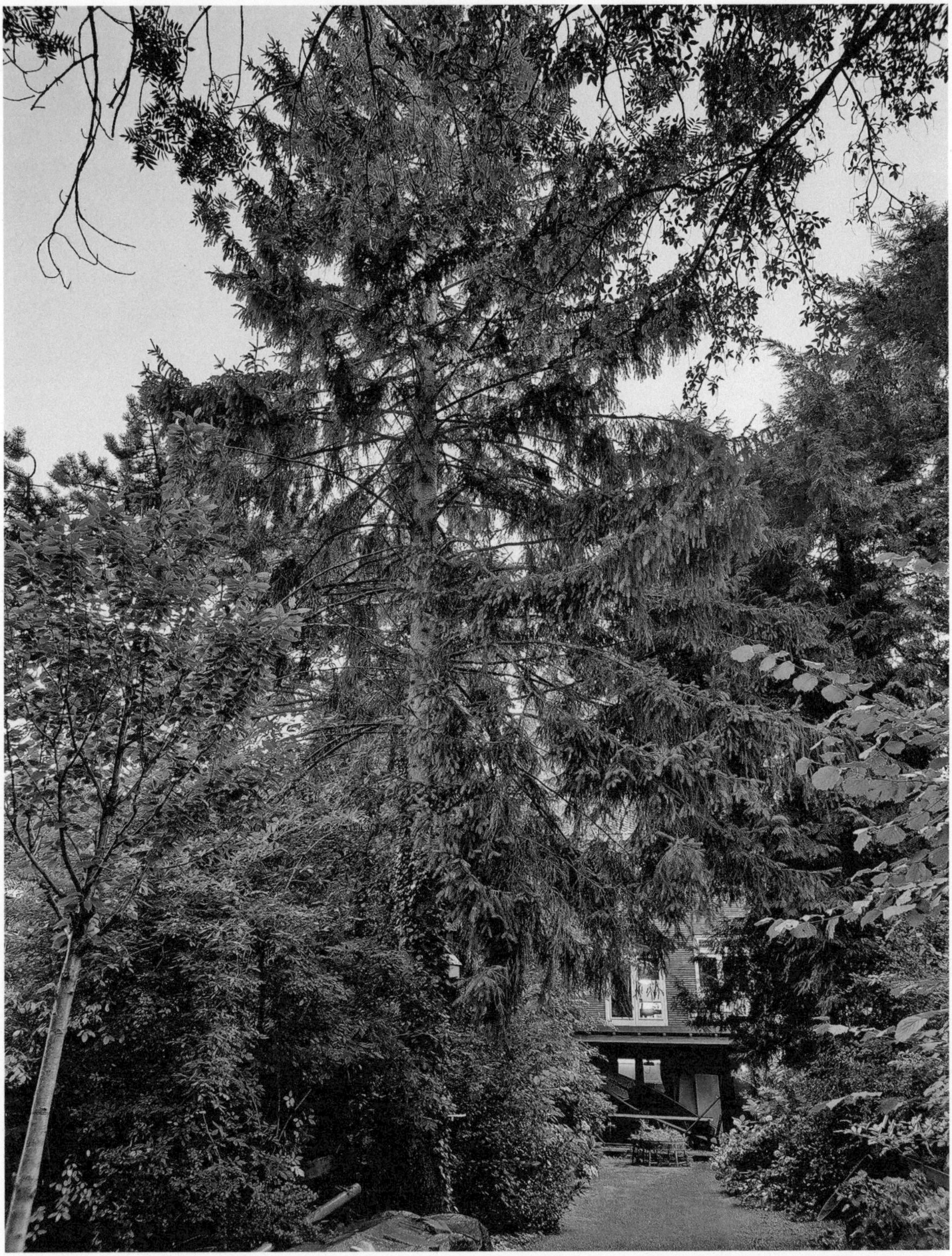

Point of Departure

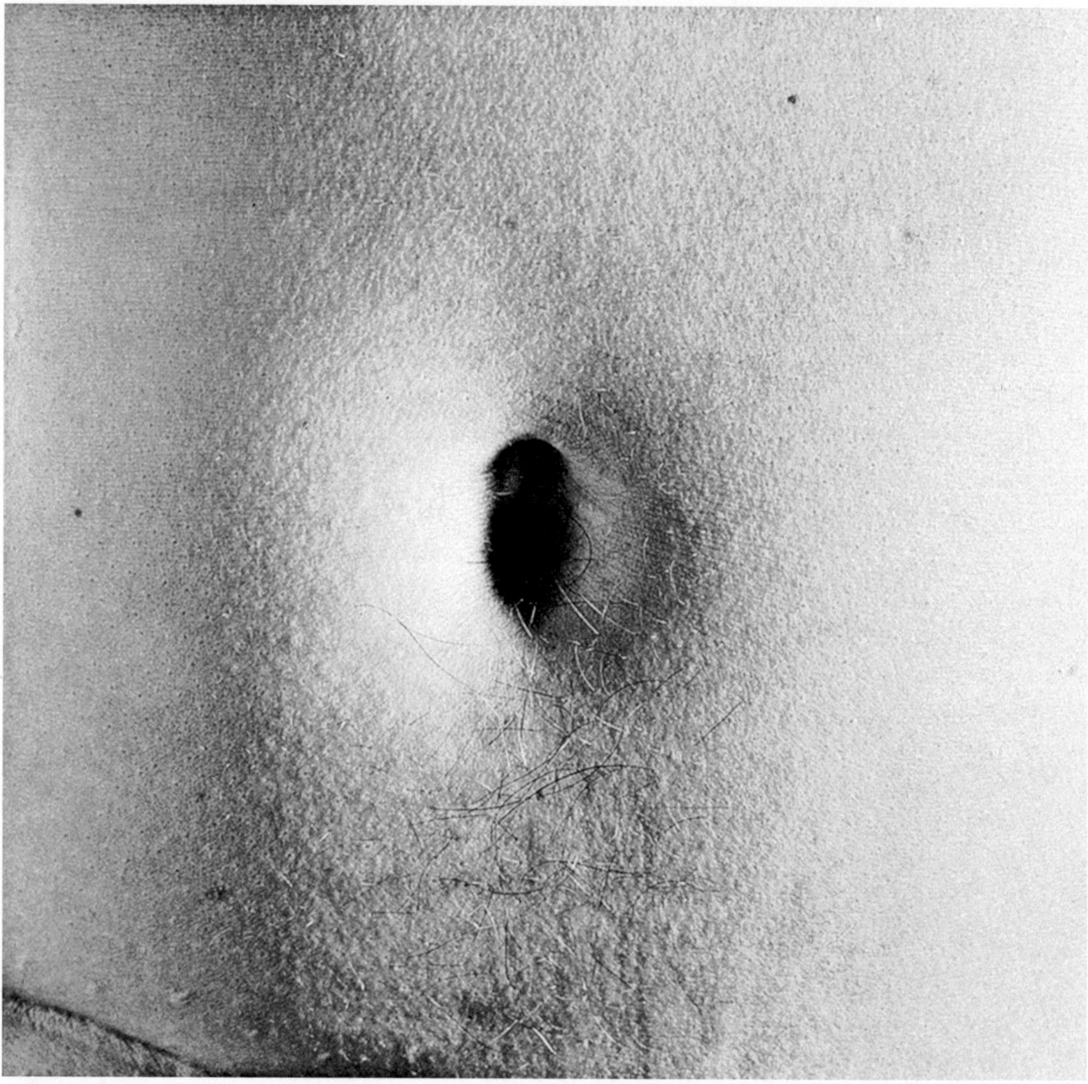

Jeannette Christensen

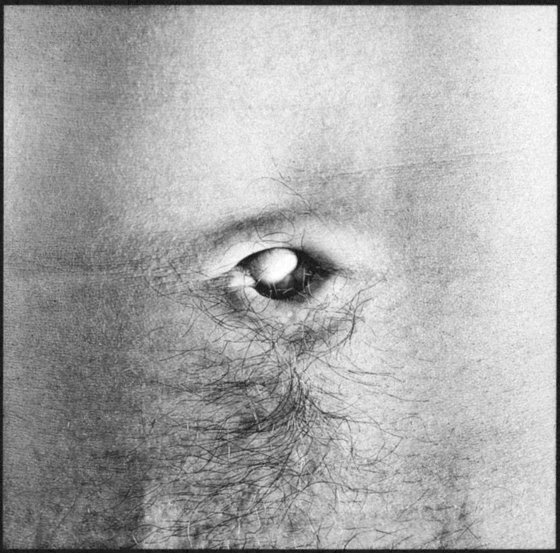

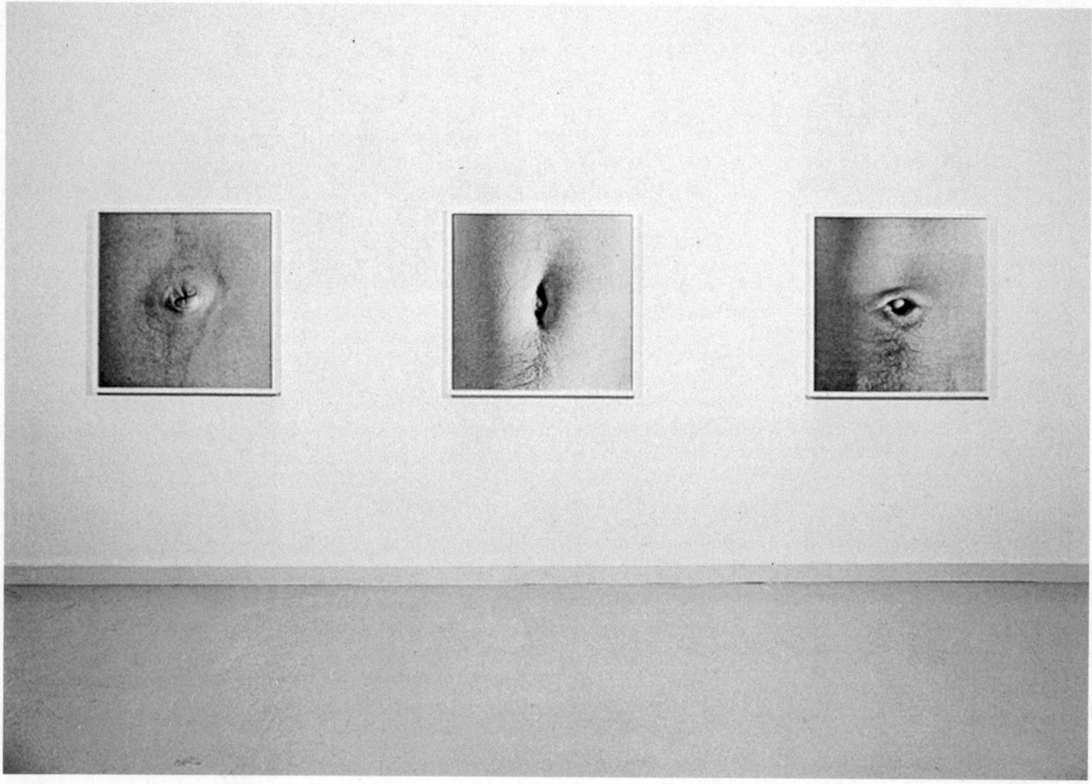

Jeannette Christensen,
Point of Departure, 1999
B/W photography, 86 × 86 cm

Shown at: Overgaden, Kulturministeriets utstillingshus for Nutidigkunst, Kopenhagen, 2000

Jeannette Christensen

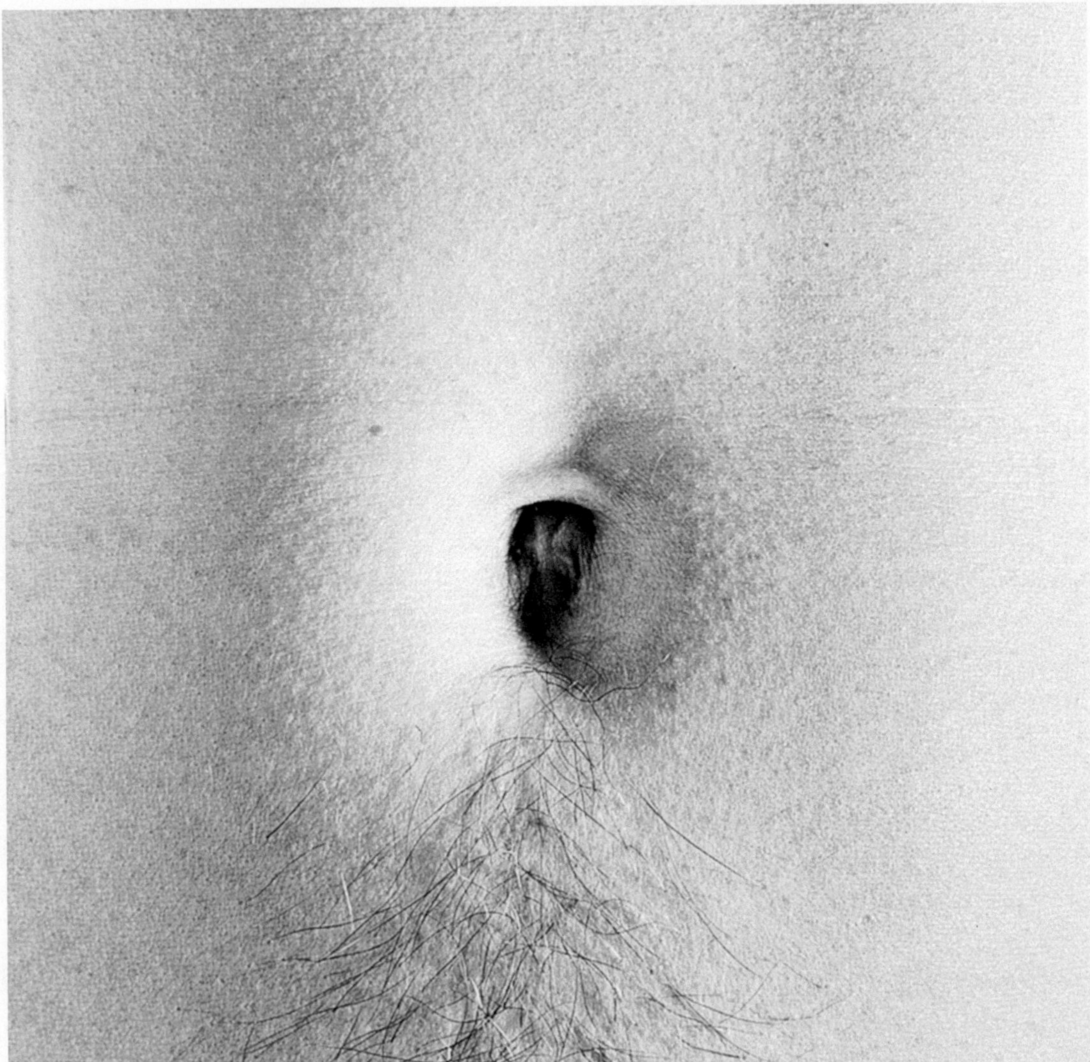

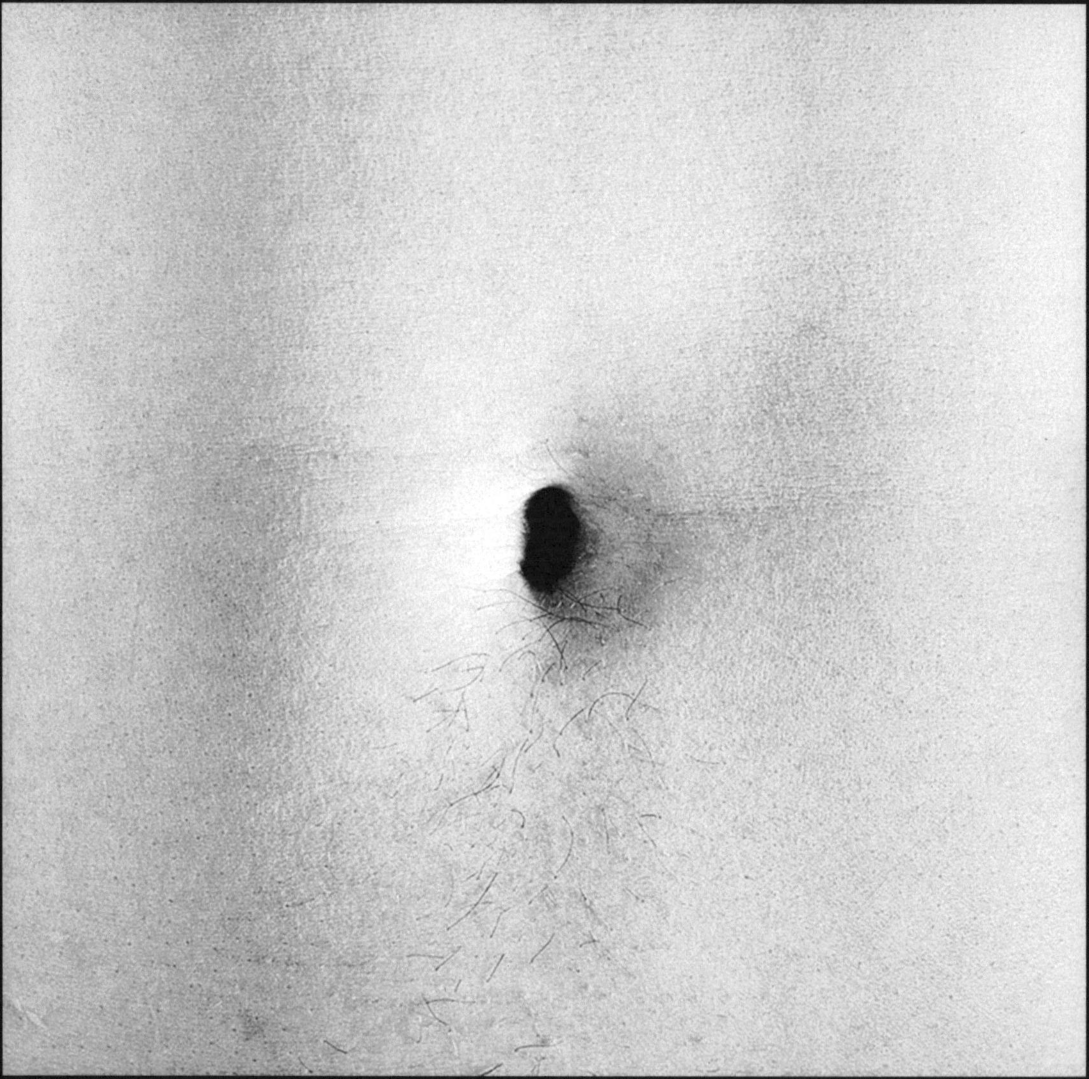

Jeannette Christensen

Jeannette Christensen,
Point of Departure, 1999
B/W photography, 86 × 86 cm

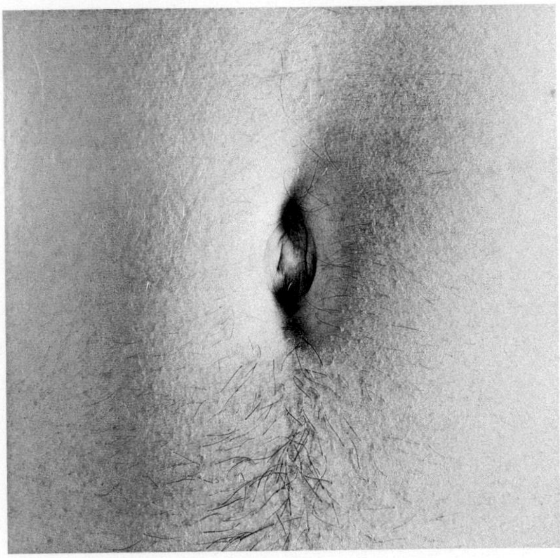

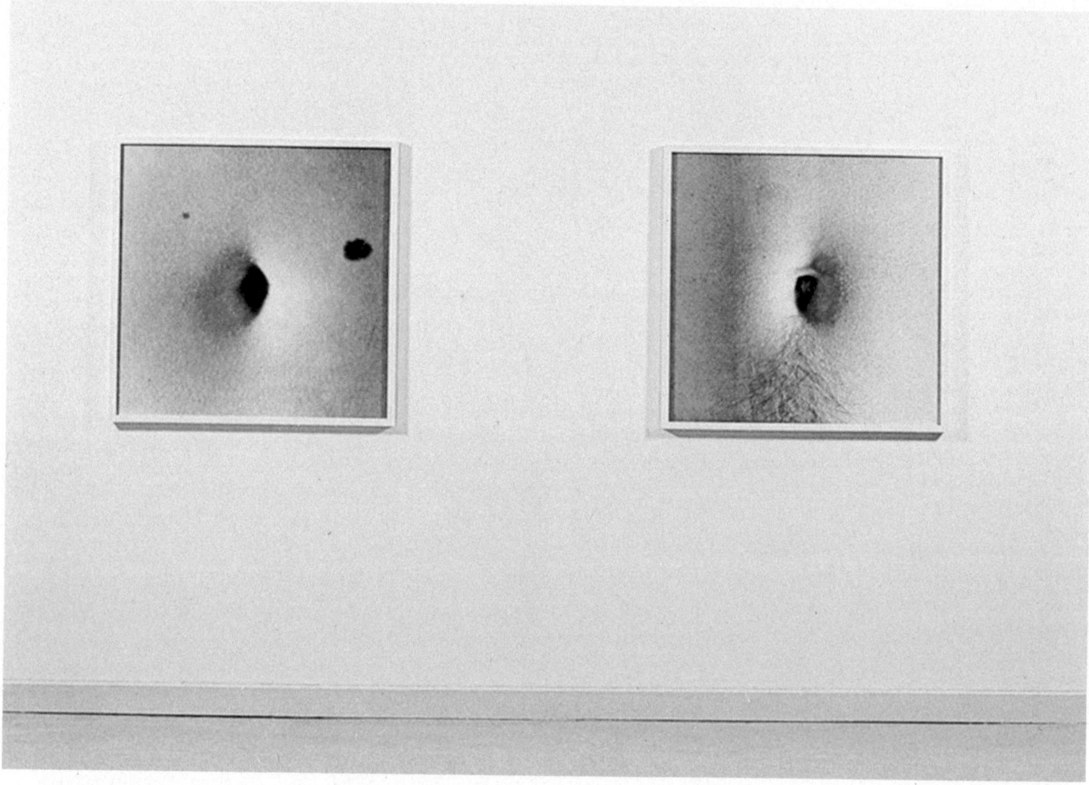

Jeannette Christensen

Jeannette Christensen,
Point of Departure, 1999
B/W photography, 86 × 86 cm

Shown at: Overgaden,
Kulturministeriets utstillingshus for
Nutidigkunst, Kopenhagen, 2000

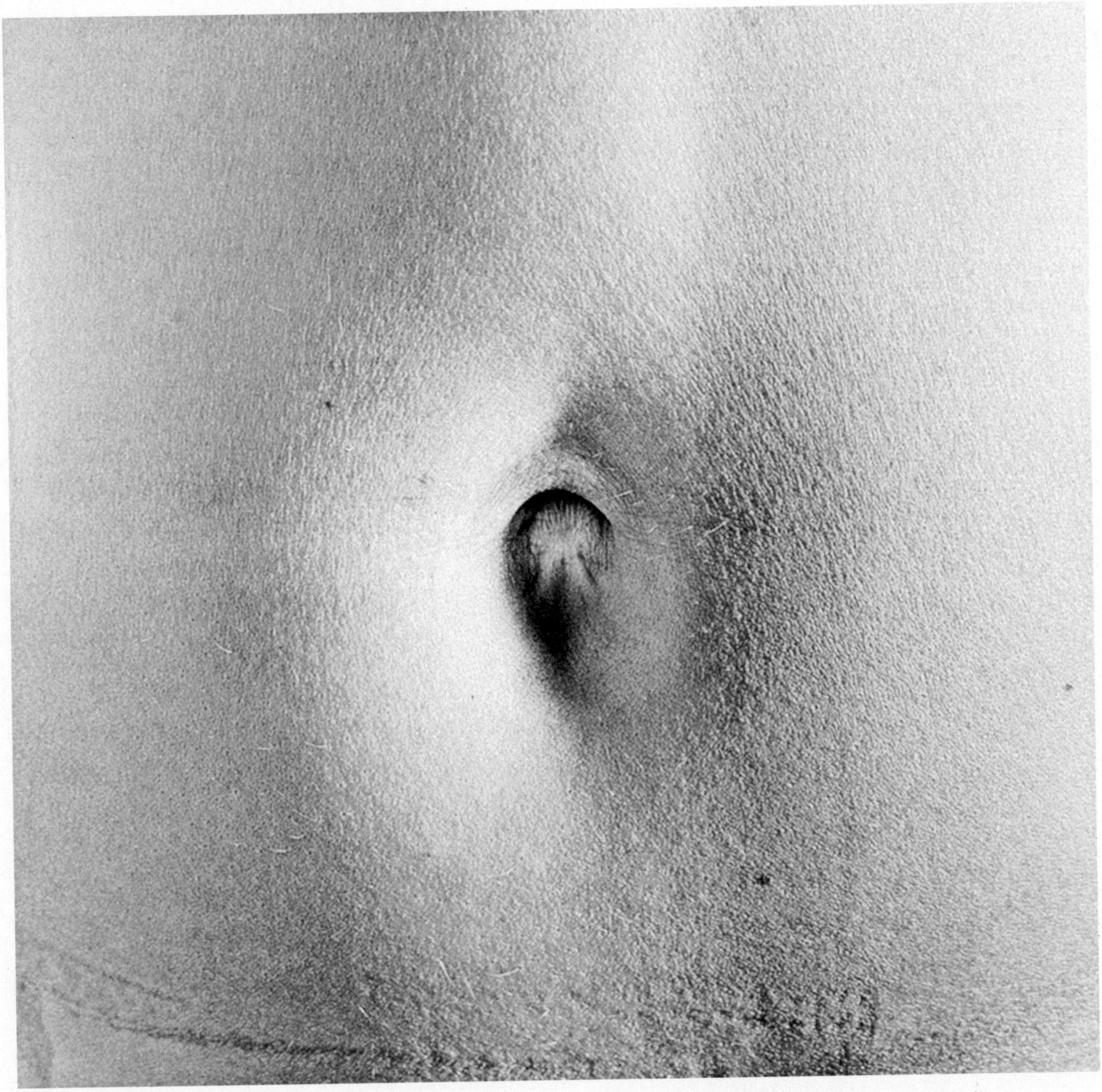

Biographies

Ernst van Alphen (b. 1958, NL)

is professor emeritus of Literary Studies at the Leiden University Centre for the Arts in Society. His research focuses on modern and post-modern literature—and its relation to visual arts. Recent book publications include *Seven Logics of Sculpture* (Valiz, 2023); Shame*! And Masculinity* (ed.) (Valiz, 2020); *Failed Images: Photography and its Counter-Practices* (Valiz, 2018); *Staging the Archive: Art and Photography in the Age of New Media* (Reaktion Books, 2014). Van Alphen lives and works in Amsterdam and Paris.

Aleida Assmann (b. 1947, DE)

is professor emerita of English and Literary Studies at the University of Konstanz. She studied Egyptology and her work has focused on cultural anthropology and Cultural and Communicative Memory. Over the past decades, she has been a visiting professor at numerous universities (Chicago, Princeton, Vienna, Yale). She is known for her key-publications about cultural memory. In 2014, she received the Heineken Prize for history from the Royal Netherlands Academy of Arts and Sciences. In 2017, she was awarded the Balzan Prize for Collective Memory together with her husband Jan Assmann. In 2018, she was awarded the Friedenspreis des Deutschen Buchhandels together with her husband, honoring their work on 'sustainable peace and understanding among the peoples of the world'. In 2021 she was elected a corresponding fellow of the British Academy.

Gianfranco Baruchello (1924–2023, IT)

has created works in varying mediums throughout his career, expressing his belief that anything can be art, from running a farm, to a pair of cutoff shorts. Baruchello's oeuvre includes wall-mounted 'box showcases' in which he displayed paper cutouts and various objects.

Jeannette Christensen (b. 1958, NO)

is a visual artist, living and working in Oslo. Since the beginning of the 1990s, she has worked with installations, sculpture and photography. A discussion revolving around the concept of sculpture, time and materiality has been a common theme. The citation, appropriation and combining of elements from art history with contemporary art, and the position and presence of art in society are recurring interests. Christensen has worked with a broad range of materials and is especially known for her installations made of Jello. She has studied at the Academy of Art and Design in Bergen (Vestlandets Kunstakademi) and Ecole Nationale Supérieure des Beaux Arts in Paris. She has been professor at the Academy of Fine Art in Oslo since 2010.

jeannettechristensen.no

Annet Dekker (NL)

is assistant professor in Media Studies: Archival and Information Studies at the University of Amsterdam and Visiting Professor and co-director of the Centre for the Study of the Networked Image at London South Bank University. She has previously been Researcher Digital Preservation at Tate, London, core tutor at Piet Zwart Institute, Rotterdam and Fellow at Het Nieuwe Instituut, Rotterdam. She also worked as web curator for SKOR (Foundation for Art and Public Domain 2010-2012), was program manager at Virtueel Platform (2008-2010) and curator/head of exhibitions, education and artists in residence at the Netherlands Media Art institute (1999-2008). She has published in numerous collections and journals and is the author of *Curating Digital Art: From Presenting and Collecting Digital Art to Networked Co-curation* (Valiz, 2021) and *Collecting and Conserving Net Art* (Routledge, 2018). She is also the editor of several volumes, including *Lost and Living (in) Archives: Collectively Shaping New Memories* (Valiz, 2017); and *Speculative Scenarios, or What Will Happen to Digital Art in the (Near) Future?* (Baltan Laboratories/ Virtueel Platform, 2013).

aaaan.net

Amie Dicke (b. 1978, NL)

is a visual artist currently based in Amsterdam. She found her approach while still a student at the Willem de Kooning Academy in Rotterdam when she used marzipan and icing to cast the negative space between her legs. Dicke has a profound and enduring interest in presence and absence, solids and voids.

amiedicke.com

Sebastián Díaz Morales (b. 1975, AR)

is a visual artist who lives and works in Amsterdam, the Netherlands. Díaz Morales' conception of reality has been shaped by the living conditions and landscape of his birthplace, Comodoro Rivadivia, an industrial city located on the Atlantic coast, in a rugged area between the Atlantic Ocean and the Patagonian Desert in southern Argentina. His questioning of reality in film, whether concerning landscape, the urban, or even the sociopolitical, has been marked from the very outset by a fundamental distrust of the belief in a single, unified reality. He attended the Universidad del Cine de Antin in Argentina from 1993-1999, the Rijksakademie van Beeldende Kunsten in Amsterdam from 2000-2001, and Le Fresnoy, Roubaix, France from 2003-2004. His work has been exhibited widely at many prominent venues—such as the Tate Modern, London; Centre Pompidou, Paris; Stedelijk Museum; De Appel, Amsterdam; Le Fresnoy, Tourcoing; CAC, Vilnius; STUK, Leuven; Art in General, New York City; Ludwig Museum, Budapest; Biennale Sao Paulo; Biennale of Sydney; Miro Foundation, Barcelona; MUDAM, Luxemburg; Calouste Gulbenkian Foundation, Lisbon; and the Biennale di Venezia and Documenta.

sebastiandiazmorales.com

Lars Ebert (b. 1976, DE)

is the Secretary General of Culture Action Europe, the major European network of cultural networks, organizations, artists, activists, academics and policymakers. Previously, he was deputy director of the European League of Institutes of the Arts (ELIA) and has co-founded EQ-Arts, where he currently chairs the board. H401 in Amsterdam has been his professional and private basecamp since 2003. From there he has initiated and implemented a series of EU-funded multilateral projects on heritage, participation, education and research in and through the arts, among other activities. Lars publishes regularly and teaches cultural management. He lives and works alternately in Amsterdam, Brussels and Athens.

lars-ebert.net

Anne Geene (b. 1983, NL)

is a visual artist based in The Hague. In her work she counts, measures, inventories and photographs nature. She looks for visual similarities or patterns, repetitions and small deviations, which she then interprets and catalogs according to strictly personal criteria.

annegeene.nl

Monika Huber (b. 1959, DE)

is a visual artist living in Munich. In recent years she has created her own archive *OneThirty*, based on television coverage showing uprisings, unrests and protests around the world. One minute and thirty seconds, *EINSDREISSIG*, is the journalistic term for the average length of time allotted to a story in a news block to convey all the essential information about an event. is the average length allotted for a news block feature. For the last ten years, Huber has been daily photographing news images of Western television networks with a focus on protest, riots, war, violence and the consequences thereof. The protests of the Arab Spring, at the end of 2010, were followed by many others, such as the Gezi Park protests, the protests on the Maidan, the umbrella protests in Hong Kong, the protests in Myanmar and Belarus, the protests of the Black Lives Matter movement and many more. The documentation of news images currently comprises about 35,000 photographs. Based on these news images, Huber develops hybrid *EINSDREISSIG (OneThirty)* photographs, which will become components of the ARCHIVE EINSDREISSIG. The photographic material is currently being entered into a database and linked to the corresponding content, contexts and search terms. The archive pages can be read like a walk through politically motivated events of the last ten years. Through the search function of the database, new levels of connection and perception can be created. The ARCHIVE EINSDREISSIG is designed as a long-term documentation.

monikahuber.com

William Kentridge (b. 1955, SA)

is a multidisciplinary artist who works in and across the mediums of drawing, writing, film, performance, music, theatre and collaborative practices, to create works of art that are grounded in politics, science, literature and history, whilst maintaining a space for contradiction and uncertainty. His art has been exhibited at Documenta (Kassel), Tate Modern (London), Museum of Modern Art (New York) Albertina Museum (Vienna), Musée du Louvre (Paris), Louisiana Museum (Copenhagen), Reina Sofia Museum (Madrid), the Kunstmuseum (Basel) and the Venice Biennale. His work can be found in the collections of art museums and institutions across the globe.

As an opera and theatre director, Kentridge has also worked with the Metropolitan Opera in New York, the Royal Opera House in London, and Holland Festival. Opera productions include Mozart's *The Magic Flute*, Shostakovich's *The Nose*, and Alban Berg's operas *Lulu* and *Wozzeck*.

In 2016 Kentridge founded the Centre for the Less Good Idea in Johannesburg: a space for responsive thinking and making through experimental, collaborative and cross-disciplinary arts practices. The Centre hosts an ongoing program of workshops, public performances and mentorship activities. He is the recipient of honorary doctorates from several universities including Yale and the University of London. Prizes include the Kyoto Prize (2010), the Princesa de Asturias Award (2017) and the Praemium Imperiale Prize (2019). He was elected as an Honorary Academician of the Royal Academy of Arts in London in 2015.

kentridge.studio

Pablo Lerma (b. 1986, ES)

is an image-based artist, publisher and educator, based in Amsterdam. His artistic practice is developed at the intersection of image & text with a focus on visual archives and vernacular materials that deal with the concepts of time, erosion, identity and counter-narrative. His work takes various forms, from photographic installations to publications. He holds a BFA in Painting and an MFA in Studio Art from the University of Barcelona, a Diploma in General Studies of Photography from the Institut d'Estudis Fotogràfics de Catalunya, Spain, and an MFA in Image & Text from Ithaca College in New York. He has been awarded with the Grand Prize of Curators Award PDN (US), Fundació Guasch-Coranty (ES) and Sala d'Art Jove (ES). Currently, he is a lecturer in Social Art Practice at Willem de Kooning Academy in Rotterdam (NL) and a faculty member in Media & Photography at Webster University in Leiden (NL). In the last decade, he served as a faculty member in Photography & Social Justice at the International Center of Photography in New York (US) and as a professor in Photography at Kean University in New Jersey (US). He is the founder of the publishing house Meteoro Editions (US-NL). A platform to create art publications with a focus on projects that deal with vernacular photography, archives, utopias and fictional representations of the world.

pablolerma.com

Inge Meijer (b. 1986, NL)

works across media of photography, analog film, digital culture, and installation. She studied visual arts at the Academy of Fine Arts and Design Arnhem (2012) and completed a two-year residency at the Rijksakademie van Beeldende Kunsten in Amsterdam (2016-2017). In 2019 she participated in the ACC-Rijksakademie Dialogue and Exchange program in Gwangju, South Korea. Her work has been exhibited at the Stedelijk Museum Amsterdam, UNSEEN, Museum Arnhem, Asia Culture Centre in Gwangju, South Korea, and the Australian Centre for Contemporary Art in Melbourne, Australia. Her publication, *The Plant Collection*, was selected for The Best Dutch Book Designs 2019. In 2021, she participated in the artist-in-residency program at Kunsthuis SYB.

ingemeijer.com

Santu Mofokeng (1956–2020, SA)

was a South African news and documentary photographer who worked under the alias Mofokengâ. Mofokeng was a member of the Afrapix collective and won a Prince Claus Award. As an artist he made the archival book *Black Photo Album / Look at me: (1890-1950)*.

Merapi Obermayer (b. 1947, ID)

is an artist, poet and writer, born on the island of Java during the Indonesian war of independence. Her visual work consists of photographs, which she calls 'dream images.' Her poetry is clear and short in form, characterized by a strong rhythm. In 1952, Obermayer left Indonesia for the Netherlands with her parents and sister. There, she grew up in a boarding school and spent the holidays with her parents in a leper colony somewhere on the edge of a village surrounded by forest and heathland which, like the boarding school, was isolated from Dutch society. The 'Indo no man's land' in which she found herself became a source of inspiration. With the help of all sorts of artists, Merapi developed herself into a visual artist. She owes a lot to Oey Tjeng Sit in particular. He encouraged her to walk her own artistic way and to find her own language. Her first international exhibitions took place in Brazil, later she also exhibited on New York, Paris, and Germany. In 2001, her autobiography *Insulinde's Dochter* (Bert Bakker) was published, which was rewritten and put on stage by director Patrizia Filia, under the title *The Island.* In 2022, her work was included in the exhibition *Revolusi! Indonesia Independent* at the Rijksmuseum, Amsterdam.

Mathieu Pernot (b. 1970, FR)

is a photographer living and working in Paris. During his time at the École Nationale Supérieure de la Photographie, Pernot met with Tzigane families in Arles, among whom the Gorgans, a family he's worked with continuously thereafter.

mathieupernot.com

Ronit Porat (b. 1973, IL)

works with photography, and includes archival materials and biographical texts in her installations. Her work was exhibited internationally in group and solo shows, and can be found in the Tel Aviv Museum of Art Collection, Shoken Collection and private collections.

ronitporat.com

Walid Raad (b. 1976, LB)

is an artist whose works include photography, video, mixed media installations, and performances. He teaches in The Cooper Union in New York (USA), and in Ashkal Alwan's Home Workspace in Beirut (Lebanon). The Atlas Group is a fictional collective, the work of which is produced by Walid Raad. The work of this fictional collective consists of an archive of images and texts concerning the Lebanon and its many wars. In 2018 he had an exhibition at the Stedelijk Museum Amsterdam.

walidraad.com

Ana Paula Saab (AR)

holds a Degree in Educational Sciences and a PhD from the University of Leiden. She is a member of the Research Project 'The schooling of the initial reading and in the primary school of Argentina' (1880-1975 circa, HISTELEA) in the Department of Education, National University of Lujan (UNLu), Buenos Aires. She teaches Theories of Education for the Bachelor degree in Education Sciences. She is currently a beneficiary of the research fellowship based at UNLu, for a project on conceptions of memory in education programs during 2006-2016 in Argentina.

Drew Sawyer (USA)

is an art historian and a curator, who holds the title of the Phillip Leonian and Edith Rosenbaum Leonian Curator at the Brooklyn Museum. He has previously held curatorial positions at the Museum of Modern Art and the Columbus Museum of Art, where he co-founded the Center for Art and Social Engagement (CASE) through a major grant from the Institute of Museum and Library Services. He received a 2020 Award for Excellence from the Association of Art Museum Curators. Sawyer holds a PhD in Art History and Archaeology from Columbia University, focusing on North American art and photography and their intersections with social histories around labor, class, race, gender, and sexuality. He is a regular contributor to scholarly volumes, exhibition catalogues, journals, and magazines.

drewsawyer.com

Carla Subrizi (b. 1958, IT)

teaches History of Contemporary Art and Contemporary Art Semiotics at the Sapienza University in Rome and is artistic director of the Baruchello Foundation. Among many other works, she published *Azioni che cambiano il mondo. Donne arte e politiche dello sguardo* (Postmedia, 2012), *Europa e America, 1945-1985* (Aracne, 2008), *Introduzione a Duchamp* (Laterza, 2008), *Cesare Viel. Azioni 1996-2007* (Silvana Editoriale, 2008), *Imagine/Image* (Rome-London 2007), *Verifica incerta. L'arte oltre i confini del cinema* (DeriveApprodi, 2004), *Il corpo disperso dell'arte* (Lithos, 2000). She is also a curator, art critic and historian.

Marjan Teeuwen (b. 1953, NL)

is a visual artist and curator, especially known for her *Archive* series and *Destroyed House* series. She creates large-scale architectural installations in buildings that are demolished after her interventions. She tears and strips, disrupts construction and with the remaining material she builds a new artistic image. Based on these installations she realizes autonomous photographic works. In her work the constructive force of building goes hand in hand with the power of destruction and decay.

Recent commissions of her work are by De Nederlandse Bank (2021), Les Archives Nationales de France (2021), FRAC Alsace (FR, 2023); Kyotographie, Kyoto (JP, 2020).

marjanteeuwen.nl

Daria Tuminas (b. 1984, RU)

is a Rotterdam-based writer and freelance curator, currently at Fotodok in Utrecht, NL. One of the exhibitions she curated was Private Stories, Public Histories (2020–2021). She regularly teaches courses and episodical workshops at educational venues, including: FOTOfactory, Amsterdam; Webster University, Leiden; docdocdoc, St. Petersburg; Fotodepartament, St. Petersburg; The Royal Academy of Art, The Hague; The HKU University of the Arts, Utrecht. From 2017 to 2019 she was Head of Unseen Book Market and Unseen Dummy Award at Unseen Amsterdam. Previously, she worked a Johan Deumens Gallery in Amsterdam. She holds an MA in Film and Photographic Studies from Leiden University (2011), for which she wrote a thesis questioning narrative in photography. In 2010 she graduated with an MA in Russian literature and folklore from St. Petersburg State University.

dariatuminas.com

Renée Turner (USA)

is an artist and writer whose practice engages with digital narratives, archives, and interdisciplinary collaborative inquiry. Her research is informed by feminist perspectives, and the entanglement of sites, histories, material encounters, and embodied subjectivities.

narrativeresonance.net

Jeffrey Wallen

is professor of comparative literature at Hampshire College, and was Dean of the School of Humanities, Arts, and Cultural Studies (HACU) from 2012-2015. He has also taught as a visiting professor at the Free University Berlin and at the University of Toulouse, and has been the director of Hampshire's semester-long study abroad program. He has published widely on nineteenth- and twentieth-century European literature; on biography and literary portraiture; on testimony, Holocaust literature, and Berlin Jewish history; and on debates about education.

His book *Closed Encounters: Literary Politics and Public Culture* (1998) was published by the University of Minnesota Press. Some of his most recent publications are 'Au Seuil, entre la vie et la morte' (in *Traces de vie à Auschwitz: un manuscrit clandestin*),'Facing the Sonderkommando: Son of Saul and the Dynamics of Witnessing,' 'Circuitous Journeys: The Migration of Objects and the Trusteeship of Memory,' 'The Witness Against the Archive: Towards a Microhistory of Christianstadt,' 'The Lure of the Archive: The Atlas Projects of Walid Raad.' He is currently working on a study of the archive in contemporary thought and art.

sites.hampshire.edu/jwallen/

Michelle Williams Gamaker

(b. 1979, UK)

is a moving image and performance artist based in London. Her work explores the fiction-making machine of twentieth-century British and Hollywood studio films by restaging sequences to reveal cinematic construction, and recasting characters to propose alternative endings that counter their often doom-laden plight. She recently completed *Dissolution*, a trilogy of films comprising *House of Women* (2017), *The Fruit is There to be Eaten* (2018) and *The Eternal Return* (2019) in which characters from Powell and Pressburger's 1947 *Black Narcissus* unravel as they become aware of their screen and staged realities. Williams Gamaker's key focus is the development of 'fictional activism': the restoration of marginalized characters as central figures, who return in her works as vocal brown protagonists challenging the fictional injustices to which they have been historically consigned. Collaboration is also a crucial element of Williams Gamaker's work; since 2009 she has worked with American artist Julia Kouneski, revisiting the psychotherapeutic work of Brazilian artist Lygia Clark, as inspiration for interventions with the body, architecture and landscape. Williams Gamaker has also completed several videos and installations exploring migratory aesthetics, mental health, and the emotional complexities of capitalism and gender ideology. This overlaps with her eleven-year collaboration with artist and cultural theorist Mieke Bal, and their experimental films which explore making as theoretical fiction.

Williams Gamaker holds a PhD in Fine Art from Goldsmiths College, University of London, is a Lecturer in BA Fine Art at Goldsmiths College, University of London, Chair of Trustees at Pavilion in Leeds and co-founder of the Women of Colour Index (WOCI) Reading Group working with the group between 2016-2019 with Samia Malik and Rehana Zaman

michellewilliamsgamaker.com

Lotte Lara Schröder _Design

is an graphic designer, interested in ecological and natural phenomena. Her 'free' work consists of drawings, paintings, and collages, often combined with sound or objects. Lotte created the overall book and cover design choosing to literally pigeonhole the book. Mixed with graphics taken from test photography.

@termsofcircumstance, @speculativepress

Valiz _Publisher

is an independent publisher, addressing contemporary developments in art, design, architecture, and urban affairs. Their books provide critical reflection and interdisciplinary inspiration in a broad and imaginative way, often establishing a connection between cultural disciplines and socio-economic questions. Valiz is headed by Astrid Vorstermans (b. 1960) and Pia Pol (b. 1985).

valiz.nl, @valiz_books_projects

Index of Names

Colophon

Editor_
Ernst van Alphen

Image research_
the authors

Contributors_
Ernst van Alphen, Aleida Assmann, Jeannette Christensen, Annet Dekker, Sebastián Díaz Morales, Lars Ebert, Monika Huber, William Kentridge, Pablo Lerma, Inge Meijer, Santu Mofokeng, Merapi Obermayer, Mathieu Pernot, Walid Raad, Ana Paula Saab, Drew Sawyer, Carla Subrizi, Marjan Teeuwen, Daria Tuminas, Jeffrey Wallen, Michelle Williams Gamaker

Project editor_
Simone Wegman / Valiz

Copy-editing_
Leo Reijnen

Index_
Elke Stevens;
Nic de Jong

This publication was made possible through the generous support of Prins Bernhard Cultuurfonds

PRINS BERNHARD
CULTUURFONDS

Lithography_
Mariska Bijl, Wilco Art Books, Amsterdam

Printing and binding_
Wilco Art Books, Amersfoort

Paper cover_
Natural Strongboard 265 gr

Paper inside_
Holmen TRND 70 gr, 2.0

Graphic design_
Lotte Lara Schröder

Cover & Theme images_
Lotte Lara Schröder

Typefaces_
ABC Marfa (Dinamo)

Publisher_
Valiz, Amsterdam, 2023
Astrid Vorstermans & Pia Pol

V

This publication has been printed on FSC-certified paper by an FSC-certified printer. The FSC, Forest Stewardship Council promotes environmentally appropriate, socially beneficial, and economically viable management of the world's forests.
fsc.org

International distribution_
NL/LU: Centraal Boekhuis, www.centraal.boekhuis.nl
BE: EPO, www.epo.be
Europe/Asia (except GB/IE): Idea Books, www.ideabooks.nl
GB/IE: Central Books, www.centralbooks.com
USA/Canada/Latin America: D.A.P., www.artbook.com
Australia: Perimeter Books, www.perimeterbooks.com

Individual orders
www.valiz.nl; info@valiz.nl

ISBN 978-94-93246-16-4
Printed and bound in the EU, 2023

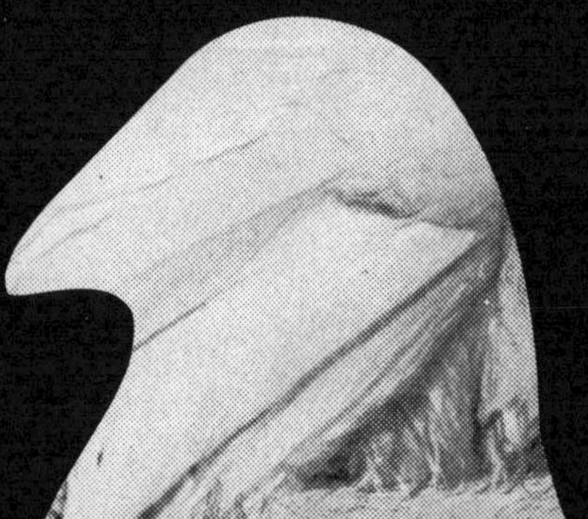